9(

D1339700

Palgrave Studies in European Union Politics

Edited by: **Michelle Egan**, American University, USA, **Neill Nugent**, Manchester Metropolitan University, UK and **William Paterson OBE**, University of Aston, UK.

Editorial Board: **Christopher Hill**, Cambridge, UK, **Simon Hix**, London School of Economics, UK, **Mark Pollack**, Temple University, USA, **Kalypso Nicolaïdis**, Oxford, UK, **Morten Egeberg**, University of Oslo, Norway, **Amy Verdun**, University of Victoria, Canada, **Claudio M. Radaelli**, University of Exeter, UK, **Frank Schimmelfennig**, Swiss Federal Institute of Technology, Switzerland.

Following on the sustained success of the acclaimed *European Union Series,* which essentially publishes research-based textbooks, *Palgrave Studies in European Union Politics* publishes cutting-edge research-driven monographs.

The remit of the series is broadly defined, both in terms of subject and academic discipline. All topics of significance concerning the nature and operation of the European Union potentially fall within the scope of the series. The series is multidisciplinary to reflect the growing importance of the EU as a political, economic and social phenomenon.

Titles include:

Ian Bache and Andrew Jordan *(editors)*
THE EUROPEANIZATION OF BRITISH POLITICS

Richard Balme and Brian Bridges *(editors)*
EUROPE-ASIA RELATIONS
Building Multilateralisms

Thierry Balzacq *(editor)*
THE EXTERNAL DIMENSION OF EU JUSTICE AND HOME AFFAIRS
Governance, Neighbours, Security

Michael Baun and Dan Marek *(editors)*
EU COHESION POLICY AFTER ENLARGEMENT

Derek Beach and Colette Mazzucelli *(editors)*
LEADERSHIP IN THE BIG BANGS OF EUROPEAN INTEGRATION

Tanja A. Börzel *(editor)*
COPING WITH ACCESSION TO THE EUROPEAN UNION
New Modes of Environmental Governance

Milena Büchs
NEW GOVERNANCE IN EUROPEAN SOCIAL POLICY
The Open Method of Coordination

Kenneth Dyson and Angelos Sepos *(editors)*
WHICH EUROPE?
The Politics of Differentiated Integration

Michelle Egan, Neill Nugent, William E. Paterson *(editors)*
RESEARCH AGENDAS IN EU STUDIES
Stalking the Elephant

Kevin Featherstone and Dimitris Papadimitriou
THE LIMITS OF EUROPEANIZATION
Reform Capacity and Policy Conflict in Greece

Stefan Gänzle and Allen G. Sens *(editors)*
THE CHANGING POLITICS OF EUROPEAN SECURITY
Europe Alone?

Heather Grabbe
THE EU'S TRANSFORMATIVE POWER

Eva Gross
THE EUROPEANIZATION OF NATIONAL FOREIGN POLICY
Continuity and Change in European Crisis Management

Wolfram Kaiser, Brigitte Leucht, Michael Gehler
TRANSNATIONAL NETWORKS IN REGIONAL INTEGRATION
Governing Europe 1945–83

Palgrave Studies in European Union Politics
Series Standing Order ISBN 978–1–4039–9511–7 (hardback) and
ISBN 978–1–4039–9512–4 (paperback)
(outside North America only)

You can receive future titles in this series as they are published by placing a standing order. Please contact your bookseller or, in case of difficulty, write to us at the address below with your name and address, the title of the series and one of the ISBNs quoted above.

Customer Services Department, Macmillan Distribution Ltd, Houndmills, Basingstoke, Hampshire RG21 6XS, England, UK

Europe, Regions and European Regionalism

Edited by

Roger Scully
Professor of Political Science, Department of International Politics, Aberystwyth University, UK

Richard Wyn Jones
Director, Wales Governance Centre, School of European Studies, Cardiff University, UK

palgrave
macmillan

First published 2010 by
PALGRAVE MACMILLAN

Palgrave Macmillan in the UK is an imprint of Macmillan Publishers Limited,
registered in England, company number 785998, of Houndmills, Basingstoke,
Hampshire RG21 6XS.

Palgrave Macmillan in the US is a division of St Martin's Press LLC,
175 Fifth Avenue, New York, NY 10010.

Palgrave Macmillan is the global academic imprint of the above companies
and has companies and representatives throughout the world.

Palgrave® and Macmillan® are registered trademarks in the United States,
the United Kingdom, Europe and other countries.

ISBN-13: 978–0–230–23178–8 hardback

This book is printed on paper suitable for recycling and made from fully
managed and sustained forest sources. Logging, pulping and manufacturing
processes are expected to conform to the environmental regulations of the
country of origin.

A catalogue record for this book is available from the British Library.

A catalog record for this book is available from the Library of Congress.

Printed and bound in Great Britain by
CPI Antony Rowe, Chippenham and Eastbourne

Contents

List of Figures and Tables

Figures

Tables

List of Contributors

Martin Brusis is Research Fellow at the Centre for Applied Policy Research at the University of Munich.

Noreen Burrows holds the Jean Monnet Chair of European Law, and is Dean of the Faculty of Law, Business and Social Sciences at the University of Glasgow.

Giandomenico Falcon is Professor of Administrative Law at the University of Trento.

Grzegorz Gorzelak is Professor of Economics and Director of the Centre for European Regional and Local Studies at Warsaw University.

Katy Hayward is Lecturer in Sociology at Queen's University, Belfast.

Gyula Horváth is Professor of Regional Policy and Director General of the Centre for Regional Studies at the University of Pécs.

Tarvo Kungla is Lecturer in Public Administration at the University of Tartu.

Anders Lidström is Professor of Political Science at Umeå University.

Carolyn Moore is Lecturer in German and European Politics at the University of Birmingham.

Francesc Morata is Professor of Political Science and Director of the University Institute of European Studies at the Autonomous University of Barcelona.

Romain Pasquier is a researcher, and head of the research team on 'Territorial governance and comparative analysis of public policies' at the Institute of Policy Studies at the University of Rennes.

Daria de Pretis is Professor of Administrative Law at the University of Trento.

Roger Scully is Professor of Political Science and Director of the Institute of Welsh Politics at Aberystwyth University.

Wilfried Swenden is Lecturer in Politics at the University of Edinburgh.

Anna Tucholska is Assistant Professor in the Centre for European Regional and Local Studies, Warsaw University.

Richard Wyn Jones is Director of the Wales Governance Centre at Cardiff University.

1
Introduction: Europe, Regions, and European Regionalism

Richard Wyn Jones and Roger Scully

Europe's regions. To the extent that this phrase conjures up any images at all among the wider public – those men and women whom the English fondly imagine as traveling on the apocryphal Clapham Omnibus – then it is surely a series of images from those parts of Europe whose obvious, confident sense of their own identity and importance sets them apart from mere 'localities', even while they lack the trappings of sovereign statehood. This is the Europe of Catalonia and Scotland, two regions whose capital cities exude an almost palpable sense of status that far surpasses that cramped and slighting des- ignation of 'provincial' sometimes bestowed upon them by their respective metropolitan centers. This is a Europe of deep roots and ancient tradition: the Europe, above all perhaps, of *bürgerliche Gesellschaft*, of bourgeois soci- ety. This is a solid, occasionally stolid, Europe which can pride itself in real and lasting civic achievement. Enterprise is another key bourgeois virtue and to invoke regional Europe is also to invoke the dynamic Europe implied by the use of the prefix 'motor' to describe a grouping of four of the most successful regions – Baden-Württemberg, Rhône-Alpes, Lombardy, as well as Catalonia.[1] This is a Europe that takes pride in its past achievements and looks to the future with confidence.

Until quite recently, it had been widely assumed that Europe's regions were gaining an ever-greater role in the continent's governance. Having been thrust to prominence most notably by the rhetoric and actions of the Delors Commission (1985–1994), the regions were posited as one of two main beneficiaries of a process that would see the powers of the traditional, sovereign state simultaneously devolved to the regional tier and central- ized to European level institutions. For some this was a development to be both lauded and encouraged. This was certainly the case among fully fledged European federalists. Indeed, Helen Wallace was once moved to suggest that the development of linkages between the Commission and the regions was 'the only available stepping stone to a truly federal system' (Wallace 1977).

Many of Western Europe's regionalist and minority nationalist movements and thinkers also began to envisage a 'Europe of the Regions' that would

1

completely eclipse the Europe of states.[2] The former is an idea that has deep roots, which may be traced back to Proudhon and beyond. In the 1980s, this notion was given new life and prominence through being appended to a European integration agenda that appeared to be firmly in the ascendant. The Europe of nation-states was, it appeared, being diminished both from above and below; by working with the EU, regions would be able to win a new status, as well as greater independence of action from the old controlling forces of the state capitals. To this end, extravagant hopes were invested in the European Union's Committee of the Regions (CoR), a 'body' of the European Union (EU) established in 1994 as a result of the Maastricht Treaty (on the origins of the CoR see Borras-Alomar et al. 1994; Loughlin 1996, 1997; Millan 1997).[3] The Committee would one day become the second chamber of the European Parliament, a pan-European *Bundesrat* – or so hoped the Welsh nationalists of Plaid Cymru and the Basque nationalist Eusko Alkartasuna (Plaid Cymru 1999; Acha 2006: 80).[4] At the opposite, state-nationalist end of the spectrum, European regions and regionalism elicited diametrically different reactions. Some of the more conspiratorially inclined Euro-skeptics viewed, and, indeed, continue to view, European regionalization as part of a deliberate ploy by the Commission to undermine the state.[5] But whatever the other differences between these two poles of opinion – or indeed the nuances of the various, intervening positions – there was broad agreement that regions had a centrally important role to play in Europe's future.

Or so it seemed. Viewed in retrospect, however, the mid-1990s appear to represent not so much the beginnings of the inevitable 'Rise of Regional Europe', to invoke the title of Christopher Harvie's splendid period essay, but rather its zenith (Harvie 1993). Few hopes have been more regularly disappointed than those focusing on the withering away of the state. Yet there is more to the fading of the aspirations for regionalism than simply the inevitable puncturing of overly inflated expectations. Geo-political developments have done most to tarnish the prospects of regional Europe. Following the collapse of Communism, the dominating issue in European politics at least since the mid-1990s has not been that of the rise of regionalism, but rather the enlargement of the EU into Central and Eastern Europe. In these circumstances, whatever momentum that was once enjoyed by the agenda of regionalism has almost entirely dissipated.

But why precisely is this the case? The undeniable fact that enlargement has consumed a great deal of political capital and energy is hardly sufficient explanation in itself. At least three interrelated factors may be adjudged crucial in this regard. First, enlargement has served to further cement the dominant position of states within the Union. As has often been remarked, states that had only just regained their sovereignty after decades of Soviet oppression were hardly likely to be in the van of moves towards a 'Euro-federalism' that might see them having to give up that sovereignty, albeit in a voluntary and cooperative arrangement, to a new center of authority in Brussels. So it has proven as Poland, the Czech Republic and others among the ranks of the newer members have joined with longer-standing inter-governmentalists, such as the UK and Denmark, in resisting further moves in the direction of supranationalism (Koenig et al. 2008). This is significant in itself, given that regionalism (in its stronger forms) may be regarded as the handmaiden of supranationalism. A further barrier to regionalism in this regard is the fact that so many of the newer states have little or no substantive tradition of regional government. Enlargement has brought very few by way of reinforcements to the regionalist camp.

Second, and relatedly, size matters. A Europe of 27 states is also a Europe of many, many more regions. Exactly how many regions is a moot point – the vexed issue of definition is returned to below as well as in many of individual chapters that follow. The Union's own statistical agency has developed a standardized three-fold classification for regions, with each level being known respectively as NUTS 1, NUTS 2 and NUTS 3 – the spectacularly unattractive acronym NUTS being derived from the French *nomenclature des unités territoriales statistiques*. Europe has 95 NUTS 1 regions, 268 NUTS 2 regions and 1,291 NUTS 3 regions.[6] To give a concrete example of what this means in practice, Scotland is a NUTS 1 region, but is itself made up of four NUTS 2 regions. NUTS 3 delineates yet smaller units of territory. Scotland's 32 unitary local authorities form the basis – either individually or in combination – for 23 NUTS 3 regions. It is important to note that there is no necessary relationship between the borders of these regions (be they NUTS 1, 2 or 3) and the meaningful loci of political authority. So while the Scottish NUTS 1 does indeed have its devolved parliament and executive, the four NUTS 2 regions in Scotland have no real administrative personality. Furthermore, as has already been noted, some of the country's NUTS 3 regions represent a combination of existing administrative units.

On the whole, the NUTS 2 regions are dominant in terms of the EU's presentation of statistical data. But whether we decide that Europe comprises of 268 regions, or more, or less, it is immediately clear that coordinating any kind of common position between so many actual or potential actors would represent a major challenge. The lowest common denominator of agreement is likely very low indeed. It certainly makes it unlikely that the regions could ever successfully coordinate a common position among themselves, let alone become important actors in the development of policy, rather than simply its implementation. (The key distinction between the role of regions as policy-makers as well as policy-takers is returned to below).

The burgeoning number of regions has also served to re-emphasize a third key factor, namely that Europe's regions are, by any standards, an extraordinarily diverse group. To a great extent it was ever thus, with regions differing widely in terms of their economic strength, constitutional powers, senses of identity and so forth. But the addition of so many new EU member states with little meaningful tradition of regional government has served only to reinforce the extent of the gulf between them. Bluntly put, and as we will see in further detail in later chapters of the book, there is a world of difference between the regions of Bulgaria or Hungary, on the one hand, and Scotland and Catalonia on the other. Of course, the objection may be made that states also differ markedly from each other, and has not the EU always contained among its number states as different as (West) Germany and Luxembourg? The differences between regions are, however, far greater even than those dividing sovereign states. For whatever divides the latter, they are nonetheless united by the fact of their membership of what may be considered the world's most exclusive club; a club whose rules of membership provide the very foundation stone for the whole edifice of international law. Sovereignty is their common denominator. No such common ground exists between regions.

The huge and almost certainly unbridgeable gulf that divides Europe's regions is most vividly brought into focus by the CoR, a body that has proven to be a sorry disappointment to those who invested great hopes in its establishment. Spanning entities that range from historic nations to mere administrative conveniences, and representing politico-constitutional units that range from something approximating proto-states to essentially notional shells that are wholly subservient both to the state-level and more localized layers of government (the latter of which are *also* members of the CoR itself), the Committee has achieved very little of note. Even if the powers of the CoR were not so slight – it was assigned powers by the Maastricht Treaty that are perhaps most generously characterized as contemplative – nothing has suggested that its membership are capable of agitating effectively for a more genuinely substantive role (Jeffery 2004a). Given the lack of common ground between its members, the CoR is a talking shop of very marginal utility either for the regions themselves or the Union more broadly.

Given all this, it is not surprising that the ardor of those regions and political movements who were previously among the most prominent advocates for an increased role for the regions in European governance has cooled significantly in recent years. As noted in particular by Charlie Jeffery, the German Länder appear to have concluded that they are more likely to influence relevant decisions at the European level via their own (constitutionally entrenched) relationship with the federal government rather than acting directly as regional actors on the European stage (Jeffery 2003). Partly because of this, they have tended to retreat from their previous commitment to the development of European regional institutions. However, there is more to this shift than a simple cost-benefit analysis of how best to make their voice heard. Implicit, at least, in their new stance is a sense that their role and status within the *Bundesrepublik* sets them apart from many others among Europe's regions. Indeed, rather than enhancing their standing, too close an association with units that play a marginal role within their own polities may diminish it.

At its height, the form of regionalism once espoused by the Länder, and by sections, at least, of the European Commission, seems to have envisaged the development of the regional tier as a third pole of European governance, interacting with and balancing state-level and European-level institutions.

The strongest form of regionalism was espoused, however, by Euro-federalists as well as some of Western Europe's minority nationalist parties – Plaid Cymru has already been mentioned, Jordi Pujol's *Convergència Democràtica de Catalunya* and sections of the *Bloque Nacionalista Galego* are other prominent cases in point. Among the latter party-movements, regionalism held out the prospect of the eclipse – *de jure* if not necessarily *de facto* – of one of those poles, namely the sovereign states. It is a sign of the times that Plaid Cymru has recently embraced independence for Wales within the EU as its long-term constitutional aim (Elias 2006), while the more conservative Basque nationalists of the Partido Nacionalista Vasco (PNV) have begun to espouse some form of special 'associated' status within the European Union (Pérez-Nievas 2006: 51–53). While there are several reasons for these developments, one is a sense of disillusionment with the prospects for European regionalization, at least in the strong form originally envisaged.

If those who were previously the most ardent regionalists have apparently lost faith in their cause, it is tempting to conclude from this that European regionalism is, more generally, a busted flush. But while this is tempting, it is also mistaken. For strong regionalizing dynamics remain evident in contemporary Europe. As is shown in many of the chapters in this book, the powers and responsibilities of regions within several significant EU member states continue to be enhanced, whether because of state-wide reforms (as in France) or as a response to pressure from regions themselves (Scotland and, to a lesser extent, Wales, being the obvious examples here). Furthermore, even if many are artificial constructs put together only to satisfy the (perceived) membership criteria of the EU, it nonetheless remains a fact that such top-down pressure has led to the development of a regional tier in Central and Eastern Europe. While they may fall far short of the aspirations of regionalists, these regions play a significant role in European structural funding programs. Furthermore, economic development models that focus on the regional scale – to utilize the language of political geographers – retain their vogue among policy-makers across Europe, as among European academics, a fact that suggests a continuing and even enhanced role for regional organizations.

The picture that emerges of regions and regionalism in contemporary Europe is, therefore, variegated and even confused; it is certainly not a picture that can be encapsulated within any single narrative of rise or, indeed, of decline. Maximalist hopes have been disappointed. But regions defiantly continue to play a role, not only within their respective states, but also in processes of pan-European governance. But what kinds of role do they play or seek to play? What are the various constitutional and politico-economic frameworks that variously serve to constrain and enable their actions? How are the regions organizing their relationships both with each other and at the European level? In order that the current state of play can be brought into clearer focus, a detailed reckoning is required, one that has as its starting point an explicit acknowledgement of the sheer diversity of Europe's regions. This book provides just such a reckoning. While no book could ever claim to provide comprehensive coverage of every European region, our aim as editors has been to ensure that this volume captures much of the kaleidoscopic variety and complexity of European regions and regionalism.

Understanding Europe's regions

Before previewing the specific contributions of the chapters in this volume, we will highlight three issues that are central to the study of European regions, and regionalism more generally, and which form key themes running through the different contributions that follow. First, there is the vexed question of definition: 'What is a region?' Second, we will briefly examine 'The dynamics of regionalism', focussing on the very different forces encouraging the development of the regional level within member states. Third, we will pose the question 'What do regions do?' suggesting, by way of response, some broad conceptualization relevant to understanding their activity – both actual and possible.

What is a region?

As has already been implied, defining Europe's regions is difficult. So difficult, in fact, that most scholarly treatments of regionalism eschew any such attempt and rather stress the flexibility and ambiguity of the term 'region'.[7] This is both understandable and sensible given that, even confining ourselves exclusively to the sub-state level, there are at least three different senses of 'region' identifiable in the theory and practice of contemporary European politics; three senses of region that are often only tangentially related to each other. These may be summarized as the *statistical*, the *administrative* and the *affective*.

The existence of three different layers of regions as the basis for the presentation of European statistical data has already been mentioned. Indeed, data on the NUTS regions, and in particular NUTS 2 regions, has become a vital aid to European policy-making, especially with regards to the division of structural funding. However, there is no necessary relationship between those units of statistical measurement and anything that might be termed a region in everyday parlance. So, for example, despite the fact that NUTS represents an attempt to develop a relatively standardized categorization system of regions, the combination of the widely varying sizes or scales of the

27 member states and the state-centric foundations of the Union means that, in many cases, the boundaries of NUTS 1 regions correspond to those of the smaller sovereign states. As of writing, this is currently the case with 12 of the 27 members.[8] The borders of eight of those 12 are also regarded as constituting the borders of NUTS 2 regions.[9] Indeed, in the case of Luxembourg and Cyprus, the boundaries of all three NUTS divisions are regarded as corresponding to boundaries of the state itself. So 12 of the 95 NUTS 1 regions are in fact full member states, as are eight of the 268 NUTS 2 regions, and so on. At which point one may be forgiven for asking the (rhetorical) question, what if anything does 'region' mean in these cases?

Turning to the Union's larger states, as has already been pointed out there are many cases in which the boundaries of NUTS regions do not correspond with the boundaries of any actually existing unit of administrative authority. While the borders of the regional map respect administrative boundaries, it is regularly the case that the boundary of a particular region – be it a NUTS 1, 2 or 3 region – is made up of several smaller units of administrative authority. Furthermore, even where such units exist, their powers vary widely both between and within member states. This is because the NUTS delineations have been overlaid onto local government structures that embody markedly different state traditions of political and administrative organization. There is no standard European model of sub-state governance, nor is there the remotest prospect that one will be developed.

The relationship between statistical regions and administrative regions is therefore a weak one. Neither is there any simple or straightforward relationship between the borders of statistical or administrative regions, on the one hand, and 'regional' consciousness and identity on the other. Scotland, already referred to several times in this chapter, is in fact rather exceptional in that it is a case of a NUTS 1 region that is also a very long-standing administrative unit, whose boundaries are coterminous with those of a distinct 'regional' – or in this case 'national' – identity. Historically speaking, Catalan identity – and certainly the Catalan language – traverses administrative boundaries; indeed, it traverses several state boundaries. There are other cases where 'regional' identities are subsumed within larger regional administrative units. Cornwall, for example, home to a distinct regional and perhaps even national identity, is part of the much larger South West England region. This is an example of a recurrent theme in the chapters that follow. There are also many examples of administrative or statistical regions which engender little or no affective attachment amongst their respective populations.

The dynamics of regionalism

With regions serving very different administrative and bureaucratic functions, as well as eliciting widely varying levels of affective identification, it is unsurprising that there are a number of distinct regionalizing dynamics identifiable in contemporary Europe. Again a three-fold classification of these various dynamics is useful, distinguishing in this case between *Euro-regionalism, state-regionalism* and *regional-regionalism*.

Euro-regionalism refers not only to the various NUTS designations but also to the perceived pressure on member states to regionalize their governmental structures as part of the broader integration process. The importance of perception should be underlined here. It has been widely assumed – not least by the states of Central and Eastern Europe themselves – that the development of a regional layer or administration was a requirement of the expansion process itself; that regionalization was part of the *acquis communautaire*. Subsequent research – in particular by Martin Brusis – has, however, demonstrated that this widely held assumption is not in fact well founded (Brusis 2002, 2003). The Commission was far more circumspect and limited in its demands than has been suggested. Nonetheless, this perception may well have had a self-fulfilling aspect to it, inasmuch as those states seeking membership saw it as being in their interests to develop their regional structures.

State-regionalism refers to regionalizing pressure emanating from the state-level itself. Such pressure may reflect any number of factors, including considerations of governmental efficiency and economic development. The key point is that this represents another form of 'top-down' regionalism, whereby levels of government above the region itself are the prime movers in the regionalizing process. By contrast, regional-regionalism refers to a bottom-up pressure for regionalism: a situation whereby the main pressure for an enhanced role for the region emanates from within the region itself, very often – though not always – as a manifestation of a 'regional' identity.

While these three forms of regionalist dynamic are analytically distinct, it is important to remember that all three dynamics can and do interact with each other in practice. So, for example, state-regionalizing tendencies may well be an attempt to contain, direct and balance particular regional-regionalizing pressures. Regional-regionalizers may well attempt to secure recognition of their particular region within a broader state-regionalizing project. Regional-regionalizers may also seek to take advantage of the possibilities opened up by Euro-regionalism, as well as the integration process more generally. And so on. In fact, the following chapters are replete with examples of the complex ways in which the various regionalizing dynamics impact on each other. It is also important to recognize that these impacts can be negative as well as positive, in the sense that, for from being mutually reinforcing, these dynamics may work against each other. Take for example a development that has already been alluded to, namely the changing attitudes among prominent regional actors towards what might be termed the European regional project. In the case of both the Länder and various regionalist movements, this has taken the form of a distinct cooling towards any notion of a 'Europe of the regions' and a maximalist vision of the integration process. These developments become easier to understand and explain when reframed in terms of the different regionalizing dynamics. So, for example, the regional-regionalists of the Länder seem to have concluded that the constitutionally entrenched state-regionalism of the *Bundesrepublik* offers stronger guarantees for their position than the weaker, more amorphous force of Euro-regionalism.

What do regions do?

One of the reasons why some of the stronger and more ambitious European regions appear to have adopted a somewhat more skeptical attitude towards the possibilities inherent in Euro-regionalism is the rather limited role allotted to the regions in the European policy process. It is useful at this point to distinguish between the role of regions as *policy-makers*, on the one hand, and regions as *policy-takers*, on the other. Regional-regionalists, be they a self-consciousness proponent of a regional identity or not, covet a role as policy-makers as well as policy-takers; as contributors to the policy-making process as well as implementers of policy developed and decided elsewhere. The position of those European member states that have a regional layer of governance on whether those regions should be able to develop as well as implement policy varies widely, reflecting the various different state traditions ranging from Jacobin centralism to formal federalism. So while in some cases regions have extensive policy-making capabilities and powers, in others regions are little more than administrative conduits for policy decided at 'higher' levels (Keating 1999).

How then is the role of the regions viewed from the European level? Structural funding provides an instructive example here. While the criteria for allotting Structural Funds, as well as the broad parameters within which the various programs operate, are decided at the European level, regions clearly have considerable (if constrained) discretion in terms of their day to day implementation. It is clear, moreover, that this degree of discretion is wide enough to allow the regions to pursue their own priorities and policies. Indeed, for some of the constitutionally weaker regions, involvement with structural funding programs has represented a major expansion in their role and capacity as relatively autonomous, policy-making actors. But the pattern varies. For constitutionally stronger regions, and certainly for regional-regionalists, discretion with regards implementation, even if welcome, is not enough. They want and have sought more influence on the policy-making processes at the European level. They have done so through the Committee of the Regions, although to little avail. The more assertive, 'constitutional' regions have also formed their own organization, REGLEG (regions with legislative powers), which has attempted to lobby for – *inter alia* – greater representation for the regions at the Union level and a direct right of appeal for the regions to the European Court of Justice.[10] These efforts seem to have largely fallen on fallow ground (Lynch 2004). Indeed, for reasons already adduced, it is difficult – though certainly not impossible – to imagine that the role of the regions in policy formulation will be strengthened in the foreseeable future. While regions remain vital in terms of implementation, their role in EU policy-making will remain, in Bagehot's terms, largely 'decorative' rather than 'effective'.

Mention of the REGLEG highlights an aspect of the activities of at least some of Europe's regions discussed in several of the chapters in this book, namely their 'paradiplomatic' activities – as the international relations of sub-state actors has become known. This is an aspect of European and indeed international politics that remains understudied by the scholarly community (Aldecoa and Keating 1999 is a pioneering work in this respect). As is made very clear in the following chapters, this is not due to a lack of effort on the part of regional actors themselves, a number of whom have invested significant resources in their paradiplomatic activities, be they bilateral or multilaterally oriented. It remains an open question, however, whether the actual influence secured as a result of these activities matches their symbolical significance in the eyes of the regional actors themselves.

The cases examined

The chapters that follow concentrate on the regional layer within a particular state, or in the case of Scotland, a particular nation-region within a state. They range across the spectrum: from historic regions such as Scotland and Catalonia, to the non-historic such as Ireland's Euro-regions; from regions within those states that are traditionally centralist, like Jacobin France, to Flanders in the now quintessentially decentralist Belgium; from those states in which the position of regions is both settled and constitutionally embedded, such as Germany, to those like Sweden in which regions remain very much a work in progress. The state of the regions in Eastern and Central Europe is subject to particular attention with chapters on focusing on Bulgaria, Hungary, Poland and Estonia.

Thus, we have deliberately chosen not to concentrate only on instances of powerful regions. The study of such exceptional cases can undoubtedly be of great interest in indicating the potential of regions and regionalism. However, it tells us much less than the whole story. We have, therefore, sought to look well beyond the 'usual suspects' of European regionalism, and have sampled a number of salient characteristics: the degree of powers enjoyed of the region(s), the constitutional 'embedded-ness' of the regions, the size of the state, the level of relative economic development of the state and specific regions, geographic location in Europe, and the length of time for which the state has been both a consolidated democracy and a member of the EU. Overall, while this volume cannot claim encyclopedic scope – we do not examine every state and region in Europe – we can be confident that there will be few major types of region, or regionalist dynamic, not addressed at all in this study.

Bearing in mind the broader context of European integration which provides the common framing for all of these studies, the chapters have been arranged in order of the respective state's accession to the EU. One of the interesting and instructive effects of this choice of ordering is to bring into focus the extent to which it is the earlier members that tend to have the strongest state-traditions of regional government, while among more recent members they are either entirely absent or, at best, have been very deeply submerged under the accretions of recent history. While there are obviously exceptions to this pattern, nonetheless, and as already been argued, this general tendency is surely significant.

Significant also is the way that the ordering of the following chapters serves to underline the importance of what one might term the 'demonstration effect' of the more established regional actors: that is, the way that some of the more advanced and developed regions serve as an example to be emulated by more recent additions to the regional club. Whatever the differences in their respective domestic constitutional status, in case of their paradiplomatic activities at least, a model has now been established which newly established regions (of both Western and Eastern Europe alike) appear almost compelled to follow. A Brussels Office, as well as numerous bilateral and multilateral links with other regions: like Structural Funding Euros, these are the common currency of European regionalism.

Given the variety and variegation of regional Europe, we have not thought it appropriate to impose a common structure or template on each chapter: issues and questions relevant to some case studies are often irrelevant in others. Legal-constitutional aspects are therefore emphasized in some of the chapters, such as that discussing Italy, while politico-economic dimensions are stressed in others, including the discussion of Poland. We have, however, ensured that the contributors focus on common themes. Thus, all the following chapters sketch the particular historical context for, as well as the current role of, the regional layer in their particular case study. The role of regions in implementing European policies is also a common theme, as well as their attempts to influence the contents of those policies. The paradiplomatic activities of the various regions is also highlighted.

The first chapter discusses what is now arguably the most regionalized of all 27 member states, namely Belgium. In it, Wilfried Swenden brings into focus the dialectical relationship between Europeanization and regionalization: the way in which the integration process has served to both facilitate and constrain regional autonomy. Romain Pasquier's chapter, by contrast, outlines the continuing search for a suitable structure and role for the regional level in traditionally centralist France.

Germany is the subject of Carolyn Moore's chapter. That country's well established and powerful regional layer is, of course, constitutionally entrenched through its federal constitution. Moore's discussion underlines the increasingly apparent constraints – and resulting frustrations – that European integration creates for the more powerful regions, with various compensatory mechanisms enacted at the national level proving a poor substitute for the competences lost to the European level through integration. Moore traces recent debates and developments in Germany aimed at making the country's federal structure 'fit for Europe'. Another member of the original 'six' and another of the large EU states, Italy, is the subject of the next chapter by Giandomenico Falcon and Daria de Pretis. Here the constitutional position of the regions has been changing with some rapidity. Falcon and de Pretis provide an overview of the constitutional reforms of 2001, the role of the Italian regions in the implementation of European rules and regulations, and the regions' attempts to influence the content of European decisions.

Katy Hayward's chapter on Ireland focuses on the development of regionalism in one of those states that was part of the first wave of European enlargement; a state, moreover, that is relatively small in terms of size and population, and which has no modern tradition of regionalism. The UK, another first wave state, is now home to a famously asymmetrical form of regionalism (or devolution, as it is known there). The most powerful of the UK's regions, Scotland, is the specific focus of Noreen Burrows' contribution. As a nation with a very long tradition of regional governance, albeit one which has only recently been made directly democratically accountable to the Scottish electorate (as opposed to the UK electorate) by the devolution reforms introduced after 1997, and in a constitutional structure where regional autonomy continues to lack any formal constitutional status even while it is politically highly embedded, Scotland represents a very unusual case in comparative terms.

In Spain, part of the third wave of enlargement, Europeanization has gone hand in hand with both democratization and regionalism – as is the case in Eastern Europe more recently. The crucial difference with much of Eastern Europe is that the Spanish state is challenged by powerful regional regionalist tendencies. Francesc Morata's chapter focuses on the complex interplay between European integration and the Spanish 'State of the Autonomies'. Sweden was part of the fourth enlargement. Anders Lidström analyses how the development of the regional layer has proceeded in parallel with both Europeanization and the related transformation of the country's rather centralist traditional welfare state model.

The remaining chapters all focus on countries that were part of the (two-stage) enlargement of the Union into Central and Eastern Europe following the demise of the Soviet bloc. Tarvo Kungla's chapter focuses on one of the enlarged Union's smaller member states, Estonia. It is Estonia's small size and apparent unsuitability as a test-bed for regionalism that makes it a particularly interesting case: it is, after all, one of many such small states in the Europe of 27. Gyula Horváth's chapter discusses the particularly difficult challenges facing regionalism in Hungary, a country that even before its submergence in the Soviet bloc, was home to one of the most centralized and 'uni-polar' societies in Europe. Grzegorz Gorzelak (with Anna Tucholska) provides a detailed account of the regional structure in post-transformation Poland, tracing the process that has led to the gradual empowerment of that country's regions. Finally, Martin Brusis provides a path-breaking analysis of the development regional layer in Bulgaria, one of the Union's most recent members, and another eastern European country whose highly centralist state-tradition actually predates the Soviet era.

Regions seem destined to continue to play a significant role in European governance and to constitute an important puzzle for those who seek to take the study of European governance seriously. Given that the story of these regions is, above all, a story of almost bewildering variety and variegation, taking regions seriously means serious engagement with their individual circumstances and characteristics while remaining mindful of broader trends and contexts. We are confident that this is precisely what readers will find in the following chapters.

Acknowledgements

The project from which this book has resulted was made possible by a generous grant from the Higher Education Funding Council for Wales (HEFCW). Their support enabled almost all the participants to spend time working alongside the editors at our home Department of International Politics at Aberystwyth University. It also made possible a joint meeting of participants at beautiful Gregynog, in the heart of the mid-Wales countryside, where draft chapters were discussed collectively. We would like to take this opportunity to thank HEFCW for its generosity.

The organization of the individual visits to Aberystwyth as well as the Gregynog conference was left in the very capable hands of Aled Elwyn Jones to whom we owe a debt of gratitude. Gwenan Creunant was, as ever, an invaluable source of advice and support. Hazel Henriksen at NUPI (*Norsk Utenrikspolitik Institut*) in Oslo – RWJ's sabbitical base – was also generous with her time as we attempted to trace some of the less immediately accessible references in the Bibliography.

This book was conceived in close collaboration with Richard Rawlings, now Chair of Laws at University College London. He also participated in the Gregynog conference, providing exceptionally useful comments on earlier drafts of the chapters. Without wishing to embarrass him, we would simply state that it was a great privilege to work with – and learn from – such a distinguished scholar.

Finally, we would like to thank our contributors for the commitment to and support for this project. It has been a pleasure both to work with them and to get to know them. In their company the 'Europe of the regions' became a living reality on the coast of west Wales.

Notes

1. The presidents of the four signed a 'Memorandum' in Stuttgart on 9 September 1988 pledging greater economic and social cooperation. On the 'Four Motors for Europe' group see http://www.4motors.org/.
2. One interesting visionary statement of the Europe of the Regions notion was provided by the Breton Yann Fouéré in his *Towards a Federal Europe: Nations or States?* (1980), a translation from the original French language version published in 1968 under the striking title *L'Europe aux Cent Drapeux*.
3. The Union's own terminological distinction between 'body' and 'institution' is key here. The CoR is an advisory 'body' of the Union (like the Economic and Social Council) rather than a full Union 'institution' with the same status as the European Parliament, the European Commission, and so on. The CoR has tried and failed to get itself upgraded to institutional status on several different occasions. See Loughlin (1997) and Jeffery (2004a).
4. In the case of Plaid Cymru, the party had actually advocated a second chamber at the European level since 1990 (Wyn Jones 2007: 245–246); the subsequent establishment of the CoR was perceived in terms of the creation of an institution that could eventually grow into that role.
5. This is a particularly familiar trope among British and, in particular, English Eurosceptics who regularly accuse the UK government of conspiring with 'Brussels' to divide Britain (or, increasingly, England) by 'balkanising it into a set of artificial euro-regions', to quote a recent parliamentary speech by the prominent right-wing Conservative John Redwood (*Hansard*, 6 November 2007, Column 51). Redwood's views of the twin threats to British sovereignty posed by integration and regionalization are set out at greater length in his *The Death of Britain?* (1999).
6. For an overview see Eurostat's *Regions: Statistical Yearbook 2007*. Available at: http://epp.eurostat.ec.europa.eu/portal/page?_pageid=1335,47078146&_dad= portal&_schema=PORTAL.
7. The literature on European regions and regionalism now very substantial indeed. A key contributor to that literature – arguably *the* key contributor – is Michael Keating (his developing views may be traced through, *inter alia*, Keating 1998, 1999, 2001, 2003, 2004a; Keating *et al.* 2003; Keating and Hughes 2003; Keating and Jones 1985; Keating and Loughlin 1997). It is significant, therefore, that Keating has not attempted to define 'region' in his work. On the contrary, he has frequently commented on the difficulty of doing so, arguing rather that the sheer multiplicity of meanings attached to the term render the search for a single definitive definition pointless. The following passage, from Keating's introduction to a Reader on 'Regions and Regionalism in Europe', is quoted *in extensio* to give a flavour of that multiplicity.

> The problem is that the term 'region' can mean many things and be approached from many different angles. It is a geographical space, but this can be conceptualized at several different spatial scales, from the local to the supranational. The concern here is with the region as a level below the state but above the locality or municipal level, but even this definition leaves a lot of possibilities. A region may have a historic resonance or provide a focus for the identity of its

inhabitants. It may represent a landscape, an architecture or a style of cooking. There is often a cultural element, perhaps represented by a distinct language or dialect. Beyond this, a region may sustain a distinct civil society, a range of social institutions. It can be an economic unit, based either on a single type of production or an integrated production system. It may be, and increasingly is, a unit of government and administration. Finally, all those meanings may or may not coincide, to a greater or lesser degree.

(Keating 2004a: xi)

8. Luxembourg, Ireland, Sweden, Cyprus, Denmark, the Czech Republic, Slovenia, Malta, Slovakia, Hungary, Estonia, Latvia and Lithuania.
9. Luxembourg, Denmark, Slovenia, Cyprus, Malta, Estonia, Latvia and Lithuania.
10. On REGLEG see http://www.regleg.org/ where the aims of the organization are described in the following terms:

The aim of REGLEG is to strive for an enhanced role of those regions in the Europen Union. This means an increased political and legal status of the regions with legislative powers in all domains of EU-governance (legislative, executive and judicial power), according to their competences and responsibilities. This implies *inter alia* an enhanced role in the Council, a better involvement of the regional Parliaments and the right to bring an action before the European Court of Justice so as to preserve their prerogatives.

2
The Belgian Regions and the European Union: Unintended Partners in Unravelling the Belgian State?

Wilfried Swenden

Belgium has long been one of the most Europhile members of the European Union (EU). The current attachment of Belgium to the EU may seem a paradox: when it joined the European Economic Community, Belgium was still a unitary state. Since 1993 it has been a federal state, made up of two types of regions: three communities (the Flemish Community, the French Community, and the German-speaking Community) and three regions (Flanders, Wallonia and Brussels; for a schematic overview of the Belgian federal system, see Swenden and Jans 2006). Can an increasingly decentralized agenda be successfully combined with an increasingly supranational one, or is there a point where the objectives of those who seek to regionalize powers clash with the policies of the EU?

This chapter provides some tentative answers to that question. I argue that while Belgium kept its Europhile credentials intact, the regions have deployed various strategies to offset the less welcome effects of European integration. They have largely tolerated the adverse affects of European integration on their domestic levels of autonomy, but only in exchange for greater involvement in inter-governmental coordination mechanisms at home (where they pertain to EU affairs) and for much higher levels of regional autonomy in general. Hence, despite (or to some extent because of) Europeanization, the Belgian state has become more decentralized than in the pre-Maastricht or the pre-Nice eras, and the regions have gained further instruments to develop their role as 'paradiplomatic' actors in European affairs. Nonetheless, notwithstanding the fact that for all Belgian regions the domestic approach takes precedence over the European route to regional interest representation, and despite the mechanisms that allow for regional representation in European policy-making, the chapter's concluding section shows that Flanders' 'state-building' ambitions are not entirely satisfied with the present status quo.

Belgium and the European Union

Pro-European political elites supported by a permissive public opinion

The Belgian political elite have been supportive of the process of European integration throughout. Even in 2006, when most European political leaders shunned the use of the term federal or put their 'supranational' ideas on hold, Belgian federal prime minister Guy Verhofstadt toured around Europe to promote his provocative manifesto for 'the United States of Europe'. To solve its current socio-economic problems and to strengthen its political influence, he argued, the EU needs more and deeper integration. Although the EU lacks statehood, Verhofstadt claimed that only a 'federal' Europe can give political meaning to a structure which seeks to unite so many different European nations (Verhofstadt 2006). Verhofstadt's analysis was welcomed by most of the political parties and the press across both sides of the linguistic border. Since all Belgian policy-makers (and even the two most recent Belgian monarchs) have subscribed to the notion of a federal Belgium, supporting a 'federal' or 'multi-layered' EU seems a logical and relatively small step.

The pro-European attitude of the Belgian political elite is shared by the public at large. For instance, when a sample of Belgian citizens was asked in the second half of 2005 whether 'generally speaking, Belgian membership of the EU is a good thing', 59 per cent agreed, compared with an average of 50 per cent for the EU as a whole (Eurobarometer 2006: 11). The corresponding share of approval was only higher in Luxembourg, Ireland, the Netherlands and Spain. Half a year later, the gap between Belgium (60 per cent) and the EU average (49 per cent) had increased to 11 per cent (Eurobarometer 2006).

Belgium is not strongly divided along regional or linguistic lines on most European issues. In general, European (as well as Belgian) political institutions are most favorably assessed by citizens who live in Brussels and less favorably by Walloon and Flemish citizens. For instance, a recent study measuring citizens' trust in a vast array of political institutions shows that 18.2 per cent of respondents in Flanders trust the European Parliament, compared with 25 per cent in Wallonia and 30 per cent in Brussels. By comparison, the corresponding levels of trust in the Belgian federal parliament are 19.1 per cent (in Flanders), 25.8 per cent in Wallonia and 27.8 per cent in Brussels (Billiet and Maddens 2007). The relatively high levels of support for the federal parliament in Brussels are consistent with the more 'pro-Belgian' attitude in that part of the country.

However, in contrast to Wallonia and certainly Flanders, Brussels is also the only region in which the European Parliament is trusted more than the federal parliament. Since Brussels hosts the most important European institutions, the relatively high levels of support for the European Parliament should not come as a real surprise. Recent Eurobarometer data confirm the more stridently pro-European attitude of citizens who live in Brussels, yet do not confirm the small gap between Flanders and Wallonia on the previous question. Of citizens who live in Brussels, 70 per cent trust the 'institutions of the European Union', compared with 56 and 55 per cent of those citizens living in Wallonia and Flanders, respectively (Eurobarometer 2006).

Despite the still widely diffused support for European integration, in recent years, the Belgian consensus on European integration has come under challenge. First, while popular support for the EU is still high, not all EU policies are warmly embraced. This is particularly apparent with attitudes in Belgium vis-à-vis (further) enlargement. Belgian citizens are even more likely to oppose (further) EU enlargement than citizens in most of the 15 member states prior to Eastern enlargement. Eurbarometer survey data show that half of Belgium's citizens oppose further enlargement (some 60 per cent if the aspiring member state is Turkey) against 39 per cent for the EU 25 as a whole (Eurobarometer 2006: 55). These data contrast sharply with the support for a European Constitution, which at the end of 2005, was more favorably viewed in Belgium than in any other member state (77 per cent of the Belgian Eurobarometer respondents supported it, against 63 per cent for the EU as a whole). Sixty per cent of all Belgians even support the idea that negotiations on a European Constitution should be revived (Eurobarometer 2006: 57). The Flemish and Walloons are united in their skepticism towards enlargement and in their support for renewed European constitutional talks.

Second, not all political parties unconditionally support European integration, with some regional variation in the nature of the criticisms voiced. In Flanders, criticism has primarily emerged from the extreme right-wing *Vlaams Belang* and the now defunct ethno-regionalist party *Volksunie*. Their fear was/is that the EU is eroding some of the hard-fought gains of regional autonomy, particularly the recognition of Dutch (Flemish) as a significant European language. On the other hand, (Dutch and Francophone) Greens and Social Democratic parties increasingly argue that the current policies of the EU are too market-driven and, in light of monetary union and enlargement, require some form of social correction (for instance by adding specific social criteria in a renegotiated Constitutional Treaty).

The third voice of criticism stems from the regions. Before specifying why the regions (in particularly Flanders) have become more critical of European integration in recent years, we should ask more generally what have been the costs and benefits of European integration from their viewpoint.

European integration and the Belgian regions

European integration has offered major opportunities to the regions. The four freedoms that came along with the creation of an internal market certainly contributed to a further opening up of the Belgian economy. At present, exports make up about 60 per cent of Belgian GDP, making the Belgian economy one of the most open economies in the world. Significantly, the Belgian regions export more to other countries (mostly other EU member states) than they trade with one another. Although we cannot estimate what the economic position of the regions would be *without* a European internal market, European integration has certainly strengthened their economic health and well-being. Increasing trade with other member states or regions has also made them less dependent on the federal government. This is particularly the case for Flanders, which at present accounts for 70 per cent of all Belgian exports.

Although the EU regulates in many fields earmarked as regional affairs in Belgium's domestic distribution of competencies, the country's regions have occasionally been able to use EU policies to their advantage. For instance, the constitutional reforms of 1980 gave the Belgian regions the most important role in regional economic policy: public investment, economic development, land use, and aspects of energy and employment policy became regional competencies. The European Commission was therefore keen on engaging with the Belgian regions when developing its revamped cohesion policies (De Rynck 1996: 136–143). However, in 1985 the Belgian regions lacked the right to conduct foreign (including European) affairs in matters over which they held domestic competence. Hence, the Belgian Permanent Representation and the Department of Foreign Affairs insisted that *they* should play the lead role in these negotiations, particularly since some aspects of the proposed cohesion package also touched upon what then were still national competencies (agriculture and vocational training for which the regional agencies still had to be set up). Yet, as De Rynck put it, 'the regions took advantage of the lack of clarity to strengthen their position on the European forum. They deployed an offensive strategy, claiming that they had the "implied power" to monopolize contacts with the EC in the preparation, decision-making and implementation of structural fund policies' (De Rynck 1996: 141). This strategy paid off. Further constitutional reforms (1988, 1992) made the regions responsible for nearly all aspects that are covered by EU cohesion policies. Furthermore, they strengthened the opportunities of the regions (regions and communities) to engage directly with the EU on matters in which they hold legislative competencies at home (see later discussion). Even before 1988 and 1992, the Commission bypassed the Belgian center by preferring to negotiate partnership agreements with the Belgian regions instead.

Yet European integration also imposes costs on the regions. The 'Maastricht' budgetary criteria bind all public authorities and thus also constrain the borrowing and spending capacity of sub-state authorities. Meanwhile, European policies undermine levels of regional autonomy in areas over which the Belgian regions have gained domestic legislative and administrative competence such as agriculture, environmental policy, competition policy, vocational training or energy policy. Most of the above-mentioned policies are regional policies. Community policies (such as education and culture) tend to be less affected by European integration. The same holds for federal competencies such as foreign policy, defense, the most important taxes (personal income, VAT and corporate income tax) and almost the entire social security field; energy policy and monetary policy represent two obvious and significant exceptions.

Furthermore, regional adaptation costs are high because in three respects the European multi-layered structure is at odds with the Belgian federal order. First, constitutional reforms which brought about the federalization of Belgium made little reference to the process of European integration. Hardly any thought was given on how the domestic distribution of competencies would match the European legal order. European regulation sometimes crosscuts the domestic distribution of competencies. For instance, environmental regulation touches upon policies of the federal *and* the regional governments.

Second, the *method* for allocating EU competencies does not comply with that of distributing competencies under federalism, Belgian style. The bulk of EU legislation requires member state implementation. This 'functional' form of federalism has much more in common with the German than with the Belgian federal order (Börzel 2005). The Belgian regions and communities are not used to implementing policies on which they do not legislate. Furthermore, provided that the EU regulates within its assigned or 'conferred' competencies, EU regulation pre-empts incompatible member state regulation (i.e. the supremacy of EU law). Again, this is reminiscent of the category of 'concurrent' legislation which is found in the German Basic Law. Yet in Belgium, federal and regional laws stand on equal footing, and the number of concurrent bills is kept to an absolute minimum.

Finally, and perhaps most importantly, although Article 203 of the Maastricht Treaty opened access to regional representatives in the Council, Belgian votes cannot be split up along regional lines. Thus, even EU regulations which touch upon competencies which the Belgian Constitution assigns as exclusively regional require a common viewpoint in the Council. In this sense, the EU reduces the capacity for regional policy divergence on issues in which European and regional interests intersect.

Before discussing the strategies that the regions have deployed to overcome the above challenges, one should note that the Flemish government and administration have voiced the greatest concern about European regulatory intrusion. This should not come as a surprise. Of all three regions, Flanders has the strongest sense of regional (national) identity and state-building ambitions. Despite its dominant position in the Belgian federation, demographically and economically, it is more sensitive to cultural and linguistic issues.[1] By comparison, the Walloon government has taken a more relaxed attitude. The Walloon government has lower 'state-hood' ambitions and European integration has never threatened (or has been perceived as a threat to) the prominent role of French in Brussels and its periphery. The greater reliance of the Walloon government on European regional development funds may also partially account for this attitude: of 1.1 billion Euros which the EU pledged to the Belgian regions as regional development aid between 2000 and 2006, 870 million Euros went into Walloon coffers (645 million Euros of which were earmarked as transitional support to the Walloon province of Hainaut which is set to lose its Objective 1 status thereafter; see Regional Development Programmes 2000–2006).

The regional response to the challenge of European integration

In the following paragraphs I will seek to illustrate the strategic response which the Belgian regions have developed to try to reduce the adverse effects of European integration on their levels of autonomy. The Belgian regions have always deployed a double strategy to strengthen their position. On the one hand they have joined other European regions in calling for a better enforcement of the subsidiarity principle, a clearer delimitation of competencies, improved access to the Council of Ministers, and a stronger role for the Committee of the Regions. On the other hand they have tried to maximize their position at home, by securing a right to be involved in foreign and European policy. We focus here mainly on the second strategy and first consider the position of the Belgian regions in external relations more generally. Arguably, no other EU member state (even those with federal constitutions) have granted its regions an equally strong right in foreign policy-making. In this regard, the Belgian solution is more '*con*federal' than 'federal'.

High politics or the role of the regions in external relations and in debating EU treaty reform

The constitutional reforms of 1992–1993 adopted the principle '*in foro interno, in foro externo*' (Alen and Muylle 2003). It remains one of the most radical features of Belgian federalism. According to this principle, the regions and communities are entitled to sign treaties and represent Belgium abroad in areas that fall within their domestic sphere of competence. Hence, the communities could sign a treaty with a state or region seeking closer educational or cultural cooperation *without* the concurrent consent of the federal government. Similarly, the regions could sign a treaty with another state or region, joining efforts in promoting (trans-border) tourism. There are few *domestic* constraints to the treaty-making capacity of the regions in areas in which they are competent. The federal level can stop the regions from signing treaties with states which Belgium (i.e. the federal government) does not recognize or with which it has no diplomatic ties. Furthermore, the regions cannot conclude treaties which would violate Belgium's supranational or international obligations (Alen and Muylle 2003: 637). Treaties that affect the competencies of the regions, either in part or in their entirety require the consent of the parliaments of the affected regions. This provides the regions with a potentially powerful weapon, for at least in theory they could refuse to endorse an agreement that does not sufficiently represent their interests, or that centralizes Belgian federalism through the international backdoor. Paradoxically, regional parliaments must consent to treaty changes that affect their domestic competencies whereas their explicit consent is not required for *domestic* (constitutional) changes with the same effect.

However, the international environment raises some direct constraints. Two of these feature in the context of the EU. First, international organizations, such as the United Nations or OECD only recognize treaties among states. Thus, even if issues are discussed that exclusively touch upon regional competencies, delegates, even if they are delegates appointed by the regions, will officially represent Belgium. As a consequence, Belgium will have to speak with one voice. International organizations do not leave room for three distinct regional or three distinct community viewpoints on the same matter. Conversely, international courts only hold *Belgium* to account for a failure to comply with international norms, although the regions may be responsible for transposing such norms into domestic law. Second, even if the regions had autonomous capacity to sign treaties in a multilateral context, treaties may often pertain to a subject matter that is partly federal *and* partly regional (so called 'mixed treaties'). The domestic answer to both challenges has been to strengthen domestic inter-governmental mechanisms, allowing all the relevant domestic players to be involved in timely fashion in the negotiations leading up to such international decisions (Alen and Muylle 2003: 626–648). Where authorized by the international organization concerned, regional representatives are included in the relevant international delegation. As is the case for inter-governmental relations at home, there is little room for central pre-emption: common action is the fruit of common sense, not of hierarchical control by the center.

In practice, the position of the regions is not always as strong as the theoretical picture would suggest. The federal government alone retains responsibility for selecting and appointing diplomats. Regions and communities can appoint *attachés* who work together with the federal diplomats, but they are answerable to the local head of mission (Ambassador, Permanent Representative or consul), who is always a federally appointed diplomat.

In the context of the EU, the equivalent of 'Treaty-negotiations' are inter-governmental conferences (IGC). Regional representatives can be included in the Belgian negotiation team, either at the ministerial level or at the highest diplomatic level (i.e. COREPER I and II). For instance, regional negotiators took part in the sessions discussing employment policy, traffic, environmental policy, health policy, the subsidiarity principle and the Committee of the Regions in the IGC, which produced the Treaty of Amsterdam (Kerremans 2000a: 502). Yet, as Kerremans observes, before long the federal level gained the upper hand in these negotiations. For starters, regional representatives made up only a quarter of the Belgian negotiation team. Furthermore, the Belgian regions became the victim of their own consociational working methods, at least in the 'European' arena. Here, Belgian regions observe a rotation practice: a region or a community only takes up the regional seat in a Belgian delegation for a period of 6 months, prior to passing it on to the next region or community in line. The federal government can (mis)use its representative *continuity* to persuade the regional representatives that there is limited room for maneuver at the European negotiation table. Domestic fragmentation may 'strengthen' the position of the international negotiator vis-à-vis other state delegations (Putnam 1988), but in the Belgian case the effects work as much in the opposite direction. The federal government can play out discussions which took place more than six months ago as a tool to bring the regional delegations in line with its own preferences. Finally, since IGCs decide by unanimity, the effects of a non-agreement are draconian (a Belgian veto). The alternative – withholding regional parliamentary consent – during the ratification phase is equally drastic.[2]

Despite the unusual style of the negotiations which led to the recently failed draft constitutional treaty, the Belgian regions did not improve their access compared with preceding IGCs (Bursens 2004). The Convention which preceded the IGC created more room for participation of European and national parliamentary delegates in discussions on a new draft treaty, but this did not necessarily increase the role of the regions. During the Convention, the coordination of the Belgian viewpoint rested not only with the federal department of Foreign Affairs (and the federal prime minister) but also with various *ad hoc* groups. Some of these groups were rooted in the Belgian Presidency of the EU (2001) and therefore provided for a larger input from the federal prime minster and his entourage. Others brought together all Belgian members of the Convention, and thus included former Prime Minister Jean-Luc Dehaene (as vice-president of the Convention), the then first minister ('Minister-President') of Flanders and a Flemish minister in the Brussels regional executive. The Flemish and Brussels' ministers attended the Convention as members representing the Committee of the Regions. In the view of Peter Bursens they operated more as representatives of their respective political groups than as regional actors. Since the main foreign policy actors as well as the federal and regional prime ministers represented the same party family, intra-party coordination partially compensated for the lack of direct regional input in the Convention debates (Bursens 2004: 346–347).

The role of the regions in 'low' politics: Regional representation in the council and domestic coordination of the 'Belgian viewpoint'

In contrast with the negotiations leading up to treaty reforms, the Belgian regions are in a stronger position to make their mark on routine Council business, although they must again forge a common viewpoint in this perspective. Article 203 of Maastricht opened the way for direct involvement of regional representatives in the Council. A cooperation agreement between the federal state and the regions (regions and communities), regulates the representation of the regions in sessions of the Council (ministerial meetings and COREPER; Alen and Muylle 2003: 644, fn. 83). In several ways the representational rules run parallel to the mechanisms that determine the participation of the regions in international treaty negotiations:

- The regions are represented by only one region or one community.
- With the exceptions of discussions of agriculture and fisheries, where represented regions usually apply the rotation principle: i.e. after six months, a community or region will pass on its seat to the next community or region in line. Because there are so many different functional Council meetings, each region or community will always represent Belgium in at least one of them (Kerremans 2000b).
- Regions do not participate in meetings on matters that are exclusively federal. This provision applies to Council meetings on general affairs, ECOFIN, budgetary negotiations, justice, telecommunications policy, development aid and civil protection.
- In meetings which primarily yet not exclusively pertain to federal matters, Belgium is represented by one federal lead negotiator and one regional assistant negotiator. The latter has no speaking rights, their main role is to liaise with the regions should Belgium depart from its initial negotiating position, and to communicate the outcome of the negotiations to the regions. This provision applies to Council gatherings on internal market policy, health policy, environmental policy, transport policy and social affairs. When assuming the status of 'assistant negotiators' regions are not normally represented by a regional minister but by one of his/her representatives instead.
- In meetings which primarily, yet not exclusively, deal with regional matters, the opposite provision applies: Belgium is represented by one regional lead negotiator and by one assistant negotiator, who represents the federal government. Currently this provision applies to Council meetings on industrial and R&D policy.

- In meetings which exclusively touch upon regional issues, Belgium is exclusively represented by a regional lead negotiator. This provision applies to Council meetings on culture, education, tourism, youth policy, housing policy and spatial planning.
- The Belgian viewpoint on fisheries policy is determined exclusively by the Flemish region (since the other regions lack a coastline).
- Council meetings on agricultural policy are attended by the federal minister for agriculture (or his/her representative) and sometimes also by the Flemish or Walloon minister of agriculture. However, the domestic inter-governmental mechanisms which determine the Belgian position in the Council are dominated by representatives of the Flemish and Walloon regional governments which hold an effective veto-right (since there is no significant agricultural industry in the Brussels capital region, a representative of this region only occasionally participates in such meetings but does not normally impose an opinion; similarly, the federal government merely 'provides information and opinions'; see Beyers and Bursens 2006).

Although these mechanisms make Council meetings 'fit' the Belgian domestic setting, they do not guarantee an effective representation of regional interests at the EU level. Intensive domestic inter-governmental negotiations are needed to that purpose, from which members of the affected federal and regional legislatures are largely sidelined. Indeed, as is often the case in parliamentary federations, inter-governmental relations strengthen the executive within the policy process (see Watts and Smiley 1985 for comparative observations).

In addition to strengthening the role of the executives, the need to coordinate European policies across different levels of government strengthens the federal government and thus implicitly centralizes the Belgian polity (Beyers and Bursens 2006). This is so because even for areas of EU legislation in which the regions play a more prominent role than the federal government, inter-governmental coordination is required. The federal government is instrumental in bringing the relevant regional parties together. As is the case for inter-governmental conferences, the Department of Foreign Affairs plays an important role, particularly its cell on 'European Integration and Coordination' (P. 11). P. 11 assembles representatives of the federal and regional governments who specialize in European affairs. It convenes on a weekly basis and discusses the issues which the Council will debate in the following week. P. 11 works as a general coordination body in European affairs. Additional coordination meetings are needed at a lower functional or sectoral level. For instance, in the field of environmental policy (a shared federal-regional competence), a coordination committee on international environmental policy operates. It brings together representatives from the federal and regional governments as well as federal and regional attaches who work in the Belgian Permanent Representation to the EU (Kerremans 2000b; Bursens 2002: 182). A failure to reach consensus in P. 11 can trigger a meeting of the Inter-Ministerial Committee for Foreign Affairs. Unlike the former this is composed of ministerial representatives.

Importantly, all forums for inter-governmental coordination require unanimity. Hence, each player (federal government or any of the regions involved) has a veto-right. In theory, this would even apply to meetings which seek to bridge inter-regional differences of opinion on matters for which the regions hold exclusive domestic competence (in practice the federal representatives play the role of mediators).

Belgian domestic inter-governmental relations *on non-EU related matters* frequently end in stalemate: inter-governmental relations regularly emerge as a measure of last resort, and no government is really in a position to push through its view. Traditionally the federal government played a key role in brokering a solution because it comprises representatives from both language groups. Furthermore, at least until 2004 the federal and regional governments were usually made up of representatives from the same parties (so-called 'congruent coalitions'; see Deschouwer 2006). Without a solution emerging from the federal (often six-party) coalition, matters were left unresolved, or, in the worst case scenario an early parliamentary dissolution ensued. Since 2004 the presence of incongruent coalitions at the federal and regional levels of government has increased the need for regular inter-governmental coordination meetings, but has not increased the success rate of issues that end up at the domestic negotiation table. Sometimes parties can spin electoral fortune out of such a crisis, particularly if they can shift the blame onto a government that they do not participate as a coalition partner.

The nature of inter-governmental relations is different, however, when inter-governmental negotiations are needed to work out a Belgian viewpoint *on EU matters*. The pressure to reach an agreement is much higher. Tanja Börzel's observation with regard to the coordination of the Spanish regions in EU decision-making applies to the Belgian case as well (Börzel 2002). In the context of the EU, regions are more willing to compromise than in a purely domestic coordination game. This is so because they have nothing to gain from fighting it out on EU affairs. A failure to compromise implies that Belgium has to abstain in Council meetings. Abstentions do not count as negative votes, hence they cannot block Council decisions which require unanimity. However, abstentions can have a more negative effect when the Council decides by a qualified majority, since they are not counted among the votes in favor of a decision. With 25 member states, the likelihood that the Belgian indecisiveness would affect the overall outcome of a Council vote is rather small. More importantly, a failure to agree on a common viewpoint reduces Belgium's authority in the Council (and by implication also that of the regions; Kerremans 2000a: 494–496). One region's veto may reduce the willingness of another region or even that of the federal government to compromise on the next or a further occasion requiring inter-governmental coordination (the rotation principle means that regions may have to rely on the goodwill of a partner region to defend their interests). The frequency of negotiations needed to work out a domestic viewpoint leave ample room for domestic 'log-rolling' (or 'revenge taking'). Ultimately, Belgium would still have to comply with legislation on which it could not formulate a common viewpoint. Abstentions, therefore, have been very rare.

Despite all the efforts made to coordinate and agree a negotiating position, an agreement on how to vote in the Council does not guarantee that Belgian representatives will ultimately vote for *that* position in the Council. Belgium is only one of 25 member states and, as negotiations proceed, the contours within which a compromise solution may be framed can shift. The Belgian negotiator has to know what room for maneuver she has in moving away from the domestically sanctioned proposal. In the first instance, the lead negotiator will have to assess whether a suggested compromise solution would still fall within acceptable limits of the domestic position. Sometimes such an assessment is difficult, particularly if the assistant negotiator is a civil servant or a member of a ministerial *cabinet*, rather than a minister himself. As Kerremans asserts, this is often the case when the regions assume the position of assistant negotiators. A regional civil servant is not likely to contradict the viewpoint of a more senior federal minister (Kerremans 2000a: 501). Therefore, policies may be adopted to which a regional minister would have objected (thus, decision-making implicitly shifts from the regional to the federal policy level, contributing to implicit centralization). When the regions delegate the lead negotiator, the presence of a regional minister is almost guaranteed and the risk of 'over-riding' regional interests is much lower. Yet, even here, regional ministers must agree a common viewpoint. If such matters cannot be discussed 'on the phone' the lead negotiator may take a decision 'ad referendum'. She will then notify the Council that Belgium needs an extra three days to confirm or adjust its decision. This short reflection period should be sufficient to convene informal gatherings, a more formalized P. 11 meeting or even an inter-ministerial conference. However, in practice, ad referendum decisions are rarely departed from, particularly if they could upset a hard-fought compromise solution involving all EU member states (Kerremans 2000a: 502).

The role of the regions in low politics: Regional involvement in different phases of the European policy cycle

Meetings in the Council may be very important, but they are only a part of the European policy cycle. The Commission still holds the prerogative in drafting legislation, but often does so after extensive discussions with member states, relevant interest groups and other non-state actors. The question arises whether the Belgian regions have sufficient access to the Commission or its relevant directorate-generals and whether the regional executives and parliaments are informed in a timely manner of any legislative proposals which the Commission has made.

Despite the Commission's attempts to liaise with the regions, for instance in developing partnership agreements with regions as part of its cohesion policy framework, there is little evidence to suggest that the regions are systematically involved in the policy preparation phase. Although the Belgian Permanent Representation passes on draft legislative proposals to all the affected Belgian governments and parliaments, most of the consultation process will have already been completed when these reach the Belgian regions. Peter Bursens and Sarah Helsen have pointed to various weaknesses in the Belgian coordination mechanisms as well as in the interaction between the European and Belgian (regional) authorities (Bursens 2002; Bursens and Helsen 2003).

With regard to the domestic coordination mechanisms, they point to the absence of a clear linkage between those who negotiate on behalf of Belgium in the Commission, Council and European parliament, and those who are responsible for implementing these policies. For instance, *cabinetards* or civil servants in the Belgian Ministry of Foreign Affairs who assist in the preparation of a Belgian position in the Inter-Ministerial Conference for Foreign Affairs and P. 11 hardly cooperate at all with civil servants in the same ministry who monitor the implementation of EU policies. Unlike P. 11, the latter has a 'judicial character' and is mainly staffed by lawyers (Bursens and Helsen 2003: 9). This artificial separation between both types of civil servants produces a discontinuity in information and can contribute to an inconsistent implementation of EU policies.

With respect to the interaction between the European and Belgian regional authorities the following three weaknesses arise (Bursens 2002; Bursens and Helsen 2003). First, Belgian regional authorities are not widely consulted in expert meetings that precede the issuing of draft legislation. Second, although adequate regional involvement in the Council is provided at the ministerial level and that of the Permanent Representation (COREPER I and II), this is not the case at the level of the working groups. Nonetheless, the working groups often establish the contours of a European-wide compromise. Finally, regions are also insufficiently involved in committees which discuss the implementation of EU legislation. The *comitology* committees are always made up of delegates from the national governments. A more coordinated approach between the federal and regional governments is needed to ensure that the regions adequately (and uniformly) implement EU policies.

The paradox of Belgian Euro politics: Euro-skepticism on the ground?

There is a paradox in the Belgian attitudes towards the EU. On the one hand, the political elite strongly support the cause of European integration and even embrace a level of European integration which at present the European Commission and European parliament (the two most 'supranational' political institutions) do not dare to support. On the other hand, Belgium does not have the strongest of records in terms of implementing EU legislation. In 1997, Belgium notified the Commission of the transposition of 91.8 per cent of all EU directives, then the worst record of all EU member states. Aware of its bad performance, the federal government (in cooperation with regional governments) launched an effort to improve the Belgian record. For instance, shortly after Guy Verhofstadt became federal prime minister in 1999, a junior minister was appointed whose primary function was to oversee the timely and correct implementation of EU legislation, to establish a databank to this effect and to liaise with the regional authorities on such matters.

This effort paid off. By the end of 2000, Belgium had already notified the Commission of the transposition of 97.9 per cent of all EU directives; by March 2006, this percentage had gone up to 99.04 (European Commission 2006). Although a significant improvement in absolute and relative terms, notifications are based on a member state's subjective perception as passed to the European Commission. Hence, member states with a better notification record could be confronted with higher infringement rates (Bursens 2002: 177). In this respect the Belgian picture looks less promising. For instance, in its most recent *Annual Report on Monitoring the Application of Community Law*, Belgium is certainly ranked among the bottom group of countries who allegedly have not or have incorrectly transposed EU legislation, or have failed to communicate transition measures to the European authorities (European Commission 2004). In 2004, Belgium featured in 16 new cases submitted to the Court of Justice, the fourth highest number of court referrals after Greece (involving 27 cases), Italy (26 cases) and France (23 cases; see European Commission 2004). In the same year, the Commission observed 79 infringements of EU law by Belgium, the sixth highest figure for the 15 'old' member states of the EU (European Commission 2004). The Commission's statistical overview does not allow us to consider which policy sectors have caused more infringement procedures and to establish whether the infringement is caused by negligence of the federal or some or several of the regional governments.

The question arises whether the defaults in the domestic coordination mechanisms that were highlighted above, or the sheer complexity of these mechanisms could be held responsible for the relatively poor Belgian performance? We can only provide some provisional answers here, since more systematic research is needed to identify the role of 'domestic complexity' and 'federalism' as crucial explanatory variables. In fact we could offer three rival hypotheses.

The first hypothesis predicts that the implementation record is better in policy areas which require relatively little inter-governmental cooperation. The inter-governmental complexity that must be overcome to formulate a common viewpoint slows down decision-making. Environmental policies exemplify such a complex policy area. The federal government still controls product standards, protection from radioactive radiation, transit of waste materials and maritime environment, but the regions control the other aspects of environmental policy. For instance, the 'packaging waste directive' touched upon the competences of no less than four governments (Bursens 2002: 182). Furthermore, environmental rules sometimes affect other regional competencies, such as agriculture, transport or public health. Thus, they may require further interdepartmental coordination within and across levels of government. As Kerremans has demonstrated, next to a coordination committee on international environmental policy, which functions as part of the P. 11 machinery, dozens of functional sub-committees or working groups have been established to prepare the Belgian viewpoint in the Council (Kerremans 2000b). The complexity of these mechanisms prevents the formation of a prominent and timely Belgian viewpoint in the Commission's expert committees. In environmental policy, Belgium comes closer to being a 'policy-taker' than a 'policy-maker', which contributes to lowering its implementation rate. This record contrasts with the more favorable implementation score for labor directives (Bursens 2002): labor policies are still largely controlled by the center and thus involve a more simplified coordination mechanism at home. Labor policies also affect well organized and relatively centralized interest groups who are allowed to play a more prominent role in the Commissions' expert groups. Therefore, EU labor directives are more in tune with Belgian domestic preferences and stand a higher chance of being faithfully implemented (Bursens 2002).

A second hypothesis suggests that the cause of different implementation records with regards in different policies is related less to the complexity of the domestic arrangements than to the overall enthusiasm and expertise which a member state or its regions can put forward in these policies. For instance, one could make the case that even if environmental policy were entirely regulated by the center or the regions, Belgium's implementation record would not be much higher. Belgium was an environmental laggard long before the regions gained responsibility in this field; by comparison, Belgium always enjoyed a strong reputation in labor law. More research is needed to show which of both explanations has the strongest predictive power.

The final hypothesis draws parallels between the implementation records in domestic and in European legislation. Although there are no comparative databanks which allow us to assess how well a member state implements its own legislation, researchers are aware of differences in political culture with regard to the significance which citizens attach to the law. In comparative terms Belgian citizens are rather 'open to a flexible interpretation of the law' (Maesschalk and Van De Walle 2006). Belgium may in fact fit better into a Latin or South European than a Northern legal culture: many and relatively detailed pieces of legislation are produced, but not all of them will be fully implemented, let alone faithfully observed (in this regard the survey data suggest that Flanders is at least as 'Southern' as Wallonia).

Conclusion: Future strategies and grievances of the Belgian regions

Compared with regions from other member states that are discussed in this book, the Belgian regions are entrusted with extraordinary instruments to make themselves heard at the European level. Yet they are not entirely satisfied with the current status quo. The requirement that Belgium must cast one vote, and the central role of the federal foreign ministry, P. 11 and the Permanent Representation in coordinating the Belgian viewpoint, are said to 'centralize' Belgian federalism through the European backdoor (Beyers and Bursens 2006). This view should be nuanced. After all, Belgian federalism is now much more decentralized than 10 years ago, even in policy areas that are most affected by Europeanization such as agriculture and environmental regulation (indeed, 20 years ago both policies were still entirely controlled by the center). Yet, one could argue that Europeanization has slowed the unravelling of the Belgian state, by forcing the regions into cooperative behavior and by making them partially reliant on federal assistance for that cooperation.

At one level the Belgian regions pursue similar strategies to further enhance their voice in Europe. They all liaise with regions with which they share common interests or constitutional levels of autonomy: the stateless nations of Catalonia, the Basque Country or Scotland, or important regions with legislative powers such as Bavaria, Piedmont or Lombardy. In recent years, Flanders, in particular, has been one of the most active members of REGLEG. Unlike the Committee of the Regions, REGLEG is more homogeneous in membership, as it unites a group of regions with directly elected assemblies which control genuine legislative powers. Yet the European regions are very heterogeneous and one could argue that their collective strength has weakened as a result of enlargement (most new entrants are small member states or lack a significant regional tier of government). Therefore, the Belgian regions also seek to strengthen their role in the *domestic* coordination of EU policies by lobbying the federal government. They are in a strong position to do so: the Belgian federal government is made up from representatives of non-state-wide parties whose organization and electoral reach largely correspond with the borders of the two dominant regions: Flanders and Wallonia. In recent years, the share of regional or community representatives in the Permanent Belgian Representation has steadily increased to above 20 per cent. Regions have also commissioned research into strengthening their input in the 'uploading' and 'downloading' phase of European decision-making. In this regard, Bursens and Helsen have advocated the creation of a 'European Co-ordination Body': horizontally, it would do away with the artificial separation between negotiators and implementers of European policy, vertically it would integrate representatives of the affected federal and regional ministries in regular policy cooperation. Such a body should be staffed with permanent personnel, rather than with civil servants who temporarily leave their functions at the federal and regional administrations (Bursens and Helsen 2003: 16). The Belgian regions are also united in their effort to advocate direct access to the European Court of Justice and to involve the regional parliaments in testing the subsidiarity principle.

At a different level, however, the strategies of the Belgian regions do not run on parallel tracks. As the region with the strongest national identity, Flanders has pursued bilateral strategies which clearly tried to 'circumvent' the federal government or the other regions. In September 2006 (and therefore, perhaps, surprisingly late in the day), the Flemish government established a regional office in Brussels to liaise directly with other European regions, member states and the European institutions. The Flemish government has also expressed discontent with the EU requirement to vote as one country. It has asked Flemish researchers to look into the possibility of 'splitting up' the vote in the Council (Vlaamse Standpunten 2003). In 2003, it suggested that in areas decided by the regions, the then ten Belgian Council votes could be divided between the regions, with 5 Flemish, 4 Walloon and 1 Brussels vote. With regards community competences the distribution between the communities could be Flanders 5, *Bruxelles-Wallonie* 4 and the German-speaking community 1. However, there was little European support for this solution, not even among the regions of the other federal EU member states. What may work for Belgium would not work as well for Germany (where the number of sub-units is much higher). Furthermore, to split a national vote along regional lines is like opening up Pandora's Box: why not divide the votes of member states along party-political lines as well? For instance, the German votes could be split among the two major parties of its present grand coalition government. Nonetheless, the current situation leaves the Flemish government frustrated: the Baltic States or Malta have a stronger input than Flanders, which represents more people. The centrifugal and dual logic of Belgian federalism clashes with the centripetal and cooperative logic of European multi-level governance: cooperation just goes against the prevailing domestic mood, and Flemish frustration suggests that Flanders sometimes reaches comprises on European policies because it has to, not because it wants to.

With only partial backing from other European regions for its suggestions, and without the immediate prospects for a renegotiated constitutional treaty, Flanders is more likely to place greater emphasis on the domestic strategy. Half the federal government is made up of Flemish delegates representing Flemish (i.e. non-state-wide) parties. These federal ministers are more receptive to regional demands than say the members of federal governments elsewhere who usually represent (a regional branch of) a state-wide party.

Already in the lead up to Maastricht, several European regions warned their national governments against ceding authority to Europe in areas of regional competence (Jeffery 1997). Indirectly, they contributed to slowing down the transfer of competencies from the domestic to the European arena. Paraphrasing Alan S. Milward, Charlie Jeffery has referred to this process as the 'regional rescue of the nation-state' (Jeffery 2006). In Belgium, however, there is a more straightforward option: with a federal government that is already 'captured' by representatives of non-state-wide parties, the unravelling of the center will gain further speed. Most Flemish parties now advocate more regional powers in health and social policy as well as taxation. Although such decisions can be blocked by the French-speakers who are not served by most of these proposals, following the 2007 general elections Flemish pressure to regionalize more powers is high. A failure to reach an agreement on future Belgian state reform could jeopardize the formation of a federal government.

In the short term, campaigning for more regional autonomy at home may be the most feasible Flemish strategy. Gains in this regard could offset any losses incurred by EU regulatory centralization past and future. In the *long* run, the loser could well turn out to be the federal government whose role would be effectively reduced to that of a regional interest broker in EU affairs.[3] Without Belgian media or parties it is hard to see who would speak up for the Belgian center. Therefore, the federal government may be hollowed out too much before the Belgian regions could come to its rescue, even if they wanted to. In this sense Europeanization may speed up the process of domestic unravelling, albeit unintentionally.

Notes

1. For instance, in the 1990s Belgium postponed extending voting rights for (non-Belgian) EU nationals resident in Belgium for European and municipal elections (Kerremans and Beyers 1998: 28). The Flemish parties insisted on a Belgian exemption because it was feared that granting those voting rights earlier could upset the delicate balance between Dutch- and French-speakers in Brussel's suburbs. The latter are situated in Flanders but comprise a majority of French-speakers. Most (non-Belgian) EU citizens who live there are more likely to speak French

than Dutch, and thus it was assumed that they would more likely vote for a French-speaking party.

2. However, this option was once seriously contemplated. The Treaty of Amsterdam affected federal, regional and community competencies. Therefore, in addition to the federal parliament, the Flemish parliament, the Walloon parliament, the Brussels regional parliament, the parliament of the German-speaking community and the French community parliament had to endorse it. Although Brussels is a region and not a community, the Dutch and French-speaking members of the Brussels capital regional parliament constitute separate Community Commissions with implementing authority in Community legislation (in the case of the French Community Commission, that authority has been extended to primary legislation in educational matters). Therefore the Treaty also required the consent of the Flemish and French Community Commissions in Brussels. Due to a political crisis among the Dutch-speaking members of the Brussels executive, the executive of the Flemish Community Council temporarily lacked majority support in the Council. The crisis revolved entirely around a *domestic* issue since few members rejected the Treaty of Amsterdam. Nonetheless, the Flemish opposition parties threatened to withhold their support unless the then Brussels executive first made concessions with regards regional politics. Consequently, of all EU member states, Belgium was the last to ratify the Amsterdam Treaty.

3. Importantly, this process may take a long time: the center still holds important competencies and the French-speakers have less interest in unravelling the center given the current flow of redistributive payments. They can use their veto-position in the center to stop or slow down the regionalization of powers (such as regional fiscal autonomy) which would work against their interests.

3
The French Regions and the European Union: Policy Change and Institutional Stability

Romain Pasquier

The French state, like other European nation-states, has been confronted for some years by the dual pressure of European integration and the growing desire for autonomy on the part of sub-national political levels. On the economic front, the growing internationalization of the economy calls into question voluntarist policies of territorial planning, while the promise of a post-Fordist model of production based on the flexible specialization of local units of production suggests the necessity of reinforcing intermediate levels of government (Amin 1994). On the political level, 'globalization' has tended to accelerate European integration and, with it, the emergence of multi-level governance (Hooghe and Marks 2001; Le Galès and Lequesne 1997; Keating 1998). Since the mid-1980s, European regional policy has been identified as a key variable in the reorganization of public action at the territorial level within the European Union (EU). More generally, the process of 'Europeanization', i.e. the 'processes of a) construction, b) diffusion and c) institutionalization of norms, beliefs, formal and informal rules, procedures, policy paradigms, styles, "ways of doing things" that are first defined and consolidated in the EU policy process and then incorporated in the logic of domestic (national and sub-national) discourse, political structures, and public policies' (Radaelli 2003), has been analyzed as a new political opportunity structure, providing political and economic resources for regional actors to strengthen their positions vis à vis central administrations (Börzel 2002; Bukowski et al. 2003; Pasquier 2004a).

In France, the central authorities have been forced to face the emergence of a rival supranational 'center,' the European Commission, which has sought to establish relations of exchange and cooperation with sub-national authorities either through the EU's regional policies or through the institutional representation of these authorities (local as well as regional) in the EU's Committee of Regions (Jeffery 1997). This ongoing process notably questions the center/periphery relations in France and the traditional domination of the central state. Does the EU empower the French regions? Does the implementation of EU policies accelerate regionalization '*à la française*'? To address these questions, I first analyze the process of regionalization in France and the role played by the regions in the institutional architecture of French decentralization. Regionalization '*à la française*' follows a specific trend in comparison to other European states. Although in most of the European states, regionalization or decentralization processes try to regulate secular cultural and political claims coming from specific territorial communities, a functional vision of the region has been dominant until the 1980s in France. This explains the current structural handicap of the French regions in terms of identitary potential and political capacity compared to other countries. However, I argue that the implementation of EU policies produced significant changes in French center/periphery relationships. The Europeanization of the French multi-level game gives new economic and political resources to the regions. They use these EU norms and resources to empower their territorial governance. However, the political impacts vary among the regions. More broadly, if this Europeanization process has really produced policy and strategic changes for the French regions, it has failed to modify the main political structures of the French decentralization until now. The implementation of the last decentralization act in 2003–2004 shows the resistance of the decentralized Jacobin state.

France: the two faces of the regionalization process

Most of the structural limits of the French regions are to be found in the history of the regional question in France. Since the end of the nineteenth century, regionalization has been one of the key issues inside the debate between centralization and decentralization. However, the regionalization process followed a specific trend in comparison to other European states. This notably explains the ambiguous position of the regional level in the first decentralization reform led by Gaston Deferre in 1982–1983. In most of the European states, regionalization or decentralization processes have tried to regulate secular cultural and political claims coming from specific territorial communities. In France, the regional issue is quite different. Two main representations of the region have emerged and competed since World War II: the region defined as an economic and planning space, and the region defined as a political representation level (Pasquier 2003a, 2004a). For a long time in France the first definition of the region has been largely dominant because it was not contradictory with the local Republican administration. From the 1960s and 1970s, the political vision of the regions arose, so the decentralization reform led by Gaston Deferre in 1982–1983 appeared as a compromise between these two ideas. So, to understand this French exception we must take into account the structuring of the local Republican administration and the state's capacity to promote cultural standardization on one hand and, after World War II, economic development through regional planning on the other.

The region: a functional space or a political level?

The French system of local administration that was defined by statute following the 1789 Revolution became the model on which local government systems were to be based throughout most of Western Europe. It resembled the Bourbon system that preceded it in its centralization of power and in being based on the same town and village. However, the Jacobin governments codified this centralization process into a uniform structure of 83 *départements*, headed by a central government official, the *préfet*. The prefects not only tended to dominate the proceedings of departmental councils (*conseils généraux*) but also exercised powers of supervision over decisions by the communes.

This system of centralized direction stayed basically unchanged for over 180 years through two imperial, two royal and four republican regimes, while local powers developed step by step towards local democracy. *Départements* were recognized as local authorities in the 1830s and they obtained full recognition as '*collectivités territoriales*' in 1871. In the *départements*, the prefects were the chief executives until changes introduced in March 1983. The mayors, the executives of the communes, became popularly elected in 1882 and full budgetary competence was conferred together with a general competence for communal assemblies. However this uniform politico-administrative structure would not have functioned without a great process of cultural standardization. It was crucial for French central elites to consolidate the institutional structures by building a strong national ideology (Rokkan and Urwin 1982). At the end of the nineteenth century, the Third Republic gave this role to schools and the army. This task was done through an intense project of national education led by the republican teachers known as the '*hussards noirs de la République*', and the development of the lines of communication inside the territory (Weber 1977; Thiesse 1997). In addition, World War I definitively convinced millions of individuals that they were French and not Breton, Basque etc. This cultural standardization explains why ethno-regionalist claims remained marginal in France until the 1960s, contrary to other European states (Izquierdo and Pasquier 2004). A first wave of regionalism emerged between the end of the nineteenth century and World War II, when elites in economic decline used the cultural and linguistic traditions of some regions to struggle against the republican project. This regionalism expanded in underdeveloped and peripheral regions such as Brittany, Languedoc and Corsica, areas increasingly left aside by the changing trade patterns characterizing the French economy. This first regionalism had an important intellectual influence through the *'Fédération Régionaliste Française'* of Jean-Charles Brun (Wright 2006) although it never obtained real electoral impact.

On the other hand, a class of political leaders known as 'notables' developed throughout the nineteenth and twentieth centuries. They 'managed' relations with representatives of the government, including prefects and subprefects and sometimes members of the government in order to advance the interests of their ideas and maintain political support. The more able and ambitious could acquire great prestige and authority, often through the accumulation of electoral offices, which gave authority and influence (*le cumul des mandats*). The more eminent became known as *grands notables*, able to direct the power of the state in the interest of the locality by their own elective and informal power. The system has been described as 'tamed Jacobinism' by Pierre Grémion (1976), implying that the Lion of Jacobinism has been tamed by local interests. This system established interdependence between local leaders, central politicians and senior government officials. This phenomenon also explains why claims for local autonomy have been well controlled by the French state over such an extended time period. Political leaders were at the same time local and national representatives.

After World War II, the French state had to embark upon economic and industrial rebuilding. Government policy was expansionist, aimed at promoting growth in the provinces and correcting the imbalances between Paris and the rest of France. In this context, local and regional actors mobilized to develop less wealthy territories as, for example, the *'Comité d'études et de liaison des interest Bretons* (CELIB)' in Brittany. A second wave of regionalism took place between the beginning of the 1950s and the end of the 1960s. This new regionalism was linked to the regional planning policy developed by the French central administration and its central planning agencies during this period.[1] Regional coalitions led by the CELIB forced the French state to regionalize national planning policy (Pasquier 2003a, 2003b). In 1956, the central administration officially established a regional map of France with 21 regions.[2] A new state economic development framework was set up in 1964 with consultative bodies to bring together local economic, social and cultural sectors with political leaders and state servants in consultative bodies to participate in regional planning and programming. Some regional groups and elites organized coalitions to pressure the national government to associate regional actors with the so-called *'aménagement du territoire'* policy (Pasquier 2003a). This second wave of 'functional regionalism' definitively failed with the failure of the General de Gaulle's referendum on regionalization in 1969. However, from the 1960s, cultural and political claims were raised in several regions: the Basque Country, Brittany, Corsica and Languedoc-Roussillon (Lafont 1967; Fournis 2005). This was a left regionalism structured in cultural movements and political parties like the *'Union démocratique bretonne'* in Brittany or the *'Action régionaliste corse'* in

Corsica. Some of the claims of these movements were adopted by the French Socialist party,[3] which implemented the decentralization reform from 1982 in France.

The decentralization against the regions?

The reforms, led by Gaston Defferre in 1982–1983, gave to the regional institutions the status of corporate public entities and the presidents of regional and departmental assemblies (the *conseils régionaux* and the *conseils généraux*) real executive powers. *Préfets* remained to head government staff within their regions and departments. The 22 metropolitan regions obtained competences in economy, vocational training, education (secondary schools), regional railway transport planning,[4] environment, culture and research, but their budgets remain quite small.[5] The first regional elections took place in 1986. However the devolution process did not really revolutionize the French local system. It is a fundamental principle of French law that no territorial unit below the level of the nation can be hierarchically superior to any other. Regional authorities are in no position, therefore, simply to impose their will on 'lower' units; they must negotiate and convince (Pasquier 2004a). This clearly results from the functional vision of the French regions: regions are often considered as constituting a coordinating level rather than a political level imposing norms and policies. It is also a way to protect the *départements* from potential regional hegemony.

In addition, the proportional representation system used for the regional elections produced an important institutional instability in most of French regions from 1986 to 1998. Small parties from across the political spectrum – including the *Front national (FN)*, *Chasse pêche nature et traditions (CPNT)*, *Les Verts*, *Lutte ouvrière* (LO) and the nationalist parties in Corsica – utilized the system to obtain new political positions and resources. Thus, political parties that were traditionally excluded from the majoritarian political game, populated the regional institutions. The multiplication of political parties' electoral lists affected the governability of the French regions. In 1986, nine regions had no clear political majorities. The FN obtained several vice-presidencies in, for example, Franche-Comté, Provence-Alpes-Côtes-d'Azur (PACA) and Haute-Normandie. The consequences of the 1992 regional elections were still more undermining for regional institutions.[6] The right obtained an absolute majority in three regions (against eight previously) and a relative majority in 13 more (eight previously). For its part, the left, which had held an absolute majority in two regions (Limousin and Nord-Pas-de-Calais) and three relative majorities (Aquitaine, Languedoc-Roussillon and Haute-Normandie), retained only one absolute majority (Limousin) and a relative majority in four regions. The height of the crisis was reached during the winter 1996–1997 in the region of Haute-Normandie, when the regional *préfet* had to impose a budget because of a lack of agreement among the parties. Faced with this instability, Lionel Jospin's government decided in March 1998 to give a new institutional tool to the regional presidents: the so-called '*49.3 régional*'.[7] The president of the region has the possibility to adopt the budget even if they do not have a majority, except if an alternative budget is proposed and voted by the absolute majority of the regional councilors.

Moreover, 1986–1998 witnessed the nationalization of the regional elections. The main French parties mainly used the regional lists to thank deserving militants without any regional feeling or strategy. The regional campaigns were mainly based around national issues. For example, for the 1998 regional elections, the key issue was the national agenda of the '*gauche plurielle*' government (the 35-hour working week and measures to address unemployment). Regional debates remained very weak: indeed the region could hardly be said to exist as a meaningful public space. During the campaigns, regional projects, regional policies and the potential reforms of decentralization were viewed through national political logics. The centralization of public media played an important part in this. Except in some regions, such as Brittany, the main public media work at local and national levels rather than at the regional one. France 3 TV has regional branches but they do not have the capacity to seriously cover the debates, in contrast to the situation in some other European regions. Furthermore, the French region does not really exist as a space for collective action. For example, trade unions in the education or agriculture policy sectors seek to preserve centralist modes of action. Key trade unions in these policy sectors, the FSU and the FNSEA, have in fact been notably resistant to Raffarin's reform and its 'regionalist' orientation. For these sectoral actors regionalization could mean a loss of power and influence.

Finally, by using *départements* as electoral districts from 1986 to 1998, the electoral rules weakened the French regions relative to the *départements*. The *département* remains a very strong political level in France. Political parties and media are always organized at this sub-regional level. Local leaders in the *départements* control their candidates on the regional lists. So, logically enough, regional councilors often end up defending their department's interests during the regional policy-making process. All this is reinforced by the overlap between regional elections and cantonal elections (elections for the *départements*). The law of 11 December 1990 established that regional and cantonal elections take place simultaneously. The resulting confusion of campaigns, as well as the concurrence of candidatures, acts to weaken the visibility of the French regions and their elites.

Thus, the decentralization process has not really empowered the regional level of the French political system (Schrijver 2006). Table 3.1 shows the feeling of belonging according to the different territories. It is immediately clear that most people in France refer to their commune and to France if they have

Table 3.1 Territory to which respondent feels main attachment, %

Attachment to*	1985	1990	2000
Commune	38.8	40.5	34.2
Département	5.8	9.1	9.3
Région	12.4	15.8	15.4
France	38.3	31.8	39.8
NA	4.7	2.8	1.6

Question asked: « Auquel de ces lieux avez-vous le sentiment d'appartenir avant tout ? La ville, commune où vous habitez; votre département ; votre région, la France, aucun ? »
*Only Alsace, Aquitaine, Centre, Franche-Comté, Languedoc-Roussilon, Limousin, Midi-Pyréennées, Nord-Pas-de-Calais, Pays-de-la Loire, Poitou-Cahrente and PACA were included in all years.
Source: Observatoire du Politique 1985, 1990, 2000, author's elaboration.

to say to which territory they have the strongest feeling of belonging. The *département* and the region are much less popular, even if the latter of those two meso-level territories scores better as primary source of identification. However, Table 3.2 underlines that the differences between the regions are considerable. In 2000, Brittany, Corsica and Alsace had a much higher proportion of respondents who placed their region above other territorial units. At the opposite end of the spectrum, regional identity is very low in Ile-de-France and Centre. This variation between the regional identities in France has not, however, had a significant impact on the strength and significance of ethno-regionalist claims and/or movements in France.

In contrast to other European countries, ethno-regionalist parties have had very little political impact in France (De Winter et al. 2006). Although several French regions exhibit very similar identity potential to Belgian, Spanish or Italian regions in terms of culture and language, until now the organization and the development of autonomist parties has remained very limited. Except in Corsica, which has had a specific statute since 1991, ethno-regionalist parties have not really developed with the decentralization process. Two main factors explain this French exception: the relatively easy cohabitation between regional identities and the national one and the electoral regime (Pasquier 2006). In France, the relationship between national and regional identification is not really conflictual. In contrast to Catalonia, Flanders, Lombardy or Wales, 90 per cent of the population feels as much Breton, Basque or Corsican as French. In other European regions the situation is radically different.[8] For instance in Wales, around a quarter of the population view themselves as exclusively Welsh rather than British. It means that in French regions such as Brittany or Aquitaine, any ethno-regionalist discourse has more difficulty in attracting support because very few persons feel exclusively Breton. The weak

Table 3.2   Attachment to the region, by region, 1999, %

	Very attached	Fairly attached	Not very attached	Not all attached	NA	Total
Alsace	59.1	29.8	8.1	2.8	0.1	100
Aquitaine	50.9	38.1	9.1	1.7	0.1	100
Bourgogne	43.6	37.1	15.6	3.7	0.0	100
Bretagne	65	27.5	6.1	1.3	0.1	100
Centre	36.3	39.2	17.5	6.9	0.1	100
Corse	78.3	16.2	4.1	1.1	0.3	100
Franche-Comté	52.7	32.6	10.5	3.8	0.3	100
Ile-de-France	30.2	36.6	23.5	9.7	0.1	100
Languedoc-Roussillon	59.3	26.1	9.8	4.7	0.0	100
Limousin	55.2	31.7	10	2.7	0.4	100
Lorraine	53.9	30.4	13.4	2.3	0.0	100
Midi-Pyrénées	58.9	31	7.6	2.6	0.0	100
Nord-Pas-de-Calais	58.1	29.4	8.4	4.1	0.0	100
Basse-Normandie	49.9	36.6	10.8	2.7	0.0	100
Haute-Normandie	43	39.7	12	5.1	0.1	100
Pays-de-la Loire	41.5	41.3	13.7	3.1	0.4	100
Picardie	46.1	32.1	15.9	5.4	0.4	100
Poitou-Charentes	46.3	36.9	12.4	4.3	0.1	100
PACA	59.9	28	8.3	3.9	0.0	100
Rhône-Alpes	51.7	34.3	10.6	3	0.4	100

Question asked: « Pouvez-vous me dire si vous êtes très attaché, plutôt attaché, pas attaché ou pas attaché du tout à votre région ? »

Source: Observatoire Interrégional du Politique 1999, 1997, author's elaboration (Because of rounding, percentages for each row do not necessarily add up to exactly 100).

differentiation between regional and national feelings presents a serious handicap for ethno-regionalist parties in France. In addition, the electoral rule adopts a two-round system at the local level (communes, départements). To participate in the second round in local elections, it's necessary to get 10 per cent of the votes. This system forces parties to bargain and compromise, accepting a 'second best', and gives the advantage to national parties, limiting the ethno-regionalist representation. At the regional level, the situation is quite similar. To be represented in the regional assembly the list must obtain 5 per cent of the voters in the electoral district. Hence, the method of election selected for regional councils has further contributed to limit ethno-regionalist representation.

The European Union: Empowering the French regions?

The EU has often been conceived of as a new political opportunity structure, which provides new resources to regional actors, while constraining others (Hooghe and Marks 2001). This Europeanization can cause a significant redistribution of power among domestic actors and result in institutional change. However, this sort of 'resource dependency model' presents contradictory expectations about outcomes (Börzel 2002; Bourne 2003; Carter and Pasquier 2006). Some claim that Europeanization, institutionalizing new political arenas and policy networks, creates direct opportunities for regional mobilization and has strengthened the regions at EU level (Hooghe and Marks 2001; Keating and Loughlin 1997). Others argue exactly the opposite: the centralist tendencies of the European integration process reinforce the centralization of power at the center, including a centralist institutional decision-making structure to which regional actors have limited access (Bourne 2003; Weatherill 2005). Considering the French case, the implementation of EU policies appears as a new structure of political opportunities for the French regions giving them new norms and resources for action. This has clearly produced policy and cognitive changes for French regions. They have notably developed a set of new local policies (local development) and strategies (paradiplomacy) which has empowered the territorial governance capacity of the French regions. However, these policy and cognitive changes have not led to a regionalization of French decentralization. The implementation of the new decentralization act since 2003–2004 confirms the resistance of the traditional political system.

The Europeanization of French multi-level governance

Most analysts today agree that the manner in which public authority is wielded in France has evolved considerably. The combined effect of decentralization and of the EU's regional policies has been a regionalization of the stakes of public policy in France. The effects of this regionalization on the interaction of actors and of levels of administration and decision-making are not always easy to interpret. The central state is pursuing its own reorganization by 'deconcentrating' power to its own agents in the field and adapting itself to European integration. The regions, for their part, are also seeking to position themselves in the most advantageous way. This said, however, the relative intensity and importance of these various levels of action remains the subject of considerable debate (Balme and Le Galès 1995; Négrier and Jouve 1998; Jouve and Warin 2000; Pasquier 2004b). Accordingly, any analysis of policy at the regional level in France must avoid two dead ends. In the first place, it is important to avoid overestimating the autonomy of regional political institutions. As we have underlined above, considerable structural constraints continue to handicap their potential for action. At the same time, however, we must not underestimate the political capacity of regional institutions. In the French case, it is clear that, over time, EU regional policy has led to substantial policy change. In nearly all the French regions from 1988 until the end of the 1990s, adapting traditional methods of encouraging spatial developments to fit the EU's rules led to a number of significant changes (Smith 2006). In particular, the pluri-annual planning of development objectives and funding mechanisms frequently led to more detailed negotiations between the different public authorities and social actors (associations, chambers of commerce) involved. A significant proportion of regional budgets is now committed to multi-year development programs in which the regional councils, local authorities, the French national state, and the EU all participate. Indeed, the regional planning contracts (*'contrats de plan Etat-Régions'* – CPER)[9] and the EU's regional policy have become the most important policy tools for territorial development in France today. Revitalizing the planning process, the CPER have become the principal institutional mechanism for the organization of center/periphery relations in the domain of public policy (Balme and Bonnet 1994). Through planning contracts, the French national state and the regions establish common objectives for development priorities and public investment in each region on a multiyear basis. To date, four generations of planning contracts (1984–1988, 1989–1993, 1994–1999 and 2000–2006) have seen the light of day. Investment in the context of the plans represents between 20 per cent and 30 per cent of the global budgets of French regions. The EU's regional policy, as implemented through the various structural funds, follows a logic similar to that of the CPER. In France, the two policy exercises are now closely coordinated.[10] First, introduced in mid to late 1988, at a time when decentralization began to take effect, the reformed structural funds provided regional and local actors with additional finance but also a set of new policy norms such as partnership, programming, concentration, subsidiarity, development project and/or evaluation (Smyrl 1997; Pasquier 2005). In interpreting and using these norms, new relationships between local actors, national administration and representatives of the Commission had to be forged in each region. Pushed strongly by the Commission, the obligation to evaluate these programs ex-ante, at mid-point and ex-post also led to more systematized forms of governing regional development. Socialized into this EU policy mode, several French regions used it as a cognitive resource to implement new local development policies and finally to empower their territorial influence. For instance, French regions have used the European model of local development diffused through varied programs (Leader, Interreg) to implement new territorial policies, and notably the policy of *'pays'*, which institutionalizes new territories of local development in France. The Europeanization process is also a cognitive process passing by regional and local actors (Pasquier 2002, 2005).

The application of the subsidiarity principle has given rise to very different hierarchical configurations in France. In this complex game of mutual interdependence, the challenge is to combine two central, but often contradictory principles: the free exercise of delegated power by sub-national authorities, and the reaffirmation of the state's coordinating and leadership role.[11] If they are to make a difference in this process, the regions must be able to bring together the various public and private partners within the region's territory around a shared vision of the regional interest. To face these changes, the strategies of French regional elites have diverged widely. In some, such as Brittany, relatively harmonious partnerships between state prefectures, regional councils and department-level authorities were concocted. However in many others, such as Rhônes-Alpes, Languedoc-Roussillon or PACA, implementing the structural funds has produced a battleground for regional-national and regional-local relations (Smith 2006; Smyrl 1997). In Brittany, the Breton regional council is at the center of the planning and implementation process for European regional policy in its region (Pasquier 2003a, 2003b). As in the case of the regional planning contracts, evoked above, the regional council and the *préfecture* have worked together to establish a list of concrete projects based on jointly determined regional priorities. While the final elaboration of the resulting plans is the privilege of the regional level (council and *préfecture*) they are based on a broader consensus, derived from the systematic consultation of officials and interests at the local and *département* level. In this context, the role of council and *préfecture* is complementary. While the former coordinates the regional coalition that ensures a working consensus, the latter uses its technical capacity and its influence in the administrative networks of the state (and, increasingly, of the EU) to defend the regional interest in Paris and Brussels. Together, they have established clear financial priorities, as well as procedures to implement these jointly. Through this ongoing relationship, they have brought about a genuine regionalization of European regional policy in Brittany. In Languedoc-Roussillon, the situation is more problematic. Despite the will of its president, the regional council does not occupy a central integrating role in the planning and implementation of European regional programs. In no case have genuinely regional priorities or strategies emerged. Rather, the field has been left open to local or sectoral actors, including the *conseils généraux* of the region's component *départements* or the field offices of national ministries. One result has been a marked shift downward, to the level of the *département*, of the organizing logic of structural funds in Languedoc-Roussillon (Négrier 1998). From this has followed a number of inefficiencies, including the fragmentation of financial effort, the politicization of 'expertise', and the predominance of traditional modes of local mediation. The regional council remains in the background, and is certainly in no position to compete with the political demands coming from below.

The EU has also encouraged and facilitated the paradiplomacy strategies of the French regions. In response to the forces of globalization, regions are increasingly viewing themselves as transnational actors whose economic and political interests are predominantly mediated at the EU rather than the national level. The deepening of integration has resulted in an increase in the number of policy areas over which regions now share authority with the EU – environment, transport, culture and public services. The response to this process has resulted in the establishment of direct links with the EU, evidenced by the setting up of a number of regional offices in Brussels and the creation of regional associations and networks (Magone 2003). If we consider regional representation in Brussels, the number of regional offices has been growing steadily the mid 1980s.[12] Along with Spanish and German regions, the French regions were the first to establish such offices. However, it becomes clear that the overall pattern of representation of sub-national authorities in Brussels is quite asymmetrical and extremely dependent on the ambition and the budgetary capacity of the region. The budgetary situation is an important factor leading to a stronger engagement with the European political system. The more regions are able to mobilize institutional and financial resources, the greater the capacity for representation. The weaker regions tend to have joint offices, as is the case for the majority of the French regions, while stronger ones have more autonomy in defining their aims. So, for example, the average size of the offices of the Spanish autonomous communities is 11 staff; in contrast, French regional offices are normally staffed by no more than two or three people (Costa 2002). One of the main analytical problems raised by paradiplomacy is that its combination of formal and informal elements it quite difficult to grasp (Aldeoca and Keating 1999). Three main activities can be distinguished in the paradiplomacy of the regions at the European level (Marks et al. 2002): influencing EU decision-making; liaising with regional counterparts in the same or other countries, as well as national and EU institutions; and networking and information gathering. All the representation offices of French regions tend to do the two last activities. However, some of them also try to elaborate real European strategies of projection and influence. For instance, since the 1970s, the political elites of Brittany have been very sensitive to European issues. In 1973, the CELIB was one of the founding forces of Europe's first cross-border inter-regional partnership, the Conference of Peripheral and Maritime Regions (CPRM), which is today the largest territorial lobby in the EU.[13] The new president of the regional council, Jean-Yves Le Drian, also created in 2006 a new *'ambassade de Bretagne'* in Brussels to symbolically reinforce its presence and, in 2005, a new 'European conference', which brings together the four *'départements'* and the main cities of Brittany to define common positions around European issues. So, the European approaches of the French regions depends on several factors: the framework of exchange among political, economic and cultural elites; the relations of cooperation or competition of regional-level political institutions with both national and local institutions and with relevant interest groups; and the strategy selected by regional leaders concerning relations with European integration and institutions.

The resistance of the decentralized Jacobin state

If the EU has impacted on the development of multi-level politics, this has not really led to significant institutional changes in French decentralization. From 2003–2004, a new decentralization reform was implemented in France. The objective of the prime minister, Jean-Pierre Raffarin, was clearly the empowerment of the regional level in France, notably to give to the French regions more resources in the EU context. During his period as prime minister, Raffarin, the former president of the regional council of Poitou-Charente, tried to give a regionalist orientation to the French decentralization. In doing so Raffarin was working with public opinion. Tables 3.3 and 3.4 show that, by the end of the 1990s, a clear majority of French people with an opinion on the matter were in favor of more regionalization (Schrijver 2006). This applied to all regions and there were only minor differences. Of those regions whose inhabitants identify closely with their region, only Corsica really showed a divergent pattern.

The reform was based on three main acts. First, the constitutional law, promulgated on 28 March 2003, established the '*organisation décentralisée de la République*' and recognized the regions, the municipalities and the '*départements*' as the '*collectivités térritoriale*' of the French republic. French regions now enjoyed a constitutional protection almost the equivalent to

Table 3.3 Opinion on further regionalization and decentralization, %

	1986*	1993	1997
Regionalization and decentralization should be developed	50.9	60.2	55.8
Regionalization and decentralization has reached a sufficient level	21.6	22	21.4
Regionalization and decentralization has gone too far	6.9	4.6	10
No opinion	20.5	13.2	13.1
Total	100	100	100

Question asked: « Pensez-vous qu'en France la politique de décentralisation et de régionalisation doivent être développée, a atteint un niveau suffisant, a été trop déeloppée, sans opinion ? »
*Only Alsace, Aquitaine, Centre, Franche-Comté, Languedoc-Roussilon, Limousin, Midi-Pyréennées, Nord-Pas-de-Calais, Pays-de-la Loire, Poitou-Cahrente, PACA and Rhônes-Alpes were included in all years.
Source: Observatoire Interrégional du Politique 1986, 1993, 1997. (Because of rounding, percentages for each column do not necessarily add up to exactly 100).

Table 3.4   Opinion on decentralization, those in favor of more regionalization, per region, %

	1986	1993	1997
Alsace	49	63.2	54.8
Aquitaine	53.2	60.6	61.5
Bourgogne		57.4	54.4
Bretagne		61.1	62.2
Centre	50.1	54.9	51.1
Champagne-Ardennes	44.3	53.6	
Corse		63.4	67.3
Ile-de-France		58.3	51.9
Languedoc-Roussillon	53.3	61.7	50.1
Limousin	55	72	74.9
Lorraine	48.2	54.3	56
Midi-Pyrénées	52.7	64.3	57.5
Nord-Pas-de-Calais	50.2	58.4	50.3
Basse-Normandie		66.1	56
Haute-Normandie	52	56	52.6
Pays-de-la Loire	51.1	57.2	53.4
Picardie	44.8	55.6	56.4
Poitou-Charentes	49.4	55.5	61.2
PACA	54.1	56.5	52.9
Rhône-Alpes	49.6	59.9	47.9
FRANCE	50.5	59.6	56.4

Question asked: « Pensez-vous qu'en France la politique de décentralisation et de régionalisation doivent être développée, a atteint un niveau suffisant, a été trop développée, sans opinion? »
Source: Observatoire Interrégional du Politique 1986, 1993, 1997.

that pertaining in federal or quasi-federal states. Second, the law of April 2003 transformed the electoral rule for regional elections with the establishment of regions as electoral districts. This law should reinforce regional democracy in France. Third, the law on 'local freedoms and responsibilities', promulgated on 13 August 2004, gave new competences to the regions in different fields (education, economic development, management of the European structural funds, vocational training, tourism, regional transports and culture) and allowed them to experiment in different policy areas.[14]

If we consider these different elements, the 2004 regional elections could appear as a real turning point for the French regions. First, the changes to the electoral system mean that regional elections take place now in a two-round system inspired by the system in use in French municipal elections, mixing proportional representation and majority system. To participate in the second round in regional elections, it is necessary to get 10 per cent of the votes. Parties can merge between the first and the second rounds. The party gaining a plurality of the votes is allocated 25 per cent of the seats, with the remainder being distributed proportionally between all the parties. This system enabled the stabilization of political majorities in all the French regions after 2004. Each French region had a stable government with the left-wing parties controlling 20 of the 22 metropolitan regions. The new electoral arrangements have also permitted new alliances. In Brittany, for example, bargaining between the ecologist and regionalist parties on the one hand, and the Socialist and Communist parties on the other hand, facilitated the election of regionalist candidates for the first time in the history of the Brittany's regional council (Pasquier 2006).[15] The campaign was also, for the first time, characterized by debates on different regional issues (European funds, transport, environment, agriculture, culture, local democracy). By contrast, the cantonal elections were largely ignored with almost all media attention concentrating on the regional elections. Of course, it is not possible to compare this campaign to the debates taking place in the Spanish or Italian regions, for example, but something seems to have changed. Moreover, new regional leaders have emerged. Younger than traditional French notables, these leaders represent new projects and a new style of government. For example, Ségolène Royal, the president of Poitou-Charentes, built an innovative project based on the implementation of participative democracy in all regional policy fields. Many of these new leaders prefer now to obtain a regional position than a local one in a *département*. Ten years ago this type of choice was unthinkable.

However, the key structures of French decentralization have not changed. The Raffarin reforms have, rather, frozen the balance of power. The principle that any territorial level cannot be hierarchically superior to any other has been maintained. The institutional design of the French decentralization and the regional map remained unchanged (Pouvoirs Locaux 2003). The government also renounced its initial proposal to extend competences over health, agriculture and roads to the regions. Why? Two main variables have affected the reform: the change of the political climate and strong opposition from the *départements*. The political climate has heavily affected the reform orientation. In May 2003, huge demonstrations by those working in education denounced the pension and decentralization reforms. In July 2003, a proposal to create a unique regional political level in Corsica was defeated in a referendum. Finally, the regional elections of March 2004 radically changed the political scene for Raffarin's government. A large majority of the regions and a majority of departments passed from right to the left. This considerably slowed the rhythm of the reform. The government was less willing to give powers to socialist regions while the regions themselves were determined to oppose the right-wing government. This resulted in significant and protracted controversies over financial transfers and regional expenditure.[16] Opposition from the *départements* also strongly constrained the government's reforms. Most notably, the government's attempts to establish the principle that the region should play the role of leader (*'chef de file'*) in the field of economic development was only partially successful due to the *départements'* opposition. The *départements*, grouped together in a powerful territorial lobby, the '*association des départements de France* (ADF)', used their political influence to limit the reform. They have notably used the French upper house, the *Sénat*, to further their political positions in the legislative-making process. Indeed, French senators represent the *départements* and the rural municipalities above all (Pouvoirs Locaux 2003).[17] Since 1969 and Général de Gaulle's referendum on regionalization, the French senate has been opposed to the regionalization of decentralization. Faced with this strong local opposition, the regions have been weak and divided. The '*association des régions de France* (ARF)' has not been able to counter the influence of the ADF. As a result of this bargaining process, the *départements* have ended up obtaining similar competences and more financial power than the regions. The regions should finally obtain €3 billion-worth of new competences, against €5 billion for the *départements*. That is one of the paradoxes of the reform: a process intended to empower the regions seems to have left the *départements* as the winners once again.

Conclusion

The combined effect of decentralization and of the Europeanization processes has been a regionalization of the stakes of public policy in France. As a result of the decentralization laws of 1982–1983, the evolution of EU policies and, most generally, the increasing globalization of the overall economic context, the central administrative organs of the French state have lost their monopoly on political initiative. The central state is pursuing its own reorganization by 'deconcentrating' power to its own agents in the field and adapting itself to European integration. The regions, for their part, are also seeking to position themselves in the most advantageous way. The Europeanization of the French multi-level game has clearly produced policy and cognitive changes for French regions. Most notably they have developed a set of new local policies (local development) and strategies (paradiplomacy) using economic and normative resources coming from the EU. However, the impact of Europeanization varies among French regions because the successful elaboration and implementation of public policy depends on more than just legal authority. Political capacity is, at least in part, a process of mediation in which elites and social groups produce a vision of the world that allows them at once to structure relations among themselves and to define the very 'interests' that they are pursuing collectively (Pasquier 2004a). In addition, these policy and cognitive changes have not led to the regionalization of the French decentralization. Since 2003–2004 the implementation of the new decentralization act has confirmed the resistance of traditional political system and its capacity to maintain the territorial status quo. The balance of powers and the main institutional architecture of the French decentralization have not been really affected by this new decentralization act. The principle that no territorial unit below the level of the nation can be hierarchically superior to any other still sharpens the competition among levels. It makes it impossible for the regional level simply to impose its will on lower levels. So the EU empowers regional governance in France, but not necessarily the regions.

Notes

1. The *Commissariat Général au Plan* and the *Direction à l'aménagement du territoire et à l'action régionale* (DATAR). Since WWI, French central administration considered the region as an efficient level to reform the Republican state. In 1917, the minister of trade, Clémentel, proposed the establishment of 17 regions to promote economic development in France. In September 1938, a law regionalized the organization of the chambers of commerce in France. The Vichy government also made different proposals to reform the Republican administration using the regional level with the notable establishment of the *'préfets de région'* (Pasquier 2004b).
2. The regional map had been modified only once since 1956. In 1971, Corsica separated from Provences-Alpes-Côtes d'Azur. France has now 22 metropolitan regions and four regions *'d'Outre-mer'* (Guadeloupe, Martinique, Guyane and Réunion).
3. In this process, the 'second left', led by Michel Rocard and the 'parti socialiste unifié' (PSU) played a crucial role.
4. Since January 2002, after experimentation from 1999 in some regions, the French regions gained the competence to organize and manage the regional railways transport (the *Trains express régionaux 'TER'*).
5. The budgets of the French regions fluctuate on average between €600 and €800 million, compared to between €200 and €500 million for the *départements*. The total of the *départements* budgets in one region is always superior to the regional budget (Pasquier 2004a).
6. From 1986 to 1992 the number of lists of candidates increased from 666 to 812.
7. In the constitution of the Fifth Republic, Article 49.3 permits the prime minister to impose a law without debate.
8. Ifop opinion poll, *Ouest-France*, 25 June 2002.
9. For the period 2007–2013, the *'contrats de plan Etat-Régions'* have been called *'Contrats de projet Etat-régions'*.
10. During the period 2000–2006 the two planning exercises have coincided in each region.
11. For the 1994–1998 planning contracts, 60 per cent of the state's contribution was tied up in 'non-negotiable' projects – a way for central authorities to impose their priorities on the regions.
12. The first of these were set up in 1984 and 1985 by the city of Birmingham and the regions of Hamburg and Sarre. By 1993, there were 54 regional offices, more than 140 by the end of 1995 and 244 in 2002 (Badiello 2004).
13. The CPMR brings together more than 150 European regions. The CPMR has recently initiated a collective campaign undertaken by both regional and local associations during the course of the European Convention to secure recognition of the regional and local tiers of government in the application of the principle of subsidiarity in EU policy-making.

14. This is the « droit à l'expérimentation ».
15. The *'Union démocratique bretonne'* obtained three seats, its leader, Christian Guyonvar'ch, becoming the vice-president for European Affairs in the new regional government of Brittany.
16. As Jean-Pierre Raffarin might have said during the senate debates, 'Between the regions and my political majority, I choose my majority.'
17. The 331 French senators are elected by 150,000 *grands électeurs*, of which 95 per cent come from small and rural municipalities. As a result the 331 senators include 128 mayors of small municipalities, 33 *département* presidents and only 2 presidents of regions.

4
'Fit for Europe'? The German Länder, German Federalism, and the EU

*Carolyn Moore**

According to Daniel Elazar, federalism is an attempt to have your cake and eat it (Elazar 1987: 33). Nowhere is this more in evidence than in the ongoing debate about the role of the German Länder in the formulation of Germany's EU policy. For many years, the primary objective of the Länder had been to secure rights of access to policy processes both domestically and in Brussels, a strategy defined as 'let us in' (Jeffery 2003); more recently, the emphasis has come to rest on securing those participation rights and protecting the autonomy of Länder competences from encroachments of both the German federal government and the EU (Grosse Hüttmann 2005: 28). This shift in approach has characterized the engagement of the Länder in both European reform debates and within the domestic arena, where a major project to reform Germany's federal system of government was harnessed by the Länder as a means to delimit their domestic responsibilities on European policy matters.

Driven by a greater desire to protect their competences, and a growing recognition that the Commission is no longer a natural ally in supporting their broader European aims, the Länder have turned their attention in recent years to a focus on their domestic powers and responsibilities. With that, the key battles over European competences and European policy priorities have been fought internally, on domestic, as opposed to European turf, as had been the case up until around the mid-1990s. What is more, the previous Länder strategy of mobilizing broad, Europe-wide sub-state support for their own policy and political objectives has also been laid to rest in recent times, with the emphasis being placed mainly on individual objectives.

This chapter seeks to understand the new strategy being pursued by the German Länder in Europe. It begins by considering how the current approach differs to earlier methods of engaging with EU issues, and contrasting the various motivations of the key actors and the drivers of change. The recent federal reform process in Germany can be regarded as a 'defining moment' of the new Länder strategy on Europe, as the deliberations within this forum allowed for the articulation of positions and tactical considerations by both the federal government and the Länder governments on how best to make Germany 'fit' for the new Europe. Länder approaches to a number of recent EU initiatives illustrate further just how closely the internal and external objectives of the delimitation of competences are entwined, and how the two discourses are mutually reinforcing.

The Länder and German EU policy

Responsibility for European policy has been a key area of conflict between the levels of government within Germany since it signed the Treaty of Rome in 1957. Yet by 2003, this permanent conflict over EU policy between the federal government and the Länder had come to be blamed for undermining Germany's ability to act in the European Union (EU). Expert opinion concurred: German federalism was seriously weakening Germany's negotiating position in Europe.

Germany's membership of the European Communities (EC) presented challenges to the domestic federal system from the outset. The Länder were affected particularly strongly by the process of European integration because, like the federation, they were continuously losing policy authority to the EC; however, unlike the federal government, the Länder had no direct role in the decision-making organs of the EC, especially the Council of Ministers, and, in addition, were obliged to implement European law in the federal republic (Naß 1989: 184). Thus, as a result of the transfer of both federal and shared competencies to the European level, the Länder were gradually being marginalized in the domestic policy-making process (Börzel 2002: 53).

This marginalization was not confined solely to the European policy sphere. Responses to the day to day challenges of government had seen a general drift towards increasing centralization of responsibility from the very beginning of the federal republic's existence, largely as a result of the pressure for uniformity in the provision of government services. This had been countered by a Länder strategy to approve the expansion of federal competences only if they were granted a co-decision right in the exercise of these at the central-state level (Börzel 2002: 51), a strategy referred to as 'compensation through participation'.

Procedures for improving Länder access to the domestic policy process on EC issues developed incrementally, focusing mainly on rights to timely provision of EC information and participation rights within domestic arenas for the formulation of the German EC negotiating position. A key turning point came in the mid-1980s with the relaunching of the European project and the development of the single market program. The Single European Act (SEA) took EC encroachment on Länder authority to a new level; European legislation was increasingly impinging upon their policy autonomy (Deeg 1995: 203). In response, the Länder mounted a much more vigorous campaign to win greater participation rights, applying their domestic strategy of seeking compensation through participation to the European policy-making sphere as well.

Ratification of the Maastricht Treaty (TEU) in Germany provided the Länder with a further opportunity to strengthen their domestic participation rights, arguing that by 1991, over 50 per cent of laws applied in Germany were of European origin (Bulmer et al. 2000: 34). The primary focus of the Länder strategy was again on securing greater participation rights within domestic processes of European policy formulation. Amendments to the Basic Law which were required in the wake of both German unification and the Maastricht Treaty provided the Länder with an opportunity to maximize claims for internal compensation through participation (Börzel 2002: 71). Using the threat of non-ratification of the Maastricht Treaty as a bargaining chip (Jeffery 1997a: 60), the Länder secured a constitutional enshrinement of domestic participation rights on European policy formulation.

The resulting *Europaartikel*, Article 23 of the Basic Law, redressed the territorial balance of power on European policy matters within Germany (Börzel 2002: 72), giving the Länder greater information and participation rights. First, it made transfers of sovereignty to the EU *conditional* on a two-thirds majority approval in the Bundesrat, the primary vehicle for the mediation of collective Länder opinion within German politics. Second, it provided for the selection of a Länder minister to represent German interests in the Council of Ministers. Third, it allowed for a special 'Europe Chamber' of the Bundesrat to be convened to fast-track decisions when time or confidentiality issues made full deliberation within the Bundesrat impractical (Deeg 1995: 204). Overall, the new *Europaartikel* represented the culmination of successive moves to strengthen the Länder's position within the domestic processes of European policy formulation.

An internal and external strategy

Complementary to these moves to improve participation domestically, the Länder had, throughout the 1980s, developed a clear external strategy which aimed to improve the role of regions more generally in the EU decision-making process. As some of the most powerful constitutional regions in Europe, the German Länder were in the vanguard of initiatives taken within the EU to promote a notional 'Europe of the Regions',[1] and in pursuit of participation rights within the EU for the 'Third Level' (Jeffery 1997) of authority, that is, the regions. The Länder were particularly successful in mobilizing high-level support for this regional agenda from other powerful constitutional regions, notably the Belgian regions and communities, the Spanish Autonomous Communities and later the Austrian Länder. Länder activism in Europe helped to secure the advances for the regional dimension in European policy development which were agreed at the Maastricht Inter-Governmental Conference in 1991, that is, the ability for a member state to send a regional minister to act as its delegate in the Council of Ministers, the legal enshrinement of the concept of 'subsidiarity' in the Treaty on EU, and finally, the creation of a forum for regional interest mediation in the EU, through the Committee of the Regions. This treaty therefore came to represent the culmination of Länder efforts to lead Europe's regions and secure a stronger foothold for regional actors in the EU policy process.

Yet this high point came at the time when the challenges of the 1990s began to undermine the ability of the German Länder to act collectively, either in the domestic context or at the European level. In fact, the course of European integration since the mid-1990s shows a very rapid abandonment by the Länder of the previous twin-track domestic and European strategy to secure greater involvement in EU policy matters.

By the time of the IGC, leading to the signing of the Amsterdam Treaty in 1997, three factors in particular had caused the German Länder largely to abandon their previous dual strategy. First, disappointment with the Committee of the Regions (CoR) had proved to even the most ardent German regionalists that their vision of a 'Europe of the Regions' and a strong 'Third Level' was simply unrealistic. The sheer heterogeneity of regional actors and regional preferences within the CoR proved to the German Länder that this body could never meet their high expectations, nor operate fully in the manner that they had originally envisaged (Börzel 2002: 74).

Second, the worsening economic climate and the inability of the new East German Länder to meet the economic challenges of reunification meant that the internal consensus amongst the Länder had largely dissipated. The natural coalition between the 16 Länder that had been formed between the Länder in the heady days of the post-unification era and the Maastricht IGC, had long since given way to the hangover of economic trauma and increasing economic disparities between East and West German Länder. This naturally led to increasing tension internally over the complex German system of fiscal redistribution, with stronger regions in effect 'bailing out' their weaker, Eastern counterparts. Consensus on all manner of policy issues, not least European policy, virtually evaporated.

Third, there was a general sense that the concessions won for the Länder at the time of the SEA and Maastricht Treaties, and in the wording of the new *Europaartikel* of the Basic Law, had indeed gone a long way towards counteracting the domestic participation deficit on Europe, and in fact, maximum use had been made of this strategy (Börzel 2002: 74). Together with the newly won right to access Council of Ministers' meetings in Brussels, this new sense of equilibrium compensated also for the perceived shortcomings of the Committee of the Regions. In sum, the domestic strategy was regarded as having been more significant in securing long-term participation rights, and thereby safeguarding the future of the Länder as effective political units, than had been their external strategy. Resources have subsequently been invested by the Länder primarily in pursuit of domestic aims.

This pervasive sentiment of a new relative level of equilibrium is reflected in the approach taken by the Länder to the Amsterdam Treaty, where only minimal demands were made, and fewer still were incorporated into the treaty (Börzel 2002: 75). While Länder pursuit of a common, Europe-wide regional strategy on this treaty revision was minimal, a certain number of the key regional demands put forward by the Länder at this point would continue to shape their policy on Europe for the next decade. Chief among these were, first, a bid to secure the right of the Committee of the Regions to appeal directly to the European Court of Justice over infringements of the subsidiarity principle enshrined in the TEU.

A second demand articulated by the Länder at Amsterdam for the first time became a leitmotif of their campaign strategy on shaping European affairs: the demand for a delimitation of competencies between various levels of authority across Europe, with clear lines of authority and accountability. Again, domestic and external strategies were clearly linked at this point, as this new demand for the strong delimitation of competencies was directly related to the Länder experience of German federalism and was essentially the 'Europeanization' of domestic objectives. In the German domestic experience, a delimitation of competencies was regarded by the Länder as a tool by which they could ringfence and further entrench their own authorities and competencies (Jeffery 2004b: 608); this strategy was felt to have broader European applicability, certainly within the context of clarifying how precisely the subsidiarity principle was to be interpreted and indeed implemented.

Subsequent EU treaty revisions have been utilized further by the Länder in their pursuit of this aim. Securing an autonomous sphere of action by clearly delimiting competences, in line with the subsidiarity principle, has now shifted to occupy a pivotal position in their European strategy. The 2000 IGC which culminated in the Nice Treaty offered the Länder further space to articulate the need for this clear division of competences (Jeffery 2004b: 610), and the treaty's failure to do so strengthened further the Länder resolve to champion this issue. Indeed, the Bundesrat made their ratification of the Nice Treaty contingent on proposals to take the competences agenda forward (Jeffery 2004b: 610).

Changing Länder perspectives on Europe

Disappointment and frustration with their lack of success at the EU level has encouraged the retrenchment of the Länder efforts in Europe to a mainly domestic focus. This re-emphasis on the domestic sphere has been compounded by increasing divergences between the Länder on EU policy issues, underpinned by widening economic imbalances between the Länder. Thus, the overall shift in the Länder strategy on Europe towards a more resolute focus on *autonomous* competences has been reinforced over the course of the 1990s and 2000s by a series of political developments, each of which has served further to bolster the idea that the Länder could best protect their autonomy by ringfencing their domestic responsibilities.

First, the European Commission was being viewed by the Länder with increasing skepticism. Far from being a natural ally, it began in the 1990s to promote an agenda which ran counter to many of the Länder's own objectives. A series of Commission rulings have been perceived by the Länder as setbacks for their own autonomy and political control. This shift in the relationship between the Commission and the Länder began when state aid to large industrial players in several German Länder were blocked by the Commission (Jeffery 2004b: 609). This trend towards divergent opinions between the Länder and the Commission has continued, with further disputes sharpening the discord, most recently with a stand-off over state funding for public broadcasters and their new media activities, a key Länder competence (FAZ, 13 December 2006), and internal market commissioner Charlie McGreevy's decision to block state-run Länder lottery games (Der Spiegel Online, 21 October 2006). The Länder have become vociferous in their warnings of the dangers of Europe extending its competences at their expense (Keating 2004b: 201).

Second, whereas the Commission continues actively to promote EU enlargement and debate with future accession countries, the Länder have become openly more Euro-skeptical, particularly with regard to the limits of European expansion and the contentious issue of Turkish membership (Stoiber 2004). The Commission's position on flexible limits to Europe is out of tune with the vision of a European 'community of values' championed by the Länder, which serves merely to reinforce the Länder opinion that the Commission is an opponent, rather than an ally. The number of stand-offs with the Commission led the Länder to focus further on protecting their domestic role in European policy as the primary means through which to achieve their EU-level objectives.

Reforming German federalism: Moving beyond compensation through participation

While the creation of the new Article 23 of the Basic Law in 1992 had been welcomed as improving the collective opportunities for the Länder to engage in domestic processes of European policy formulation, the reality of the 1990s and early 2000s led the powerful and richer Länder in particular to seek out new avenues through which to promote their agenda of individualization. It was for this reason that the federal reform process in Germany, which was launched in mid-2003, during a 'window of opportunity' between Land elections as a means to streamline the legislative process in general, came to be regarded as a key opportunity to revise existing mechanisms for Länder involvement in European affairs.

The problems of Germany's complex system of cooperative federal system are well documented elsewhere (see, for instance, Scharpf 2008; Jeffery 2008), but by 2003 it was generally felt that the federal order was holding Germany back, impeding its development and its ability to meet the cumulative challenges of German unification, European enlargement, economic globalization and demographic changes (Scharpf 2005).

Support for federal reform came from both sides: from the federal level, which wished to reduce the amount of federal legislation requiring Bundesrat approval, estimated to be around 60 per cent (Scharpf 2005); and the Länder, particularly the larger, economically prosperous Länder, who sought to secure their legislative autonomy within the domestic federal system. The key issue was that the leaders of the larger, economically prosperous Länder had come to regard a stronger role for the Bundesrat in policy-making as an inadequate solution to their frustrations. The post-war Länder strategy of 'compensation through participation' was now recognized as inappropriate; simply giving greater joint decision-making powers to the Bundesrat in return for the transfer of Land legislative competencies to the national or EU level did not allow the larger Länder to articulate and secure their own objectives (Bertelsmann Stiftung 2004: 8), because the majority of votes in the Bundesrat from the mid-1990s onwards had come to lie permanently in the hands of the weaker Länder, those that were reliant on federal support and fiscal-equalization payments.

This logic also held for EU policy: given that as much as 80 per cent of the legislation the Bundesrat considers today is of EU origin (Töller 2006), the larger Länder have come to rely increasingly on their Brussels offices as a means for mediating individual policy preferences and shaping legislation in its early stages (Degen 2005; Landtag von Baden Württemberg 2006: 47). By actively utilizing their Brussels outposts as a strategic tool in policy development, the more resourceful Länder have been able, in some ways, to compensate for the shortcomings of collective domestic procedures and the need to carve out what are, from their perspective, sub-optimal policy compromises within the Bundesrat. This increasing political emphasis being placed by the Länder on their independent operations in Brussels helps to explain why the Länder continue to strengthen these offices with further personnel and more prestigious presences in the city (Moore 2006a: 192, 2006b: 798). Indeed, as Bavaria's minister-president Edmund Stoiber stated at the opening of the palatial new Bavarian EU representation in 2004, 'In a number of areas, Brussels is more important for Bavaria today than Berlin' (Stoiber 2004).

In the summer of 2003, a Commission of members of both chambers of the German parliament (*Kommission von Bundestag und Bundesrat*) was established to develop proposals for improving Germany's federal system. Its voting members included the prime ministers or lord mayors of all 16 Länder and an equal number of Bundestag MPs, divided proportionally among the parliamentary parties (Scharpf 2005).

Any reform of Germany's federal constitutional order would have wide-ranging implications for the internal balance of responsibility for Europe, given the cross-cutting nature of so much of European legislation, and the high volume of German domestic legislation which originates in the EU. Yet, despite the fact that the Reform Commission was given the original aim of considering the reform of German federalism 'against the background of the future development of European integration' (Kommission *Einsetzungsbeschlüsse* 2003), the participation of the Länder in European matters was not considered at the outset as a central aspect of the discussions. It was only included in the agenda in light of the evidence from external experts (Eppler 2006a: 77), all of whom agreed that Germany was currently *unfit* for Europe.

The argument put forward by the constitutional, legal and political experts called on to inform the Commission's deliberations was that Germany's domestic EU policy formulation process was flawed. Action in the EU demands flexible leadership on negotiations, the ability to forge coalitions with partner governments rapidly at an early stage in the decision-making process, as well being able to create package deals before EU decisions are taken. However, Germany, the experts concurred, remained largely unable to do this due to the fact that its negotiating position had to be agreed domestically with too many different actors, and was then very difficult to amend during the actual negotiation process. From their perspective, there was an urgent need to improve the complex domestic Bund-Länder negotiation and policy formulation process on European matters, given that in an enlarged EU of 25 and more members, the ability to react flexibly in EU-level negotiations would be crucial. In fact, a number of experts called before the Reform Commission referred to how any form of abstention from a vote within the EU's Council of Ministers had pejoratively come to be referred to as a 'German Vote' (see for instance Professor Dr. Hansjörg Geiger, minutes of 6th meeting, Berlin, 4 May 2004).

The *Europaartikel* of the Basic Law (Article 23) had been drafted in 1993 with the express intention of strengthening Germany's overall European policy and ensuring that Germany was 'fit for Europe' (*Europafähig*). Nonetheless, since it had come into force, the provisions for inter-governmental cooperation on European matters as laid out in Article 23 had been under continuous discussion. Despite the clarity which this constitutional arrangement was intended to set out, relations between the federal government and the Länder had continued to be strained; the permanent tension between the two levels had even led Article 23 to be derided as 'institutionalised mistrust' (Chardon 2005). Put simply, it was widely felt that the time was right for a complete overhaul of the inter-governmental machinery on Europe.

The domestic 'binding' of the German negotiating position to a deal hammered out between the federal government and the Länder through the Bundesrat under the provisions of Article 23 of the Basic Law did not take into account the need for subsequent flexibility and compromise within the European arena. As a result, the provisions of Article 23 had come to be viewed both as inefficient and parochial, reflecting merely the concerns of the Länder and taking no consideration of the demands of diplomatic practice in the EU, limiting the room to manoeuvre in the run up to Council of Ministers meetings (Bertelsmann Stiftung 2004: 9). This is corroborated by the fact that since 1986, Germany has been outvoted in the Council of Ministers on more occasions than any other member state (Kommission 2003).

A second point of criticism expressed by expert opinion was that when Länder ministers led the negotiations in Brussels on Germany's behalf, they were often ill-equipped to do so (Eppler 2006a: 78). While they were generally highly competent in the specialist policy area under consideration, they lacked both the kind of political skills necessary for EU negotiations and the personal networks with EU partners which ultimately facilitate the resolution of package deals underpinning any Council of Ministers agreement. This, therefore, spoke against this particular provision being extended further.

The primacy of process over the primacy of politics?

Germany has long been considered to be the EU member state with the most decentralized and slowest process of EU policy formulation. Even before the *Europaartikel* of the Basic Law had been drafted, there had been a tendency within Germany's inter-governmental relations on Europe to put the primacy of process before the primacy of politics (Bertelsmann Stiftung 2004: 6), privileging correctness in the federal, procedural mechanics of federal-Länder relations on Europe, rather than considering the pragmatic politics necessary for effective engagement in the EU. If the federal reforms were therefore to make Germany 'fit for Europe', the balance of priorities had to be redressed, and domestic procedures would need to consider the bigger picture.

As a first step towards this goal, the Reform Commission sought to establish just how effective the constitutional provisions on inter-governmental cooperation on Europe had proven to be in practice. Analysis of the workings of Article 23 since 1993 exposed very different viewpoints between the federal and Länder levels. The Länder stressed that Article 23 was 'problem free' in practice and a necessary element of the compensation for their loss of competencies to the EU, and, contrary to the federal government's claims, did not limit Germany's ability to negotiate at the EU level (Maurer and Becker 2004: 26). The federal government, by contrast, blamed the provisions of Article 23 directly for their limited ability to engage fully in European decision-making processes (Grosse Hüttmann 2005: 30).

Empirical analysis of the workings of Article 23 in practise suggested an altogether different reality. A paper drafted on behalf of the Länder by the

Rhineland Palatinate presented an entirely positive evaluation of the working of Article 23 in practice. Every year, the Bundesrat considers around 150 to 200 EU items on which it then issues an opinion. Between 1993 and 2003, over 1500 such positions had been presented by the Bundesrat (Kommissionsdrucksache 0034).

Over the period 1998–2003, only 37 of the 900 opinions presented by the Bundesrat, or around 4 per cent, requested that its opinion be given *decisive* consideration (*maßgebliche Berücksichtigung*) in the formulation of Germany's final position. Although the federal government had rejected this demand in 20 of those 37 cases, there was only one instance where this then resulted in a public dispute between the two bodies: in the case of the EU's 2003 draft directive on environmental impact assessment (Bertelsmann Stiftung 2004: 8).

Over the same period, Länder ministers had asked to take the lead on EU negotiation of a particular policy issue in a mere eight cases, all of which were instances where the sole domestic competence (*ausschliessliche Gesetzgebungsbefgnisse*) rested with the Länder themselves. In three of these cases, the request was rejected by the federal government. Nonetheless, a pragmatic solution was ultimately found, by giving all of the participants the opportunity to speak during the Council of Ministers negotiations (Kommissionsdrucksache 0034).

The reality is that only in rare instances do Bundesrat opinions and preferences differ substantively from the position taken by the federal government. These cases have related mainly to EU legislation which cross-cuts policy responsibility within the German federal system, such as EU proposals that address issues related to general and vocational education: the former being an exclusive competence of the Länder in Germany, the latter being a policy directed at the federal level (Maurer and Becker 2004: 27). Furthermore, Bundesrat opinions tend largely to be technical in their scope, and relate primarily to administrative or procedural aspects of proposed Commission directives. This is hardly surprising, given the make-up of the Bundesrat as executives from the Länder governments and their broad experience of Länder administration. The overall picture is thus generally one of congruence on European issues in practice, contrasting sharply with the acrimonious battleground depicted by both sides in the Reform Commission.

The reason why both levels of authority took different views of the functioning of Article 23 in practise was due to the fact that they were approaching their evaluation from very different angles (Eppler 2006a: 84–85). The Länder were basing their evaluation on domestic coordination and cooperation, and the very limited number of cases of real conflict. The federal government on the other hand was evaluating the functioning of Article 23 in practise on the basis of its experience of operating in Brussels, and of being bound to a German position that had had to be coordinated domestically.

The empirical survey of the workings of Article 23 illustrates how debate over the *Europaartikel* was misplaced, given that its value is largely symbolic; it outlines normative assumptions as to shared responsibility for European policy formulation, which differed from the pragmatic approach which had in practice been taken. The significance of Article 23 should not, however, be understated; clarification of responsibilities was central to the Länder understanding of their own role on EU issues.

Across the board, there was a ground swell of support for changing Article 23. Experts who testified before the Reform Commission stressed that while Bund-Länder cooperation on Europe had worked relatively well in practice since Article 23 had been drafted, this was due largely to the pragmatic approach taken by actors at all levels of the political spectrum. Were these in future to demand a stricter interpretation of the provisions of Article 23, a very different pattern of conflict over cooperation would most likely emerge (Bertelsmann Stiftung 2004: 8), with the Constitutional Court having to rule on respective roles and responsibilities for European matters. Debate about making Germany more 'fit for Europe' therefore came to center on the issue of reforming Article 23.

Concrete reform proposals

At a normative level, the reform objectives of both the federal government and the Länder representatives appeared to intersect; both expressed the wish that Germany be 'fit for Europe' with regard to its domestic division of competencies. However, views on how to achieve this aim were divided. Indeed, debate on amending Article 23, and thus amending practices for Länder engagement in domestic European policy formulation within Germany, was one of the areas where there was no clear agreement within the Reform Commission even as deliberations drew to a close. Debates on the issue were highly charged and emotional (Eppler 2006a: 75).

The federal government position

A reform of inter-governmental practise in the area of European policy formulation was deemed a necessity if Germany was to play a full role as a member of an enlarging Europe, yet it is hardly surprising that the lines of conflict on reform of Article 23 ranged widely. At one extreme, the Länder sought to extend their responsibilities on Europe by clarifying the existing legal framework and providing more specific wording to concepts loosely characterized within Article 23 (Eppler 2006a: 75). The federal government, on the other hand, sought to exploit negotiations on this constitutional provision as a means of achieving greater independence from Länder control in the conduct of EU-level negotiations.

All expert opinion which reported to the Reform Commission concluded that a radical overhaul of Article 23 was necessary. The text of the constitutional provision regulating Bund-Länder relations on Europe was too wordy, and too complex, to allow for the practical demands of an effective German representation in the Council of Ministers, and to pro-actively engage in the European decision-making process (Grosse Hüttmann 2005: 27).

The federal government used the opinion of the experts called before the Reform Commission to reinforce its own demands for a greater ability to act and react flexibly in Brussels. Its initial negotiating position, outlined in a paper presented to the Reform Commission in April 2004, would have deleted all mention of explicit rights on Europe of the Länder, giving the federal level the right to take final decisions on EU policy matters, as well as to lead all negotiations in Brussels. This was to be achieved by reducing dramatically the cooperation framework as laid down in paragraphs three to seven of Article 23, and removing any obligation to be bound by the wishes of the Länder on EU matters (Projektgruppenarbeitsunterlage 2004). The more streamlined regulation put forward by the federal government sought to move away from the detailed procedures for Bund-Länder cooperation as they had been delineated in Article 23 of the Basic Law, allowing for more flexibility and greater cooperation with other EU member states; essentially, they argued, this would bring about an 'optimalisation' of Germany's European policy (Maurer and Becker 2004: 27).

The federal government also expressed doubts as to whether a Länder representative would be fully capable of representing 'Germany' in EU negotiations, or indeed, whether the Länder would be able to coordinate a joint negotiating position among themselves (Kommissionsdrucksache 0041). Giving the lead on negotiation to a Land ministerial representative would only contribute further to the problems of 'who speaks for Germany' in Brussels (Moore 2006a: 202), confusing the picture of relations with partner countries, and would result in 'Chaos', according to the then chancellor, Gerhard Schröder (*Die Zeit*, 18 November 2004). The federal government also contended that Länder ministers had limited experience of EU negotiations, and are not as competent in forging overarching deals with other member states. They do not have access to the necessary *diplomatic* channels in Brussels to be able to sound out other member states' perspectives in the run-up to negotiations, nor do they have the ability to build up a network of contacts over time.

The Länder position

The Länder moved quickly to adopt a line which would support their overall strategy of securing more scope for autonomous action on key policy issues. In their position paper on Europe, the minister-presidents of the Länder suggested two possible reform options (Kommissionsdrucksache 0045). The first of these, a suggestion initially put forward by the government of Baden-Württemberg, was a solution which would completely disentangle German domestic responsibility for European policy-making and negotiation. Modelled on the Belgian hierarchical separation of competences model (see Swenden in this volume), this solution would have seen the Länder take over sole responsibility for those aspects of European policy over which they had exclusive domestic policy responsibility. This, however, was regarded largely as a tactical move by the Länder to provide a radical alternative to match what they regarded as the equally radical contrasting suggestion promoted by the federal government – the complete removal of the provisions of Article 23 which provide for Länder input into European policy formulation.

The second option sought to clarify the current legal situation as enshrined in Article 23, thereby delimiting rights and responsibilities on Europe. This would also bind comprehensively the federal government's negotiating position in Brussels to the opinion of the Bundesrat on those EU policy issues which were concerned with Land-level competencies (Kommissionsdrucksache 0045). The minister-presidents repeatedly countered the criticism that the Länder would be unqualified to negotiate for all of Germany, stressing that they, like the federal government, were equally able to carry 'responsibility for the entire state'.

However, the increasing divergence of policy preferences between the 16 German Länder also had implications for the demands on European policy formulation competencies during the deliberations of the Reform Commission on federalism reform. Despite minister-presidents' pressure for greater delimitation of competencies, inter-Länder solidarity soon broke down, revealing clear dividing lines between the strong and economically powerful Länder who were strident in their demands to go it alone, and the smaller, weaker Länder whose fear of the financial implications in particular of sole competence in European policy areas quickly became apparent (Bertelsmann Stiftung 2004: 5). They were primarily concerned with the financial impact if the federal level were to provide no financial framework whatsoever for key policy areas decided at the EU level.

Nonetheless, there were a number of key aspects where Länder-wide support could be sustained. Proposals made by the Länder to support both of the reform options sought to clarify further within German law what exactly were deemed to be EU 'proposals' (*Vorhaben*), the point at which many of the existing information and participation provisions kicked in. They sought to specify directly that this related not simply to legal instruments such as EU directives, but also to other EU measures, particularly Commission documentation such as Green and White Papers or Action Plans, and instances where the Open Method of Coordination would be used in decision-making. Clarification of terminology relating to what exactly constituted a 'decisive' consideration of the Bundesrat opinion (*maßgeblich*) was a further objective of the Länder at this point (Eppler 2006a: 81). Further objectives were improved coordination on European policy at the horizontal level between the Länder themselves, as well as improved use of the Bundesrat's Europe Chamber; improved representation of the Länder within the German permanent representation in Brussels; and improved inclusion of the Länder observer into informal Council of Ministers' meetings in Brussels in order to improve communication between the levels at an earlier point in the decision-making process.

Finally, the Länder also put forward two proposals for improved intergovernmental coordination at the domestic level, which were in their view necessary due to the 'changing political demands of the EU' as a result of the draft Constitutional Treaty. First, they pushed for the Bundesrat to play a role in the nomination of judges to the European Court of Justice; and second, for the Bundesrat to be obliged to issue its agreement before Germany would allow EU accession negotiations to begin with an applicant state (Eppler 2006a: 82), effectively giving the Länder the right to veto EU expansion. Both demands reflect the increasing Euro-skeptical stance of the Länder in their bid for greater control rights on key aspects of the integration process.

Outcomes: Only limited change

During the Reform Commission's deliberations, compromise solutions on better federal-level Länder cooperation on European issues were sought somewhere between the maximum positions presented by both sides. Yet there was little consensus on a common middle ground, in view of the fact that both the federal government and the Länder were seeking to extend their European competences, and at the very least, to maintain the competences they had under the status quo (Eppler 2006b).

In the end, these efforts came to naught: the overall package deal on reforms to the federal system drafted within the Commission fell apart, largely due to the fact that they did not go far enough for the biggest Länder, Bavaria, Baden-Württemberg, Hesse and North Rhine – Westphalia. The results were seen as hardly worth the effort, or mere 'peanuts' ('Quisquilien') as one leading Land official called them (*Die Tageszeitung*, 8 May 2006).

Despite the failure of the Commission on German federalism to provide a final list of acceptable reform proposals by the end of 2004, the change of government at the federal level in September 2005, and indeed, the leadership at the federal level of a grand coalition, facilitated a reinvigoration of the reform process. While no further Commission was established, the original findings were examined by the grand coalition government in a series of short hearings in 2006, leading to the drafting of a set of constitutional amendments. These were accepted by the Bundestag on 30 June 2006, and by the Bundesrat on 7 July 2006.

The implications for European policy coordination within Germany are, however, limited. In fact, the wording of Article 23 has remained almost intact. The most significant change relates to Paragraph 6, regulating Länder ministers' participation in the Council of Ministers; this 'will' now be the case rather than the previous 'should' construction, setting a new legal norm to regulate inter-governmental behavior.

A further key change is that Paragraph 6 of Article 23 sets out the precise policy areas where Länder ministers can lead negotiations in Brussels on behalf of the federation, namely the areas of school-level education, culture or broadcasting. Given the cross-cutting nature of many EU directives with regard to the internal division of competencies within the Germany, the only condition put on this lead responsibility was that the actual content of the proposals under consideration in Brussels should relate directly to an area of exclusive Länder competence.

In other policy areas where the Länder have exclusive competences, other than those listed explicitly in the reformulated Article 23 (*Europaartikel*) of the Basic Law, the federal government will continue to lead in EU negotiations. However, the Bundesrat was given the ability to nominate members of the Länder governments to accompany federal negotiators in the Council, and to deliver explanatory reports (*Erklärungen*) to the deliberations. The key policy areas affected by this formulation are likely in future to be research policy and home affairs (Landtag von Baden Württemberg 2006: 14). One final constitutional amendment enacted in the wake of the Reform Commission's deliberations in 2006 seeks to improve the speed and efficiency of joint Länder positions on EU policy, by enhancing the function and operation of the 'Europe Chamber' (*Europakammer*) of the Bundesrat (Article 53, Paragraph 3a). In future, the Europe Chamber will also be able to provide opinions on written questions. This will enable the Länder to communicate views on EU policy issues much more rapidly and effectively than having to go through the cumbersome process of a plenary session of the Bundesrat. This change has been welcomed by both the federal government and the Länder as a move towards better European coordination (Eppler 2006b: 6).

Towards even greater complexity?

The limited changes made to Article 23 regulating inter-governmental relations within Germany on European affairs reflects the deep institutionalized mistrust between the Länder and the federal government over the scope of their respective competences. The unwillingness of both sides to compromise on some kind of middle ground position has ultimately led again to a sub-optimal solution being enacted, and one which would appear to compound further the tensions and frustrations that have characterized federal-Länder relations on Europe since Germany signed the Treaty of Rome. The likelihood of a further revision to this particular constitutional provision is underscored by the manner in which these changes work to create additional complexity rather than ringfence federal/Länder competences on European issues:

1. By specifying the three sole policy areas where a Bundesrat-nominated Land representative will represent Germany in the EU's Council of Ministers, the Länder have closed off potential new avenues for taking lead responsibility in other policy areas. Such new areas were in fact opened up by the broader federal reform agreement in 2006, which did achieve its goal of streamlining decision-making in Germany by transferring back to the Länder level a number of policy competences.

2. As a result, certain policy issues for which the Länder now have sole domestic responsibility, when they form part of an EU decision, will have to be managed jointly by the federal government and the Länder. Thus, rather than establishing autonomous spheres of competence for European matters, the new wording of Article 23 in fact necessitates further interaction and compromise between the levels of governmental authority.

Thus, whilst the new version of Article 23 does in fact provide the Länder with a strengthened, guaranteed right to take the lead for Germany in areas of their core competence (education, culture and broadcasting), and indeed in areas where consensus between 16 diverse territories will most likely be achieved, it also adds a degree of complexity to inter-governmental relations that runs counter to the larger Länder's aim to ringfence responsibilities on Europe. An agenda which set out to delimit roles has, paradoxically, now led to enhanced cooperation.

Implementation issues

Two related issues of domestic responsibility for EU legal and economic conditions were deliberated during the federalism Reform Commission's work, and have since become enshrined in German law: an acceptance of burden sharing when Germany is held to be responsible for violation of the Stability and Growth Pact or of EU directives.

Transposing EU law

The Länder have consistently battled with the German federal government for greater participation rights in the domestic European policy formulation process, not just on account of fear of the 'hollowing out' of the Länder, undermining their constitutional status as state-like entities and leaving them as little more than mere technical administration units, but also because of the fact that they are chiefly responsible for the implementation of EU law. They therefore have a wealth of experience which can be fed directly into the decision-making process in a bid to improve future EU legislative proposals, and indeed to reduce future implementation costs. For example, the Länder are primarily responsible for applying the EU's complex food safety system, and are also responsible for making the payments required through the EU's Structural Funds.

To this end, the Länder have representatives actively engaged in around 300 working groups set up by the Council of Ministers and the Commission to consider implementation aspects of EU policy (Maurer and Becker 2004: 27). These working groups in themselves serve as arenas of compromise on policy proposals between the Bund and the Länder at a very technical level. In fact, the federal government actively welcomes this collaborative forum, as it offers an opportunity for the Länder to bring their expertise in the implementation and application of EU law into the policy formulation process.

This relatively inclusive process goes some way towards explaining why inter-governmental relations alone are not the root cause of Germany's poor implementation record. While an EU Commission study of the EU15 put Germany in 13th position, with an implementation deficit of 3.5 per cent or 53 pieces of legislation (Maurer and Becker 2004: 28), analysis of the legislation concerned during this time period found that only two instances of non-implementation were directly attributable to the Länder administrations. Federal ministries have suggested that poor horizontal coordination between themselves is more likely the cause of the German implementation deficit (Grosse Hüttmann 2005: 32), a view articulated repeatedly within the Reform Commission. Experts blamed the lack of a coordinating function within the federal government, such as a Europe minister and a supporting Europe ministry, for this implementation deficit (see Professor Dr. Peter M. Huber, cited in minutes, 15 and 16 May 2006).

A new constitutional arrangement to regulate instances where Germany is fined for not meeting its EU obligations was a key success of the Reform Commission, and has since been adopted by the new grand coalition (Eppler 2006b: 7). The new Article 104, Paragraph 6 of the Basic Law sets out provisions for distributing the burden of payments in such cases, particularly through failure to implement EU directives or the mismanagement of EU funds. In these instances, the majority of the payment falls to the transgressor.

Stability and Growth Pact

Disputes between the federal government and the EU Commission over the high level of Germany's national debt in the early 2000s had domestic consequences, and had become an additional area of tension between the federal and the Länder over Europe (Hofmann 2006: 64).

The Reform Commission examined proposals for distributing any future EU fines according to the internal levels of responsibility. Debate over both the vertical and horizontal distribution of sanction payments was, as was to be expected, extremely heated. One of the earliest proposals put forward by the federal finance ministry during the Reform Commission's deliberations, was that the horizontal distribution of EU sanction payments should be calculated on the basis purely of Länder population size (Hofmann 2006: 60). This formula simply applied the system of internal transfers of payments between richer and poorer Länder within Germany, the *Länderfinanzausgleich*, which has itself become a bone of contention between richer and poorer Länder.

The final proposals put forward sought to distribute these payments both horizontally, between the Länder, and vertically, between the federal government and the Länder, through the establishment of a new 'national stability pact' within the Basic Law (Article 109, Paragraph 5), which would in future regulate the proportion of any EU fines to be paid by the federal or Länder governments. The agreement eventually reached will see future fines shared, with the federal government bearing the greatest burden, 65 per cent of the total sum, and the Länder collectively paying the remaining 35 per cent. With regard to the Länder payment, the 16 Länder will contribute 35 per cent according to their population size, and the remaining 65 per cent will be paid according to the extent to which each has contributed to the overall financial transgression.

Nonetheless, expert opinion on the economic rationale for this division of financial responsibility was resolutely against the 65:35 ratio at both levels, stressing instead that a larger share of the burden needed to be borne by the level of government whose financial mismanagement had triggered the fine – the so-called 'transgressor pays' principle (*Verursacherprinzip*). Even the widely respected German Institute of Economic Research complained that the 65:35 ratios were never given any technical explanation and that the figures appeared to have been simply plucked out of thin air. (DIW 2006: 5). Clearly, the solution which had been arrived at was part of a broader political compromise on federal reforms and Germany's interactions with the EU rather than a true reflection of the financial complexities of German fiscal federalism.

EU developments: Supporting domestic claims?

The new strategy adopted by the Länder on European issues and their prioritizing of protecting their domestic role, has led them to exploit broader EU developments in the ongoing debate with the federal government over the extent of their rights and responsibilities. While a limited degree of cross-border activism with other EU regions is in evidence, this can be understood primarily as supporting further claims for greater domestic autonomy and a ringfencing of Länder competences. Recent EU developments have been harnessed by the Länder in support of their claims for greater autonomous competences in the domestic realm over the formulation and application of EU policy.

Convention process and the Draft Constitutional Treaty

Länder activism with regard to the Convention was muted; unlike during the pre-Maastricht era, the Länder were not in the vanguard of any new regional agenda, and focused their efforts on issues with domestic relevance. The Länder demands of the Convention were hampered further by the low salience of 'the regional dimension' to the debates of the Convention in general (Keating 2004b: 197). During the Convention process, the Länder had, however, led calls for the inclusion in the treaty of rights for constitutional regions, those with legislative competences across Europe to appeal to the European Court of Justice against supposed breaches of subsidiarity (Jeffery 2004b). While this right was afforded by the Draft Constitutional Treaty both to national parliaments and to the Committee of the Regions, it was not extended to the constitutional regions. Nonetheless, the Länder still championed this move as a new approach to European policy matters; it was an approach, they argued, which needed to find some echo within the work of the domestic federalism reform debate (Kommissionsdrucksache 0045).

In the context of the Convention's deliberations on the future of Europe, one clear dividing line did emerge, however, at the European level between those regions with legislative competences and the other regional and municipal governments. The German Länder have been powerful advocates of the new 'RegLeg' group, as its aims underline their own demands both internally to Germany and at the EU level – that their competences and indeed responsibilities for implementing EU legislation put them in a separate bracket similar to that of member states, and that they should as such be afforded special treatment (Keating 2004b: 201).

Support for the Constitutional Treaty and the subsequent Lisbon Treaty among the Länder is widespread on account of a number of clearly related factors. First, the treaty moves European political responsibility closer to the model the Länder themselves support, both in the domestic and the European context: a clear separation of authority through an articulated and legally enforceable delimitation of competences. The Lisbon Treaty also gives teeth to the subsidiarity principle as a guiding concept in European policy formulation, through the institutionalization of a 'subsidiarity watchdog' system (Grosse Hüttmann 2006: 151–152). Third, the Länder also support the full ratification of this treaty, given that it will finally make a reality of a long-held aim of theirs – dating back as far as Maastricht – to give the Committee of the Regions the right to appeal to the European Court of Justice when they feel decisions are in breach of the subsidiarity or proportionality principles.

Ratifying the Draft Constitutional Treaty

German ratification of the Draft Constitutional Treaty was again an opportunity for the Länder to push for some of their EU-related demands from the federal government, particularly given the time constraints of the domestic ratification process. There was a general sense among German elites that a strong positive endorsement of the Constitutional Treaty was essential to send out very clear positive signals which it was hoped would help stimulate the 'yes' vote in the French Referendum on the treaty in May 2005. Thus, the timetable for ensuring German ratification was tight: Bundesrat support for the treaty was given on 27 May, two days ahead of the 29 May French referendum.

The Länder were able to mobilize rapidly to put forward a number of the key demands on domestic EU responsibilities that had already been articulated within the framework of the federal Reform Commission, and to use these as bargaining chips with the federal government in return for speedy Bundesrat endorsement. As a result, the federal government made several key concessions to the Länder that had first been put forward by the Länder during the Reform Commission's deliberations. They agreed to Länder demands for new legal rules obliging the federal government to inform the Länder earlier of EU legislative proposals and developments, a tightening up of what were legally held to be EU 'proposals' (*Vorhaben*) as well as the cooperation of the Bundesrat in the nomination of German judges to the European Court of Justice. These were set down in a new law on the 'extension and strengthening of the rights of the Bundestag and the Bundesrat in EU matters'.[2]

Ratifying the Lisbon Treaty

The Lisbon Treaty was ratified relatively painlessly by the Bundesrat, as many of the issues they had raised with regard to the Draft Constitutional Treaty had now been regulated by the draft transposition law, which would now come into force on application of the Lisbon Treaty. However, the additional time available for discussions allowed Länder politicians to vocalize further concerns on the future scope of federal-Länder cooperation on European matters. Indeed, debate within the Bundesrat on the ratification of the Lisbon Treaty allowed many of the common tensions that have characterized federal-Länder relations on European policy competences to resurface. From the Länder side, there was a push to revise the executive agreement that gives fuller legal flesh to the constitutional framework established by Article 23 of the Basic Law. This 'Law on the Co-Operation between the Federal Government and the Länder in European Union matters'[3] (known as EUZBLG) had been drafted in 1993 to accompany the original *Europaartikel*, but had not been updated to the same extent. Thus, the Bundesrat debate on the Lisbon Treaty allowed Länder politicians to call for its overhaul within the broader *spirit* of the Lisbon Treaty (Professor Dr. Wolfgang Reinhart, Baden-Württemberg, in debate, 15 February 2008). The Bundesrat debate on the treaty emphasized clearly that its ratification was not simply a rubber-stamping exercise, but rather demanded that the Länder role on European issues within Germany as a whole also be revised. While no further steps were taken to link a revision of the EUZBLG with ratification of the Lisbon Treaty, these debates in 2008 clearly show that the tensions between the federal government and Länder politicians over responsibility for Germany's European policy-making have not been entirely resolved by the 2006 federal reforms.

Conclusion

Despite having some of the most far-reaching legislative powers of any EU regions, the German Länder are no longer in the vanguard of driving change at the EU level, nor in pushing for greater inclusion of the 'regional perspective' in European policy decisions in the EU. They lag far behind some of the newer 'constitutional regions' in Europe, not least the UK regions, which have deployed a much more pro-active approach to developing opportunities for action at the EU level.

In recent years, the new approach of the Länder to EU issues has clearly come to focus primarily on promotion of autonomy in the domestic sphere, ringfencing and strengthening existing competences on Europe. Indeed, the policy and political agendas promoted by the Länder continue to individualize, to the extent where it is more appropriate to speak of 16 competing policies on Europe than a unified Länder policy on the EU. However, the recent reforms of the federal order, which set out to provide more autonomy for the Länder have ultimately resulted in a more complex arrangement that will in fact demand a higher degree of cooperation in the long run.

Inter-governmental relations on Europe within Germany remain, therefore, characterized by a high level of mistrust and mutual skepticism. The collective aim of making Germany more 'fit' for Europe, more flexible in its interactions with the other 26 member state governments, more capable of determining package deals during EU negotiations and more competent in its overall negotiating strategy, demands that the root cause of the problems be recognized. If German federalism is to withstand the future and increasing challenges of an enlarged EU, both the federal government and the Länder must seek to institutionalize a new culture of mutual trust on European matters.

Notes

* An earlier version of this chapter appeared as Moore, C. and Eppler, A. (2008) 'Disentangling Double *Politikverflechtung*? The Implications of the Federal Reforms for Bund-Länder Relations on Europe' in *German Politics*, vol. 17, no. 4, pp. 488–508.

1. Though note the subsequent rise and fall of this concept: see Elias, A. (ed.) (2008) 'Whatever Happened to the Europe of the Regions? Revisiting the Regional

Dimension of European Politics', special issue of *Regional and Federal Studies*, vol. 18, no. 5.
2. 'Gesetz über die Ausweitung und Stärkung der Rechte des Bundestages und des Bundesrates in Angelegenheiten der Europäischen Union.'
3. 'Gesetz über die Zusammenarbeit von Bund und Ländern in Angelegenheiten der Europäischen Union.'

5

'Loyal Cooperation': Italian Regions and the Creation and Implementation of European Law

*Giandomenico Falcon and Daria de Pretis**

The participation of Italian regions in the creation and implementation of Community law has been given added impetus by the 2001 constitutional reform (Constitutional Act 3, 2001), which has modified 'Title V' of the Constitution regarding Italian autonomous regional and local authorities, such as regions, provinces and towns (municipalities) (Falcon 2001b; Caravita 2002; Pizzetti 2002; Gambino 2003a, b). Changes in Article 117 of the Constitution have given the state and the regions apparently similar legislative powers, 'in compliance with the Constitution and with the constraints imposed by EU legislation and international obligations' (Pajno 2003).

It must be immediately observed, however, that on the whole the legislative powers of the regions are very limited in scope (dealing essentially with policy matters); those of the state on the contrary are very wide (including exclusive power with regards private and commercial law, criminal law and all the law concerning the court system and procedure). Furthermore, the state continues to exercise exclusive legislative power in many matters, including environmental protection, health protection and competition protection: the specificity of this public reserve consists basically in the possibility to recognize the legislative power of the national parliament in all of those cases where the subject matter, as an object of the discipline, requires the consideration of these interests (D'Atena 2003b). Such a circumstance can also occur with reference to the discipline of matters assigned to the regions. Therefore, it is clear that the situation of abstract 'equality' between the state and the regions does not match entirely the reality, because in those matters the state can always exercise its own competence to regulate 'transversal' interests (Mangiameli 2003).

Article 117 also ensures that, regarding matters over which they have competence, regions and autonomous provinces may participate in decisions regarding the creation of community law ('The Regions and the autonomous

Provinces of Trent and Bolzano take part in preparatory decision-making process of EU legislative acts in the areas that fall within their responsibilities') and, on the other hand, that they implement EU law, according to Italian procedural rules ('They are also responsible for the implementation of international agreements and EU measures, subject to the rules set out in State law which regulate the exercise of subsidiary powers by the State in the case of non-performance by the Regions and autonomous Provinces.') (D'Atena 2003a; Chieffi 2004; Mabellini 2004).

The description of the process of regional participation in EU matters is normally divided into two phases: the *bottom up* or *ascending phase* (the decision-making process of EU legislative acts) and the *top down* or *descending phase* (the implementation of EU law). We will start with the descending phase.

Descending phase

First, let us consider the transfer and implementation of European law into the Italian legal system. For self-executing community law such as treaties and regulations, no special problems exist: obligations of this kind are meant to become operational regardless of national or sub-national inaction or the adoption of conflicting national or sub-national rules. The Italian state, its regions and its autonomous provinces are legally bound to comply with supranational rules without any delay between the time of the enactment of a community law and its implementation at state level. That does not mean, as it is known, there is no Community law, even if directly enforceable, that expressly requires a detailed rule that can assure an immediate effectiveness of the supranational rule. However, even in those cases, discretion by the 'internal' (state or region) legislator is limited and, therefore, it is very hard for his role and articulation to assume a definite importance.

Things are different when dealing with community law that is not self-executing, such as directives, where the national legal system has a role to play, at least in principle. The rules regarding the national system of the sources of the law influence the way in which European law is implemented. This principle, already expressed in Article 117 of the Constitution and mentioned before, is reasserted by Article 1 of Parliamentary Act 131, 2003 (the so-called *La Loggia Act*), which provides that 'according to Article 117, section 1, of the Italian Constitution, international legally recognized obligations such as those in Article 10 of the Constitution, agreements of mutual limitation on sovereignty, as indicated in Article 11 of the Constitution, Community law and international Treaties represent legal constraints on the legislative power of the State and its Regions' (Cavalieri and Lamarque 2004; Falcon 2004).

Article 117 of the Constitution also ensures that legislative power is allocated either to the state or to the regions, according to matters of jurisdiction. This would imply that, broadly speaking, in the implementation of rules pertaining to non self-executing community law, the Italian regions may act, in some cases, autonomously and directly, in all matters that fall within their jurisdiction.

The way in which the new basic law defines the field of the regional legislative power or jurisdiction is very significant. Unlike in the previous system, and as already noted in the introduction to this chapter, the state now has exclusive jurisdiction over some matters (as indicated in Article 117, Section 2) while the regions have jurisdiction on all remaining matters. More specifically, regions have two kinds of legislative powers:

- First, over matters where the state also has competence in defining basic principles (Article 117, Section 3, on concurrent competence between the state and the regions).
- Second, over any other matters that have not been expressly attributed to the state (Article 117, Section 4, on residual regional competence).

The characteristics of the new constitutional framework have been implemented by Parliamentary Act 11, 2005 (also called the *Buttiglione Act*), which indicates the 'general rules' regarding Italian participation in the European Union (EU) legislative process and the procedures to be followed to implement community law within the Italian state (Bona Galvagno 2005; Califano 2005; Cartabia and Violini 2005). Article 8, Section 1, of this Act states that state and regions 'shall promptly implement European directives pertaining to areas of their competence'. This general principle is thus adopted and emphasized with regard to non self-executing community law.

The new allocation of competences to either the state or the regions and the autonomous provinces is not the exclusive result of the 2001 constitutional reform and the new Acts of 2003 and 2005, by which it was officially implemented. The general principle that states the need for the Italian Republic to comply with community law at regular intervals had actually already been established in Act 86, 1989 (the so-called *La Pergola Act*), which was, in effect, the original source of the principle (Onida and Cartabia 1997; Bienintesi 2004). This important Act introduced a special legislative procedure called the 'Communitarian Act' (*legge comunitaria*). It is a parliament Act especially dedicated to the 'transfer' of the laws produced in Europe during the previous year to the Italian system. The Italian government proposes it annually to parliament. The Act also states that, in matters over which the Constitution does not impose the adoption of a parliament Act for the implementation of community law at national level, its implementation may be achieved through administrative regulations, or through other government administrative measures. Furthermore, it is stated that, in matters that do not fall under the exclusive jurisdiction of the state as required by the Constitution, community law may be implemented directly by the regions.

A further modification was the introduction (by Article 13 of Act 128, 1998, which considered the possibility that Italian regions participate in the community law-making process) of a special body called the '*Conferenza Stato-Regioni*' (State-Regions Conference), a consultative body that represents regional interests (established and regulated by legislative decree 281, 1997). The 'Communitarian Act' requires that parliament be informed of the views of the Conference (Woelk 2003).

The introduction of the 'State-Regions Conference' was very important. It is a special institution that gives organizational expression to the demand for a structured institutional link between the central apparatus and the regional autonomies, and the need to provide an appropriate forum for the sharing – by the state towards the regions – of some important functions of general interest. In other words, it embodies the constitutional principle of 'loyal cooperation' (Bartole et al. 2005). The Conference is made up of presidents of the regions and it is summoned and presided over by the prime minister, who also determines the agenda. The work of the Conference is preceded by a 'Conference of Presidents' at which an attempt is made to identify common ground between the often very diverse positions of the various regions.

The Conference operates not only in the field of the regional activity of Community law implementation and enforcement. It represents a more general tool. It gives compulsory advice on the content of government bills, decrees and regulations in all the regions' areas of competence; it is the place where the state and regions reach the 'agreements' required by law; in all cases required by law it sets criteria for the distribution of the funds allocated to the regions; and it appoints regional representatives to the different bodies, including state bodies, in which their presence is mandated.

Since the already-mentioned reform of Title V of the Constitution, an important ruling of the Constitutional Court (decision, 1 October 2003, No. 303) has conferred another new and significant function on the Conference. With regards the definition and distribution of administrative functions, if the state decides to exercise its administrative powers in areas which, even when falling within its area of responsibility and having general interest to the whole territory of the Republic, nevertheless impact on the regions' exclusive areas of competence (e.g. public works), the content of administrative acts will have to be the result of a previous 'agreement' reached within the Conference (Falcon 2005).

This solution was reached as an enforcement of the new Article 118 of the Constitution, ensuring that municipalities are responsible for administrative functions, and that a different allocation by the state, aiming at guaranteeing a 'unitary outcome', be motivated by criteria of subsidiarity, differentiation and appropriateness. As a matter of fact, according to the court, this provision compels the state to comply with a 'relational' conception of subsidiarity: it can provide by law the attribution of certain administrative functions, the majority of which concern the protection of 'transversal' and 'general' interests, such as competition, environment and welfare. Nevertheless, such a provision will always have to take into account the need for some procedural mechanisms that will allow regions, where competent in one particular sector, to find solutions that can be chosen in agreement with the state. Evidently it is not easy to concretely implement such a project. Yet this is a clear example of the 'cooperation' philosophy that inspires the procedure of 'Community law' approval by the state, and that is today integrated in a wider context that amplifies and emphasizes its importance.

Of the 20 Italian regions, five enjoy a higher level of autonomy (Valle d'Aosta/Vallée d'Aoste, Trentino-Alto Adige/Südtirol and Friuli-Venezia Giulia, in the North of Italy, plus Sicily and Sardinia, Italy's largest islands). The autonomy of the Trentino-Alto Adige/Südtirol region was subsequently transferred to its two provinces, Trento and Bolzano. The *La Pergola Act* granted the autonomous regions and provinces authority to also directly implement community directives pertaining to matters over which they had exclusive jurisdiction. At the time this possibility wasn't granted to the other regions. It is only through subsequent modification of the already-mentioned Article 13 of Act 128 (1998) that the latter were also given permission to act on matters where they have concurrent jurisdiction, but only within limits allowed by the state (Chieffi 2003).

As mentioned, the instrument of the so-called 'Communitarian Act' (*legge comunitaria*) is very important as it represents the true 'center of gravity' for the whole system of implementation of community law. It has to be stressed that – although the regions have concurrent legislative power on their own relations with EU (Article 117, Section 3) – the relationship between Italy (as a whole) and the EU and its institutions comes under the exclusive legal jurisdiction of the Italian state, as clearly stated in Article 117, Section 2, of the Italian Constitution. As already noted, the Italian regions have a right to take part in the related decisions, according to Article 117, Section 5, of the Constitution, on the basis of rules defined by an Act of the Italian parliament. The 2005 Law (Article 8 of Act No. 11) keeps the old 'Communitarian Act' (*legge comunitaria*) basic framework, but introduces more details in the regulation of the regions' participation to the process of its elaboration. It states that the prime minister, or the minister for community policies

> shall promptly inform both Houses of Parliament and – through the Conference of the Regional Presidents, the Presidents of the autonomous Provinces of Trento and Bolzano, and the Conference Presidents, the presidents of the Regional Councils and the Councils of the autonomous

Provinces – the Regions and the autonomous Provinces about the rules and guidelines issued by the EU and the European Communities.
(Article 8, Section 2) (Cannizzaro 2005; Pitino 2005; Tiberi 2005)

The evident purpose of this procedure is to provide advanced information on the new 'Communitarian Act' and to assist all local authorities in its prompt implementation. Once this initial phase is completed,

The Prime Minister, or the Minister for Community Policies, shall verify – with the cooperation of all relevant administrations – the level of conformity of the national legal system and the Government's policies according to that described in the second paragraph. In order to allow interested bodies to take the necessary measures to ensure such conformity, the Prime Minister, or the Minister for Community Policies, shall then report on his/her findings to the relevant parliament bodies, to the permanent Conference for the relationship between the State, the Regions and the autonomous Provinces of Trento and Bolzano, and to the Conference Presidents, the Regional Councils and the Councils of the autonomous Provinces within four months, for their comments.
(Section 3)

In matters that fall under their own jurisdiction, 'the Regions and the autonomous Provinces shall check the level of conformity of their own legal systems and advise the Council of Ministers' Office / Department for Community Policies about the measures to be undertaken'.

At the end of this rather complex verification process, 'The Prime Minister or the Minister for Community Policies, in agreement with the Minister for Foreign Affairs and other concerned Ministers, shall prepare a bill for Parliament by 31st January of each year indicating "Dispositions for the implementation of the obligations deriving from Italy's European Union membership" ' (Section 4).

Regulating the 'Communitarian Act' (legge comunitaria), the 2005 Law requires the prime minister to convene a special 'Community session' of the State-Regions Conference every 6 months (Article 17 of Act 11 (2005)). The Conference is called upon not only to express its opinion on the 'Communitarian Act', but also to act as a consultative body in matters pertaining to the implementation of community law at the regional level (Cartabia and Violini 2005).

Having said this, the state maintains a general power for substitution of the regions 'in case of non-compliance to international or European Union law and Treaties' (Article 120 of the Italian Constitution; and also Article 117, Section 5). To this end, it is provided that the state, and more precisely the Italian government, puts into operation a rather complex mechanism

that involves the participation of the Permanent Conference between state, regions and the autonomous provinces of Trento and Bolzano (Article 10 of Act 11 (2005)) (Caliandro 2004).
Through the same mechanism, the state may proceed to the urgent and immediate implementation of non self-executing community law. In other words, the state is not obliged to wait for the start or the completion of the 'annual Communitarian Act' (*legge comunitaria*) procedure. This happens whenever community rules impose a deadline 'before the presumed date the Communitarian Act of the current year will come into force' (Article 10).

It must be pointed out that the faculty of the state to implement directly European law is used most, and most decisively, when dealing with the 'individual' determinations of the European institutions. Such determinations are directly applicable and require prompt implementation. If they are of great importance for the national interest, the national government may challenge their legitimacy before the European Court, or it may choose to enact them by issuing all necessary measures. These measures may also be taken when the community law to be implemented pertains to regional matters. In this case, though, the president of the region or of the autonomous province involved may intervene in the government's deliberations by lodging a consultative vote (Article 14, Act 11, 2005) (Cartabia and Violini 2005).

To summarize, Italian regions may participate in the descending phase of the transposition of community law in two different ways. First, the regions may participate in procedures that are the exclusive domain of the Italian parliament or government (such as the elaboration of the 'Communitarian Act' (*legge comunitaria*) or other measures, including administrative decisions); in this domain, regions primarily have just an advisory capacity, and have to take into account the needs of national unity. Second, the regions may produce their own laws in order to implement community law, either in accordance with state 'principles' laws in matters that the Constitution has assigned to both state and regions, or working alone in their own fields of competence, as provided for by the Italian Constitution.

This second point needs to be further clarified. The new law provides that the report that the government must prepare annually by 31 January, as an annexe of the 'Communitarian Act' (*legge comunitaria*), must refer back to the 'annual implementation acts that may have been passed by the Regions and the autonomous Provinces during the year' (Article 8, Act 11, 2005). This is an unequivocal acknowledgement of the possibility that even the regions directly utilize the technique of the 'Communitarian Act' in areas over which they have jurisdiction, according to the different implementation methods that the law grants them (such as the possibility of using delegated legislation) (Adinolfi 2004; Cartabia and Violini 2005).

It is significant that some regional 'Statutes' (the statute may be viewed as the equivalent of the Basic Law of the Region) already include articles that deal with this option (among others, Article 11 of the Statuto of the Lazio Region, regional Act 1, 2004; Article 42 of the Statute of the Piedmont Region, regional Act 1, 2005; and Article 12 of the Statute of the Emilia-Romagna Statute, regional Act 13, 2005). The regions too, for matters that fall within their jurisdiction, may give immediate implementation to non self-executing community law through their so-called 'secondary' regulation: Section 6 of Article 117 of the Italian Constitution provides that the regions have general regulatory powers (also through 'secondary' legislation) over matters that are not the exclusive competence of the state.

In their own areas of competence, Italian regions may approve acts for the implementation of the community directives. However, we must remember that regions may have either *concurrent* legislative jurisdiction or *exclusive* legislative jurisdiction. In the case of *concurrent* jurisdiction, regions must adhere to fundamental state principles (Article 117, Section 3, of the Italian Constitution). Regions must, therefore, adhere to 'fundamental principles that cannot be derogated by Regional or provincial law, which prevail over any acts that may have been passed by the Regions or autonomous Provinces' (Article 16, Section 1, Act 11, 2005).

In the case of those areas of public policy over which the regions enjoy exclusive jurisdiction, they may pass regional acts implementing community law. This does not, however, apply whenever matters that are the exclusive competence of the regions are nevertheless disciplined, in actual fact, even if only partly, by state law enacted by parliament in the exercise of its exclusive jurisdiction in a matter falling under the competences of the state.

An example will clarify this point. Italian regions have exclusive legislative power on hunting matters. Nevertheless, it is the state alone that has the power to adopt rules for the safeguard of the environment and the ecosystem. The Italian Constitutional Court ruled (decision, 26 June 2002, No. 407) that Italian regions cannot establish hunting seasons that differ from those established by the state. If they do so, they would contravene the constitutional law that grants the state exclusive jurisdiction over the ecosystem and, more specifically, each animal species, especially during breeding times. This means that, whenever the state has the power to intervene with its own law in matters where it has exclusive jurisdiction (such as the safeguard of the environment, but also health matters and business competition matters), the regional jurisdiction, even though exclusive as in the case of hunting (or, among others, in 'vocational education'), may in fact be much more constrained than might otherwise appear to be the case. The Italian regions have to accommodate themselves to the rules established by the state in matters of its exclusive competence. The state, in turn, may be compelled to accommodate itself to community directives governing those matters over which it has exclusive competence. This is the reason why the implementation of directives concerning matters that fall under the exclusive jurisdiction of the regions should, in any case, go through the mechanism of the 'Communitarian Act' approved by the Italian parliament. On the basis of the dictates of the 'Communitarian Act', the regions would then be free to legislate over the remaining areas that fall under their jurisdiction. As has already been mentioned, the state may autonomously implement non self-executing community law pertaining to matters that fall under its exclusive jurisdiction. To that extent, when there are community directives to be implemented, the government must prepare administrative guidelines 'that must be adhered to by the Regions and the autonomous Provinces in order to comply with needs of unity, pursue economic strategies and meet international obligations' (Article 16, Section 4, Act 11, 2005). This is done to further an agreement with the State-Regions Conference through a decision of the national government, according to the general principle of loyal cooperation. This principle also governs the relationships between the state and the local autonomies as guaranteed by the Constitution.

It has been suggested that this governmental power could be deemed to be unconstitutional, as it appears to be the expression of a general, typically governmental, power of policy and coordination, which had apparently been overthrown by the 2001 reform to the Constitution. In the absence of constitutional dispositions that provide for such a power, it should not be provided for based on ordinary (instead of constitutional) law (Cartabia and Violini 2005). This is a hotly debated issue, involving as it does to questions and problems pertaining to the whole gamut of the Italian legal system, especially from the point of view of a regional system.

The general issue of the implementation of community law also includes cases where the Italian legal system does not comply with community law. An example could be the requirements from EU Institutions that are deemed to be in conflict with the treaties. The Italian legal system includes this possibility. The actions to be undertaken, such as an appeal before a European Court, are subject to a 'shared' and 'complex' procedure. The Italian regions have an explicit right to participate in all proceedings the Italian government may enter to appeal against EU law before the European Court of Justice or the Court of First Instance. Article 5, Section 2, of the *La Loggia Act* states that, in matters that fall under regional jurisdiction, the state may consider appealing at the request of the regions. However, when the request is issued by the State-Regions Conference, through an absolute majority resolution that has been adopted by the regions and the autonomous provinces, the state is obliged to appeal and cannot ignore the request (Cartabia and Violini 2005).

The ascending phase

As to the 'ascending' stage, it is useful to focus initially on a different issue area, namely the allocation of European structural funds, both through specific regional policies and the recognition of the regions' power to manage all administrative procedures that are fundamental to the concrete determination of the receivers of funds, to their dispersal, and to the assessment of impact of resultant spending (Caretti 1997; Profeti 2006). As regards the first point, it is important to state again that the situation varies according to the area over which the region has concrete legislative power. For example, the autonomy enjoyed by regions in the vocational training sector – an area where European structural funds can have a key impact – is remarkably extensive: indeed, in this field, the regions' role is more decisive than that of the state itself.

Nevertheless, such a statement must not be misunderstood. The state still plays a fundamental role, even though the effect of its interventions in this area may on occasion be to produce some curious 'short circuits', and may sometimes even be in contrast with the fundamental principles of community law. With regards to this point, there is a telling example concerning vocational training, a field in which the regions have wide-ranging powers and where there are considerable possibilities for the use of European structural funds to generate growth and to improve the average level of education and abilities of the workforce. These possibilities have been put to good use by a number of regions. However, in order to achieve even better results, and to make the regional vocational training system accessible to a higher number of companies, the Italian state intervened with a law allocating further sums to the regions in order to finance renovation activities and safety measures improvement in private training schools. This was designed to make it easier for these schools to obtain authorization from the regions to take part in the distribution of community funds.

This state intervention, however, created a peculiar situation: while the state had attempted to make it easier to meet, on a territorial basis, the objectives for which structural funds are allocated, at the same time it had created 'State Aid' that was incompatible with community law and, for this reason, was condemned by the EU Commission. Specifically, an EU Commission ruling (2 March 2005, No. C.22/2003), adjudged that this intervention by the Italian state had advantaged companies operating in Italian regions, thus creating a competitive advantage that might alter exchange relations within the vocational training single market.

State intervention does not always engender such results. Sometimes it favors such positive phenomena as the integration of procedures between social parties, local authorities and regions. The collaboration dynamics that have permeated labor market policy are a typical example of just such an outcome. In this case, the state's mediation role, together with its setting of general objectives, has allowed the regions' policies to achieve significant results through the utilization of structural funds, especially with regards re-skilling and the reinsertion of the unemployed into the labor market.

Turning from regional development to the role of the regions in community law-making, current practices are based on Article 117, Section 5 of the Constitution, and also on very detailed state Acts (Article 5 of the *La Loggia Act* and Article 5 of Act 11, 2005) (Cartabia and Violini 2005). The Italian Republic, one and indivisible, cannot be defined in monolithic terms, but rather as a complex entity, 'composed of the Municipalities, the Provinces, the Metropolitan Cities, the Regions and the State. Municipalities, provinces, metropolitan cities and Regions are autonomous entities having their own statutes, powers and functions in accordance with the principles laid down in the Constitution' (in the words of the new Article 114 of the Italian Constitution).

Whenever the Republic is called upon to operate as such at European community level, there are procedures to ensure that the interests of the state, the regions and the local authorities, based on their respective areas of competence, have been taken into account and will be followed in order to reach a valid expression of the 'national will'. Regions are guaranteed participation in national decisions aimed at influencing EU decision-making processes. As mentioned earlier, Article 117, Section 5 of the Constitution ensures that the regions and the autonomous provinces of Trento and Bolzano may participate in 'preparatory decision-making process of EU legislative acts in the areas that fall within their responsibilities', and that they can also act in 'proceedings for the creation of Community law', involving matters that fall within their jurisdiction.

National law specifies in more detail how regional participation is achieved. A first example is the paradiplomatic role that the Italian regions can play in EU institutions. On matters over which the Constitution gives them legislative powers, representatives of the regions – together with national government representatives – may attend 'proceedings held by the Council, its working groups and Council Committees, and meetings of the EU Commission, according to procedures that have to be agreed by the State-Regions Conference (Article 5, Act 131, 2003). Moreover, in matters over which the regions have exclusive legislative competence, the 'Delegation Head' may be the president of a region or of an autonomous province, who will be appointed by the government, 'based on criteria and procedures that have been established through an agreement of general cooperation between the Government, the Regions [...]. during the State-Regions Conference' (Article 5, Act 131, 2003).

A second example is the right of regions to be kept promptly informed by the government on any projects involving community law from the very early stages of development. Further to the receipt of information, the regions have two options: on the one hand, they may submit detailed comments to the government; on the other hand they may ask, individually or collectively, that a special session of the State-Regions Conference be called. The region(s) will then be able to express its (their) own views at the meetings, and either reach an agreement with the state government or force it to enter a 'reserve of examination' (*riserva d'esame*) with the EU's Council of Ministers pending further consultations within the Conference (Article 5, Act 11, 2005).

None of this is enough, though, to stop the government's activity. Once 20 days have elapsed after the communication to the State-Regions Conference of the issue of a '*riserva*' the government may proceed with its participation in the process of elaborating European decisions; this can also happen should the Conference fail to respond. Moreover, even when the State-Regions Conference replies promptly, the resolution is not considered mandatory by national law.

The regions have the right to be informed and consulted when parliament deals with matters that are relevant to the regions. Conversely, the law recognizes the same rights to the national parliament. This is seen as an attempt to give regions and state the same importance. However, parliament may, as regulator of the government's actions, provide the necessary guidelines, which allows it to partially direct the ensuing activity of the national representatives in the EU institutions. Such a role is not granted to the regions, which therefore have a weaker position.

The weaker role of the regions becomes apparent when we look at the fate of agreements that may have been reached in the State-Regions Conference. The government, in fact, may decide to proceed even though an agreement has not been reached – either because the matter being dealt with is considered an urgent one, or by simply allowing the 20 days that the law fixes as a deadline to reach an agreement to elapse.

A third example of the participation of the regions in the making of European decisions lies in the possibility for the regions to attend governmental ministries' meetings to coordinate positions in the community decision-making process. These procedures are rather complex and require mechanisms of connection between national and regional institutions. To that end, Article 2 of Act 11, 2005, provides for an Interdepartmental Committee for European Community Affairs (CIACE). Its task is to prepare the Italian government's position on European issues. If the Committee has to deal with matters of regional relevance, the president of the Regional Presidents' Conference (or the president of a region or an autonomous province that has been appointed as his/her official representative) may attend the meetings, although his/her vote only has a consultative value. The Committee is assisted by a permanent group of experts, whose task is to provide guidance to the Committee. The experts are drawn from various ministerial administration departments. The participation of regional administrative personnel is provided for, with the same constraints as those indicated for the Committee.

It should be noted, however, that the regions' role in the field of community law issuing is partially influenced, both in a negative and positive sense, by the evolution of regulations concerning the 'foreign' powers of the regions themselves (Palermo 1999, 2002; Florenzano 2004), regulations that are part of *La Loggia* law. On the one hand, as recently restated by the Italian Constitutional Court, regions can carry out international activities but in no case can they carry out a foreign policy of their own (decision, 1 June 2006, No. 211). On the other hand, as can be seen in the practise established by regions on the basis of their participation in community institution activities, it is now evident that regions are often engaged in initiatives that demonstrate their exertion of significant 'external' prerogatives, particularly in regard to 'paradiplomatic' relations established with representatives of other countries, regions or international organizations.

The potential contradictions and tension are evident. They are moderated to some extent by the fact that these activities are carried out 'in the shadows' of very strict regulations designed to ensure that regions have to communicate in advance with the government about any proposed 'international' action. The government has the power to judge whether the action is compliant with the general guidelines of national foreign policy, of which it is the sole custodian from an institutional point of view. Nonetheless, some regions chafe against such restrictions and search for new and innovative methods of international collaboration and cooperation (Palermo 2006).

All that said, contradictions and tensions should certainly not be overstated. In European matters relations between the state and regions tend to be characterized by cooperation. Nor can this cooperation be reduced to the letter of the relevant legal and constitutional procedures. Relations between state and regions not only overlap and reflect the rigid constitutional scheme of division of competences, they sometimes even surpass it.

Conclusion

Some closing considerations may usefully summarize the Italian situation. The rules governing the participation of the Italian regions in proceedings to create and implement community law have been greatly affected by the 2001 constitutional reform. Difficulties in the interpretation and the implementation of the new rules, which are not always self-explanatory and complete, make a definitive characterization difficult. Although the 2001 reform was intended to strengthen and give more visibility to regions this goal has not always been achieved. More specifically, regional autonomy has been weakened by the way the national parliament and the government have identified areas that fall under the state's legislative and administrative jurisdictions. The Italian Constitutional Court has been working hard to prepare a more comprehensive reference framework, in an attempt to avoid conflicts between the regions and the state; conflicts which have been numerous since 2001.

In the so-called descending phase pertaining to the implementation of community law, the current system of the 'Communitarian Act' (*legge comunitaria*) only partly favors regional prerogatives. Even when there is a provision for a State-Regions Conference consultation, the level of cooperation between the various public bodies is often biased towards central government interests.

A similar problem can be found even when the regions, as holders of exclusive jurisdiction in certain matters, could directly implement community law. As we have seen, the fact that the state has exclusive legal jurisdiction in certain matters, creates a special phenomenon: since the state competence prevails in areas of overlapping competence, areas of regional competence are, in effect, absorbed into the state field, despite the original distribution of the powers. The same process may also be observed in the descending phase. However, the state has developed new institutional mechanisms for communicating with the regions, and has strengthened the role of the State-Regions Conference, and the agreements that can be reached therein. In other words, the requirement that the central government and the local governments have to cooperate and share responsibility is helped by the provisions that allow regional representatives to participate in meetings where the Italian state decides upon its European policies. However, the weaknesses that are found in the descending phase are again present in the ascending phase. The agreements that are reached between the state and the regions are not always honoured. The nature of the State-Regions Conference as a mere consultative body often renders its work ineffective.

On the latter point we may make further observations. During recent years the role of the State-Regions Conference has been weakened by the fact that the viewpoints of various regions are frequently divergent: this is due in particular to the different political allegiances of presidents and the majorities that support them. Conflicts between the state and regions are frequent where the state and a region are controlled by different political majorities; a clash with the government is generally avoided by regional governments that are supported by the same political forces that enjoy majority at a national level. The best illustration of this point can be found in the number of appeals lodged by regions with the Constitutional Court in order to oppose the state's attempts to issue laws on various matters: since 2001, the more 'active' regions have generally been those governed by political forces hostile to those that have supported the national government. As a consequence, when a new political majority emerges at the state level, regional activism is far more likely to appear in those regions that are dominated by opposition political forces. However, it is not only this conflict that weakens the role of the State-Regions Conference. With regards to the issuing and implementation of EU law, it is often the case that the regions – particular the more important regions – fail to make their voice heard within the

Conference, but rather act autonomously in seeking access to government, community institutions or other countries' governments.

Finally, the issue of the EU Constitutional Treaty and its failure has to be taken into account. In Italy this event does not seem to have influenced in any particular way the relations between state and regions in the field of community law-issuing and implementation. Rather, experts and law interpreters in Italy still conceive the debate on the 'community' role of regions as a direct consequence of the constitutional reorganization of relations between state and regions. Reforms of the Italian Constitution are, now and always, at the heart of the debate, together with the problems pertaining to the need to give voice and wider legislative and administrative powers to the richer and more developed areas of the country, without overlooking uniformity and the equalization needs of poorer and less developed areas.

Note

* The authors would like to thank Dr. Fulvio Cortese for his research assistance and comments.

6

Divide to Multiply: Irish Regionalism and the European Union

Katy Hayward[*]

The relatively recent phenomenon of Irish regionalism owes much of its shadowy existence to a fortuitous combination of political pragmatism and European funding. The movement toward regionalization in modern Ireland has been a definitively 'top-down' process, driven by assessments of national advantage rather than by local pressure for devolved power. The latter stages of this process have been indelibly shaped by the European Union (EU) – the priorities of its integration and the ramifications of its enlargement. The Commission's (1997) blueprint for the pre-accession strategy of the EU in *Agenda 2000* rang warning bells for Ireland that receipts from the EU would rapidly diminish in preparation for the new member states. If it remained a single region in the next round of structural funding, the 'Objective 1 in transition' status was to apply to the whole country; the expected consequences of this included a substantial reduction in EU subsidies and a near and firm end date for their removal altogether. The Irish government's response was to divide the country into formalized administrative regions in order to extend its eligibility for structural funding. The following year (1998), it lodged an application with Eurostat to have Ireland classified into two NUTS 2 regions: Border, Midlands and Western (BMW) and Southern and Eastern (S&E) (Boyle 1999: 738). This enabled full Objective 1 status to remain with a large part of the territory, the relatively underdeveloped northwest. The creation of these Euro-regions in Ireland, in accordance with the definition presented by Wyn Jones and Scully in the introduction to this volume, is a fascinating case study of a state's response to a perceived overlap between its own interests and the requirements of European integration.

The Irish case, therefore, stands somewhat in distinction from other examples of decentralization in the EU, including many elaborated in this volume. The main players in the story of Irish regionalism in the EU context are not local actors but national politicians and, even more pivotally, government officials. For this reason, perhaps, this aspect of Ireland's experience of EU membership can be seen to exemplify the typically *ad hoc*, agenda-driven and reactive nature of the Irish public administration's response to the

conditions of European integration critiqued by Brigid Laffan (2000, 2001).
Indeed, Rees, Quinn and Connaughton's (2004: 402) detailed social network analysis of the 'institutional realignment' of one Irish NUTS 3 region
leads them to conclude that 'Ireland's adaptation [to Europeanization] has
been politically pragmatic, administratively ambitious and institutionally
limited.' This chapter develops this theme in outlining the form and function of regional governance in Ireland, its relationship to and development
through the EU, and its limited public impact.

The EU and sub-national government in Ireland

Local government

Sub-national level government was first given clear constitutional status in
Ireland in 1999 following a national referendum on the subject.[1] Until that
point it had only had a basis in Acts of the Oireachtas (parliament) and
had changed little since the 1898 Local Government (Ireland) Act enacted
prior to independence (Coyle 1997: 76). This Act historically meant that
the primary unit for sub-national government has been the county and
not the region. This was reaffirmed by the 2001 Local Government Act
which divided the state for the purpose of local government into 34 units
(O'Sullivan 2003: 41). These so-called county and city councils, supported by
the small municipal councils, make up the core of the local administrative
system in terms of power, functions and finance. The members of these local
authorities are directly elected using the system of proportional representation with single transferable vote (as is the case for elections to Dáil Éireann,
the national parliament). They have an extensive range of responsibilities,
including waste services, environmental protection, recreation amenities
and development incentives/controls. However, in many instances, the local
authorities' role is subordinate to the state agencies responsible for policy delivery and enforcement in specialized areas, such as the National
Roads Authority, the National Educational Welfare Board and Bord Pleanála
(the planning appeals board). The number of these quasi-autonomous bodies has grown substantially in the early twenty-first century in a process
that has been described as 'agencification' (Collins and Quinlivan 2005:
392; McGauran et al. 2005). By 2008 there were approximately 200 such
agencies, with government-appointed boards but with employees who are
neither elected representatives nor, typically, civil servants (MacCarthaigh
2007). They fulfil a range of cultural, commercial, developmental, advisory
and regulatory activities without being subject to direct ministerial control
(MacCarthaigh 2008: 86–92).

The trend to create these single-function executive agencies in response
to the demand for new services from government – as opposed to upgrading local authorities and devolving responsibilities to them – typifies what

Adshead (2003: 117–118) describes as a system whereby 'practical problems are often solved at the expense of democratic accountability'. The devolution of power to officials rather than to local politicians has been held as a precaution against corruption since the first such measures (which gave dominant power to managers rather than councilors in local authorities) were taken by the new state in the 1920s (Chubb 1992: 270). The history and structuring of regional-level governance exemplifies on an even greater scale the prioritizing of pragmatism and task-led efficacy over representative democracy in sub-national public administration in Ireland. Acting as a significant bolster to this agenda has been the EU's influence in the construction of regional administration in Ireland. In a comprehensive study of regional and local public service bodies in Ireland, MacCarthaigh (2007) found that the EU played a major part in both the funding and legislation for the establishment of sub-national bodies, over 80 per cent of which were created after 1990 (following the EU's move toward emphasis on the sub-national level). These bodies most commonly serve to directly implement and coordinate policy. Encouragement of 'social partnership' aside, the EU has not been able to do much by way of enhancing the democratic credibility of these new institutions.

The EU context for regionalization in Ireland

The very meaning of regionalism in Ireland is contested; the boundaries of even the official bodies deemed to be 'regional' cover a conflicting variety of geographical areas.[2] Reflecting the lack of popular use of regionalism as a political or social reference, the recent establishment of regional-level public institutions has been by way of executive discretion rather than bottom-up mobilization or lobbying. By far the most important factor in this process of deconcentration ('decentralization' would be too strong a term) has been an assessment of the economic interests of the state. The dallying with regionalization that occurred on a somewhat sporadic basis in the 1970s and 1980s was primarily due to recognition that major regional imbalance was injurious to Ireland's economic welfare. At that time, the government response (such as it was) essentially took the form of extending the aforementioned state-agency sector to the regional level, adding regional arms to national organizations (such as the Irish Development Agency) (Whelan 1976: 284, 288; Boyle 1999: 742).[3] Somewhat ironically, as the EU was coming to prioritize the regional level as a focus for intra-European cohesion in the late 1980s, Ireland's main public regional bodies (the Regional Development Organisations, established in 1969) were abolished as part of budgetary cost-cutting measures. Nonetheless, the requirements for EU structural funding were too important for the Irish government to overlook, and so in order to fulfil the Commission's demand for regional consultation, it quickly constructed a regional structure (based this time on seven regions) for the purpose of assisting in the preparation of the National Development Plan

(NDP) for 1989–1993.[4] However, the concurrent designation of the whole state as a single underdeveloped region meant that the Irish government remained in effect *the* regional authority for the purposes of EU structural funding (Coyle 1997: 81). The cosmetic nature of regional participation (merely taking the form of Sub-Regional Review Committees) at this time was glaringly apparent and a cause of explicit 'regret' from the then EU commissioner for regional policy, Bruce Millan (Coyle and Sinnott 1993: 82).

When it came to the negotiation of the next Community Support Framework (CSF) for 1994–1999, Ireland's National Development Plan again placed a strategic emphasis on national over regional development. However, an embryonic conception of multi-level development and administration was present in the form of the eight NUTS 3 regional authorities established at the start of this period (see section below). Ireland began to experience vibrant economic growth during the course of this NDP, but it continued to be spatially imbalanced in a pattern of regional deprivation (i.e. substantially poorer in the north-west than in the south-east). Hence, one of the four specific objectives of the subsequent National Development Plan for 2000–2006 was for 'balanced regional development' (Ireland 1999: 8). To this end, the NDP revised regional boundaries (allowing for allocation at NUTS 2 level for the first time) and included (in addition to the three national Operational Programmes) a Regional Operational Programme in each region, to be managed by the two newly constructed regional assemblies. This division of Ireland into two regions facilitated the devolution of responsibility for the regional programs away from central government. Perhaps most significantly, the conjuring up of these two regions also enabled Ireland to receive Objective 1 level structural funding for as long as possible, phasing out funding to the prosperous Southern and Eastern region up to the end of 2005/2006 while retaining Objective 1 status for the poorer Border, Midland and Western region (see Figure 6.1). Nonetheless, it should be acknowledged at this point that, due to the unprecedented economic growth referred to above, the 2000–2006 National Development Plan was the first that was not primarily designed to draw down EU structural and cohesion funds. Receipts from these funds of around €3.8 billion (of which approximately €600–700 million was secured through the delineation of the new NUTS 2 regions) were but a small part of the overall NDP budget of €57 billion (National Treasury Management Agency 2002: 23).

By the time of the National Development Plan of 2007–2013, Ireland's economic standing was such that virtually all the €184 billion investment planned was anticipated to be domestically funded (Ireland 2007: 43). Even more importantly, in relation to our considerations here, the motivating priority of EU structural funding itself had moved from regional development to 'niche investment' (Bennett 2008). Of the €3 billion expected from the EU in this period (not this time included in the NDP calculations), most is targeted at rural development (€2.3 billion) and then at selected programs

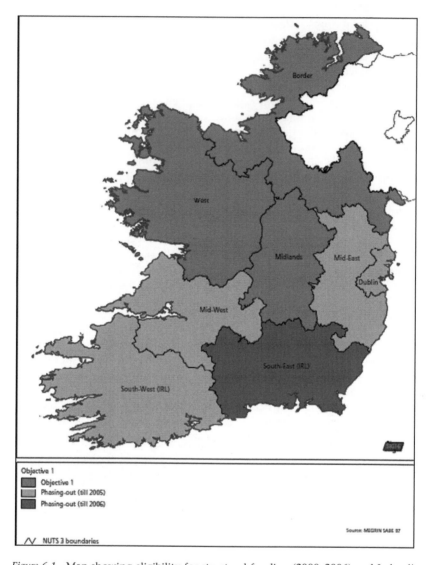

Figure 6.1   Map showing eligibility for structural funding (2000–2006) and Ireland's eight Regional Authorities (NUTS 3) © European Union, 1995–2010
Source: CEC Directorate-General for Regional Policy http://ec.europa.eu/regional_policy/sources/ graph/maps/cnat/ir_obj1_en.pdf (Accessed May 2010).

such as research, 'youth in action' or lifelong learning (Ireland 2007: 43; Bennett 2008). Indeed, Ireland ceased to be entitled to cohesion funding by 2004 and its receipts from structural funds, although a far from insignificant €0.9 billion, will be approximately 75 per cent less in the period 2007–2013 compared to 2000–2006 (BMW and SERA 2008: 4; Bennett 2008). From 2007 onwards, both NUTS 2 regions qualified only for Objective 2 status. Nonetheless, half of the structural funding budget is dedicated to the Border, Midland and Western region for 'phasing in' to its new status (€457million); the Southern and Eastern region will receive nearly €3 million to meet targets for regional competitiveness, and approximately €150 million will be received across the country for territorial cohesion (Bennett 2008). Most of this money is set to be delivered by 2010, after which point the BMW region will no longer receive a differential amount of funding from the EU (BMW and SERA 2008: 5). As this was one of the motivating factors behind the division of Ireland into two regions in 1999, it is worth considering what the legacy of a decade of more active regional structures in Ireland will have been.

Regional authorities

There are no directly elected provincial or regional authorities between central government and the local authorities in Ireland. What exists in place of elected bodies are the regional authorities and assemblies, to which elected councilors from the member local authorities are nominated and which are essentially run by centrally appointed (albeit small) managing authorities. The eight NUTS 3 regional authorities (see Figure 6.1) came into existence in 1994 (through the 1991 Local Government Act) and served to review the implementation of the Operational Programmes for the 1994–1999 period. According to Carroll and Byrne (1999: 174), the nature of the powers and functions assigned to the regional authorities shows that they were designed to be weak and uninfluential. They have two main functions. The first is to coordinate the provision of public services by the local authorities; the other is to monitor the delivery of EU structural and cohesion funding in the region. Members of these authorities are nominated by elected members of the constituent city/county councils from among themselves, with the number of seats (from 22 (Mid-East) to 38 (Border)) being based on the population size of the area. Each regional authority has a chairperson, a director, a designated city/county manager (to enhance links between the local and regional authorities), and policy and administrative staff (see Figure 6.3 for an illustration of the structures of the regional authorities). The work of the authority is assisted by an operational committee and an EU operational committee responsible for reviewing progress in the various EU operational programs in place in its NUTS 3 region. This involves the preparation of regional strategies, which are specifically intended to monitor the delivery of EU structural funds as well as to promote the coordination of public services in the region (DELG 2003). The fact that these regional strategies have now been developed to incorporate the Regional Planning Guidelines, which must be regarded by all other planning authorities in

Ireland, means that the regional authorities evolved to have substantially more influence and import than commentators (and perhaps policy-makers) originally envisaged.[5]

Regional assemblies

As noted above, prior to the programming period of 2000–2006, the Irish government designated the country into two NUTS 2 regions: Border, Midland and Western (BMW) and Southern and Eastern (S&E) (see Figure 6.2). These assemblies were established in 1999 under the same parent

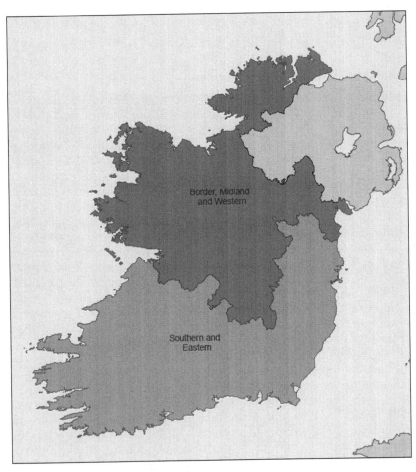

Figure 6.2   The two regional assemblies (NUTS 2) © European Union, 1995–2010
Source: CEC Directorate-General for Regional Policy http://ec.europa.eu/regional_policy/images/
map/eligible2007/conv_comp_0713_ie.pdf (Accessed May 2010).

legislation as the regional authorities in order to have them in place at short notice.[6] Each of these regions has a regional assembly whose members are nominated by constituent city/county councils from among their elected representatives who are also members of a regional authority. There are 29 members in the BMW region and 41 in the Southern and Eastern region, given that membership is based on population rather than territorial size. The tasks of the regional assemblies are closely aligned to those of the regional authorities. Their general function is to promote coordination in the provision of public services among the public, regional and local authorities in their regional areas. Most particularly, however, each regional assembly is charged with being the managing authority for its respective Operational Programme (i.e. BMW or S&E). These Regional Operational Programmes for EU structural and cohesion funding very much reflect the trends of policy priority and definition at the EU level. For example, in the NDP 2000–2006, they were designed to target investment at local production, infrastructure (such as urban renewal) and social inclusion. The Regional Operational Programme for the 2007–2013 NDP is somewhat different, reflecting the EU's so-called Lisbon Agenda in prioritizing: 'innovation and the knowledge economy', 'sustainable urban development' and 'environment and accessibility (S&E)/risk prevention (BMW)', and, an additional priority for the BMW region alone, 'transport and information communication technology services' (Ireland 2007). Not only is each assembly responsible for the financial management and control of the Operational Programme, it has a statutory duty to provide guidance to implementing bodies/final beneficiaries to ensure the sound financial management of the structural funds (BMW 2006: 12). Moreover, a particularly interesting function of the regional assemblies – and one illustrative of some deconcentration of responsibility away from central government with respect to 'European' tasks – is that of national coordinators of the transnational and inter-regional strands of the INTERREG program. This role was previously held by the Department of Finance, but now the members of selection committees for transnationally funded projects are appointed by the regional assemblies rather than the Department of Finance. For example, the BMW regional assembly was a partner in the INTERREG IIIC 'Futurreg' (Futures for Regional Development) program. And the S&E regional assembly is managing and certifying authority of the Ireland-Wales Programme of INTERREG IVA 2007–2013 on behalf of the Welsh assembly government and the Department of Finance.[7] The assemblies also have to monitor and evaluate the impact of the various measures of the Regional Operational Programmes, provide information and publicity on these measures, and ensure compatibility with community policies such as gender mainstreaming (BMW 2006: 23). The costs incurred by the assemblies in their function as managing authorities for the Regional Operational Programmes are covered jointly by the technical assistance budget in the programs themselves (which comes from the EU and the Irish exchequer) and by the Department of Finance; other costs of the assemblies are paid by the local authorities, as is also the case with the regional authorities.

The structure of the authorities and assemblies

The structure of the regional authorities and the regional assemblies (see Figures 6.3 and 6.4) immediately gives a clear impression as to the priorities of the Irish government in creating these regional institutions. Both the authorities and the assemblies are bottom-heavy in that the committees that run under their aegis are substantially larger and have more specific responsibilities than the forums in which the elected councilors meet. Moreover, the fact that these councilors are not directly elected to either type of institution, plus the fact that they meet so infrequently (approximately monthly in the authorities, bi-monthly in the assemblies) suggests that it would be difficult for even the most motivated members to have much more than a symbolic role. For the most part, the EU Commission's requirements for broad participation and consultation have been met via committee-contact with appointed representatives of social, sectoral and public interests rather than active democratic politics.

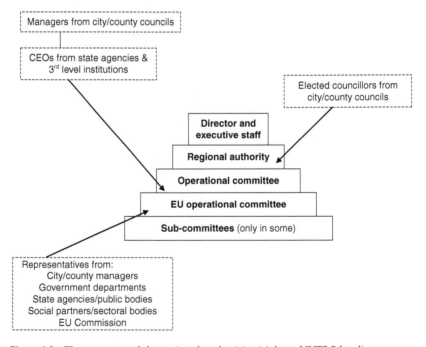

Figure 6.3   The structure of the regional authorities (eight at NUTS 3 level)

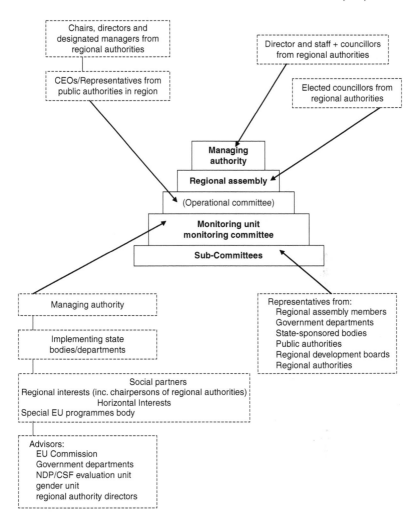

Figure 6.4   The structure of the regional assemblies (two at NUTS 2 level)

There are two main committees that operate in the regional assemblies. First, the Monitoring Committees of the Regional Operational Programmes, which are established in accordance with EU structural funding regulations (99/1260/EC). The Monitoring Committee for the BMW Regional Operational Programme has been chaired by an elected member since its inception in October 2000 and usually has a handful of elected members on it (from both the regional assembly and the three constituent regional authorities). The regional assembly also provides the secretariat for the Monitoring

Committee. Second, the operational committees were established to 'advise and assist the Regional Assembly in the discharge of its functions'.[8] These operational committees are far less significant than their Monitoring Committees, as is reflected in, first, the poor level of attendance at their meetings (as recorded in minutes of the BMW assembly, for example) and, most definitively, in the fact that the frequency of such meetings was reduced by the Department of Environment, Heritage and Local Government in 2004 from a fixed basis to 'as and when required' by the assembly. This has been put into effect as, at the time of writing (spring 2009), the operational committee of the S&E assembly has not met since August 2005 (SERA 2006). At the same time, a growing emphasis has been placed on the role of sub-committees, which are dedicated to the 'National Development Plan' and 'Regional and Rural Affairs' in the BMW assembly and to 'Enterprise and Productive Investment', 'Employment and Social Inclusion', 'Planning and Infrastructure' and 'Agriculture and Rural Development' in the S&E assembly (SERA 2008). A consequence of this emphasis on governance by a multiplicity of agencies and (sub-)committees is, Marshall (2002: 2) contends, that Ireland's regions have among the most convoluted and inscrutable structures of governance in Europe. This is illustrated in Figures 6.3 and 6.4.

Evaluating the role of the regional institutions

The limited effect of the programs toward redressing the significant regional disparities between levels of development and living standards across the territory of Ireland,[9] was in part due to the fact that the Regional Operational Programmes only accounted for around 15 per cent of the National Development Plan budget. The majority of elements that directly relate to the task of decreasing regional disparity, e.g. energy, roads, transport, research and development, are still largely addressed and coordinated on a national basis. The substantial amounts of under-spend (59 per cent) that hindered development of the less-developed BMW region in the first part of the 2000–2006 National Development Plan was in such areas as these and, therefore, beyond the remit of the assembly-managed Regional Operational Programmes. (e.g. just 4.6 per cent of spending forecast for regional innovation and 1.2 per cent for waste management had been spent by the time of the 2004 mid-term evaluation of the NDP) (Finn 2004). This was due in some part to a slowdown in the economy around 2002 and delays and cutbacks in the distribution of government funding. Yet even those areas in receipt of full funding were not without their problems, not least of which were the persistent concerns outstanding about value for money (Finn 2004).

More general problems arose in part from the need for further coordination between the various bodies and plans involved in regional governance. Cohesion had been damaged in part by shifts in the government's own priorities (as seen in the substantially altered plans of the exchequer for regional development). Moreover, the decisive policy-making process at the national level does not substantially factor-in the Regional Planning Guidelines or the Consultation Documents that regional bodies spend so much time and effort compiling. There is concern that, although regional structures overlap at various levels and effort is being made to coordinate planning within the regions, intra-regional development is not taken into account. This problem is simultaneously tackled and exacerbated by the National Spatial Strategy – yet another initiative for balanced development across the country, and one which came before the full potential of its Regional Operational Programmes could be realized.[10] So, good management remains imperative at this level. Perhaps unsurprisingly the director of the S&E managing authority proposed that the managing authorities in the regional assemblies be strengthened (Blair 2004). Certainly, the work of the committees have been improved with professional support services and targeting issues of particular need via the sub-committees active in the 2007–2013 NDP. There is also opportunity here for devolution of particular functions in another direction, i.e. to local authorities. Such a response would, however, need to ensure that it does not exacerbate the ultimate problem, which is the lack of clarity in the working of the sub-national bodies in general and the regional institutions in particular. Some complaints in this area directed at the regional authorities argue that pressing needs are obscured by the complex details the various committees have to deal with. The complex bureaucratic structure of these regional-level institutions plus, most pressingly, the fact that their existence and functions are not widely known, can have the effect of dissuading other actors working at the sub-national level in a wide variety of areas from engaging with them. One evaluation argued that even members of the committees from various sectors (from EU Commission to social partners) found it 'difficult to engage meaningfully with the process and to contribute effectively in influencing the implementation and progress/performance of the O[perational] P[rogrammes] in the areas which are of critical interest to them' (Farrell 2003: 159). This is not due to an inactivity or unwillingness on the part of the regional institutions, particularly the assemblies, to be responsive, innovative and informative, but is perhaps one symptom of the location of these bodies outside of the realm of directly elected representation, and the media focus on national-level policy and decision-making (as Irish representatives of EU institutions will attest).

Inputs from Irish regions into the EU

The role of central government

Benz and Eberlein (1999) found, in case studies of regionalism in France and Germany, that European-style multi-level governance can cope with the challenge of coordinating decision-making among a large number of

actors and arenas as long as the national institutional setting was supportive of functional and territorial differentiation. There have always been
concerns as to the capacity of the Irish administrative structures and institutions to adapt as necessary for successful regionalization. Addressing the
specific question of the conditions necessary for regional development in
post-accession Ireland, Barrington (1976: 354–358) argued that success in
this area would depend on resources, political will, promotional and supportive policies, and institutional machinery. Each of these four areas were
identified as in need of much advancement at the time. Thirty years later, the
effects of continued neglect and underdevelopment in these four areas are
apparent, exemplified in some of the problems encountered by the regional
bodies, particularly with regard to the relationship between sub-national
actors and the EU. The fundamental cause of this weakness is the belief of
the national government, vocalized at the start of regionalization in the EU
and sustained fairly consistently since, that central control is fundamentally
necessary for 'the requirements of efficiency, effectiveness and expediency'
(Haughey 1989). The Department of the Environment, Heritage and Local
Government (and its forebears) has traditionally held enormous power over
local authorities, exercising financial and administrative control as well as
regulating their relations with central government (Coyle 1997: 81). Because
the department is relatively peripheral to EU negotiations in areas outside
its remit, local authorities have as a consequence been effectively held back
from input into policy formulation in the EU. It was only in the mid-1990s
that sub-national authorities gained any sort of direct contact with EU institutions. This contact – and confidence – has increased over time, to such
a degree that regional-level actors engaged in the drafting of the Regional
Operational Programmes for 2007–2013 noted that the control of central
government over their negotiations with the Commission had 'relaxed considerably'. The suggestion is that this may be both because the scale of the
co-financed programs under negotiation is so much smaller than previously
and because the staff involved (for example in the regional assemblies) are
now more experienced and familiar with the EU's requirements than their
counterparts in the Department of Finance.[11]

Ireland's informal policy style on EU negotiations mirrors the *ad hoc*
nature of consultations between central and local administrations (Callanan
2002: 73). The limited (and sometimes fairly sporadic) amount of dialogue
between central and local government in Ireland is reflected in the fact that
expertise from the local level in Ireland is rarely incorporated in negotiations on new EU legislation (Coyle and Sinnott 1993: 102; Callanan 2002:
73). Insight into why this is the case was given in a comparative report by
the Council of European Municipalities and Regions (CEMR 1999), which
found consultations between central government and local authorities in
Ireland 'usually involve lobbying actions or information meetings rather
than genuine negotiations producing binding decisions'. It is not surprising,

therefore, that there has been no cohesive or coordinated local authority perspective on EU issues (Coyle 1997: 81). More generally, this has meant that general discontent at the local level regarding the decentralization of powers has not been channeled into any concerted campaign to improve or enhance it (Coyle and Sinnott 1993: 101, 103).

Regional capacity

The Irish government has traditionally been wary of allowing direct links to develop between the EU Commission and the local authorities, preferring to act as mediator for all relationships between the EU and the Irish state. This has gradually changed, however, shifting from what was in effect a prohibition on local authority-Brussels links in the early years of membership, to reluctant permissiveness in the early 1990s, to cautious support at the present time. Yet the government remains watchful of EU-related activities at the sub-national level, aided by the role of its departments in managing, monitoring and implementing EU programs (Coyle 1997: 90; Rees et al. 2004). The position of local and regional authorities in Ireland contrasts with that of the majority of their EU counterparts in terms of their democratic standing, capacity and powers. It is the managers of the local and regional authorities who have been bestowed with most autonomy and discretion at a sub-national level. Yet the City and County Managers' Association can be credited with having invited the Institute for Public Administration to provide a consultancy service and, later, a training program for local authority officials on the workings of the EU. As local officials have gained knowledge and confidence in working in and with the EU institutions, it has become more common for local government to look for support from the EU in negotiation with central government departments (Callanan 2003a: 425).

Access strategies to the EU

Direct contacts between sub-national authorities and EU institutions have, indeed, become increasingly necessary with the growing amount of EU legislation directed at local governance. These have been fostered through a variety of means but primarily for specified purposes related to local authorities' role in the management of EU funding/legislation or to their representation in EU policy-making. First, the role of regional and local authorities and assemblies in monitoring and managing EU structural funds and programs has led to direct links being formed with the European Commission. For example, representatives from the Commission (particularly from directorate-generals dealing with regional policy, fisheries and agriculture) sit on the Monitoring Committees of regional assemblies and the EU operational committees in the regional authorities. Analysis of the minutes of the meetings of these committees indicates that the role of Commission representatives at these meetings is one of a benign, albeit fairly strict, mentor (offering, for example, encouragement on progress made, suggestions for new 'innovative tools' and reminders of good practise). More generally, Irish delegates regularly attend the range of seminars, training programs and study visits hosted by Brussels for local authority members and officials. Expanding upon this role are the projects funded by the EU to encourage links between other regional players in the EU. For instance, the Southern and Eastern assembly was involved in the ReAct project, funded by the ERDF. This 2-year project sought to learn from the combined experience of eight regional partners in managing INTERREG funding in order to help the EU improve the quality of INTERREG projects and their management at the NUTS 2 level (SERA 2006). Regional authorities are also active participants in projects funded by the EU, typically through INTERREG – such as the South-West Regional Authority's involvement in the amusingly named e-bygov INTERREG IIIC project to improve the use of communications technology by public services.

The Committee of the Regions (CoR) is the most important formal forum for Irish sub-national government at the EU level – a fact that, as Wyn Jones and Scully's evaluation herein confirms, does not necessarily indicate any substantial move beyond central government control. Ireland's nine members are nominated by the minister for the Environment, Heritage and Local Government from local authorities (although it is also in the remit of regional authorities to nominate CoR members if requested to do so by the minister). Although they are first and foremost local councillors, because they represent their region in the CoR all members are automatically given membership of their regional authority upon nomination and are required to brief it on developments within the Committee. There are also the offices in Brussels established to promote direct contact between sub-national authorities in Ireland and the EU. As far back as 1992, six local authorities in the west of Ireland set up a liaison office, known as NASC, in Brussels (see www.nasc.ie); their example was followed by Údarás na Gaeltachta (for the development of Irish-speaking areas) and the West Regional Authority. NASC is the largest and most successful of such initiatives and works to inform local actors about developments in the EU, facilitate partnerships and support dialogue between the various levels. This is especially notable because the limited remit and power of local authorities in Ireland means that they do not fit particularly well into the large transregional organizations (such as the CEMR) that work to lobby the EU on local authorities' behalf. Nonetheless, participation in smaller, direct partnerships, especially in projects funded by EU Community initiatives such as INTERREG and RECITE, has generated genuine cooperation and an exchange of experience.

A government initiative in this area is the Irish Regions Office (IRO) established by the Department of the Environment, Heritage and Local Government in 2000. In Brussels, it is a resource for the Irish members of the Committee of the Regions and their regional authorities and serves to assist sub-national authorities in influencing EU policy. At the local level, it seeks to maintain awareness of developments within the EU and to identify funding opportunities.[12] Its role at this level has been expanded through collaboration with local authority managers and the Association of Irish Regions, the national organization of the regional authorities and regional assemblies. As well as facilitating communication between its members, the Association represents them in relation to central government, offering advice on economic development in the regions, for example. The Association is, however, constituted of chairpersons and directors from these regional bodies rather than a wider body of elected representatives. If there is, therefore, any burgeoning 'paradiplomatic' role for Irish regional actors in relation to the EU, it remains limited in scope (due to the restricted remit of the regional bodies to begin with), by and large confined to the involvement of officials rather than politicians and, consequently, beyond the public eye.

Outputs from the EU to Irish regions

Experience of EU laws and directives

As Ireland settles into being a net contributor to the EU, the costs associated with implementing a large body of EU legislation are being felt increasingly acutely, not least at the local level. The micro-detail of EU legislation, policies and funding has meant that the burden of EU membership has become increasingly heavy for local authorities. In their role as service providers, property owners, employers, development agencies etc., local authorities are responsible for implementing nearly three quarters of EU legislation (Callanan 2003a: 408). The experience of EU directives can be both direct and indirect for local authorities. A direct impact can be seen in the large-scale administrative and financial costs of managing and maintaining the infrastructure needed to meet the Urban Waste Water Directive (91/271/EC), for example, or in compliance with the Landfill Directive (99/31/EC). Indirect effects of EU legislation may affect local government activity in such areas as health and safety, employment, recycling targets or the protection of habitats (Callanan 2003a: 408–410). Although national governments are responsible for implementing EU legislation *de jure*, local authorities tend to be responsible in practise, and thus growing Commission vigilance regarding infractions of EU legislation may become a source of increasing tension between local and central administrations (Callanan 2003a: 411). Moreover, because a large proportion of the observation, implementation and enforcement of European legislation occurs at a sub-national level, the EU itself is increasingly dependent on local authorities (Callanan 2002: 67). In recognition of this fact, the European Commission's White Paper on European Governance (2001) proposed enhanced involvement for local government at all stages of EU policy-making (Callanan 2002: 66, 70).

Recent alterations to the structure and functions of sub-national government in Ireland have not substantially altered the centralized nature of the Irish state. Indeed, it may be said that, while the EU has facilitated significant change in the role of regional and local authorities in Ireland, the central government's mediation of Ireland's experience of EU membership has prevented such changes from having wide or deep implications for governance in Ireland more generally. This is in part because much of the strength of Irish public administration in response to the requirements of EU membership has resided in its use of centralization (Laffan 2001: 88). In addition to this, the multi-level nature of the impact of the EU has, if anything, served to complicate rather than coordinate the workings of sub-national government in Ireland. Critics may see this 'multiplicity' as a direct effect of the notoriously bureaucratic nature of EU influence, whereas a more sanguine observer would interpret it as the (necessarily complex) operation of network-building. Certainly, Carroll and Byrne (1999: 177) identify the embedding of some EU principles such as networks, partnership and sustainability in Irish regional development strategy, 'even if the other key principle of subsidiarity has yet to gain a firm foothold'.

EU funding

Over the course of the four programming periods 1989–2006, Ireland received around €17.5 billion in funding from the EU that was aimed at improving development and rectifying regional imbalance across the country, including through cohesion, structural and rural development funds (Bennett 2008). Cohesion funding ran from 1993–2006 and was concentrated on improving transport and the environment in member states lagging behind in development. Given that cohesion funding was determined on a national rather than regional basis, Ireland ceased to be eligible for this from the end of 2003 (see Table 6.1).

Local authorities acted as the implementing bodies for cohesion funding in the areas of water treatment/supply (with the Department of the Environment, Heritage and Local Government) and national roads (with the

Table 6.1   GDP per capita levels in Ireland and its NUTS 2 regions (EU average = 100)

	State	S&E Region	BMW Region
1988	64	–	–
1993	81	–	–
1998	108	119	79
2000	115	126	74
2004	141	157	100
2006	140	163	104

Source: Bennett 2008; Central Statistics Office.

Department of Transport and National Roads Authorities). EU structural funds have been used to establish and finance a range of local development groups (such as area partnerships and county/city enterprise boards) largely independent of local government (Callanan 2002: 67). A contemporary study by Hart found that, even in the early 1990s, local authorities were tending to over-concentrate on EU structural funds to the neglect of the numerous directives associated with the European Single Market (see Coyle 1997: 86). This perhaps shows another dimension of Irish regionalism and the EU: Ireland has from the start and from all levels been concerned much more with the extraction of inputs from the EU rather than with the wider contextual and more complex legal effects of membership.

The Community Initiative programs enabled interests not covered by the National Development Plan but within the interests of the EU as a whole to be met by additional funding. This provided a new opportunity for subnational authorities and organizations to communicate directly with the Commission in applications for local funding requirements. Even by 1993, two-thirds of local authorities in Ireland had participated in at least one of the Community Initiative programs (Coyle 1997: 89). The most significant Community Initiatives for the regional level have been INTERREG (particularly the Ireland-Wales and Ireland-Northern Ireland programs), LEADER (for rural development) and RECITE (exchanges between local and regional authorities). As cohesion and structural funding diminished in the 2000–2006 programming period, sub-national organizations became even more motivated to apply for funding from the Community Initiatives, raising their importance for local and regional authorities.

New ways of making policy

Sub-national authorities in Ireland have traditionally had little involvement in major policy areas or the negotiation of central government policy (Coyle 1997: 78). Yet one indirect consequence of EU membership has been the changing relationship between central civil servants and their local government counterparts. In 1987, Collins found that that civil servants in government departments viewed local authority managers as 'troublesome functionaries'; yet, 10 years on, their political autonomy and policy focus has made the two key allies (Asquith and O'Halpin 1998: 88–89). Indeed, in their optimistic vision, Asquith and O'Halpin (1998) foresee a future 'steering' role for local authorities in the EU context: developing 'a multitude of working relationships with other state, semi-state, not-for-profit sector and private business sector organisations'. However, this overestimates the capacity for leadership in local politics in a context long-inhibited by tight party discipline, the persistence of clientelism and localism, and (until recently) the dual mandate by which individuals could simultaneously hold seats both as local councilors and members of the Dáil (Coyle 1997: 80).

The increasing complexity of policy-making and delivery in the context of EU membership has not served to counteract the relative invisibility/obscurity of elected representatives at the sub-national level. Nor has the development of the regional level of administration in Ireland had a substantive effect on democratic input to policy delivery, given that members of the regional authorities and the regional assemblies are not directly elected but rather nominated from constituent authorities. Any effects of deconcentration in responsibilities across the local, regional and national spheres have therefore primarily impacted on public servants rather than politicians. This fact is, one might argue, reflected in the low-level impact that changes to sub-national governance in Ireland have had on public opinion, including in EU-related matters.

Attitudes toward the European Union

Citizen opinions

Despite the blows dealt to Ireland's reputation as a strong pro-European member state by the results of the first referendums on the Treaties of Nice (2001) and Lisbon (2008), Ireland continues to come first in Europe when it comes to positive attitudes toward membership of the EU.[13] This reflects a perceived complementarity between a pro-European and pro-national attitude in Ireland that has been consistently supported by successive Irish governments. A strong national identity is central to this belief that EU membership suits Irish interests. To take results from the 2004 survey: while 80 per cent say they are 'very attached' to Ireland and 78 per cent are 'very proud' to be Irish, 72 per cent still describe themselves as 'fairly attached' to Europe and 33 per cent are 'very proud' to be European.[14] The general pattern of attachment to territorial area in Ireland – strongest for the nation and weakest for Europe – is replicated throughout the EU. In between the nation and Europe, regional identity is less important to Irish people than even that of their town or village, with only 64 per cent admitting to feeling 'very attached' to their region (Eurobarometer 2004a). Holmes and Rees (1995: 236) contend that Irish citizens have tended to identify more closely with the lower tiers of governance than with the region because of the historical lack of regional institutions in comparison to the long-standing city or county administration; this does not appear to have changed since the establishment of the regional authorities and assemblies. When it comes to the regional policy of the EU, however, the routine reaction of Irish respondents is one of enthusiastic support. A 1991 Eurobarometer study of regional attitudes to the EC showed that, while levels of identification with the region and with the EC were relatively low, Ireland had high awareness of the EC's regional policy and high expectations of the benefits it could bring.[15] Over a decade later, support for regional

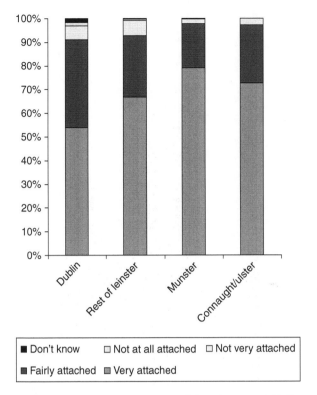

Figure 6.5 How attached are you to your region? (Eurobarometer 62.0)
The sample size for all Eurobarometer data used here is 1000

policy remains high – 70 per cent believe that support for regions in economic difficulty should be organized on a joint European basis. Indeed, they are so motivated by principle/idea over knowledge/information, that, although only 27 per cent of respondents have ever even heard of the Committee of the Regions, 36 per cent consider it to 'play an important role' (Eurobarometer 2004a).[16]

A breakdown by regional location to the Eurobarometer standard survey of 2004 shows that there is little differentiation between the regions of Ireland when it comes to attitudes to the EU.[17] The chart below (Figure 6.5) shows that, unsurprisingly, identification with one's region is weakest in the Dublin area and strongest in Munster, which is the most historically established and cohesive of the four survey respondents.

Regarding the question of whether Ireland has benefited from EU membership (see Figure 6.6), there is little to distinguish between the regions, although Connaught-Ulster has, at 11 per cent, almost twice the average

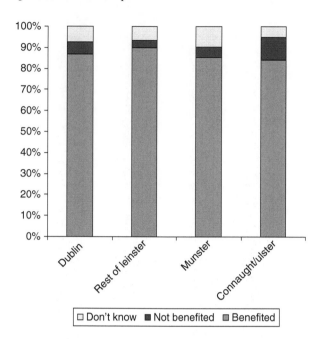

Figure 6.6   Has Ireland benefited from EU membership? (Eurobarometer 62.0)

number answering in the negative. This finding is borne out in the fact that counties Donegal and Louth in this region also had among the highest level of 'no' votes in the referendums on the Treaty of Nice in 2001 and 2002.[18] Coming from an area that has received proportionately the most in structural and cohesion funding, this suggests that more receipts from EU funds do not automatically equate to greater pro-European sentiment.

The relative insignificance of regional location in answers to Eurobarometer surveys in Ireland is also seen in the reports of the National Forum on Europe, established after the 'no' vote in the first referendum on the Treaty of Nice in 2001 to 'facilitate democratic engagement on European issues affecting Ireland' (National Forum on Europe 2005: 2). A large part of the Forum's mandate is to hold regular 'regional meetings' (i.e. 'outside Dublin') for public debate. Any regional differentiation in the topics of concern expressed by the participants at these meetings regarding 'European issues' is not to be found in relation to European enlargement or the Lisbon Treaty but rather reflects the socio-economic character of the particular locality, for example fisheries policy or the agricultural policy. Despite the Irish government's acknowledgement of the Draft Constitutional Treaty of the EU upholding the principle of subsidiarity (DFA 2005), there was no evidence of the national government encouraging debate around the treaty along these lines nor, indeed, of the Constitutional Treaty instigating much of a response at the level of sub-national government in Ireland. It appears that attitudes toward the EU are shaped most definitively by the national-level debate and by the outworking of party politics in the local constituencies rather than by regional needs or interests. This is also evident in analysis of the results from referendums on EU treaties, which are constitutionally required in Ireland.

Results from the 2001 referendum on the Treaty of Nice, which was rejected by 53.9 per cent to 46.1 per cent, show relative uniformity in a virtual mid-way split in every constituency across the country.[19] The same is true for the 2002 referendum on the same treaty (with minor clarifying amendments), which showed a greater degree of differentiation in the final results (37 per cent 'no' to 63 per cent 'yes') but again this did not seem to have a regional basis. In fact, the most movement from the general trends in both referendums occurred within Dublin. The only two 'yes' votes in 2001 (60 per cent, 54 per cent) and the highest 'yes' votes in 2002 (around 73 per cent) came from southern Dublin while the highest 'no' vote in 2001 (62 per cent) and among the highest in 2002 (around 46 per cent) also came from within Dublin. This pattern was replicated in the referendum on the Lisbon Treaty in 2008, in which Dublin contained the constituency with the highest 'no' vote (Dublin South West, 65 per cent 'no') and the constituency with the highest 'yes' vote (Dún Laoghaire, 64 per cent 'yes'). Although again constituencies in the far north-west and at points along the coast of Ireland voted most strongly against the Lisbon Treaty in 2008, the general pattern of discontent with the Treaty was countrywide. This suggests that opinions of European integration are primarily shaped by factors other than regional location. Even when it comes to voting on issues that directly relate to sub-national governance, regional location does not appear to be a decisive factor. Support for the referendum for constitutional recognition of local government in 1999 did not vary widely throughout the country, with the average 'yes' vote being 78 per cent and ranging from a low of 75 per cent in South Dublin County to a high of 83 per cent in County Mayo. When these results are put alongside those of the elections to local authorities and to the European parliament held on the same day in June 1999, again there is no notable regional differentiation. The most important factor that differs between constituencies is not location in a particular geographical region but the role of local political personalities and their use of both very localized issues and larger national debates (even in European parliament elections) in their election campaigns.

Complication and obfuscation

The sub-national system of public administration and governance in Ireland has long been highly complicated and difficult for the majority of citizens to understand let alone relate to. Chubb (1992: 263) argued that the 'jungle' of administrative areas, 'is both impenetrable to the ordinary citizen and frequently inconvenient for any kind of business that involves more than one authority or regional organisation'. Bearing this in mind, the former leader of Fine Gael, Alan Dukes, suggested that citizens' lack of identification with or comprehension of the EU is unsurprising given that very few have good comprehension of the directly elected local authority within which they live.[20] The impact of EU and other initiatives toward the goal of regional area development have, if anything, served to complicate this 'jungle' even further. This is partly because of their aim 'to incorporate an ever wider circle of policy actors into sub-national government' (Adshead 2003: 119), reflecting the social partnership trends with insufficient clarity as to the purpose and ideal outcome of this networking. Underlying this classification of Ireland as a single region for such a long time in the EU undoubtedly contributed to the lack of popular and political debate about regional disparity within Ireland particularly in relation to representation of local interests at the EU level.

Conclusion

Early on in Ireland's EU membership, the process of European integration was predicted to make the very aim of balanced regional development 'increasingly hard to hold' (Barrington, 1976: 364). It is possible to contend that this has indeed been the case, in light of the fact that development in Ireland remains heavily skewed in favor of Dublin and the Eastern region. The bulk of the burden of responsibility for this failure must undoubtedly rest with the Irish government's approach to devolution of power at both the supranational and sub-national levels. The central administration's insistence on a gatekeeping role in sub-national EU links, the flip-flop nature of decisions on regional policy and development within Ireland, the reluctance to trust substantial policy-making roles or democratic powers to the sub-national level, and the emphasis on function over form in regional bodies... all these factors have contributed to a largely inauspicious beginning for regionalism in Ireland. Nonetheless, the case of Ireland also provides valuable lessons for the EU in its encouragement of regionalization. The huge amount of bureaucratic complexity associated with the new regional institutions in Ireland relates directly to the EU's use of structural funds as a 'carrot' for regional-level development in member states. As it now stands, the strength and effectiveness of sub-national administration in Ireland may depend less on official devolution than on a growing multiplicity of networks and channels of communication between the local, regional, national and European levels. Yet, given the fact that there are still no strong conduits – nor demand for – for political participation, knowledge and identification alternative to the nation-state,[21] the development of sub-national governance in Ireland and the EU's influence therein is likely to remain a bureaucratic and technocratic rather than a democratic phenomenon.

Notes

* I am grateful for post-doctoral funding support from the Irish Research Council in the Humanities and Social Sciences (2005–2007) and wish to thank Colin D. Shaw and Muiris MacCárthaigh for their advice in compiling some of the data contained in this paper. Warm thanks are also extended to the Wales in a Regional Europe Centre, and particularly to Aled Elwyn Jones, for assistance during my study visit there.

1. Article 28a of Bunreacht na hÉireann, the Constitution of Ireland, inserted following the referendum of June 1999, gave constitutional recognition to local government 'in providing a forum for the democratic representation of local communities' and established that local elections be held at least every five years.
2. For example, the administrative structures classified as 'regional bodies' include the regional authorities (of which there are eight), the regional fisheries boards (of which there are seven), the regional tourism authorities (of which there are seven, very differently aligned to the fisheries boards), regional area health boards (of which there are three) and regional assemblies (of which there are two).
3. Notably, even today, the only Irish government-owned agency dedicated to regional economic development is Shannon Development, which was established in 1959 in order to reap benefits from the location of the Shannon airport for tourism and investment in the wider locality (see www.shannon-dev.ie).
4. The National Development Plans were originally drawn to facilitate negotiations between the government and the European Commission prior to the designation of the Community Support Framework through which EU structural and cohesion funds are distributed. The EU-motivation for NDPs has greatly diminished since the change in Ireland's economic fortunes.
5. I am grateful to Kieran Moylan, assistant director of the Border, Midland and Western region assembly, for drawing this to my attention and, indeed, for the other detailed and insightful comments he made on an earlier version of this paper.
6. This means that, strictly speaking, the assemblies are classified as regional authorities under the 1991 Local Government Act (Callanan 2003b: 437).
7. Kieran Moylan, correspondence with the author; see www.irelandwales.ie/ and www.futurreg.net
8. Source: S&E Regional Assembly www.seregassembly.ie/assembly/oc/oc_committee. asp?temp=&lang=en (Accessed May 2010).
9. The percentage difference in Gross Value Added for the Southern and Eastern region and the rural Border, Midlands and Western region actually increased (from 39.5 to 42) between 2002 and 2005 (BMW 2006). However, it should be noted that the significance of such figures and the causes of such disparities are disputed (Morgenroth 2008).
10. The National Spatial Strategy was launched in 2002 as a response to the European Spatial Development Perspective. It aims to 'drive development in the regions' through building 'a network of gateways and hubs' (see www.irishspatialstrategy.ie).
11. Kieran Moylan, correspondence with the author.
12. Source: Irish Regions Office (www.iro.ie/).

13. For example, in Eurobarometer 65 (spring 2006), 87 per cent of respondents viewed advantages of EU membership positively. The next most positive score came from Denmark, with a result of 75 per cent.
14. The EU25 average showed just 48 per cent 'very proud' of their nationality and 16 per cent 'very proud' to be European (Eurobarometer 2004a).
15. Awareness of EC regional policy in Ireland was third highest in the EC, as was expectation of raised living standards through this policy and attachment to the country, while identification with the EC was the third lowest (Eurobarometer 1991).
16. This pattern of Irish respondents never having heard of certain EU institutions yet still considering them to play an important role is replicated in relation to the European Ombudsman, the Economic and Social Committee, and the European Court of Auditors (see Eurobarometer 2004a).
17. It is notable that, in line with the inconsistency in the definition of regions in the Irish case, the regional breakdown for the Eurobarometer surveys in Ireland is idiosyncratic, with a vague nod toward the ancient provinces of Ireland, together with a need for relatively proportionate population size: Dublin, rest of Leinster, Munster, Connaught/Ulster.
18. All electoral data extracted from http://electionsireland.org/results/referendum/ (accessed 21/06/10).
19. All electoral data in this section extracted from http://electionsireland.org/results/ referendum/ (accessed 21/06/10).
20. 'People are just not very well informed about governance in general. I think the same applies whether you talk about EU governance, national governance, or even people's county council. There are a lot of people who know less about their county council than they do about their government.' Extract from interview with the author, Institute for European Affairs, Dublin, 9 September 2004.
21. The government's abortive attempt at decentralization in the mid-2000s was doomed to failure by their reliance on the willingness of civil servants to move out of Dublin. In a symbol of the reversal in Ireland's economic fortunes, newspaper headlines have focused on the cost of land purchased by the government at the height of the property boom to build property for the relocation of state bodies outside Dublin that is now unused and unsellable 'Decentralisation sites that cost Government €16m lying idle' (*Irish Independent on Sunday*, 16 November 2008).

7
Scotland's European Strategy

Noreen Burrows

The United Kingdom's system of devolution is famously asymmetrical. In so far as Scotland is concerned, the Scotland Act (1998) created the Scottish Parliament with powers to legislate in any area that was not reserved to Westminster. Powers were transferred from ministers of the crown to Scottish ministers in areas of devolved competence. As if to demonstrate the subordinate position of the Scottish Parliament, the Scotland Act specifically provides that the Act does not affect the power of the UK Parliament to make laws for Scotland (Section 28(7)). International relations, including relations with the EU, are reserved matters with the exception that observing and implementing obligations under Community law are not reserved, and neither is assisting ministers of the crown in EU matters (Schedule 5.7). Given the general reservation of EU matters, it is perhaps surprising that in 2004 the (then) Scottish Executive published *The Scottish Executive's European Strategy*, implying that a strategy for Europe could exist independently of the UK strategy (Scottish Executive 2004). This chapter deals with actions and issues arising from that strategic approach.

The strategy was developed by a ministerial group established by the then first minister, Jack McConnell, following the second elections to the Scottish Parliament. The stated primary objective of the Scottish Executive's European Strategy was to grow the Scottish economy; this objective was supplemented by two overarching strategic goals. The first was to position Scotland as one of the leading legislative regions, with a thriving and dynamic economy, and the second was to bring effective influence on the UK government, EU member states, regions and institutions on EU on policy issues affecting Scotland. The strategy focused on three aspects of the Executive's work:

- promoting Scottish interests in Europe both indirectly via the UK and directly by developing bilateral links with the EU institutions and multilateral links within organizations such as REGLEG.

- maximizing influence with the UK government to secure automatic recognition and understanding of Scottish interests.
- enhancing the Scottish profile in Europe by building strong regional ties, supporting and expanding business connections with Europe and attracting fresh talent and tourists to Scotland.

The strategy committed the Executive to prioritizing those aspects of EU policy likely to have most impact on the lives of people in Scotland. That said, the range of policy priorities set out was enormous, covering matters ranging from the Lisbon Agenda, engagement in the reform of the structural funds, transport policy, fisheries policy, agricultural reform, Justice and Home Affairs, environment, the role of regions in the constitutional structure of Europe and expanding the role of Scotland in Europe. The mechanisms to deliver the strategy included working at the European level through a number of different multilateral and bilateral links and engagements, working with the UK and working within Scotland. Following the May 2007 elections, the SNP developed its *Action Plan on European Engagement* (Scottish Government 2008).

This chapter examines the mechanisms open to Scotland's government to promote Scottish interests in Europe, to maximize influence within the UK government and to enhance Scottish profile in Europe. As with any other regional government in Europe, Scotland is constrained in conducting its European affairs both by its constitutional position in the UK and by the relatively weak constitutional position of regional governments in the European Union (EU). To put the Scottish Executive's European Strategy in context this chapter first explores the concept of Scotland as a region within the UK and Europe and the limits faced by regional governments in Europe that have been imposed by the European legal framework.

Scotland as a UK 'region'

Devolution was brought about in the UK by the enactment of separate Acts of the UK parliament for Scotland, Wales and Northern Ireland. Devolution is asymmetrical in terms of the extent of devolved powers and the size and shape of the devolved institutions (Burrows 2000). No attempt has been made to regularize these constitutional arrangements into any kind of constitutional framework that would be recognizable to a constitutional lawyer in most European traditions. While devolution has shaped UK constitutional law, it has not given us a written UK constitution as yet. A key conceptual problem is the difficulty in defining Scotland as a 'region', as a category of political and legal analysis in this constitutional context. Depending on the discipline, approach and context, Scotland can be, and has been, defined variously as a nation, a national society, a sub-national entity, a stateless nation, a country or a region. Even among lawyers, the geographical territory situated north of the English border is defined in different terms.

A constitutional lawyer discussing the constitutional history of the formation of the United Kingdom might concentrate on the idea of Scotland as a nation. Tierney, for example, writes in the following terms in discussing that history: the 'UK is composed of a plurality of nations' or 'England, Scotland and Wales are each discrete national societies with distinctive histories and traditions.' In historic terms 'the constitutional nations came together [...] in a process of legal union' to form 'a multinational union' (Tierney 2006). The Union state approach stresses an historic tradition of independence and autonomy, of distinctiveness and separateness with the inherent possibility that the separate nations that currently form the UK might choose to dissolve that union at a future date.

The term 'nation' or 'national society' is a sociological and cultural as well as a constitutional construct. As a sociological construct it imports a sense of identity and belonging and difference from (at the extremes, exclusion of) others not of the nation or not sharing that identity. The nation is bound by a shared understanding of history, institutions unique to the nation such as the education or legal systems, a common language or languages, shared traditions, memories and so on. There is a sense that the concept of 'nation' is a rich and proud concept, defying a tradition of assimilation and homogeneity. The concept of the Scottish nation has been kept alive both by its institutions, and by its symbols: its parliament and system of government, its system of education and law, the Saltire (the Scottish national flag), the thistle, tartan or plaid, the rugby and football teams, a distinct Scottish literature, a Scottish Arts Council and so on. The unofficial national anthem of Scotland, *Flower of Scotland*, calls on Scotland to rise up and 'be a nation again'.

A private international lawyer would not see Scotland as a nation but might see Scotland as a country (or law district). Himsworth points out that, in Scotland, jurisdictional boundaries are aligned with governmental boundaries and that in the UK the three jurisdictions of England and Wales, Scotland and Northern Ireland 'define for the purposes of the rules of international private law or the conflict of law, the "countries" into which the UK is divided' (Himsworth 2007). In this sense the term 'country' relates to the area in which a particular legal system operates. The separate Scottish legal system, legacy of the independent state of Scotland, protected and preserved by the Acts of Union, with its separate system of courts and its separate body of law, defines Scotland, in legal terms, as a country. This is also the sense of the term as it is used in Section 29(2)(a) of the Scotland Act where it is made clear that an Act of the Scottish Parliament is not law in so far as any of its provisions 'would form part of a country or territory other than Scotland, or confer or remove functions exercisable otherwise than in or as regards Scotland'. The Scottish Parliament cannot legislate for England, Wales or

Northern Ireland any more than it can for France, Italy or Spain. It seems obvious that the latter are different countries; but, for these purposes, so are England, Wales and Northern Ireland.

While the term 'country' may resonate with some lawyers, it lacks the sociological richness and depth of the term 'nation'. It does not suggest the same sense of identity or of shared values; it is a more neutral term. It lacks the incipient nationalism and independence in the term 'nation'. However, it is a term that has been used to brand Scotland – as in the marketing message 'the best small country in the world', previously used for several years by the Scottish Executive to encourage investment and to market Scotland abroad. The 'best small nation in the world' is a very different message and would play to a nationalist agenda precisely because of the depth of the meaning attached to the idea of nationhood.

Perhaps it is better to be a country than a region however. In the UK domestic constitutional context, the term 'region' has no meaning in terms of defining the constituent elements of the UK and is not used in a political, sociological or legal sense within the UK to describe Scotland. Moreover, unlike countries such as Spain, where there is a common language to describe the units of government below the state level – autonomous communities – or other federal structures such as Germany with the term Länder being used, there is no common constitutional language to describe Northern Ireland, Scotland, Wales or England. No one would describe England as a region of the UK. Our system of devolution and our constitutional law has not devised a language that can describe the constituent parts of the UK. The Scotland Act simply uses the term, Scotland, which is itself not defined but includes, according to Section 126 of the Scotland Act, 'so much of the internal waters and territorial sea of the United Kingdom as are adjacent to Scotland'. The term 'region' in the Scotland Act refers not to Scotland but to the eight regions of Scotland which had originally been constituencies for the purposes of elections to the European Parliament and are now electoral regions for the purposes of elections to the Scottish Parliament (Schedule 1.2 (2).

In fact, the term 'region' is only used to describe Scotland in the context of EU arrangements. The term is often prefaced with the adjective 'legislative'. Scotland is a member of REGLEG, the group of legislative regions or 'regions with legislative powers' as defined in the Laeken Declaration. The Scottish Executive's 2004 European Strategy sought 'to position Scotland as one of the leading legislative regions in the European Union'. In 2006, Scotland, via Scottish Development International and Scottish Enterprise, competed for and was named as 'European Region with Best FDI Strategy' and 'European Region with Best Human Resources'.

Operating at a European level, therefore, Scotland has been content to use the language of 'the region' alongside other sub-national units and, where possible, to use it to its economic and strategic advantage. The term is a convenient, if imperfect, shorthand, whereby Scotland can display its distinct characteristics within the EU. It is a useful but artificial construct – artificial in the sense that it does not reflect the sense of nationhood or the sense of being a separate country that characterizes Scotland – that enables it to inhabit the European space on a level that is more or less understandable to other 'regions', which may themselves be equated with historic communities or may be merely administrative units. Given the absence of any European definition of a region and the existence of historic nations elsewhere in Europe, Scottish administrations have used the term for their own purposes.

As noted above, the Scotland Act provides that relations with the European Communities (and their institutions) are reserved matters. The Scotland Act does not reserve observing and implementing obligations under Community law. European policy is therefore a UK responsibility, but the devolved institutions have the authority and obligation to implement and observe Community law. The obligation to observe Community law is secured by the Act by providing that it is outwith the legislative competence of the Scottish Parliament to enact any law that is incompatible with any Community law obligation (Scotland Act s.29(2)(d)). These provisions ensure that the UK complies with the Community law requirement that a member state, as represented by its central government, is responsible for enforcing Community law in its territory, irrespective of the internal constitutional rules of the member state.[1]

Much community law is implemented in the UK by secondary legislation in the form of regulations. Following devolution, powers delegated to ministers of the UK government under the European Communities Act 1972 have been transferred to Scottish ministers in so far as they are within devolved competence (Scotland Act s.53). Scottish ministers are therefore empowered to make Scottish subordinate legislation to implement community law in Scotland in matters which have not been reserved. Under the terms of the Legislative and Regulatory Reform Act 2006, Scottish ministers now have the power to implement community obligations in devolved matters by order, rules or schemes in addition to the use of regulations. They have no power, however, to make any subordinate legislation or do any other act that is incompatible with Community law (Scotland Act s.57(2)). In addition, the Scotland Act provides that, despite this transfer of powers to Scottish ministers, the power to make subordinate legislation to implement a Community law obligation remains with UK ministers (Scotland Act s.57(1)). Thus, a concurrent power is created with both Scottish ministers and UK ministers having powers to implement Community law in Scotland.

The decision as to how Community obligations will be implemented in the UK post-devolution is governed by the Memorandum of Understanding and Supplementary Agreements including the Concordat on Co-ordination of EU Policy Issues (2002) between the UK government and the Scottish ministers (hereafter the Concordat). The key principle in relation to implementation is to achieve consistency of effect and, where appropriate, timing in relation to the implementation of community law in the UK as a whole. Officials in the lead Whitehall Department notify officials in the counterpart Scottish Executive Department of any new EU obligation for which the devolved administration has the duty of implementation. It is the responsibility of the Scottish Executive to determine, in consultation with Whitehall, whether an obligation will be implemented by separate Scottish measures or by GB or UK legislation. Where the decision is taken to have separate Scottish implementation measures, Scottish Executive officials must consult so as to achieve consistency of effect. Separate measures are notified to the Commission via UKRep; there is no separate reporting line from the Scottish Executive to the Commission. Consistency of effect might be achieved by amending Scottish implementing provisions to bring them into line with equivalent English provisions (fish sellers and buyers) but, despite similarity of wording the Scottish Executive and UK government departments may not necessarily interpret implementing provisions in the same way (waste incineration).[2] Consistency of effect, therefore, may not always be achieved.

In areas where the division of competences between Westminster and Holyrood is clear, transposition of community obligations is relatively straightforward. However, there is often an element of overlapping competences and it may be expedient to allow Westminster to legislate even in areas of devolved competence. In these circumstances, following the so-called Sewel Convention, a legislative consent motion is placed before the Scottish Parliament by the relevant minister to transfer powers to Westminster to legislate for Scotland. For example, implementation of the EU Framework Decision on attacks against information systems deals with computer-based crime, a devolved matter. Its nature is, however, transnational and the Scottish Executive took the view that UK-wide legislation would provide a single legislative text (the Police and Justice Act 2006) to make enforcement simpler.

Should Scotland fail to comply with any community obligation, the Concordat specifies that the Cabinet Office will coordinate the UK response but, where a matter falls within the devolved competence of the Scottish Executive, the devolved administration must draft the response. If a matter is referred to court the devolved administration must assist in preparing the proceedings and would take a lead in cases in a matter within its responsibility. Overall coordination, however, lies with the UK Cabinet Office and the Treasury Solicitors Department. Any financial penalties fall on the devolved administration where the failure to comply lies with it.

Under the devolution settlement, therefore, it is clear that in legal terms, it is the UK government which retains overall responsibility for EU matters, and the devolved administrations have obligations to comply with community law and the authority to implement community obligations in devolved matters. It is this context that makes it imperative that Scotland, using whatever means it has at its disposal, is able to maximize the scope provided for at European level and at UK level to influence European policy development in a direction which takes into consideration Scottish interests.

European limits to regional powers

Much has been written about the 'blindness' of Europe toward regional governments. That literature has focused on the absence of the regional dimension in policy-making at the European level (Kottman 2001; Wakefield 2005; Weatherhill 2005). In fact Europe is far from completely blind to regions and their interests, but the signals from Europe are mixed. The 1980s and 1990s saw the development of a stronger regional dimension to the work of the European institutions. The intensity of the transfer of powers from the member states to the EU by both the Single European Act and the Treaty of Maastricht significantly eroded the powers of the regions in Europe. The absence of compensation for the erosion of their political autonomy led to demands from the regions to have a say in policy-making at the European level (Bourne 2003). Regional demands, supported by the Commission, led to the creation of the Committee of the Regions to give them a direct voice in the institutional policy-making processes, the amendment of Article 203 EC to allow for participation of regional ministers in the Council of Europe and the inclusion of the principle of subsidiarity in the treaty – extending only, however, to the division of competences between the EU and its member states.

At the same time, the negative impact of the single market on the peripheral regions, enlargement, as well as the growing demands of the regions themselves, led to the development of a regional policy with substantial funding to be spent via the structural funds. In order to access funding, regions had to turn to lobbying at the European level as well as at the national level. The Commission's emphasis on partnership working brought local authorities and regional governments into the European frame. Internal boundaries were redrawn in order to ensure that certain areas could benefit from European funding. Compensation for lack of political autonomy was to some extent achieved by financial contributions.

In the period before devolution it was clear that Scotland needed to position itself in Europe in order to lobby on matters such as structural funds, but also on other aspects of European policy that had impacts on Scottish interests. Even prior to devolution, Scotland maintained a distinct presence in Brussels. Created in 1992 as a cooperative venture between Scottish Enterprise, local authorities, the universities and other partners, Scotland Europa provided a distinct Scottish presence in Europe.

Networking, information gathering and lobbying were seen as key tools to the successful exploitation of the Single European Market for Scottish interests.

The need for a Scottish presence in Brussels to ensure that the EU understood Scotland is apparent from the way in which Scotland appeared to be categorized by the EU institutions in the 1990s. The perception of northern Scotland in the 1990s by civil servants in the European Commission was 'in terms of their rural or upland character – indeed, grouping the Highlands with parts of Greece, southern Italy and north-eastern Portugal – rather than recognizing their distinctive character' (Bachtler et al. 1999: 6). The Scottish Office sought ways in which to influence the regional policy debate – for example, by forming a key alliance from 1994 with the Nordic applicant countries, the Nordic-Scottish Cooperation. According to Bachtler et al.:

> The impetus for the Nordic-Scottish cooperation stems from the proposals for the 'fourth enlargement' of the European Community to include Finland, Norway and Sweden (as well as Austria). In the run-up to enlargement, there was considerable, spontaneous activity from the then applicant countries to explore Scotland's experience of the Structural Funds. In turn, the Scottish Office identified a long-term strategic interest in establishing a broad relationship in the applicant countries. For example, it represented an opportunity to increase the profile given to peripheral, sparsely populated areas (the Highlands & Islands) within the EU.
>
> (1999: 6)

Networking as a means of influencing policy was an important part of Scottish Office thinking prior to devolution and the networks established in this period continued post-devolution. The Nordic-Scottish Cooperation came to an end in 2006.

It could be argued that regional policy is marginal to the central goals of the EU and, aside from regional policy itself, European strategies tend to underestimate the importance of regional governments in delivering on key strategic goals. For example the EU, through its Lisbon Process, has set ambitious targets for economic performance of the member states. By 2010, it aims to be 'the most competitive and dynamic knowledge based economy in the world'. Despite the fact that regions are in a position to help deliver on these objectives, they appear to be the 'missing' element in the Lisbon strategy (Scott 2005). Scott argues that:

> it is now generally accepted that regional authorities are well placed to devise and implement a range of policy instruments designed to enhance the economic growth and employment prospects within the region.
>
> (2005: 10)

He cites the following as economic policy advantages of regions: 'knowledge of local labour market conditions; delivery of local education and training facilities; responsibility for quality of local transport links and other communications facilities; stimulating local and inward investments; enhancing local amenities; provision of dedicated business services; and a raft of measures which can help attract, or encourage the creation of dynamic knowledge based industries' (Scott 2005: 10). Despite this, the Lisbon strategy fails to focus on the undoubted benefits that resilient regional governments can deliver.

One explanation for the absence of a regional dimension is the fear that regional governments might resort to policies and strategies that would contravene EU state aid rules. In particular, measures to stimulate growth must not distort or threaten 'to distort competition by favoring certain undertakings or the production of certain goods' (Article 87(1)(EC)). Infraction proceedings have been brought by the Commission against several member states because of assistance given by regional governments to local enterprises to encourage regional development (Burrows 2002; Wakefield 2005). In addition, EMU constrains regional economic policy choices (Hallett and Scott 2003).

It is within these constraints, both at UK and EU level that the Scottish Executive's European Strategy operated.

Promoting Scottish interests in Europe

The Scottish Executive's European Strategy was to promote Scottish interests in Europe indirectly via the UK, directly by establishing bilateral links with EU institutions, and multilaterally within organizations such as REGLEG. At the European level the Scottish Executive worked on a number of fronts to engage with European matters. The Scottish Executive has maintained a physical presence in Brussels since July 1999. Situated in Scotland House alongside Scotland Europa, the Scottish Executive EU Office (SEEUO) supports the EU-related work of the Executive in attempting to boost Scottish influence in Europe. It provides operational support for the Executive in the sense of information gathering, assisting in influencing EU policies, raising Scotland's profile in the EU and developing links with other regions. In that sense it is a regional office which seeks political influence rather than exerting political pressure (Marks et al. 2002).

SEEUO works closely with UKRep which is responsible for representing the views of the UK as a whole to the European institutions. Because of this link with UKRep it has been said that Scotland and Wales are 'uniquely well-placed in Brussels because they are treated as separate units within the UK Representation to the EU. This gives them a diplomatic status and a much higher level of access to the EU institutions than is enjoyed by most other regional representations, including the German Länder offices'

(Constitution Unit 2005: 10). However, SEEUO must act in a manner consistent with the responsibility of the UK government for European matters; its position is therefore subordinate to that of UKRep (Concordat B3.27). In that sense, SEEUO augments UKRep in the framework of a 'single UK "voice" in Europe' (Bulmer et al. 2006: 83).

SEEUO also facilitates Scottish dialogue directly with the European Commission. It is difficult to evaluate this dialogue in terms of assessing Scottish influence in Europe or Scotland's impact on key European debates as a whole. However, there is evidence that Scotland has had some impact on governance debates within the EU and, in particular, has influenced Commission thinking. A recent example of such influence is the work undertaken in the context of the Commission's White Paper on a European Communication Policy (European Commission 2006b); itself part of the Commission's Plan D for democracy, dialogue and debate (European Commission 2005). Bringing together Scotland's experience of devolution and examining some of the features of its legislative processes, a project involving the Commission and the Scottish Executive was established to examine ways in which decisions can be brought closer to the people through 'two-way initiatives between citizens and institutions'. The project, *Building a Bridge*, was a Scottish Executive-European Commission project, led by Jack McConnell and Margot Wallstrom, which explored how communication and engagement can help deliver further progress on the Lisbon Agenda for Jobs and Growth (Scottish Executive 2007a–d).

Scotland can also promote Scottish interests by participating in those European bodies open to regional governments (representation in the Council is discussed below). The principal institution is the Committee of the Regions (CoR) established by the Maastricht Treaty. The CoR is an advisory body advising the Commission and Council on matters specified in the treaty (Art 7 EC) such as environment (Art 175 EC), public health (Art 152 EC) and economic and social cohesion (Art 161 EC). Without exception, all the areas in the treaty which require involvement of CoR fall within the devolved competence of the Scottish Parliament. Active participation in the CoR is therefore essential, despite its very limited powers, if Scottish interests are to be promoted within the EU's decision-making processes.

CoR is composed of elected representatives of regional or local authorities (Art 262 EC). Four of the UK's 24 representatives are from Scotland (with four alternates). Four representatives are nominated by the Scottish Executive and the Scottish Parliament and four by the Convention of Scottish Local Authorities (COSLA). It is the task of the first minister to coordinate the Scottish nominations but it is the UK government which adopts and approves all 24 UK representatives. Until he lost power after the May 2007 Scottish election, the first minister, Jack McConnell, was a member of the Scottish delegation.

Scotland has worked with other regions in the context of REGLEG to mobilize regional interests in the constitutional design of the European

Union. REGLEG grew out of regional cooperation to prepare for discussions on the regional dimension of European Strategy in the Intergovernmental Conference in 2000. It is today an informal association of regions with legislative powers, and it has scored some notable successes, not least in securing agreement on the term 'regions with legislative powers' and ensuring recognition of their constitutional importance in the Laeken Declaration. There are 73 such regions in the EU; they have comparable powers with the member states of which they form part and are responsible for transposing EU law directly into domestic law within their area of competence. They argue that they have a particular legitimacy within the EU since they are closer to the citizens within their territories. Their aim within the framework of REGLEG is to achieve a greater role in the EU for legislative regions, including an enhanced role in the Council, an appropriate involvement of regional parliaments and the right to bring actions before the European Court of Justice where the prerogatives of the region are threatened.

Scotland engaged actively in REGLEG during the debates on the Draft Constitutional Treaty; however, it was not entirely clear whether the Scottish Executive supported all the Laeken objectives. The first minister, Jack McConnell, held the presidency of REGLEG in 2003–2004 and Scotland hosted the REGLEG summit in 2004. While endorsing the general ambitions of REGLEG, McConnell refused to be drawn on whether the standing of regional governments should be enhanced to enable them to bring actions before the European Court of Justice in defence of their prerogatives. In addition, he refused to come before the European and External Affairs committee of the Scottish Parliament to discuss his presidency of REGLEG referring the committee to the minister for finance and public service who has portfolio responsibility for European matters on behalf of the Executive but who is not involved in REGLEG (Burrows 2006). McConnell may have been reluctant to discuss the European Court issue with the committee since the UK government, and his own political party, do not support that particular demand.

It was on the initiative of REGLEG that the Committee of the Regions set up an inter-regional group within CoR to enhance the visibility of the regions with legislative powers without calling for a full reform of CoR (Declaration of Munich 2005). The key purpose of this group is, however, to apply a subsidiarity test to legislative proposals. This is an interesting example of how regions can mobilize their interests within the framework of both informal and formal institutional structures.

Scotland engages in other networks to attempt to influence European policies which impact on regions. For example, both the Scottish Executive and some Scottish local authorities participate in the Conference of Peripheral Maritime Regions (CPMR). The CPMR highlights the particular problems and disadvantages of geographically peripheral regions, and in particular campaigns for increased investment in these regions and in their maritime industries. It is also interested in governance matters supporting greater regional involvement in European level decision-making.

Maximize influence within the UK government

Prior to devolution, the UK was characterized by a strong central government that included separate arrangements for Scotland, Wales and Northern Ireland. Disputes were settled at Cabinet or departmental level although, historically, there were no formal dispute resolution mechanisms in place. Policy was decided in Cabinet Committees. Post-devolution, arrangements needed to be put in place to provide both a dispute resolution mechanism and a negotiating forum for policy-making on European matters. The latter is particularly important when so many matters are governed both by a devolved and European competence.

The arrangements for Scottish involvement in EU policy-making are set out in the Concordat. The Concordat is based on the premise that effective exchange of information is essential in order to allow the devolved administrations to participate effectively in EU decision-making. It commits the UK government to providing information in full and as early as possible on matters which appear to the United Kingdom government to be likely to be of interest to the devolved administrations. The devolved administrations in turn agree to respect the confidentiality of such information.

The Concordat places heavy reliance on exchange of correspondence between officials and departments, both as a way of resolving differences of view and as a way of determining the UK position on EU matters. The Joint Ministerial Council (JMC) Europe, provided for in the Concordat, was intended to provide a forum for discussion of EU matters at ministerial level. Several commentators have noted the success of these arrangements. The JMC Europe is the only inter-governmental formation to have survived the 'withering away' of any appetite for mutual cooperation between UK ministers and Scottish ministers (Trench 2004). The term 'cooperative governance' was coined to define the working relationships within JMC Europe (Carter and McLeod 2005). When research has focused on specific areas, it has shown that officials and ministers have attempted to make these arrangements work effectively. For example, in agriculture officials from both sides of the border appear to cooperate and liaise closely on EU matters (Burrows 2006). One reason why arrangements may have run smoothly to date is the continued existence of a unified home civil service in the UK. The Scotland Act states explicitly that 'the Civil Service of the State is a reserved matter' (Schedule 5.8 (1)). Thus, the Concordat arrangements make explicit the working relationships between departments within a unified service. However, it is clear that to make these arrangements work as they were intended, and to avoid conflicts, it is essential that consultations and negotiations are based on effective exchange of information. The key is to avoid surprises so that differences in approach on both bigger issues and on details of implementation and timing do not lead to disputes (Bulmer et al. 2006).

One post-devolution difference in these arrangements is the need to liaise with officials in the Scottish Executive departments as well as officials in the Scotland Office. Many EU matters straddle both devolved and reserved functions meaning that the lead ministry, always a UK department, must understand fully the devolution settlement plus the complexity of the EU matter in hand. There is some evidence that officials in Whitehall departments do not understand devolution:

the main variable is a lack of salience in Whitehall. Scotland and Wales with their local politics are mentally marginalised as long as they do not cause trouble. Even when there is a concern (most often with regard to Wales) the formal mechanisms of control (Concordats, Civil Service codes) are not invoked for fear of ratcheting up the stakes. All this might change if a devolved administration that was a political rival of the UK government sought to impede collegial civil service relations in order to advance its political agenda. Devolution works most smoothly if there are no surprises and neither side picks fights.

(Parry and MacDougall 2005)

Problems are beginning to be reported due precisely to the marginalization of Scottish interests by Whitehall departments. Michael Aron, head of the Scottish Executive EU office (SEEUO) is reported to believe that, at times, UK departments have developed a UK line that is directly counter to Scottish interests, for example in discussions relating to regulations on spirits. He has also stated that Whitehall officials simply forget to consult on EU matters and do not share information (*Herald* 2007). This may be simply that some UK departments are not in the habit of consulting across departmental structures and, in the absence of appropriate mechanisms to prompt Whitehall departments on the need to consult the Scottish Executive, it is treated like any other department of government. The devolution desks originally created in Whitehall departments as a process of adjusting to the need to consult on devolved matters have been disbanded, leading to a 'patchy record of consultation by the UK government about policy developments' and a failure to mainstream expertise on devolution matters (Trench 2005).

Some Whitehall departments have a preference for central control and this is manifested in the way in which the devolved administrations are kept at arms length in the policy-making process. Thus, whereas in agriculture and rural affairs 'they are treated as fully engaged partners' the same was not true in the review of the post-2006 structural funds, an area where all the devolved administrations have substantial interests. In this area 'the initiative was maintained by Whitehall with the DTI and Treasury in the lead along with ODPM [...] only once the package was determined in broad terms were the devolveds and the English regions formally consulted' (Burch et al. 2005: 470). Although it could be argued that this was a politically sensitive area, there seems no clear justification for failure to involve the devolved administrations at an early stage.

Whitehall departments cannot claim that they are unaware of Scottish EU priorities. SEEUO produce a 'Forward Look' paper at the start of each presidency, outlining the presidency priorities and the state of play with various dossiers with relevance to Scottish interests. These documents are published on the Scottish Executive website, and are intended to disseminate information not just within the Scottish Executive but to the wider, in particular the business, community. These attempts to systematize issues make for greater transparency in understanding the Scottish Executive's strategy and its priorities, allowing relevant stakeholders to engage with the Scottish Executive on EU matters. Prior to the publication of these documents it had been difficult to track Scottish European policy. The Forward Look documents have become increasingly sophisticated in reporting on those EU issues that are of direct relevance to Scotland.

It may be the case that the Scottish Executive has improved its own capacity to articulate its European agenda. Certainly in the early days of devolution it appears that neither the Scottish Executive nor the Scottish Parliament had a fully formed view of Scottish priorities. With experience has come a greater willingness to articulate specific Scottish needs. The Forward Look for 2007, for example, clearly set out the Scottish interest in, and position on, the draft Spirit Drinks Regulation:

> it will significantly improve the process of protection for geographical indications. It also provides the basis for proposed new domestic Scotch whisky legislation which is a key priority for the industry. Any delays caused by the remaining wide differences in the definition of vodka[3] would therefore be very unwelcome for Scotland.
>
> (SEEUO 2007: 8)

On the Draft Constitution, the Forward Look again spells out the Scottish Executive priorities, 'to ensure that any statement of competences within a new Treaty text takes account of Scottish interests and defends the recognition of the regions and the regional dimension of subsidiarity contained within the original draft Constitutional Treaty' (SEEUO 2007: 3).

Once a UK line is determined, both Scottish ministers and UK ministers must defend that line within the Council of Ministers. The Concordat specifies that the decision on attendance by ministers at Council meetings is taken by the lead UK minister. Scottish ministers, therefore, do not attend Council meetings as of right even where matters are being discussed which relate directly to Scottish interests. Where they do attend their role is 'to support and advance the single UK negotiation line which they will have played a role in developing [...] the UK lead Minister will retain overall responsibility for the negotiations'. The lead minister also determines how each minister can best fulfil his/her role in the UK team. This may amount to having a Scottish minister lead in negotiations but it may also, it appears, lead to Scottish ministers waiting in anterooms during crucial talks (*Herald* 2007). Scottish ministers have attended some 10.2 per cent of Council meetings since devolution, a slight reduction in the percentage of meetings attended by ministers from the Scottish office in the 3 years prior to devolution (Burch et al. 2005: 474). Devolution does not appear to have encouraged Whitehall-led ministries to have relaxed their control.

Enhance Scottish profile

To enhance Scotland's profile, the Scottish Executive's Strategy has been to build strong regional ties, to support and expand business connections and to attract fresh talent and tourists to Scotland.[4]

In developing regional ties, Scotland has focussed on a limited number of European regions and countries with whom the Executive believes it shares common concerns: Flanders, North Rhine Westphalia, the Nordic countries and the Czech Republic. As an extension of these close working relationships Scotland has entered into four bilateral cooperation agreements with Catalonia (2002), Tuscany (2002), NordRhein Westphalia (2002) and Bavaria (2003). Each cooperation agreement is supported by an action plan detailing areas of practical cooperation. Such cooperation agreements have no legal status although they are written very much as legal documents. They are, for that reason, highly symbolic quasi-treaties between regional governments committing the parties to cooperate in specific policy areas. With Catalonia, for example, commitments include the development of projects in the areas of e-government, research to support innovation, education and training, substance misuse, culture, environment and food, and agriculture. The cooperation agreement also commits both parties to collaborate on EU matters of mutual concern.

From the perspective of the Executive, these agreements demonstrate 'the benefits of the constitutional settlement which allows Scotland to operate within the significant international influence of the United Kingdom yet at the same time participate in cooperation with European partners where that falls within our own powers' (Scottish Executive News Release, 2 May 2002). They are, according to the Executive, a sign of an outward-looking country, seeking to forge partnerships to enable each partner to learn from the successes and failures of the others. One way of evaluating such agreements is to see them as the beginnings of a form of 'paradiplomacy' in the sense of 'a form of sub-national "foreign policy" unmediated by the traditional foreign policy institutions of the state' (Jeffery 1997). In 1997 Jeffery saw no evidence of such paradiplomacy within the EU, but devolution has created the potential for Scotland to enter into regional-level alliances and to develop into a transnational actor in its own right within the limits of the constitutional settlement.

It is all the more disappointing, therefore, that there appears to have been a failure to engage successfully with the diplomatic corps based in Edinburgh and Glasgow. There are some 48 consulate missions in Scotland promoting contact between their countries and Scotland. The Executive appears to have missed key opportunities to engage with them: possibly fearful that the UK government would suspect the Scottish Executive of attempting to replicate the Court of St James in Edinburgh, and thus incur censure from the UK government. 'Diplomatic representatives stationed in Edinburgh speak quite openly at the lack of initiative and response to suggestions of greater activity at international level, activity which would benefit Scotland and the UK without necessarily putting the Foreign and Commonwealth Office's nose out of joint' (Munro 2006).

Conclusion

In the first two terms of the Scottish Parliament, the Scottish Executive slowly defined its European Strategy. It is a strategy which has been far from ambitious in terms of developing new policy opportunities and the Executive has not sought to challenge the 'conditional' and 'dependent' relationship it has with the UK in relation to EU matters (Bulmer et al. 2006: 86). This is partly because of the nature of the arrangements which have been put in place, which have opened a window of opportunity for the Executive to work with the UK government on EU policy-making. In some areas, this has resulted in benefits both to the UK and to Scotland. It is also the result of political cohabitation, a *pax laburista*, north and south of the border (Ruggiu 2004). In what were essentially bilateral arrangements, Whitehall ministers were dealing with Scottish ministers within the context of Labour Party dominance where there was goodwill on both sides to make devolution work. It was not in the interest of either side to rock the boat. The UK government was dependent on Scottish MPs to get its legislative program through the British Parliament and it had no interest in alienating the Scottish Labour Party. Goodwill and party discipline combined to ensure that neither side was prepared to challenge the other openly and a system of at best cooperative governance or at worst accommodatory governance on EU matters emerged. For these reasons, the Scottish Executive maintained the position that Scotland benefits from the strong negotiating power of the UK as a large and powerful member of the EU. Furthermore, given the constitutional limitations on the devolved administration in Scotland, it was not perhaps worthwhile investing much political capital in pushing the boundaries of a European strategy when the domestic agenda was sufficiently challenging.

However, the status quo on European matters is untenable in the long run. While they might be an efficient way in which to coordinate policy, the mechanisms created by the Memorandum of Understanding and the Concordat on EU Policy Issues have two inherent flaws: they lack transparency, and hence accountability; and they have no legal status, and there is no certainty that the devolved administrations will continue to be as involved now that the *pax laburista* has broken down with Labour's defeat in the May 2007 Scottish election.

The limitations imposed on Scotland by UK constitutional arrangements have long been a source of irritation to the Scottish National Party. The SNP's first preference is, of course, independence in Europe whereby Scotland will assume a place at the top table. In the context of a EU where Scotland is bigger in both population and size of economy than one third of the current membership of the EU, the prospect of being a small state in a wider union does not appear to seem so problematic to the Scottish electorate. Scots attitudes to Europe have become more positive over the past 30 years. An opinion poll in 1975 suggested that the majority of Scots would vote against continued membership of the European Community, whereas by 1997 almost 40 per cent of Scots believed that membership of the EU had been good for Scotland and a similar percentage were neutral (Mitchell and Leicester 1999). Of the peoples in the UK, it is the English, and not the Scots, who have had the greatest difficulty coming to terms with a future in Europe (Kumar 2003). Scots seem to have a more pragmatic and instrumental view of Europe – ranging from SNP supporters who see continued membership of the EU as a means of achieving independence, to others who see the benefits of European funding (Haesly 2001). A future vision of an independent Scotland in Europe does not seem as unrealistic in 2007 as it did in 1997. Young people, perhaps more likely to support independence, are also the most pro-European group of Scottish voters (Scottish Executive 2007b).

Even if independence is rejected by the Scottish electorate, there will be pressure to increase the powers of the Scottish Parliament, in particular in economic and fiscal policy. The Scotland Act provides for a limited tax-varying power of up to three pence in the pound for income tax, to date unused (Scotland Act, Section 73). At present, there is no direct link between Scottish citizens and the spending departments of the Scottish Executive. A bloc grant is provided to the Scottish Executive based on the Barnett formula. 'The formula is a way of sharing changes (not the level) in public spending plans between the participating countries of the Union. Scotland receives a population-based share of the total charges in planned spending on analogous programmes in England or England and Wales. Since the formula is based on population shares, it does not necessarily reflect spending needs' (MacDonald and Hallwood 2004: 50). This lack of fit has led to calls for fiscal decentralization to parallel political decentralization as a means of imposing fiscal discipline on Scottish politicians and of introducing political accountability for spending decisions. (MacDonald and Hallwood 2006)

European law, however, would impose limits on the extent to which the Scottish Executive could exercise any additional fiscal competences, particularly should the Executive wish to lower tax rates below those applied in the rest of the UK. To avoid classification as state aid any such reductions would require to meet the four tests set out by the European Court of Justice.[5] First, whether the measures are adopted in the exercise of powers are sufficiently autonomous vis-à-vis the central power: typically the regional government must occupy a 'fundamental role in the definition of the political and economic environment in which the undertakings on the territory within its competence operate'. It will have a separate and political and administrative status. Second, the measures must apply to all undertakings within the region. Third, the measure must have been adopted without the central government being able directly to intervene in determining the content of the measure and fourth, the financial consequences of the measure be borne by the regional government and not offset by aid or subsidies from other regions or central government. These criteria were set out by the European Court of Justice in a case involving the Commission and Portugal with the UK intervening, anxious to preserve the devolution settlement with the possibility of differential tax rates in Scotland and Northern Ireland in view. These criteria may prove unduly restrictive for further devolution of the kind of fiscal freedoms that are currently being debated in Scotland. If so, this might lead to further demands for independence.

Another possible change on the constitutional landscape may be the adoption of the amended Constitutional Treaty. As noted above, the Forward Look for 2007 states that the Scottish Executive supports the proposals in the original draft treaty that would have strengthened the position of constitutional regions. Scotland has also worked with its partners in REGLEG to secure those aspects of the treaty that would enhance regional democracy. Both the Munich and Cardiff Declarations of REGLEG, supported by Scotland, note that the presidents 'continue to believe that the Constitutional Treaty includes important provisions that would enhance the contribution of the regions with legislative powers to the democratic life of the Union. These provisions include explicit recognition of the role of the regions with legislative powers within Member States and the contribution that regions make to the national identity of Member States, strengthening the provisions on subsidiarity, introducing an early-warning mechanism and recourse to the European court of Justice for the Committee of the Regions.' All of these provisions are acceptable both to the UK government and to the Scottish Executive as they do not challenge current devolution arrangements in the UK.

These constitutional changes may well affect the way in which Scotland's European strategy develops in the future. To date, its strategy has been to work within the boundaries of the devolution settlement and the exigencies of EU law to try to establish a distinct Scottish voice in the EU. Scotland has worked with other regions to enhance the visibility of the regional dimension in Europe and with other regions to develop a learning cycle. It has also engaged directly with the Commission. In all these activities it has enhanced the 'symbolic capital' of Scotland as a distinct part of the UK. Working with the UK government on EU matters has been portrayed by the Scottish Executive as a way of strengthening the Scottish position in Europe, in the face of arguments that Scotland as an independent nation would have direct access to decision-making and would not be dependent on the UK to represent Scottish interests. It is likely that the SNP administration will pursue a different course.

Notes

1. Case C-33/90 *Re Toxic Waste: Commission v Italy* [1991] 1 ECR 5987.
2. Inquiry into the Transposition and Implementation of European Directives in Scotland, European and External Relations Committee Report, 2nd Report 2007.
3. Vodka forms a small part of Scottish export of spirits, whereas England is the largest exporter of vodka in the EU.
4. This chapter does not discuss the policies of the Scottish Executive in terms of building business connections or encouraging fresh talent to Scotland because of constraints of space.
5. Case C-88/03 *Portugal v Commission* [2003] I ECR 7115.

8
Europeanization and the Spanish Territorial State

Francesc Morata

Europeanization studies focus on the different impacts the process of European integration has on the member states and the effects that derive from them (Radaelli 2000; Börzel and Risse 2001; Cowles et al. 2001; Schmidt 2003; Bulmer and Lequesne 2005). Most of Europeanization literature has devoted attention to the policy process in various forms, while there has been less concern about how European integration affects the member states' polities (Börzel 2002; Kassim 2005; Schmidt 2006) and much less about the impacts on central-regional relations and sub-national structures (Börzel 2002; Morata 2004; Bursens 2007). This chapter aims at reducing this gap looking at the interactions between European integration and the Spanish territorial ('autonomic') state.

One of the most salient domestic impacts of European integration is the territorial redistribution of power in decentralized members that benefits central governments. Even though there is some room for regional participation in the Council of Ministers (Art. 146 TUE), the EU treaties are still 'blind' to the territorial organization of the member states since they do not consider the division of competencies between the different levels of government (Weatherill 2005).[1] Hence, Spain's accession to the EU has caused a double centralization (Jáuregi 2005; Morata and Ramon 2005). On the one hand, the ACs, like the central institutions, have been deprived of decision-making powers transferred to the EU; on the other, the Spanish government, as the representative of the state's interests in the Union's council, participates in the adoption of decisions for which, internally, the ACs are responsible.

Since 1985, Catalonia and the Basque Country have frequently raised the need to be involved in the EU decision-making process to preserve the constitutional balance. The evolution of the issue can be viewed as a process of adaptation prompted by domestic variables and, more especially, by the specificities of the Spanish multi-level party system through which the sub-national parties can exert strong pressures at the central level when their support becomes crucial to guarantee political stability. Ironically, the inter-governmental agreement on regional participation in the EU which was reached in 2004 almost replicated a central government's proposal of 1986. At the same time, quasi-constitutional reforms, such as the new Catalan Statute of Autonomy of 2006 have sought to increase sub-national influence at the EU level.

Regional actors have also attempted to circumvent the central state to gain more institutional influence in Europe. However, the outcomes were rather disappointing. Their performance was more convincing when they have used the European opportunity structure to establish policy networks with other regions, although the degree they take advantage of it depends on their capacity to mobilize their own resources, in terms of socio-economic structure, administrative capacities and the mobilization of civil society. Moreover, institutional developments of the EU have provided the ACs with strategic tasks vis-à-vis the central government and the European Commission concerning the implementation of supranational policies. In general, the impacts have proved to be differential, from incremental political-administrative adaptations to EU requirements in areas such as the CAP and Cohesion Policy (CAP), to strong difficulties in complying with environmental directives in many cases.

Drawing on some conceptual assumptions deriving from Europeanization literature, this chapter reviews how the autonomous communities (ACs) have faced the domestic effects of Spain's membership. First, it examines the processes that have either hindered or enhanced regional participation in the decision-making process of the EU through the state, highlighting the domestic 'mediating' variables that explain differentiated responses. Second, it shows the high relevance assigned to the EU by the Catalan statute of 2006 as an example of quasi-constitutional Europeanization. Third, it looks at regional mobilization in the EU arena as a response to the domestic limitations and to the opportunities entailed by EU policies. Finally, it briefly illustrates the role of the ACs in the implementation of some relevant Community policies, underscoring some important limitations.

Europeanization

Literature on Europeanization reflects a growing concern about the differential impacts of European integration upon the member states and the domestic changes or adaptations triggered by it (Cowles et al. 2001; Börzel 2001; Featherstone and Radaelli 2003; Bulmer and Lequesne 2005; Graziano and Vinck 2007). Although it would be premature to portray Europeanization as a 'theory' (Bulmer 2007), the emergence of the concept can be viewed as an attempt to test alternative approaches to traditional theories of European integration, namely neofunctionalism and inter-governmentalism, to explain member states' performance. Yet both theories have focused on the interpretation of institutional and policy developments at the EU level, paying little attention to the concrete impacts on the member states (Graziano and Vinck 2007). The concept of Europeanization itself remains ambiguous. Olsen has identified five variants – or 'faces' – involving different types of effects of transformations resulting from European integration (Olsen 2002: 923–924): changes in external boundaries (enlargements), the development of institutions at the EU level, the EU penetration into the national systems of governance, exporting forms of political organization and a political unification project. The third definition implies a multi-layered European political system seeking to preserve 'unity' through national adaptations to central (EU) requirements. In this regard, Radaelli lists a detailed set of processes related to Europeanization (Radaelli 2003: 30): '(a) construction (b) diffusion and (c) institutionalization of formal and informal rules, procedures, policy paradigms, styles, "ways of doing things" and shared beliefs and norms which are first defined and consolidates in the making of EU decisions and then incorporated in the logic of domestic discourse, identities, political structures and public policies.'

This understanding of Europeanization can be put in connection with the approaches that see the EU as a system of shared governance in which the various levels of government constantly interact (Wallace 2005). From this perspective, Europeanization should not be considered as a one-way 'top-down' process, but rather as a 'bottom-up-down' one (Börzel 2002, 2005; Featherstone and Radaelli 2003; Vink and Graziano 2007). European integration entails the creation of common institutions, policies, norms and ideas impacting upon the member states which, in turn, influence the dynamics and the objectives of European integration.

When it comes to analyzing the domestic impacts of the EU, empirical research shows that Europeanization is not synonymous with convergence or progressive homogenization among the member states (Bulmer et al 2006). Europeanization is a process while convergence/divergence is a consequence of it (Radaelli 2003). Domestic changes and adaptations may entail coincidences, but also – more often – considerable variations. If Europeanization consists in any process of adjustment, change or transformation at the domestic level impinged by European integration (Caporaso et al. 2001; Börzel 2003) what really matters, therefore, is the understanding of the domestic factors that underlie such processes.

In attempting to explain the differential impact of Europe, students of Europeanization have pointed out the degree of compatibility or fit between European and domestic processes, structures and policies as the explicative variable. Börzel and Risse (2007) have identified two types of misfit: on the one hand, a 'policy misfit' between European rules/regulations and domestic policies; on the other, an 'institutional misfit' when European integration challenges 'domestic rules and procedures and the collective understandings attached to them' (Börzel and Risse 2007: 490). Two impacts are particularly relevant in this regard. They refer to the strengthening of central governments both at the expenses of the national parliaments and – in decentralized member states – the regions as a consequence of the dominant role of national executives in EU policy-making.

Domestic adaptation to Europeanization, here understood as the preservation of constitutional arrangements, will depend on 'mediating factors' such as political culture, formal and informal institutions and shared understandings (Börzel 2005). When dispute on the appropriate way to tackle the institutional misfit persists, adaptation can take place if the domestic 'losers' (i.e. the regions) gain enough power resources to oblige the central government to negotiate. Likewise, although Europeanization constrains domestic actors it also generates opportunity structures, providing them with additional resources that can be used both at the national and the EU level. As we will see below, the Spanish case fits both scenarios.

Domestic participation in EU decision-making

The regions' participation in the EU is one of the central issues dealt with in the literature on regionalism and European governance (Jeffery 1997, 2004b, 2005; Keating and Loughlin 1997; Letamendia 1999; Morata 2004). In Spain, the entry into Europe gave rise to very different attitudes between the central government (controlled by an absolute PSOE majority until 1993) and the most demanding communities, like the Catalans and Basques. Just as the main concern of the Socialists and, in general, of state elites, was to take maximum advantage of the new development opportunities, guaranteeing Spain's credibility through compliance with community law, the nationalist forces perceived membership simultaneously as a threat and an opportunity. It was a threat in the sense that the rules of the game of the EU reduced their new competencies and, at the same time, induced an internal re-centralization process. However, it was also an opportunity, because EU membership opened up for their territories an unsuspected horizon of political, economic and cultural projection beyond the state. To sum up, assuming the representation of national sovereignty in the European sphere (Hooghe and Marks 2004), the central government was mainly concerned with the respect of community law by the ACs. In contrast, the latter intended to compensate the centralizing effects of accession by claiming a direct role in European politics (Morata 2001).

1985–1993: From conflict to pragmatism

The Spanish executive took the initiative as early as December 1985 by proposing an agreement on 'cooperation on issues related to the European Community' (MAP 1995). The objective was to guarantee compliance with community laws by unifying the transposition of directives, but not participation by the autonomous communities in the decisions themselves.

The document proposed that the sectoral conferences, which had been created in 1983 as an inter-governmental coordination mechanism, be tasked with the defining of common criteria vis-à-vis implementation, and also suggested the use of other bilateral mechanisms, like the cooperation committees, anticipated in the statutes.

The Catalan government responded with a counterproposal based on three principles:

(a) The distribution of competences to be the only criterion in determining responsibility for implementing community norms;
(b) Central government to assume responsibility for informing the ACs of European developments that might effect their competencies; and,
(c) The ACs to be allowed to formulate recommendations that would be binding in those policy areas over which they had exclusive domestic competence.

The Catalan proposal also included the creation, in Brussels, of a Delegation of the Autonomous Communities for European Affairs, composed of six representatives; three from the historical communities (the Basque Country, Catalonia and Galicia). The autonomic delegates had to be a part ('with full rights') of the Spanish Permanent Representation (REPER) and take part in all the committees and working groups of the community.

The Catalan proposal was rejected by the central government and most regional governments (MAP 1995: 141), the former opposing direct participation and the latter opposing any kind of privileged position for the historical communities. In April 1986, the Spanish government presented a second draft agreement, inspired by the German model negotiated as a result of the ratification of the Single European Act (Nagel 2004) in which it committed itself to transmitting to the ACs all proposals from the European Commission that might affect their competences. On their part, the ACs could express views and positions that could be incorporated into the Spanish position 'as much as possible, as long as they were compatible with the general interests of the state and with the European integration process'. At the European level, the ACs would be allowed an observer and a joint observer, appointed by the ministry of foreign affairs and responsible for communicating information to an internal coordination committee. Both observers would have been allowed to attend the meetings of the committees and working groups of the Commission and the Council of Ministers.

The proposal did not prosper due to the insistence of Catalonia and the Basque Country that they have their own representative in the Spanish REPER and that autonomic positions should have a binding character. The aim of reaching a general agreement thus seemed impossible, not only because discrepancies between state and regional actors, but also given the lack of a common position of the ACs themselves: many of the PSOE- and PP-governed, weaker autonomies did not share the views of the more powerful ones, while others were still not sensitized to the importance of European issues (Börzel 2002).

The issue arose again in 1988 in view of the first EC Spanish presidency. The government then proposed the creation of a so-called *Sectoral* Conference for issues related to the European Communities (CARCE is the Spanish acronym). Its main task was to communicate information about the six-month presidency and to serve as a mechanism for the exchange of information and opinions between the two levels of government. It was a change of strategy based on pragmatism as well as an increased preoccupation with the conflicts deriving from the implementation of community law.[2] However, the horizontal character and the lack of pre-eminence of the CARCE with respect to the other sectoral conferences reduced its effectiveness (Morata 2001).

1993–1996: Relative majority of the PSOE

The general elections of 1993 in which the socialists lost the previous absolute majority they had enjoyed since 1982, turned the nationalist forces and, in particular the Catalan *Convergència i Unió* (CiU), into the referees of the situation.[3] This led, in November 1994, to the adoption of a new agreement on the participation of the ACs in community issues through the sectoral conferences. This agreement established the following procedure:

> Given a proposal of the European Commission, the ACs to adopt a consensus-based position, which is then transferred to the central government through the relevant sectoral conference with the objective of negotiating a common position;
>
> The ACs' position is not, however, binding on the central government, unless it deals with an issue that is an exclusive AC competence, in which case 'it is considered in a determinant way'.

In other words, autonomic participation has different degrees of intensity based on two criteria (Jáuregi 2005: 155): the nature of the affected competences (exclusive, shared, concurrent) and the degree of agreement reached in each case among the ACs. To this initial complexity of the procedure one must add the fact that it had to be adapted by each of the sectoral conferences, based on the specific – and often heterogeneous – distribution of the competences and the reach of the respective community policy.[4] In addition, the operating system of the conference has been – and still remains – very heterogeneous and irregular since it does not have the organizational means and a common criterion regarding its intervention in the European procedure. In practise, the CARCE does not exercise any hierarchic power over the rest of the sectoral conferences.

The Aznar government (1996–2004)

The Aznar government term reproduced similar trends to those of its predecessor. The first legislature (1996–2000), in which the parliamentary support of the nationalists was essential for governmental stability, included significant changes in the participation of the ACs in the EU. However, the second, in which the PP had absolute majority, ended with the paralysis of the process.

The tight electoral victory of the PP in the 1996 elections again turned the Catalan nationalists into central players in the quest to guarantee political stability. Both parties subscribed to a 'pact of investiture and governance'. This included the improvement of the regional participation in the EU, embodied in the empowerment of the CARCE; the intervention of the ACs in the formulation of the European positions of the Spanish Government; the creation of the figure of the Autonomic Advisor in Brussels; and, finally, the participation of regional representatives in the committees and working groups of the Commission and the Council. The agreements benefited all the ACs and not only Catalonia, except with respect to the creation of a bilateral State-Generalitat Commission on the EU. In practice, the central government did not respect all of its commitments, vetoing the presence of autonomic representatives in the meetings of the Union's Council of Ministers and in the committees and working groups of the Council.

The experience of these years underscores two types of problems. On the one hand, it has been difficult to formulate a common position between the ACs due to the absence of effective mechanisms of horizontal and vertical cooperation. On the other hand, central government has complained about the lack of technical preparation, and even of political interest, on the part of some communities.

The CiU-PP agreement created the post of advisor for autonomic affairs, which was incorporated into the REPER with the purpose of transmitting information to the ACs through their offices in Brussels.[5] However, the advisor was an official of the diplomatic corps, assigned to the Ministry of Public Administrations and designated by it.

In conclusion, the period of 1996–2000 is characterized by four elements:

The consolidation of the CARCE as the central axis of internal participation. However, such participation was not effective due to a host of reasons including, inter alia, the complexity of the procedure, information asymmetries, the governmental monopoly of the calls, the inability to coordinate with the other sectoral conferences, and the lack of resources and/or interest of some ACs;[6]

The creation of the autonomic advisor assigned to the REPER, but dependent on the central government;

The increasing presence of regional representatives in the consultative committees of the European Commission;[7] and,

The breach, on the part of the central government, of its commitment to facilitate the incorporation of autonomic advisors into Council of Ministers meetings.

2004: The Rodriguez Zapatero government

As a result of the victory of the PSOE in the March 2004 elections, the ACs participate regularly in the meetings of the Council of the EU. There are two explanations for this development. First, the PSOE competed in the elections with a program inspired by the mottos of 'the plural Spain' and 'the return to Europe'. The program stated a number of specific commitments seeking the revitalizing of relations between the state government and the autonomic governments,[8] including their participation in the EU, and the organizing of a referendum to approve of the Constitutional Treaty project. Second – and most important – denied an absolute majority like Gonzalez and Aznar before him, Zapatero had to negotiate the required parliamentary support through agreement with other parties, and in particular with the independence-seeking ERC and Izquierda Unida/Iniciativa per Catalunya-Verds. Both parties had among their priorities the participation of the ACs in the EU and the use of the co-official languages at the European level. From there, with all eyes set on the referendum called for the month of February in 2005, the government quickly took the initiative. In December 2004 the CARCE passed two agreements that regulate both the participation of the ACs in the working groups of the Council of the Union, and their direct representation in the various configurations of the latter.[9] Both facets will be discussed briefly in turn.

Autonomic representation in council formations

For the first time, the agreement makes possible the incorporation in the state delegation (in four of the nine formations in the Council meetings) of a regional minister as the ACs' representative in the matters affecting their competences.[10] Each one of the sectoral conferences concerned chooses the representative of an AC for a six-month period, equivalent to the presidency terms of the Union. The autonomic representative works under the supervision of the head of the Spanish delegation, and as a referee, during his mandate, in case of a conflict of interests between the ACs. Finally, the autonomic participation cannot alter the unity principle of the representation and of the Spanish action in the EU (Ramon 2006). The four relevant Council configurations are: Employment, Social Policy, Health and Consumers; Agriculture and Fisheries; Environment; and Education, Youth and Culture.

This (experimental) selection is justified on the basis that the four Council configurations cover competences exercised by all ACs. In contrast, other configurations, such as ECOFIN or Justice and Home Affairs, would only affect the Basque Country and Catalonia.

Participation in the working groups

The agreement also requires the presence of regional officials and experts to provide state officials with their views in order that the Spanish position adequately reflects the perspective of the ACs.[11] The new procedure replaces the post-1996 advisor arrangement with two advisors designated by the ACs themselves, for a period of 3 years, through a system of rotation. The latter are responsible with regards the CARCE.[12] The advisors are members, with full rights, of the REPER and, thus, of COREPER I and the Special Committee of the CAP. Their main duties consist of transmitting information about community developments that can affect AC competences through their delegations or offices of representation and to assist, or replace, autonomic representatives present in Council working groups meetings as members of the Spanish delegation.

The new system does not establish any distinction between the ACs, although the provision to name a third advisor leaves the door open to the aspirations of Catalonia and the Basque Country for their own representative (although such representations would have to be shared).

An evaluation

The first aspect that needs to be emphasized is the striking resemblances between the 2004 procedure and the proposal put forward by the central government in 1986. The second aspect refers to the intent to render compatible two apparently contradictory concerns that have been present in this debate since the beginning: the desire to ensure respect for the competences of the ACs, on the one hand, and on the other hand the desire to defend Spanish interests in the EU. Having said that, it is possible to identify the elements of continuity and change that characterize the new model.

Continuity is reflected in the predominant role of the central government within the system of sectoral conferences, in the persistence of the horizontal fragmentation and in the demand for unanimity among the ACs when formulating a joint position. In addition, the selection of the four Council configurations favors the elements of symmetry in the autonomic state. As in the German case, the new model also tends to reinforce even further the power of the executives to the detriment of the autonomic parliaments, which are still excluded from the process insofar as the regional minister that participates in the meetings of the Council represents all of the ACs, but is not accountable to his or her respective parliament.

The most important new features refer to access to information and the increase in the ACs' capacity to influence the decision-making process through the participation of regional experts in the Council's working groups and the participation of regional ministers in the selected Council configurations. The breaking of the governmental monopoly in the representation of the state interests translates into a greater transparency of Spanish positions and in a greater interdependence between the two levels of government in relation to EU issues (Ramon 2006: 29).

Finally, the new procedure is not a zero-sum game in which the regional actors benefit from losses by the central government. In contrast, it is a positive-sum game with several aspects. For the first time, the ACs are able to penetrate the central nucleus of the European decisional process, simultaneously increasing their internal legitimacy and their institutional relevance at the European level. For its part, central government reinforces the degree of internal cohesion with regards the EU, ensuring the co-responsibility of the ACs in the different phases of the negotiation process and in the final decision; at the same time it prevents potential conflicts with the regions (Ramon 2006: 34).[13]

As regards the concrete workings of the agreement, it is possible to point out some important shortcomings related to political attitudes and both the lack of regional resources and coordination capacities.[14] First, according to regional observers, some central ministries have been reluctant to enable the active involvement – or even the presence – of regional ministers in the EU Council meetings. Since the agreement does not benefit from any legal support, the ACs can only complain about, but not appeal before the constitutional court. Second, aside from the Structural Funds and the CAP, a number of ACs still do not consider European issues relevant enough to allocate financial and administrative resources to follow-up the policy processes. As a result, they are not able to put forward policy positions or they don't do it in due time. Given the lack of expertise and, sometimes, also linguistic skills, some regional authorities do not participate in the working groups of the EU Council. Third, as regards the domestic formulation of common positions, there is no a single coordination procedure among the ACs but four (one for each Council configuration) and the sectoral conferences simultaneously concerned by Commission's proposals do not interact each other. Effective mobilization depends ultimately on the political relevance assigned to EU policy processes and especially on the efforts deployed by the AC in charge of horizontal coordination. Finally, against the terms of the agreement with the central government, the two regional experts assigned to the Spanish permanent representation do not participate in the COREPER meetings, the central body of inter-governmental bargaining at the EU level. Nevertheless, even if they were allowed to particpate, they would never be able to follow up all the issues at stake for regional interests. In sum, at first sight the new procedure entails a series of political and technical challenges. The most important one remains the regional ability to influence EU decision-making at the beginning and not at the end of the process, as it is the case now.

The Catalan Statute of Autonomy of 2006 and the EU

When the Catalan Statute of Autonomy of 1979 was approved Spain did not belong to the EC. Twenty-seven years later, the new statute ratified by referendum in June 2006 devoted special attention to the institutional relations with the EU both on a bilateral and multilateral basis, although the former are predominant.[15] During the negotiation process with Madrid of the statute drafted by the Catalan parliament, the most controversial issues were the definition of Catalonia as a 'nation' and the financial arrangements.[16] Surprisingly, the set of provisions dealing with the EU remained unchanged. These include five main aspects (Articles 184–192): decision-making, implementation, financial management, judicial review and representation before the EU.

As a first general rule, the Generalitat (the Catalan institutions) participates in EU matters affecting the powers or the interests of Catalonia. This includes EU treaty-making as well as ordinary decision-making. In this regard, the Generalitat should be informed by the central government of initiatives for the reviewing of EU treaties and of signing and ratification processes. Both the Catalan executive and the parliament have the right to address observations to their counterparts at the Spanish level. Furthermore, the Spanish delegations may include Catalan representatives to take part in the negotiations in matters affecting the exclusive powers of the Generalitat. On the other hand, the Generalitat takes part in the definition of the state positions before the EU – and especially before the Council – in matters concerning the powers or the interests of Catalonia on a bilateral basis when those affect it exclusively, or in the framework of multilateral procedures with the other ACs. More importantly, 'the position expressed by the Generalitat is decisive for the formation of the State position if it affects its exclusive powers and if the European proposal or initiative could lead to especially important financial or administrative consequences for Catalonia' (Art. 186-3). The central government provides the Generalitat with complete and up-to-date information about the EU initiatives and proposals. The government and the parliament of Catalonia may address the central government and the Spanish parliament with observations and proposals in relation to these initiatives and proposals.

Catalonia also participates in Spanish delegations to the EU that deal with affairs within its legislative powers, and especially in delegations to the Council of Ministers and the European Commission. This includes the consultative committees and the working groups of the Council and, in accordance with the state, the appointment of representatives in the permanent state representation in the EU. The Catalan parliament may establish relations with the EP in areas of common interest. It is also involved in the procedure aiming at overseeing the principles of subsidiarity and proportionality established by EU law in relation to legislative proposals affecting the powers of the Generalitat.

As a second general rule, the Generalitat enforces and implements the law of the EU within its own jurisdiction. The statute clearly states that European regulations do not modify the internal distribution of powers established by the Constitution and the statute. When the implementation of EU law requires the adoption of internal measures beyond the Catalan jurisdiction that the competent ACs are unable to adopt by means of collaboration or coordination mechanisms, the state should consult the Generalitat prior to adopting the measures. The Generalitat participates in the bodies that adopt these measures or, should this participation not be possible, issues a preliminary report. In the event that the European legislation replaces the basic state regulations, the Generalitat may adopt its own legislation based on European rules.

According to the statute, the Generalitat is responsible for the management of European funds in matters within its jurisdiction. It has also access to the European Court of Justice. The government of the Generalitat may demand that the state government bring actions before the court in defence of its interests and powers. The refusal to bring the requested actions must be justified, and immediately communicated to the Generalitat.

Finally, the Generalitat may establish an official delegation to represent its interests before the EU institutions. The Catalan delegation was already set up in September 2006.

Regional mobilization at the EU level

Domestic constraints, along with new opportunities provided by the EU system of governance, explain regional mobilization beyond the state (Hooghe and Marks 2001; Morata 2003). In addition to promoting concepts such as partnership, policy networks and subsidiarity, the EU provides incentives in terms of funding, rights of representation and access to policy-making. In this way, it indirectly strengthens regional legitimacy (Kohler-Koch 2002). From a bottom-up perspective, Europeanization fosters regional mobilization in search of additional resources; from a top-down perspective it provides incentives to operate at the EU level. Setting aside participation through the Committee of the Regions, ACs' mobilization takes three main forms: permanent offices/delegations in Brussels, coalition building and regional networks.

Regional offices in Brussels

By 1986, and following the example of the German Länder, the Basque Country and Catalonia established their own offices of representation in

Brussels. By the mid-1990s all 17 ACs had established their own representation. At present, the offices of Catalonia, the Basque Country, Andalusia and the Balearic Islands are titled 'Delegations' of their respective governments – although they do not enjoy any official status at the EU level – while the remaining 13 still keep the original name of Offices.

The legal status for regional offices based in Brussels was established in 1994 when the Spanish Constitutional Court ruled against the central government in a dispute with the Basque government about the setting up of a 'Basque official delegation' to the European community. However, institutionalization has not led to homogenization. For example, the delegation of the Catalan government, with a staff of almost 20 experts, is headed by the general secretary for European affairs. The Basque representation is also of a strictly institutional nature while the Galician one acts through a public-private foundation. Most regional offices, however, are parts of their respective regional development agencies.

The performance of the various offices reflects not only relative levels of political will and expertise, but also domestic inter-governmental arrangements. In this regard, the creation of the autonomic adviser in 1996, the growing participation of regional experts in the consultative committees of the European Commission and, since 2005, the involvement of regional representatives in the Council workings have certainly reinforced the strategic role of regional offices as linkages between the three levels of government. In addition to exchanging information among themselves and with the various DGs of the European Commission as well as the European Parliament, the offices coordinate their home delegations at the CoR. Finally, AC representatives are members of a larger network made up of more than 200 regional offices.

Regional coalitions

European integration has led ACs to seek to strengthen their institutional position through the building of partnerships with other European regions. Historic nationalities such as Catalonia and the Basque Country have taken advantage of their influence in the Spanish arena. Some autonomic presidents, and especially the former Catalan presidents Jordi Pujol and Pasqual Maragall, have contributed to the strengthening of European regionalism, defining new strategies and building alliances aimed at enhancing the role of the regions in the EU.

During the 1990s, the German, Spanish, Belgian and Italian regions were strongly supportive of a 'Europe of the Regions' as part of strategy aimed at ensuring for the regions' institutional recognition as the 'third' level within the EU institutional system. For this purpose they initially focused on the Assembly of the European Regions (ARE), a common platform founded in 1985 (and chaired by Jordi Pujol from 1992 to 1996). However, the high ambitions of this period were not matched in practice:

What emerged as the institutional manifestation of the "third" level was the Committee of the Regions (CoR), established at Maastricht as a mixed regional/local body to advice on EU legislative proposals. The CoR has not established itself as an authoritative voice of the regions.

(Jeffery 2004a: 4)

Regional expectations were further frustrated by the interpretation of subsidiarity in the treaties of Maastricht (1992) and Amsterdam (1997). Such disappointment explains why the stronger European regions moved toward a new strategy at the end of the 1990s.

During the Nice IGC of September 2000, Catalonia and the Basque Country, along with 22 'constitutional' regions from Germany, Austria and Belgium reached a common position reflecting their common concerns in connection with the ongoing treaty reform. This proposal led to the first Conference of Presidents of Regions with legislative powers (REGLEG) that took place in Barcelona, in November 2000. REGLEG brings together 73 regions with 'their own Government and Parliament' in Austria, Belgium, Germany, Italy, Spain and the UK, plus island regions from Portugal and Finland. Furthermore, in May 2001, seven 'constitutional regions' (Catalonia, Bavaria, Scotland, North Rhine-Westphalia, Salzburg, Wallonia and Flanders) put forward a common Declaration as a contribution to the debate on the 'Future of Europe'. These positions, along with pressure from the Belgian regions and the German Länder on their respective central governments, led to the inclusion of an explicit reference to the role of the regions in the EU in the Laeken Declaration of December 2001 (Morata and Ramon 2005). During the workings of the European Convention, REGLEG put forward its main concerns regarding the constitutional treaty.[17] Those included (Jeffery 2004a):

a clearer allocation of competencies in the EU so that the limits of European integration can be marked out and controlled more effectively by and within member states;

a recognition of the particular status of RegLeg regions as significant law-making bodies distinct from other regional and local authorities (i.e. distinct from the rest of the members of the CoR);

the formalization of their direct right of access to the Council of Ministers in the treaty;

direct access of any REGLEG region to the Court of Justice in cases where it feels the principle of subsidiarity has been infringed;

better access to Commission thinking at the pre-legislative stage of decision-making when the broad lines of policy are set, in order to ward off the possibility of over-intrusive regulation.

Even though the Convention and the IGC did not take into account all the demands made by regional actors, the final draft of the constitutional treaty did incorporate some significant improvements regarding the recognition of local and regional autonomy, cultural and linguistic diversity or the principle of subsidiarity (Jeffery 2004a) that were kept in the new Treaty of Lisbon. The CoR would win the right to bring actions before the European Court of Justice (ECJ) in policy fields dealing with the principle of subsidiarity.

Horizontal networking

European integration has transformed state-rooted concepts like 'space' and 'border' (Anderson et al. 2003; Christiansen 2005). Although state borders are still relevant in many respects, they are strongly challenged by the advance of globalization and supranational integration. As a consequence, regions are now more dependent on the external market and on their own resources in facing up to competitive pressures (Keating 2004). However, the reduced significance of state borders within the EU also provides opportunities for the regions to define common interests and to draw up joint strategies which shape new spaces for supraregional integration (Christiansen and Jorgensen 2004). This process has been encouraged by EU policies with territorial impact (Structural Funds, trans-European networks) and especially by the INTERREG program which has been recently upgraded to a community objective of the 2007–2013 Cohesion Policy.

The INTERREG initiative has led to the creation of five Euro-regions at the two Spanish borders: Galicia-North of Portugal; Extremadura-Alentejo-Algarve; Andalucía-Algarve; French-Spanish Basque Country; and, more recently, the Euroregion Pyrenees-Mediterranean, which brings together three Spanish (Aragon, Catalunya, Balearic) and two French (Midi-Pyrenees and Languedoc-Roussillon) regions.[18] Euro-regions do not have their own 'government' but rely on voluntary cooperation within a context of pragmatically defined and mutually recognized set of rules (Perkmann 2005). In the absence of hierarchical structures and formal powers, they operate through policy networks involving public and private actors. Euro-regions therefore can be considered as laboratories of institutional innovation in line with the rationale of European integration. At the same time, the main challenge they are confronted with is the need to built governance capacities in a context of legal asymmetries. A recent survey conducted with public and private actors of the Euro-region, Pyrenees-Mediterranean Euroregion (PME) shows that institutional capacities are essential to provide the PME with adequate organizational, financial and managerial instruments.[19] The opinions expressed underline the need to build cooperation arrangements through shared multi-level strategy involving public and private actors at all levels.

Some ACs are also active members of wider multi-regional networks with general (i.e. the Atlantic Arch, from Portugal to Ireland) or single-issue purposes (the Mediterranean Technologies Arch, from Valencia to Lombardy; the South European Arch, based on transport networks). Those examples should be complemented with transregional agreements like the Four

Motors for Europe, a network made up of Catalonia, Baden-Württemberg, Rhône-Alps and Lombardy, which seeks to advance technological innovation and promote external trade cooperation.

Regional implementation of community policies

The ACs are responsible for the implementation of EU policies according to the terms of the individual statutes and the constitutional sharing of competencies. Their role is particularly relevant in three policy fields: agriculture, cohesion and the environment.

Since Spain's entry into the EU, regional administrations have been the effective managers of the CAP. In other words, there is no longer policy implementation at the national level. The Spanish ministry simply acts as national negotiator of EU legislation – since 2005 in consort with the regions – while most decisions related to the regional distribution of Community financing are taken through the Sectoral Conference of Agricultural Policy (Ramon 2006). Even though the domestic institutional framework has considerably strengthened the role of the regions, these have not been able to establish their own agricultural policies beyond promoting Community programs in favor of rural development under the LEADER initiative and the rural development program PRODER. According to a recent assessment, the lack of specific agricultural policies tailored to the individual regions has had a negative impact on the sector (Ramon 2007). At the same time, political devolution has favored the emergence of policy communities in connection with the CAP through which the regional governments seek to enhance the agricultural interests of their own territories at the EU level without any effective horizontal (inter-regional) and vertical (central-regional) coordination (Ramon 2007).

As regards cohesion policy, Spain's entry into the EU has had a significant impact on regional development. Between 1989 and 2006, assisted by EU cohesion policy, the whole country, and in particular Objective 1 regions, made considerable progress in developing infrastructure and public services. During the 1989–2006 period Spain was the member state that benefited most from cohesion policy spending. According to some estimates (Herce and Sosvilla-Rivero 2004) Community grants were generating almost 1.2 per cent additional growth in Spain during that period.[20] Moreover, between 2000 and 2006, Objective 1 funding to Spain amounted to almost 70 per cent of the Spanish structural actions budget, representing almost 30 allocations (Yuill et al. 2006).

Since the introduction of cohesion policy regulations in 1988, the ACs have played a greater role in regional development policy-making (Morata and Muñoz 1996). Regional authorities participate in programming functions on both bilateral and multilateral bases, under the coordination of the various relevant central ministries. They are also involved in multi-level monitoring meetings with Community and central government representatives. During the first cohesion policy round (1989–1993), the internal distribution of funds among the various levels of government was a permanent matter of inter-governmental contention due to the refusal of the Spanish Ministry of Economy and Finance to regionalize the central state's funds and those allocated to local government. The latter took advantage of its institutional prerogatives to allocate community funding according to its own criteria, curtailing regional autonomy. Nevertheless, after 1996, and especially during the last 2000–2006 round, the central government has progressively adapted to European requirements. Partnership with the regions has been improved, along with the creation of a single Community Supporting Framework (CSF) that is almost fully regionalized (instead of several CSFs managed by the regions and one multi-regional CSF managed by the central state).

From 1989 to 2006, most Spanish regions were able to use EU funding to modernize socio-economic infrastructure and services. In the new round, 2007–2013, of Cohesion Policy they have to compete at the EU level to achieve more qualitative objectives. The ACs are confronted with the challenge of using their expertise to achieve a more efficient use of limited resources.

Regional authorities have primary responsibility for implementing environmental policy. They can also complement and adapt Community directives according to their competencies, and central authorities are not able to control the way in which the regions perform their tasks. The Spanish government is, in the main, entrusted (though now in collaboration with the regions) with the task of negotiating at the EU level, and also with transposing EU directives and establishing general standards and programs to be implemented at the regional level. However, the ACs can also anticipate the enforcement of community legislation when the central government is not complying with its obligations. The multi-level character of environmental policy has led to the establishment of coordination mechanisms for promoting inter-governmental cooperation. Through the sectoral conference on the environment, central and regional ministers and high officials meet on a regular basis to exchange information and agree on common issues, including the formulation of common positions on EU environmental proposals, which are then sent to the CARCE. However, the lack of effective integration of environmental considerations into the other policies – especially those related to the Structural Funds – has given rise to a network of environmental authorities made up of EU Commission, central, regional and local representatives.

In practice, environmental policy decentralization in Spain means that in areas such as industrial waste, sewage, air pollution control, special protection areas and clean water, the legal implementation of Community directives depends on the political commitment and administrative capacities of regional governments. These requirements are not always fulfilled in a country characterized by rapid economic development based mainly on tourism and housing. In some coastal, mountain and large urban areas the preservation of the environment has not been among the priorities of regional and local authorities. As a consequence, over recent years the European Commission has taken legal action against Spain with regards cases of violation of EU environmental law by the ACs. These include non-compliance with directives on uncontrolled and illegal waste landfills, environmental impact assessment, protected areas and habitats, the protection of wild birds and the Water Framework Directive.

Conclusion

This chapter has addressed some of the issues raised by the process of Europeanization of the 'Autonomic State' in Spain, from both a top-down and a bottom-up perspective. We have seen that while conflict and disagreement is a necessary condition for domestic changes and adjustments (Börzel, 2005), it is the internal distribution of political and institutional resources that ultimately shapes domestic responses to Europeanization. Between 1986 and 2004, the lack of cooperation hampered any bilateral or multilateral agreement on the internal (re)distribution of competencies derived from European integration. The gradual advances achieved have not been brought about as a consequence of a shared understanding of a model of the state and its projection in Europe, but rather in connection with the occasional veto of nationalist parties in the central parliament.

Given the internal limitations, the most active ACs have taken the initiative of 'by-passing' the state barriers, acting as political entrepreneurs and developing their own strategies in the European arena. The regional offices in Brussels have facilitated informal direct contacts with the EU institutions, particularly with the Commission. Through the construction of coalitions with other European regions and to a lesser extent through the CoR, the ACs have sought to defend their institutional interests during the processes of treaty reform. Finally, the multi-level governance promoted by the EU has given the regions the opportunity to get access to the European arena through the development of transnational and cross-border networks of cooperation, the exchange of experiences and the transfer of new concepts of policy. However, empirical research shows that the institutional capacities to deal with these issues cannot be taken for granted. Many times, regional actors embark in cooperation agreements with other regions at the EU level without considering the institutional implications in terms of funding and organizational resources.

Regional mobilization beyond the state may be more or less fruitful according to endogenous or European constraints and opportunities. Yet successive treaty reforms confirm that internal arrangements continue to represent the main channel of access by the regions to the EU. Hence the importance of the agreement reached at the end of 2004 between the Socialist government and the ACs, which widens regional participation in four formations of the Council of the EU and in their corresponding working groups. This represents a qualitative leap forward influenced, undoubtedly, by electoral results, but also by a more cooperative approach to inter-governmental relations. However, the concrete application of the 2004 agreement reflects a series of shortcomings entrenched in persisting centralist attitudes, the lack of political commitment by some ACs and the need of effective coordination mechanisms and, in some cases, technical expertise.

The full integration of the EU dimension in the Catalan Statute of 2006 confirms the former assessment. It reveals the importance of European matters for Catalonia (and for the other ACs) after 20 years of EU membership. Through the protection and the enhancing of regional competences, it also expresses distrust about the central government and the political determination to play a role in Europe based on multilateral and, especially, bilateral arrangements.

Finally, the Spanish regions are entrusted with essential responsibilities with regard to the implementation of community policies and the management of EU funds. Although the central government was using its coordination powers to limit regional competences in Cohesion Policy and the CAP, it is the development of the EU regulation and funding that has increasingly empowered the ACs. Concerning the environment, the legal enforcement and the effective implementation of the policy are handled by the regions. In those areas, Europeanization can be considered as a learning process in which the regions were adapting more or less successfully their structures and procedures to the EU requirements. At present they are facing important challenges such as the progressive drop of structural funds, the territorial impacts of the CAP reform and, in some cases, scarce observance of European environmental legislation.

Notes

1. The Treaty of Lisbon devotes attention to the regions and the local governments through: (a) the recognition of regional and local self-administration; (b) the inclusion of the regional and local authorities within the principle of subsidiarity; (c) a clearer division of competencies; (d) the system of early warning regarding the control of subsidiarity; (d) the recognition of the regional parliaments with legislative competencies in the Protocol of Subsidiarity; and (e) the right to appeal by the Committee of the Regions (CoR) in case of violation of the principle of subsidiarity.

2. In 1989, the minister of Public Administration (MAP) referred to 'the conflict of competences derived from the application of the European normative as one of

the fundamental problems pending solution between the ACs and the central state with respect to European decisions'.

3. It is important to remember the commitment of the then president of the Generalitat, Jordi Pujol, to maintain the support of CiU for the Socialist government until the end of the Spanish presidency of the EU during the second semester of 1995.

4. Until 2004, only three of the 25 conferences had developed the framework procedure: Agriculture and Rural Development, Sea Fishing and the Inter-Territorial Council of the National Health System.

5. This figure is clearly inspired in the German model of the Länder *Beobachter* (the Länder observer).

6. As a confirmation of this trend, between 1992 and 2002, the CARCE only met 36 times. In 2002, four meetings were held as opposed to the 11 of the Consultative Council of Agricultural Policy for Community Affairs (Vid. MAP, 2003, *Conferencias Sectoriales,* Informe Anual, 2002).

7. However, some authors refer to the rules committees of the committology system and not to the preparation phase of European norms.

8. These included the creation of a 'Presidents Conference' and the reform of the senate to guarantee territorial representation.

9. BOE 64, 16 March 2005.

10. In 2005, six regional ministers participated in the Council meetings: Andalusia (three times), Aragon (once), Asturias (once), Castile and Leon (twice), Catalonia (three times), Galicia (once). During the first semester of 2006, another five have been incorporated: Madrid (six times), Extremadura (once), Cantabria (twice), the Canary Islands (once) and Murcia (once).

11. By the end of 2005, autonomic experts had participated in more than 40 meetings of the Council's working groups, together with the technical representative of the corresponding Ministry (web MAP).

12. During 2005–2007, the advisors belonged to Andalusia (governed by the PSOE) and Galicia (governed by the PP until June 2005 and, thereafter, by the PSG-BNG until October 2008). A new adviser from the Generalitat of Catalonia was appointed in January 2009 to replace the Andalusian one while political disagreements blocked the appointment of a Valencian PP representative until June 2009.

13. The evaluation of the new model formulated by the Department of Agriculture of the Generalitat is significant in the sense that 'it will reinforce the cohesion of the Spanish agrarian policy and the negotiating power of the Spanish Minister vis-à-vis his or her peers'. (DARP/Info 1/3/2005, quoted by Ramon 2005: 35).

14. In view of assessing the impact of the new procedure, two interviews were conducted in May 2009 with regional officials involved in domestic and UE coordination mechanisms.

15. http://www.gencat.cat/generalitat/eng/estatut/index.htm (accessed 20/06/10)

16. In 2006, the Popular Party appealed before the Constitutional Court against the Catalan Statute which they considered a 'parallel Constitution' giving Catalonia 'a privileged position over other regions in Spain and laying the foundation for a confederate system which would invalidate the current state of autonomies'. The statute came into force on 8 August 2006.

17. Vid. Resolution of the 3rd REGLEG Conference http://ue.eu.int/newsroom/ NewMain.asp? (accessed 20/06/10).

18. http://www.euroregio-epm.org/qu_presentacion.html#objetivos (accessed 20/06/10).
19. The survey was based on 1000 questionnaires which were sent to public and private actors of the five regions. It included the various levels of government as well as economic sectors and ONGs.
20. It is worth noting that, compared to other European regions, virtually no private participation was included in Objective 1 interventions in Spain (Inforegio 2004).

9

The Swedish Regions and the European Union

*Anders Lidström**

The regional level in Sweden has traditionally been comparatively weak. There is no history of federalism or of strong regional identities or governments in the Swedish polity. On the contrary, in a political system with a strong emphasis on national public welfare with equal access for every citizen, and adjustments to specific circumstances through local implementation and self-government, the national and municipal levels have been the main levels of government from the end of the eighteenth century. The major task of the intermediate level of elected governments, the county councils, has been to run hospitals and provide health services, because these required a larger population base than the municipalities could offer. Indeed, during the 1980s and in the beginning of the 1990s, an increasing number of voices were raised suggesting that the county councils should be abolished and their functions transferred to central government or to inter-municipal cooperative boards. Similar debates occurred in the other Nordic countries, apart from in Finland where a directly elected intermediate level had never been established (Sandberg and Ståhlberg 2000; Rose and Ståhlberg 2005; Sandberg 2005).

In 1995, Sweden decided to join a European Union (EU) that 3 years earlier had accepted the Maastricht Treaty with its emphasis on the local and regional levels. Not surprisingly, this came as a blessing for the county councils and changed the focus of the debate. If county councils had previously been seen as an anomaly, they now had a role to play in a Europe of the regions as the only directly elected form of regional government in Sweden. However, in practice, national as well as regional adjustments to the EU had started well before Sweden became a member of the Union (Baldersheim et al. 2001; Svenska kommunförbundet/Landstingsförbundet 2001). This included economic adjustments and public procurement, but also the establishment of regional information offices in Brussels.

This chapter aims at summarizing the experiences of the last 10 years with regard to the relationship between the Swedish regions and the EU. What are the main features of this relationship? Are there any specific characteristics that distinguish the Swedish regions from their counterparts in other countries within the EU?

The theoretical point of departure for this study is a multi-level governance perspective, in which policy-making and implementation in the EU is seen as a complex interplay between levels of decision-making. Not only does this emphasize how the local, regional, national and European levels are linked to each other, but the concept of governance also underlines that the relevant actors are not limited to formal public decision-makers but may also include non-governmental interests (Hooghe and Marks 2001).

Multi-level governance can be seen as the response to two major, and seemingly contradictory, tendencies of change – Europeanization and decentralization (c.f. Peters and Pierre 2001). On the one hand, multi-level governance is a way for EU institutions to safeguard efficient implementation of EU policies and to enhance European integration. On the other hand, multi-level governance is also a means for regions and municipalities to increase their institutional capacity by drawing on resources from higher levels of government (Lidström 2005). This chapter contributes with insights into how multi-level governance – from both the EU-down and region-up perspectives – functions in a Swedish setting.

The next part of the chapter presents the structure of Swedish local and regional government. This is followed by two sections in which the relationship between Swedish regions and the EU are discussed. The input of Swedish regions into the EU are outlined and the consequences of the Union for Swedish regions are presented. The chapter continues with a discussion about the attitudes among citizens and politicians toward the EU and whether these may have been affected by the integration process within the EU. It ends with conclusions about the distinctive features of the relations between Swedish regions and the EU.

The structure of local and regional government in Sweden

The Swedish system of government consists of three levels of directly elected government (Lidström 1999; Häggroth 2000). There are two tiers of local government, a municipal level with 290 municipalities (*kommuner*) and an intermediate level consisting of 19 county councils (*landsting*) and two regions (*regioner*).[1] One municipality (Gotland) is also a county council. The municipalities are in charge of a large range of welfare services, such as social services, day nurseries, care of the elderly, and primary and secondary schooling. They are also responsible for the local public infrastructure, i.e. streets, parks, and systems of water and sewage. They make decisions about physical planning, land use and building permissions. The municipal level is generally regarded as the stronger of the two levels, not only because of the larger range of functions but also in financial terms, as they represent approximately two thirds of total local government spending.

Also, as smaller units of government, municipalities are closer to the citizens, therefore their decision-makers are often more well-known than the county councilors.

The municipalities vary in size from Bjurholm's 2600 to the 771,000 inhabitants of the city of Stockholm. On average, they have 30,200 inhabitants. In order to be able to carry out their welfare responsibilities, municipalities have been twice amalgamated into larger units, the first time in 1952, and the second during a period in the early 1970s. At the intermediate level, the country is divided into counties (*län*). This division originates from a revision of the Swedish Constitution in 1634, when Sweden was a great power, and aimed at facilitating central control of its territory. Northern Sweden was divided into several counties in the nineteenth century, and in 1968 the city of Stockholm was included into the county of Stockholm, but otherwise the county structure remained practically unchanged until the late 1990s. In 1997, the two southernmost counties merged and became Skåne län and in 1998, three counties in western Sweden were amalgamated to create Västra Götalands län. Both these mergers were voluntary, initiated from below and only concerned a part of the country (Baldersheim et al. 2001). This contradicts the previous typical pattern of territorial reform in Sweden. For example, the reorganizations of the municipal level in the 1950s and 1970s were top-down, comprehensive and compulsory processes.

In each county, there is a directly elected county council or a regional assembly. These are unique from a comparative European perspective in that one of their tasks, health care, is very dominant (Lidström 1999). Approximately 80 per cent of the county councils' budgets concern medical care and public health, but they are also responsible for public dental services, care of the handicapped and regional cultural institutions. In addition, county councils/regions support regional development and subsidize public transport jointly with other local and regional actors. The two regions differ from county councils as they are parts of an experimental program that gives them more responsibility for regional development. The average size of the counties/regions is 430,000 inhabitants, ranging from Jämtland's 127,000 inhabitants to the county of Stockholm with 1.9 million inhabitants. The two regions and the county of Stockholm dominate, as they represent half the Swedish population.

In each county area, there is also a county administrative board. This is a central government agency with responsibility for general state administration at the county level. It performs, for example, control and support functions with regard to social services and environmental protection and issues permits, such as driving licences. However, the board also has a responsibility for, and resources to support, regional development. In the experimental regions of Skåne and Västra Götaland, the county administrative board only has a supervisory role as its regional development functions have been transferred to the directly elected regional councils. The chairman of the board – the county governor – is appointed by central government and is often a prominent politician or senior civil servant. Despite not being directly elected, the county governor is usually seen as the main representative for the county area. The rest of the board is also appointed by the government.

In addition to the county councils and the county administrative boards, there are a number of other institutional actors at regional level, some of which have an explicit interest in the development of the region. These include other state agencies, such as labor market boards, universities and higher education colleges. Municipalities are also involved, and their common interests are pursued by the regional branch of the national interest organization for sub-national elected governments – the regional association of local authorities. Some cities can also be regional actors as they may have an impact on the region as a whole. From 2003, the municipalities and county councils in a county have had the right to establish a regional development association. This takes over some of the regional development functions from the county administrative board, and may also pool resources from the county councils and the municipalities. However, these associations can only be established if all municipalities in a county agree. At the moment, there are 14 regional development associations. Other types of cooperative structures aiming at developing the region are also common. These may include private interests and do not necessarily correspond to existing county boundaries.

It is not surprising that the Swedish intermediate level is referred to as 'the regional mess' (Olsson and Åström 2004). There is a contrast between this fragmented structure and the seeming rationality that characterizes both the municipal and central government levels, where there is just one dominant institutional actor in the territory. At regional level there are a large number of actors with different sources of democratic legitimacy, with partly overlapping functions and to some extent also with different territories. Within the field of regional development, in particular, this has often caused open conflict. The main contenders have been the county administrative board, the county council and the municipalities. However, in recent years, these actors have begun to cooperate. As national and European regional policies increasingly emphasize that the regions are responsible for their own development, it has become necessary for the actors in a region to act in concert, instead of competing with each other.

The regional mess has been addressed by a parliamentary committee – the committee on public sector responsibilities – which presented its suggestions in February 2007. The committee was given the task of comprehensively reviewing the allocation of functions between levels of government in Sweden and overseeing the structure of territorial divisions at local and regional levels. It suggested that the present counties should be replaced by between six and nine larger directly elected regions. Negotiations between various local and regional actors will decide how the borders should be set. However, the committee suggested that a number of criteria that should be met, including that each region should have at least one million inhabitants and a specialized university hospital. Apart from providing health services, the new regions should have the responsibility for regional economic development. These changes are partly a consequence of Swedish EU membership. The present revision is more comprehensive than any previous reform made in modern times, as it combines a thorough review of both territorial divisions and functions. Although practically all municipalities and county councils are in favor of the suggestions, the government has only agreed to give full regional status to four regions from 2011 (the experimental regions of Skåne and Västra Götaland and two smaller regions). The rest of the country is expected to be regionalized by 2015.

Interestingly, the other Nordic countries are also carrying out similar reviews and reforms (Rose and Ståhlberg 2005; Sandberg 2005). A common theme is that the municipalities and county councils, with their responsibility for public welfare services, need to be restructured in a way that makes them better prepared to handle future challenges. These include an ageing population, but also the continuing depopulation of the rural areas and of the smallest municipalities.

Swedish regions v. the European Union

Alongside the municipalities, Swedish regions were actively involved in international cooperation and contacts long before Sweden became a member of the EU. Activities include not only twinning arrangements and memberships of international organizations but also more informal contacts between leading regional politicians. However, with the establishment of the European Economic Area, and the subsequent Swedish membership of the EU, the international activities of the regions entered a new phase. It became much more important to be informed about and to be able to influence EU decisions. In 2008, practically all municipalities and county councils/regions were involved in such activities (Sveriges Kommuner och Landsting 2008).

Generally speaking, national legislation and regulations have not restricted local authorities from pursuing their interests vis-à-vis the EU. It has usually been possible to find ways around existing legal limitations. Even though, for example, the Local Government Act specifies that all activities undertaken by municipalities and regions must concern the local authority's population or its territory, it has been possible to carry out activities directed toward the EU as these have been regarded as being in the interest of the municipality or region. Interestingly, in some cases where the current regulation turned out to be too constricting for the international aspirations of local authorities, the rules have been changed. Local authorities can now send equipment surplus to their requirements as international aid as well as being able to export their services.

A different matter is whether central government wants regions to be active, or if this is seen as a weakening of the position of the national interest. Even if these activities are not explicitly counteracted by central government, there seems to be no official view in this matter. During the first 11 years of Swedish EU membership, Sweden had a Social Democratic government, led by Prime Minister Göran Persson. The Social Democratic position was ambivalent. Some representatives of the government expressed their support for local government international activities. The previous minister of infrastructure and regional affairs even created a reference group of regional politicians, who met regularly to discuss regional development policies and national and regional policies vis-à-vis the EU.

However, Göran Persson had a different view, at least according to a book by the usually well informed journalist and author Olle Svenning. He portrays Persson as highly critical of the international activities of the county councils and regions. Persson claimed that these authorities, instead of focusing on their main areas of responsibility, prefer more extravagant activities such as lobbying in Brussels. He was afraid that regionalization would undermine the unitary character of the Swedish state. Regions might establish alternative sources of power, linked with other regions in other countries, which in the long run could challenge central government's over-all control over the country and the homogeneity of the public welfare systems (Svenning 2005). Despite these views, the county administrative boards, the extended arm of the state in the region, continued to be actively involved in regional international activities.

After the general elections in September 2006, the Social Democratic government was replaced by a non-socialist government under Prime Minister Fredrik Reinfeldt. The new government has not expressed any explicit view with regard to regional activities vis-à-vis the EU. This seems to suggest that the previous policy of not actively counteracting such involvement is likely to be continued.

Some of the inputs by regions vis-à-vis the EU are carried out by each institutional actor separately. A county council, for example, may lobby a relevant administrator in the EU bureaucracy in order to ensure that its application conforms to what the EU decision-makers expect. It may also collect information or develop networks with other regions that will improve its position in the future. Nevertheless, most of these activities are coordinated with other institutional actors in the region, or with other regions, either within the country or on a European level. As previously mentioned, there are several institutional actors at regional level, and most of them have international aspirations. Each of them has employees who specialize in the field of EU relations. In the county councils and the municipalities, this also includes a limited number of politicians. The typical pattern is that EU-related activities are handled by specialists in the field, and are not particularly well integrated into the main responsibilities of the various institutional actors. For example, politicians and officers in charge of health policies in a county council do not usually combine this with an EU perspective. Instead, coordination of EU activities takes place at the top level in the organizations, among the leading politicians and chief administrators. This makes it somewhat difficult to integrate an EU perspective into the daily activities of a county council or a major city. On the other hand, it opens up links and coordinated activities between those who specialize in EU matters. At the regional level, these various specialists are best characterized as a policy community. They have a common focus, meet regularly to discuss and coordinate their activities, share information and develop joint strategies. When necessary, the leading politicians, chief administrators and the county governor are also involved. This policy community of EU relations is a way of achieving coordination and concerted action in the institutional setting of a regional mess. However, this also means that EU oriented activities are primarily elite-driven.

Some coordination takes place on an informal basis, but it is enhanced by a number of more formalized arrangements. One is the joint information centers in Brussels. These are typically run by a regional consortium that brings together various regional interests, such as county councils and county administrative boards, the municipalities, business interests and universities. There are seven such centers, and most of them are run jointly by several counties. For example, SydSam is the information center in Brussel for the six southernmost county councils, regions and regional associations of local authorities. Together, these represent 2.3 million inhabitants. In 2004, SydSam had five employees in its Brussels office and two in its office in Kalmar, Sweden.

Typically, the information centers work both upstream and downstream. Upstream strategies aim at influencing decisions at an early stage of the process, for example when a new cohesion policy is about to take shape or a new EU directive is prepared. Downstream lobbying, on the other hand, relates to the implementation of decisions already taken by the EU institutions, for example to capture resources already allocated for specific purposes. Most of the activities of the Swedish information centers have a focus on downstream activities (Jerneck and Gidlund 2001). Among the regional information centers in Brussels, there is a clear difference in focus between, on the one hand, those representing Nordic regions and the smaller UK offices and, on the other hand, those acting on behalf of regions from federal or regionalized states. The Nordic and UK offices are more pragmatically oriented toward achieving funding and gathering information, whereas the latter are more actively lobbying politicians and representing the home region (Lein-Mathiesen, 2004).

Another form of regional cooperation is conferences on EU matters. An example is the regularly recurring conference for the four northernmost counties – *Europaforum Norra Sverige* – that brings together local, regional, national and European politicians, and representatives from the county administrative boards to discuss and develop common positions in European matters. A third example of regions cooperating around EU issues is the organization for decision-making on allocation of means from the EU Structural Funds and the special units that control how the resources have been used. These organizations are established jointly between several county councils and county administrative boards.

Regions also cooperate at the international level as members of international organizations with an EU focus. Perhaps the most important of these is the Association of European Regions (AER), with 270 member regions; 15 of the Swedish county councils and regional councils are currently members. One major task for the AER is to pursue a general regional interest vis-à-vis the EU. Both EU and non-EU regions from Europe can be members, but in recent years there has been a tendency for several regions from Western Europe to leave the organization while those from Eastern European countries have joined it. Hence, the AER is increasingly a vehicle for non-EU members to get access to EU decision-making. The AER-related activities of the Swedish regions are coordinated by one of the member regions.

Other international organizations that have a focus on influencing the decisions of the EU are also relevant for Swedish regions. Of particular relevance is the Conference of Peripheral and Maritime Regions (CPMR), in which ten of the 159 member regions are Swedish. The three largest Swedish cities are members of EUROCITIES, which is an interest organization for major cities in Europe.

In addition to the activities that the regions themselves are undertaking, either on their own or together with partners at regional, inter-regional or international level, there is also a national level of cooperation through which regions indirectly exert influence over EU decision-making. This function is performed by the Swedish Association of Local Authorities and Regions in which all municipalities, county councils and regions are members, and it is carried out mainly in three ways. First, the Association is involved in central government decision-making directed toward the EU. The links between the Swedish Association of Local Authorities and Regions and central government has developed significantly since Sweden became a member of the EU. The organization is involved in more than 20 preparatory committees, located within six different government departments. Various sections within the Association have regular contacts with relevant civil servants (Kommunförbundet/Landstingsförbundet 2001; Ansvarskommittén 2003). There seems to be no pressure in the other direction, i.e. central government does not appear to try to make local authorities act in a certain way, nor does it attempt to control or coordinate their activities.

Second, the Swedish Association of Local Authorities and Regions is represented in European organizations that are trying to influence EU decision-making. In certain organizations, such as the Council of European Municipalities and Regions (CEMR), the Association is itself a member. In the EU Committee of the Regions, which was established in 1993 with the purpose of strengthening the role of local and regional government in the EU, the 12 members from Sweden are selected by the Swedish Association of Local Authorities and Regions, even if they are formally appointed by the government. All 12 members are councilors, but only four of them are county councilors or members of regional assemblies and the rest are from the municipalities (Ronchetti 2005). This reflects the relative weight that the municipal interest has in Swedish politics. Finally, the Association has its own information office in Brussels. Its main purpose is to collect information that can be used by the Association in its EU-related activities but it has also developed an extensive network with EU institutions.

Hence, there are both direct and indirect ways for Swedish regions to influence the EU. Although engagement in EU issues is not a mandatory requirement, most regions are highly active in this field (Baldersheim et al. 2001. The typical strategy is to use several means in parallel to collect information, improve regional capacity and pursue the interests of the region. Initially, there was a certain amount of uneasiness about encountering a decision-making culture that was felt to be different from the Swedish model. During the first 10 years of Swedish membership, the actors learned from their initial mistakes and are now more skilled in knowing exactly how to work to achieve a particular purpose. Swedish regional inputs into the processes of EU decision-making have become much more sophisticated. Sweden has also shifted from a focus on extracting resources to a more general interest in EU matters (Berg and Lindahl 2007).

The European Union v. Swedish regions

Swedish regions attempt to influence decision-making in the EU because these decisions have important consequences for the regions. This section of the chapter will discuss three sets of consequences – the regions' experiences of EU laws and directives, the impact of the structural funds and the new ways of making policy at regional level that have emerged with EU membership.

When Sweden joined the EU it was generally believed that the consequences for municipalities and county councils would be fairly limited. It was expected that the EU would have an impact on market related activities, but not on the public welfare services that are the major functions of municipalities and county councils. According to the Swedish Agency for Public Management, which has evaluated the effects of the Swedish EU membership for municipalities and county councils, the effects have turned out to be more profound than envisaged. Local and regional authorities are often responsible for implementing policies and directives that are partly the results of EU decision-making (Statskontoret 2005). There has not been any radical reduction of regional self-government as a result of the introduction of EU regulation. However, in the field of public procurement, county councils and regions have been forced to accept stricter regulation, leaving practically no room for local and only limited room for environmental considerations when buying goods or services. For example, it is no longer possible to take transport distances into account when making such decisions. A new Public Procurement Act came into force already in 1994, i.e. before Sweden became an EU member. Although this Act was primarily an adjustment to EU regulations, it also set more stringent national standards by including tenders below the thresholds specified by the EU and including a wider range of services than these specified in the EC legislation (e.g. health care, social services, education and cultural services). As a consequence, public procurement is now more complex, requires more skilled personnel and has increased the administrative burden for local authorities (Svenska Kommunförbundet/Landstingsförbundet 2001; Ansvarskommittén 2003).

EU regulations aiming at improving the free movement of goods, people and services have had specific effects on medical care and health services – the main areas of responsibility for county councils and regions. For example, EU support for the free movement of labor has made it easier for employees to get their qualifications recognized outside their own country. For the Swedish county councils and regions, this has made it easier to recruit doctors from abroad, but it has also meant a net loss of nurses to countries that pay better wages. Another example is that the EU has created a system that compensates county councils when they offer medical care to people from other countries. A new system of authorizing drugs has also been introduced. If just one member country accepts a new drug, it is automatically authorized in all EU countries. This has put additional pressure on the county councils and made it necessary to set up a special governmental agency to evaluate the cost-effectiveness of drugs (Statskontoret 2005).

Indirectly, county councils are also affected by the gradual adjustment to EU alcohol policies. Traditionally in Sweden, access to alcoholic beverages has been restricted by taxation, import limitations and state monopolies for sales and retail. From 2004, anyone entering Sweden was permitted to bring the full EU ration of alcohol. This has put pressure on Sweden to reduce the taxes on alcohol purchased in the country. The increase in alcohol consumption in Sweden has been dramatic since the mid-1990s, with consequences for the health system and the county councils.

A softer form of EU coordination of local and regional activities within areas that are outside the EU's responsibilities is 'the open method of coordination'. Here the aim is to develop common views and strategies together with the national level and other levels of government that are responsible for a particular policy area. However, participation is voluntary. So far, the method has not had any substantial effect on the county councils, but it may have an impact on health and medical services in the future. The economic consequences for local authorities of EU membership are difficult to assess, as many of the effects are indirect. It is likely that the stricter regulation of public procurement has reduced costs, but on the other hand the costs for administration seem to have increased. The previously mentioned way of authorizing new drugs together with the increase in alcohol-related problems has contributed to rising costs for county councils. In 1993, the Swedish parliament established the 'principle of finance', which means that central government will provide the extra resources required if it gives local authorities new functions (Loughlin et al. 2005). EU regulation has resulted in more tasks without financial compensation for local government, but it is not clear to what extent this should be regarded as a violation of the principle of finance (Statskontoret 2005).

Perhaps the most significant effect of EU membership for many Swedish regions is the additional resources for regional development that have been provided by the structural funds. During the period 2000–2006, Sweden has received €2.19 billion for this purpose. Most support ends up in the countryside, in particular in the sparsely populated northern parts of Sweden, whereas the large cities generally get the least. EU funding is complemented by local and regional co-financing by municipalities, the county council/region and the county administrative board. The structural funds have contributed to changing the focus of Swedish regional policies. From having been mainly redistributive, they are now increasingly emphasizing that regions should develop their own assets. Hence, EU membership has facilitated a shift toward one of the aspects of new regionalism (Keating and Loughlin 1997; Keating 1998) in a country that traditionally has relied heavily on redistributive regional policies (Gren 2002; Hudson 2005).

Apart from effects in terms of local self-government and the funding of regional development, Swedish membership of the EU has also introduced new ways of making policy. Since the 1930s, Swedish policy-making at national level has been characterized by an active involvement of affected interests – in particular trade unions and employers' organizations – which has often been referred to as corporatism (Gustafsson 1995). Contacts between the government, the major trade unions and big business have been frequent. The various interests have been involved during different stages of policy-making – preparations, decision-making and implementation. With EU membership, emphasis on coordination at the local and regional levels has become much more pronounced. As support from the structural funds has required that other public and private interests are willing to contribute, partnerships have been created between various actors for joint projects. Compared with traditional corporatism, these partnerships have a clearer focus on the joint mobilization of resources, and are more concerned with regional development issues. Further, corporatism was more controlled by the state whereas partnerships are looser networks of independent actors.

Another example of the adaptation to a more 'European' style of decision-making was the introduction of regional growth agreements in 1998. Central government resources for regional development were pooled with public and private means at the regional level through a formal agreement. The county administrative boards were responsible for the process, but priorities were set after negotiations between different regional and local interests – business organizations, voluntary associations, universities, municipalities, the county council, etc. In order to get access to the resources from central government, these interests had to come to an agreement that represented a consensus view on how the region should be developed (Svensson and Östhol 2001; Hudson 2006). Emphasis was put on enhancing the unique traits of each region and on regional mobilization. However, there are also signs that central government is using the agreements to retain their control over regional development (Hudson 2005).

Clearly, Europeanization has brought the different regional actors together in closer cooperation. As summarized by a local politician:

> During all my 30 years in politics, cooperation in the region has never worked as well as now. The main reason for this is that international activities have narrowed the gap between county councils and municipalities. Membership has led to closer and more useful contacts, and the joint Brussels office has been a great help in this respect.
> (Svenska Kommunförbundet/Landstingsförbundet 2001: 13)

The EU's emphasis on the regional level has contributed to reshaping the Swedish county map. For several decades, numerous attempts were made to redraw county borders, but with few exceptions central government had been unwilling to accept any changes. However, with the additional pressure from the EU, and its emphasis on the regional level, it eventually became possible for the counties and municipalities in Skåne and Västra Götaland to establish their new regions (Gren 2002). A more comprehensive regionalization reform is expected to be implemented in 2015.

Attitudes toward the European Union

The conclusion so far is that Swedish regions are becoming more affected by decisions taken by the EU, but are also actively trying to influence these decisions. At regional level, much of this activism is limited to a policy community of regional politicians, chief administrators and professional specialists. Hence, the process is basically elite-driven, and only affects to a limited extent the daily activities of the county councils or the county administrative boards. Within these policy communities, attitudes toward the EU are generally very positive. However, is a different picture found among other politicians and the general public? Are there any signs indicating that the closer links between regions and the EU are also reflected in the attitudes of citizens and politicians, and are there differences between regions in this respect?

The most accurate measures of Swedish EU opinion are, of course, the two referendums on EU matters that have been held. In November 1994, the Swedes voted on membership in the Union and in September 2003 the question concerned whether Sweden should adopt the euro as its currency. In the first referendum, 52 per cent voted for Swedish membership but in the second, a majority of 56 per cent rejected the idea of a common currency. Surveys at the time of the Euro referendum show that almost everybody who was against EU membership voted for retaining the *Krona*. In addition, 20 per cent of the EU supporters also voted against the euro (Sollander and Öhrvall 2004).

Swedish citizens have been among the most EU-skeptical of all citizens in the EU. From 1995 to 2001, most Swedes were against the EU, and it was not until around 2001–2002 that a shift occurred. During the last few years, there has been a popular majority in favor of Swedish membership (Lindahl 2005).

Swedish citizens are much more critical of the EU than their elected representatives. Surveys in 1997 indicated that a majority of the voters were in favor of leaving the EU, but their elected representatives wanted to stay. However, there were major differences between categories of politicians. Members of parliament were most in favor of retaining membership, support was less strong among county councilors and it was weakest, though still positive, among municipal councilors (Petersson et al. 1997). Could it be that closeness to the local area fosters a more EU-skeptical attitude, whereas responsibility for larger entities, such as regions and nations, is conducive for more favorable views on the EU?

The shift in sentiment among the general public is also detected by the citizen surveys carried out by Statistics Sweden (responsible for producing official statistics). However, there are interesting differences and similarities between the regions. Table 9.1 summarizes the biannual development in support for the EU since Sweden became a member, at both national and regional levels.

Increasing support for the EU is also a feature at regional level. In Table 9.1, Sweden has been divided into ten statistical regions, each comprising a major city or a number of counties. In practically all of these regions, the pattern of change is the same: there has been a gradual but very significant increase in support for the EU with the exception of a temporary drop in 2003. The developments follow the same directions in the different

Table 9.1   National and regional variations in support for the EU 1997–2005

	1997	1999	2001	2003	2005	2007
National averages						
For the EU	32.1	38.9	42.7	44.4	42.3	50.2
Against the EU	51.0	42.2	37.1	35.5	34.9	24.0
Net EU opinion	−18.9	−3.3	+5.6	+8.9	+7.4	+26.2
Regional variations in support for the EU:						
Greater Malmö	45.7	49.0	57.6	57.6	53.2	62.4
Southern Sweden excl. Malmö	34.1	36.8	46.3	44.5	40.4	50.1
Southern highlands (Småland)	31.2	36.1	36.9	38.6	41.1	47.3
Göteborg	38.1	43.9	51.4	50.4	50.3	56.3
West Sweden excl. Göteborg	28.8	36.1	39.4	41.1	38.9	49.9
Stockholm	48.9	55.9	59.7	58.9	57.7	64.3
Stockholm county excl. Stockholm	38.9	51.2	52.4	52.6	54.3	61.0
Eastern mid Sweden	30.7	37.9	39.4	42.8	39.2	46.5
Northern mid Sweden	21.6	28.8	33.1	37.3	33.0	40.8
Mid and upper northern Sweden	22.3	27.6	30.1	33.5	29.3	34.6

Source: Statistics Sweden: Partisympatiundersökningen (PSU).[2]

parts of the country. This seems to indicate that the reasons for these changes are national, rather than specific to the individual regions.

There are striking differences with regard to the levels of EU support between the regions. It is strongest in the three largest cities and in the greater Stockholm area. In the rest of the country, there is a clear north-south cleavage: the closer the region is to Brussels, the more positive are the attitudes toward the EU. Hence, support for the EU varies in Sweden, between the major cities and the countryside and between north and south. It is almost twice as likely that a Stockholmer will be positive to the EU as someone from the far north. The differences are very distinct and they appear to be consistent over time. The same pattern emerged in the two referendums.

In part, these variations reflect differences in the demographic compositions of the regions. According to Oscarsson (2004) variations between citizens' EU attitudes are largely captured by an extended center-periphery dichotomy, where not only the geographical location is included, but also the person's socio-economic status. Apart from living in the big cities or in the south, supporters of EU membership typically have high incomes, are well-educated, work for central government or in the private sector and have international contacts. Those that are against the EU live in the countryside or in the north, have low incomes and have spent less time in education, are local government employees and have few international contacts. However, the differences between the regions are only partly explained by the socio-economic characteristics of their citizens. There is something else that makes the northerners more skeptical and the people from the large cities more positive.

The same north-south divide in support for the EU can also be found in the two neighboring countries of Finland and Norway (Detlef and Storsved 1995; Pettersen 1996). In the Finnish referendum in October 1994, most people voted for membership in the EU. However, there were majorities against membership in the six northernmost counties but a net support in the southern parts. In Norway, where the people voted against EU membership, the yes-side still captured a majority of the votes in the five counties closest to Oslo. The differences between various parts of the country were more pronounced than in Sweden. In Finnmark in the very north, only 26 per cent supported membership, compared to 67 per cent in Oslo.

Contrary to what one would have expected, support for the Union in Sweden has not increased more in those areas that received the greatest financial contributions from the EU Structural Funds. Money does seem to pay off in terms of political support from the general public. Structural Funds may be an appropriate way of stimulating regional development, but they do not make people outside the major cities and in the north happier about the EU. Again, this supports the previous observation that the change in EU attitudes among the general public that has taken place during the last 10 years is a general, national tendency, and is not influenced by specific regional traits.

There is an interesting difference between the citizens' and the regional politicians' attitudes in this respect. A study of regional politicians in the Nordic countries, undertaken in 1997–1998, indicates that in counties that receive structural fund support from the EU, the politicians have stronger regionalist attitudes. This refers to a more pronounced pro-EU sentiment, a belief that regions should cooperate with each other across national borders and that regions should have a greater influence over national decision-making (Baldersheim et al. 2001).

Unfortunately, there are no more recent studies available of regional politicians' attitudes toward the EU. However, it seems obvious that, particularly in the northern and rural parts of Sweden, there is a gap between the aspirations of the regional politicians and the attitudes of the general public. The politicians are EU-enthusiasts whereas the citizens are skeptics. As long as there are benefits such as financial support from the structural funds, the former have good arguments for continuing their efforts, but if the level of support is reduced, as has happened in the Structural Fund period starting in 2007, it may be more difficult to justify why the region should be active in EU matters. On the other hand, perhaps the lack of resources is an even stronger argument for involvement, as peripheral regions are likely to be more vulnerable when they have to take full responsibility for their own future development.

Conclusion

Swedish regions are gradually becoming more sophisticated actors in the policy-making processes of the EU. As they are gaining experience of the decision-making culture in Brussels, and learning from their initial attempts, they develop more focused strategies to reach their objectives. These include collecting information, building organizational capacity and influencing decisions. Various regional interests are working together and they use a broad range of both direct and indirect means. At the national level, the Swedish Association of Local Authorities and Regions plays an important role in enhancing the common interests of Swedish local authorities.

There are good reasons for regions to be involved. They are directly affected by EU laws and directives, for example in the field of public procurement, but are also increasingly experiencing indirect effects, such as the pressure on the medical services that has been caused by the liberalization of alcohol regulations. Regions may also be recipients of financial resources through the structural funds. They have learnt new ways of making policy at regional level, which involves closer cooperation between different public and private interests.

During the years of Swedish membership in the EU, Swedish citizens have gradually become more positive to the Union. Since 2001, those in favor of the Union outnumber those who are against it. There are, however, considerable regional differences. The enthusiasts are to be found in the largest cities and in the south, whereas citizens further north tend to be skeptical. There is no obvious connection between being a financial beneficiary of the EU, and a more positive attitude toward the Union. Citizens in regions that receive resources from the Structural Funds have not become more positive than those living in the rest of the country.

Generally, Swedish regions are no different from regions in other countries in trying to influence EU decision-making and in adjusting to the preconditions that the Union sets for how they can carry out their responsibilities. Most of the processes described in this overview are experienced by regions in many other EU countries. However, because of the history of the country, and specific regional circumstances, some features make the relationship between the Swedish regions and the EU unique.

First, some of the challenges associated with the EU have been particularly demanding for regions in a unitary, corporatist state with extensive public welfare commitments. The unitary character of the state is challenged by a diversity of different regional solutions. Corporatism is being replaced by public-private partnerships at regional level and multi-level governance. The welfare systems, for example the health and medical services, are constantly in focus in a EU debate aiming at creating more scope for private providers and increased competition.

Second, compared with many other European countries, the regional level in Sweden has traditionally been weak. It is situated between a strong national level and highly significant municipalities. In contrast, the regional level is fragmented with several institutional actors. Some of the functions of these actors are overlapping and they have also different types of democratic legitimacy. None of them has an obvious leading role. Therefore, the EU focus on the regional level has required the regional actors to improve cooperation and coordination. A policy community of leading politicians, chief administrators and specialists has reduced fragmentation.

Third, although the Swedes have become more positive about the EU, there is still a considerable majority against EU membership in many rural areas and in particular in the very north. However, the key regional decision-makers tend to be fairly enthusiastic about the EU. In the northern counties, the majority is doubtful about the EU, despite the benefits these areas have received from the Structural Funds system.

It is not likely that these traits will remain unchanged in the future. Closer cooperation between Swedish regions and the EU will contribute to a gradual transformation of the Swedish system of government. The regions are likely to be highly affected in this process. In the distant future, it is even possible that the Swedes in the most remote areas will be in favor of the EU.

Notes

* I am grateful for valuable comments on previous versions of this chapter from Åsa Edman at the Ministry of Finance, Håkan Ottosson at the Swedish Association of Local Authorities and Regions and Inge Andersson at the North Sweden European Office in Brussels.

1. Throughout the chapter, both county and region will be used as labels for the intermediate level. When specific reference is made to the two regions of Skåne and Västra Götaland, which have more extensive tasks than the county councils, this will be emphasized in the text.
2. Data from the PSU-study, carried out by Statistics Sweden. In each survey, a random sample of approximately 9000 Swedish inhabitants was interviewed. The response rate was approximately 80 per cent. The respondents were asked: 'On the whole, are you for or against Swedish membership of the EU, or do you have no opinion in the matter?'

10
Estonian Regions and the European Union: Between Transformation and Europeanization

Tarvo Kungla

Introduction

Estonian public administration has undergone considerable changes since the end of 1980s. On the one hand, after the fall of the Soviet Union and the restoration of Estonia's independence in 1991, the whole system of public administration has gone through a process of transformation from communism to a free market democracy. In fact, democratic structures were first introduced at the level of the local and regional government and only later at the level of the state. Measured in terms of the scope and number of changes, the period of transformation of public administration has continued well into the mid-1990s. On the other hand, in aiming for EU membership, Estonia has had to adapt its institutions and policies to the requirements of the *acquis communautaire*. The accession negotiations with the European Union (EU) influenced the development of the Estonian public administration from the beginning of the negotiations in 1997 (Viks 2002).

The dynamic institutional context of transition of Central and Eastern European (CEE) countries makes these countries especially interesting from the perspective of the study of Europeanization. The concepts and theories of Europeanization developed in the context of Western European countries can be analyzed in a new institutional and policy environment. Nevertheless, the context of democratic transformation makes it more difficult to distinguish domestic factors driving change from Europeanization and other external factors. The context of transformation certainly needs to be taken into account while analyzing the impact of Europeanization in the Estonian case.

As in other CEE countries, local and regional structures in Estonia have undergone a considerable change since the collapse of the communist system. Whereas the general legal-institutional framework of local and regional government has not changed much since 1993, there is still an ongoing discussion on changing it. In the cases of some transformation countries (e.g. Poland, Hungary), it has been demonstrated that Europeanization has shaped regional-level institution building (Hughes et al. 2001; Kungla 2002). The main aim of this chapter is to analyze the impact of the EU on regional-level institution building in Estonia. The focus will be on the period of accession negotiations and the resulting domestic changes following the adoption of the *acquis communautaire*. The second part of the chapter gives an overview of the role of the Estonian sub-national actors in the multi-level governance system of the EU (Hooghe and Marks 2001), analyzing their involvement at EU level and in national level EU politics.

The development and powers of local and regional government in Estonia

There is no history of federalism or strong regional identities in Estonia. Nevertheless, regions as self-government units in a modern democratic sense (*maakonnad*) existed from 1918 till 1934. In 1934 legislation was passed by the Estonian parliament that provided for the replacement of self-government at the regional level by state administration (Olle 2001). Democratic structures at local and regional levels were abolished with the outbreak of World War II and the subsequent occupation regimes. During the Soviet occupation, local and regional administration became part of the communist state administration modelled according to Marxist-Leninist principles (Illner 2002).

The collapse of the communist system seemed like a promising opportunity for the revival of self-government both at local and regional levels. With the changing political climate in the Soviet Union at the end of 1980s, a gradual political opening became possible (Uibopuu 1991; Lieven 1993; Norgaard and Johannsen 1999). In fact, the first political reform was the introduction of democratic local government. The first local level democratic elections were held in December 1989. A month before the elections were held, the basic framework for the new local and regional government system was established with the Law of the Foundations of Local Government. This law foresaw the introduction of a two-level local governmental system. The primary administrative level was formed by municipalities (*vallad*), boroughs and cities (*alevid, linnad*); the secondary level was formed by 15 counties (*maakonnad*) and six independent cities (*vabariikilikud linnad*) (Mäeltsemees 2000). The law also provided for the introduction of self-government at the regional level, with the main impetus for establishing self-government both at local and regional levels being a desire to devolve power to sub-national levels.

The two-level local government system, however, was maintained only until the adoption of the Estonian Constitution, and following changes in the local government legislation, in 1993. Three factors account for this change (Kettunen and Kungla 2005). First, despite the fact that in the early days of the transformation period county-level leaders had been supportive of institution building at the local level, by the beginning of the 1990s a more conflictual relationship had developed between both levels. Local government leaderships began to view the regions in competitive terms and advocated the reduction of their powers. Second, there was a general perception among the politicians that Estonia is too small a country for an entrenched regional level of government.

A third factor was the issue of Russian minorities. In pre-war Estonia, ethnic minorities constituted only about 12 per cent of the total population (Taagepera and Misiunas 1983). The situation changed during the Soviet period. As a result of Moscow's industrialization policies, people from other Soviet republics were resettled to Estonia. As a result, by the time independence had been restored, Russian-speaking minorities constituted approximately 36 per cent of the Estonian population, with these minorities concentrated in the north-eastern part of the country, as well as in the capital (Bungs 1998).

This large proportion of Russian-speaking minorities, combined with their geographical concentration in a few areas (in the case of Estonia's third largest city, Narva, they constitute an overwhelming majority of more than 90 per cent), created considerable potential for the emergence of regionalist demands. In July 1993, a referendum on regional autonomy was organized by the Narva and Sillamäe municipal authorities. This referendum, aimed at establishing an autonomous region in Estonia, was declared anti-constitutional by the constitutional chamber of the Estonian State Court. Since that time, the incumbent right-wing Conservative government under Prime Minister Mart Laar, as well as its successors, have ensured that regional government has not become a venue for articulating the demands of the more radical representatives of the Russian-speaking minority.

Against this backdrop, the arguments against a strong regional level of government prevailed in the discussions of the Estonian Constitution and the subsequent legislation on regional and local government. The Estonian Constitution, adopted by referendum in 1992, implies a one-level local government system. The introduction of other levels of local government is left open. More specifically, Article 155, Section 2 states that '... other units of local government [beyond municipalities and towns] may be formed in accordance with the bases and procedures established by law' (Kettunen and Kungla 2005).

Thus, the regional level of self-government was abolished altogether. Regional self-government units were transformed into general-purpose state administrative units led by county governors (*maavanemad*). County governors were appointed by the central government on a proposal by the prime minister and in concordance with the representatives of local governments of the respective county. Similarily to the French *préfet*, the most important task of a county governor is to represent the interests of the central government in the county. S/he is responsible for the supervision of local government activities. In the context of regional development, county governors should provide for the comprehensive and balanced development of the county. So, on the one hand, as a representative of central government, he/she must ensure that the interests of the state are taken into account in the regions; on the other hand, he/she must act as an advocate of local government interests at the central level. The latter role is underscored by the requirement that candidates for county governorships enjoy the support of the local governments within the counties concerned (Kettunen and Kungla 2005).

County governments are certainly not the only actors at the intermediate level. Regional governance structures are much more complex, involving other state and non-state actors. Notably, there are a number of central government agencies covering different jurisdictions that do not necessarily overlap with the counties; among them tax offices, immigration and citizenship departments, and statistics bureaus. Crucially, with regards to discussions about the future of regional governance in Estonia, regional associations of municipalities also exist, drawing together participating municipality representatives. These associations were established on a voluntary basis by the municipalities and lack a clear-cut legal basis. Although they have been assigned certain tasks by law, such as the evaluation of local civil servants and consulting with the government in the appointment of the county governor, the scope of their tasks remains relatively narrow. In addition to the functions conferred upon them by law, the regional associations of municipalities have been assigned competencies in the fields of education and development (Kaldmäe et al. 1999).

While the importance of regional government has decreased both in terms of its legal-constitutional status and tasks, the municipal level has clearly become the most important sub-national level of government. Local government fulfills a number of important public administration tasks in the areas of education, the social sphere and local infrastructure. The most costly tasks undertaken by local government include the construction, operation and maintenance of primary and secondary schools, kindergartens and art schools, sport facilities, houses of culture and community centers; vocational, hobby and sports schools; and capital investment and maintenance for municipal hospitals and polyclinics as well as maintenance of local networks and town streets. Notwithstanding their wide range of tasks, the proportion of public expenditures managed by Estonian local government is less than is enjoyed by its counterparts in the Nordic countries. Whereas in Estonia about 19 per cent of public expenditure is managed by local governments, the corresponding figure for Norway is 35 per cent (indeed, in Norway the municipal and regional levels are jointly responsible for 50 per cent of total public expenditure) (LGDK 2002). There are currently 227 local government units in Estonia: 194 rural municipalities and 33 towns.

Europeanization and territorial government reform

In several CEE countries EU Enlargement has played an important role as the catalyst of *regionalization* processes (Hughes et al. 2001; Kungla 2002). In particular, the *acquis communautaire* had significant implications for the territorial structures of the candidate countries. It contained an extra chapter on EU Regional Policy (Chapter 21: 'Regional Policy and Coordination of Structural Funds'). The CEE candidate countries had to demonstrate that their arrangements were in line with the principles of EU regional policy, match their territorial structures to the NUTS classification, ensure the implementation of the 'partnership' principle, and demonstrate that they have the 'administrative capacity' necessary for implementation (Arnswald 2000). The following sections analyze the impact of the EU accession on the debate around regionalization in Estonia, as well as the changes resulting from the country's adaptation to the EU's regional policy.

Regionalization and Europeanization

The reform of local government, and to a lesser extent regional government, has always been on the agenda of Estonian government since the regaining of independence. Almost every government since the mid-1990s has developed its own plan to redraw the boundaries of local governments. Perhaps the most radical proposal was put forward by the then minister of regional affairs, Toivo Asmer, during the period of the Reform Party (*Reformierakond*), Pro Patria Party (*Isamaaliit*) and Moderate Party (*Mõõdukad*) coalition government. It envisaged the creation of 15 + five local government units on the basis of the current counties and the five largest cities (Huang 2001).

In most instances, these plans have emerged as initiatives of the responsible ministers without commanding the support of the coalition partners or even of their own party. Whereas during the first half of the period, well up to the end of the 1990s, the discussion focused more on amalgamating local governments, more recently decision-makers have begun to treat the issue in a wider context, and have also been thinking about territorial governance in general. The following paragraphs will survey the more recent discussion on local and regional level reform from the point of view of Europeanization.

Reform discussions gained additional momentum under the three-party (Reform Party, People's Union and Res Publica) coalition government that was in power from March 2003 till March 2005. Their coalition agreement foresaw the strengthening of the local government level, by providing local government with sustainable independent revenues and transferring more tasks to them according to principles of the European Charter of Local Self-Government. It was also suggested that some self-government functions should be transferred to local government. In contrast, only lip service was paid to the regional level, saying that the county level will be reorganized and that its efficiency should be increased.[1] Taken all round, therefore, the coalition agreement appeared to promote a bottom-up model of regional governance, cutting back the powers of state administration, facilitating cooperation between the local governments and strengthening the role of associations of local government (Kettunen and Kungla 2005).

In October 2003, a reform plan for regional administration was worked out by the Ministry of Interior. At the heart of the plan was the creation of a regional level – *maakogu* – consisting of local government representatives: the reform may in fact be best understood regarded as involving the upgrading of the local government associations (Estonian Ministry of Interior 2003; Õunapuu 2003a, 2003b). This proposed reform reflects a new approach to dealing with the fragmented local government system aimed at ensuring the efficient and effective provision of public services. 'European' arguments were used to bolster support for the proposals in the subsequent public discussion. For example, it was argued that the new regions would be in a better position to absorb EU funds (Kivimägi 2003). In a similar vein, it was emphasized that the reform would create units able to act as project partners for sub-national actors from other EU countries (Allik 2003).

The necessary legislation was to be adopted within a year, meaning that the *maakogud* could convene as early as 1 November 2004. Due to disagreement between the coalition partners, however, the implementation of the reform was postponed and ultimately, of the three coalition parties, only one, the People's Union (*Rahvaliit*), eventually approved the proposed reform. The delays in implementing the reform even induced the minister of regional affairs to threaten resignation if no agreement were achieved. The whole reform of regional government had, though, been foreshadowed by disagreements between the coalition parties concerning the nomination of new county governors (Kettunen and Kungla 2005).

In spring 2004, the coalition parties reached a consensus to change the status of county governments. County governors were now to be appointed by the government upon the recommendation of the minister of regional affairs. The second very important change was the strengthening of the supervisory functions of the Ministry of Interior over the county level. These changes were controversial with opposition forces in parliament, who accused the government of concentrating too much power on the Ministry of Interior. It was also pointed out that this change would strengthen the role of the Ministry of Interior as a mediator between the county governments and other parts of the central government. There certainly can be no doubt that the status of county governments has been downgraded by this change (Kettunen and Kungla 2005).

The government coalition broke up in March 2005 and further plans to modernize local and regional government contained in the coalition agreement were not realized. The plans of the new government (made up of the Reform Party, People's Union and Centre Party) for local and regional government reform did not differ much from the ideas of its predecessor. It advocated the strengthening of local governments, the increasing of their independence and revenue basis and the strengthening of inter-municipal cooperation.[2] However, there have been no further changes thus far.

A more 'technical', expert-level discussion has always taken place in behind the public debate of these 'big-picture' issues. This is a discussion of the relative merits of special-purpose v. general-purpose administration at the regional level. Appealing to the principle of 'ministerial responsibility' and the need to supervise policies in their area of responsibility, ministries have insisted on their right to intervene or interfere directly in policy implementation. In this light, county governors have been viewed as small or minor 'rulers' who obstruct the efforts of ministers to ensure the smooth implementation of policies within their own territories. County governments have proven to be particularly vulnerable to their critics because of their inadequate legitimation. Despite that, their powers and responsibilities have not been dramatically reduced even if some competencies in the field of environmental policy have been removed. Taking effect on 1 January 2000, the environment departments of county governments were reorganized into environmental agencies directly under the Ministry of Environment. Although it does not follow from the debates in the Estonian parliament that 'European' arguments have played a role in introducing this change, the Estonian National Programme for the Adoption of the Acquis 2000 mentions this measure as providing for more administrative capacity to ensure the implementation of the EU legislation in the field of environmental policy (State Chancellery, Office of European Integration 2000).

Notwithstanding the general trend in the other CEECs, it is clear that there were no significant developments in regional-level institution building in Estonia during the EU accession negotiations. The discussion on the reform of regional-level governance has been overshadowed by a debate over the future role of local government. Although 'European' arguments have certainly been deployed in discussions on the reform of the regional level, they are best regarded as providing additional support or buttressing for arguments stressing the need to reduce the number of counties, rather than as significant arguments in their own right (cf. Committee of the Regions 2000).

Adaptations to the EU regional policy

The requirements of the regional policy chapter of the *acquis communautaire* have been often cited as a triggering factor of regional institution building in the new member states (Hughes et al. 2001). It is true that in the Estonian case, a more coherent approach to regional development – as well as the necessary institutional framework – developed only in the second half of the 1990s, i.e. parallel to the accession negotiations. However, in Estonia this institution building has taken place mostly at the level of central government.

In its 1998 progress report, the European Commission recognized progress made since the beginning of the transformation period, while also pointing out significant shortcomings. In particular, it emphasized the need to improve the coordination of sectoral policies and to strengthen administrative and budgetary capabilities. As a result the Estonian government took steps to align the country's regional policy with EU regional policy. In 1999 it adopted a new Regional Development Strategy that attempted to reinforce the process. Subsequently, new legislation was also passed allowing for the co-financing and multi-annual programming of budgetary expenditure. In order to streamline its efforts to monitor the effectiveness of regional development measures, the State Regional Policy Council was established in December 2000. Under the chairmanship of the minister of regional affairs, this body included representatives of all ministries, two elected county governors, representatives of local government associations and the Office of European Integration of the State Chancellery (European Commission 2001).

In April 2001, the Estonian government set out the basic principles for the implementation of the European Structural Funds and the Cohesion Fund Support, as well as an action plan in preparation for European Structural and Cohesion Funding. The Ministry of Finance was given overall responsibility for programming and was designated as the future managing authority for the Objective 1 Single Programming Document (SPD). It would coordinate the drafting of the SPD in consultation with other ministries. In line with the Council Regulation 1260/1999 Art. 8, social partners including local governments and county governments as well as interest groups were also involved into the process. The social partners were determined on the basis of lists submitted by the ministries. In preparing the SPD for the period 2003–2006, social partners were consulted twice. In addition, the SPD was presented to the public at large on numerous occasions (Ministry of Finance of the Republic of Estonia 2003).

The Ministry of Finance was also designated the managing authority of the Single Programming Document and charged with monitoring its implementation. In addition, several single-purpose authorities were assigned as implementing authorities responsible for the pre-selection of projects to be forwarded to the Evaluation Committee (Ministry of Finance of the Republic of Estonia 2003).

Finally, at a relatively late stage of the accession negotiations, Estonian territory was matched with the NUTS system. With roughly 1.4 million inhabitants and an area of 45,227 km^2, Estonia is a very small country. It was therefore agreed at the outset of the accession negotiations that the whole country should be considered as a NUTS 2 unit. More controversial was which level should correspond to the NUTS level 3 units. The delineation submitted by the Estonian government to the EUROSTAT in April 2001 proposed the division of the country into five NUTS 3 units: north Estonia, covering Harju County, central, north-east, west and south Estonia. The counties were seen as corresponding to NUTS 4 regions (Ruubel 2002).

In contrast to those Central and Eastern European countries that have organized their regionalization plans around the NUTS classifications (Pozun 2001; Kungla 2002), these five units, all above the county level, remained purely statistical regions.

It seems that throughout the accession negotiations the European Commission stressed the need for necessary structures and administrative capacity at the central government level, and put less emphasis on ensuring the involvement of sub-national levels in the implementation of the policy. Central government ministries, and in particular the Ministry of Finance, dominated all phases of regional policy decision-making, assigning local and regional actors only a subordinate role. From this point of view, Estonia has followed the lead of many other older member states of the EU where the influence of sub-national levels in the implementation of EU regional policy has been characterized as low or insignificant (Marks 1996).

Estonian regions and local government at the EU level

As Estonian county governments are subordinated to the central government and form part of the state administration, they are not much involved in international networks. It is rather Estonian local government that have been more active at the international and European levels. Numerous Estonian local government units have partner local authorities abroad, the majority of them being located in Northern or Baltic countries.[3]

Under the Estonian Law on the Foundations of Local Government, local governments are allowed to join their respective international organizations or develop cooperation with them. Although the government has not explicitly encouraged these kinds of activities, it seems to have a positive attitude toward local and regional governments' 'soft' networking at the European level. The government's paper on the principles of Estonian Government's EU Policy for 2004–2006 states that:

> Estonia considers it necessary to support the active participation of local governments and regional authorities as well as independent associations and social partners at the European Union level through the Committee of the Regions, the European Economic and Social Committee or through trans-European non-governmental organisations network.[4]

Thus far it is only the capital that has established its own 'one-man office' in Brussels. Other local government units rely on representing their interests at the EU level collectively via the unions of local authorities.

There are two major local government unions in Estonia that maintain numerous international contacts. The first is the Association of Estonian Cities (AEC). The AEC was originally founded in 1920 to represent common interests and facilitate cooperation between cities and rural municipalities. One of the tasks of the association is to support cooperation and twinning agreements with local governments and their associations abroad, as well as with international organizations. Thus, the AEC is a member of the International Union of Local Authorities (IUL) the Council of European Municipalities and Regions (CEMR), the Congress of Local and Regional Authorities of the Council of Europe (CLRAE), the Baltic Sea States Sub-Regional Cooperation (BSSSC) and the Joint Consultative Committee of the Committee of the Regions (CoR).

The second union of local government units in Estonia is the Association of Municipalities of Estonia that was originally founded in 1921. Like Association of Estonian Cities, the Association of Municipalities of Estonia represents the interests of its members at the international level.

In October 2005, the two associations opened a joint office in Brussels. The main aim of the office is to represent the interests of Estonian local authorities in the EU's legislation, funding and policy-making processes, as well providing a direct communication channel to EU institutions, organizations and networks. In more detail, the tasks of the permanent representative in Brussels are:

1) to represent the Association of Municipalities of Estonia and the Association of Estonian Cities and present their positions in Brussels;
2) to participate in meetings, conferences, seminars and information events to gather information on current and future policies, legislation and programs from EU institutions with direct implications for local authorities;
3) to provide Estonian local authorities up-to-date information on EU developments of specific relevance for them through – *inter alia* – the circulation of a weekly newsletter;
4) to develop cooperation with other local and regional representations in Brussels;
5) to coordinate the work of the Estonian members of the EU Committee of the Regions. Estonia has seven members in the CoR with the Association of Estonian Cities proposing four members and the Association of Municipalities of Estonia proposing the remaining three;
6) to organize meetings and seminars in Brussels for representatives of the national associations of local authorities; and,
7) to offer support in building transnational partnerships.[5]

In a nutshell, the Brussels Office of the Association of Municipalities of Estonia and the Association of Estonian Cities performs two functions typical of the EU offices of sub-national governments from the other member states: representing the interests of its members at the European level and informing the members about the relevant policy developments at the EU level. The bureau consists of one person based permanently in Brussels. Office facilities are shared with the Brussels office of the city of Tallinn. Apart from representing their interests directly at the European level, Estonian local governments can also use indirect channels to try to influence EU policy-making. Potentially at least, they can attempt to influence the formulation of the Estonian position on EU issues at the national level. The main body in charge of the coordination of Estonian position on EU policies is the Coordination Council of EU issues. It coordinates the views of different ministries with regards Estonia's positions in EU decision-making proposes and prepares the ground for government meetings concerning EU issues, as well as monitoring implementation of the *acquis communautaire*.

In principle, local government should be involved at the level of the working groups in the ministries to discuss matters falling under their sphere of responsibility (such as the environment, social policy, transport and so on). There is, however, no solid legal ground for involving local government and the regions in consultations even when their interests are at stake. In general, it is up to the respective ministries whether they want to involve and take into account the interests of local government and the regions. In practice there have been very few instances of such involvement. While both the ministries and local government may initiate local government involvement in such debates, thus far local government unions have not been very particularly pro-active in promoting such consultation.[6]

Conclusion

The restoration of independence seemed set to facilitate the revival of self-government at the regional level in Estonia. In 1989 self-government was indeed introduced both at local and regional levels. However, Estonian regions failed to establish themselves as significant actors during the first years of the transformation. Conflicts emerged between the local and regional levels. In addition, emerging tensions between Estonians and Russian-speaking minorities concentrated in the capital and north-eastern part of the country, made politically strong regions impossible to achieve. When it came to the adoption of the Estonian Constitution in 1992, regional self-governments were abolished altogether and replaced with general-purpose state administrative units.

In contrast to several other Central and Eastern European countries, the accession negotiations with the EU did not contribute to the revival of the debate on regionalization in Estonia. Rather, Estonia has matched its institutions to the requirements of the EU regional policy by making only minimal changes to its system of local and regional governance.

As Estonian county governments are state administrative units and there is no directly elected regional level, moreover, regions play only a weak role both in terms of Estonia's EU policy-making as well as at the European level itself. It is rather local government that is more active regarding the EU. Like their counterparts in other EU member states, Estonian local government unions have established a presence in Brussels which acts as an upstream and downstream communication hub for the Estonian localities and the EU. The involvement of the Estonian local governments in the Estonian EU policy is less developed, with local government being neither informed nor consulted, either formally or on an *ad hoc* basis.

It conclusion, it is clear that Estonian regions remain weak actors within the multi-level governance system of the EU. Their relatively low importance is demonstrated by the fact that discussions about the regional level are usually related to the problems of the local government. While it is generally acknowledged in Estonia that the regional level should be reformed, it seems unlikely that directly elected regions will be the result of any such reform.

Notes

1. http://www.valitsus.ee/?id=1276 (accessed 14/03/2007).
2. http://www.valitsus.ee/?id=1307 (accessed 24/02/2007).
3. Ministry of Interior, Department of Local Government and Regional Administration, Local Government in Estonia, www.siseministeerium.ee/doc.php?17432 (accessed: 21/06/10).
4. http://www.riigikantselei.ee/failid/The_Government_s_European_Policy_for_2004_2006_FINAL.pdf p. 31 (accessed: 21/06/10).
5. http://www.emovl.ee/index.php?pg=sisu&id=150&keel=eng (accessed 3/03/2007).
6. Interview, Union of Estonian Cities, 13/03/2007.

11
Regionalism in a Unitary State: The Case of Hungary

Gyula Horváth

In Europe, the state and national development processes of the nineteenth century shaped the regional structure of different countries in different ways. In the multipolar states (Italy, Germany, Spain) industrial development and the creation of a transport infrastructure involved several urban areas, which went through an almost identical development cycle, with the main driving-forces of the economy, culture and politics rooting themselves in different places. In the unipolar countries (France, Austria, Hungary, most East-Central European countries and, partially, the UK) the performance of the peripheries away from the dominant capitals was weak, and the railway network was developed in a radial structure mainly in order to serve the state center where the cultural and political functions were also concentrated. The most important industrial stakeholder circles were generally interested in the development of integrated national markets, their economic interests on several occasions forcing regional elites to concede over the issues of protectionist taxes versus the strengthening of regional autonomies.

In the Austro-Hungarian monarchy, developing along the normal lines of the multipolar economic area, similar economic interests prevailed. Due to the dominance of the Hungarian agrarian economy, relatively little attention was paid within the empire to the development of industry. Outside the capital, the largest industrial center was Pozsony (now Bratislava), whose manufacturing operations employed 6000 people – followed by Temesvár (Timisoara), Arad, Brassó (Brasov), Miskolc, Debrecen and Pécs, whose industrial labor forces each amounted to some 4000–5000 (Beluszky 1999).

The modernization programs in Hungary during the Dual Monarchy era – railway and waterworks construction, and state-financed public works – introduced serious changes in the regional structure of the country, being overwhelmingly a force for concentration. Although governments in those days did not set out spatial development policy (at least as currently understood), they nonetheless had to respond to the demands for modernization being formulated in the underdeveloped regions of the country. Various levels of action in the peripheral areas were supported by the National

Hungarian Economic Association (OMGE), while the first governmental development program was established in the NE Carpathians at the end of the 1890s as a result of decisions arrived at by the Székely Congress. A governmental 'gap-bridging' strategy for the institutional system of Székelyföld (the land of the Székely people), one of the most backward areas of the country, was formulated. Although the nation's stormy history prevented the proposals from being put into practice, the minutes of the congress even today still make interesting and useful methodological reading for specialists in regional development.

After World War I, regional development processes ongoing in historical Hungary were disrupted following the Trianon Treaty. Areas of economic development were fragmented by the intrusion of state boundaries: natural gravity zones and their hinterlands were divided; linkages between factors of production were severed. The economic structure of the new country showed an extreme degree of imbalance. The dynamic industrial development of previous decades mainly favored Budapest, with 50 per cent of industrial employment and 90 per cent of machine industry being concentrated there. Outside the capital, only Győr had a noteworthy machine-production capacity. The territorial structure of direct tax revenue, accurately reflecting the general performance capacity of the economy, portrays a clearly unipolar country: the contribution of Budapest amounting to some 59 per cent (Table 11.1). Consequently it is no exaggeration to argue that all the basic characteristics of today's regional structure were already

Table 11.1 The regional structure of direct tax revenues[1] in Hungary 1913

Region	Total of direct taxes, '000 Crowns (Korona)	Distribution %	Population '000 inhabitants	Distribution %	Allocation quotient[2]
Budapest	188,525	58.6	930	14.4	4.07
North Transdanubia	37,066	11.5	1,175	18.2	0.63
South Transdanubia	22,822	7.1	1,222	19.0	0.37
North Hungary	17,375	5.4	993	15.4	0.33
Great Plain	55,876	17.4	3,128	33.0	0.53
Total	321,664	100.0	6,448	100.0	1.00

1) The direct taxes (land tax, housing tax, earnings, income and corporate taxes, mining, transportation, capital gains and annuity tax, and other direct taxes) comprised 32 per cent of state revenues.
2) The intensity of concentration is represented by the well-known regional economic indicator, the allocation quotient, which is the quotient of the population ratio of the given region and the ratio of the direct taxes in that particular region.
Source: The author's own calculation on the basis of Edvi Illés–Halász 1921: 74.

present at the beginning of the twentieth century: the highly developed city of Budapest, the relatively well developed region of North Transdanubia and the remaining – underdeveloped – two-thirds of the country. Between the two World Wars, the structural differences between the regions remained essentially unchanged. Indeed, the modernization of the machine industry's sector once again served only to strengthen the position of the capital; in 1930, 60 per cent of industrial employees were concentrated there. The centers of the dynamically developing industry lay – almost without exception – in the capital; R&D facilities were almost exclusively established here and, in 1938, 54 per cent of the country's 13,000 university students studied in Budapest institutions.

The regional imbalance of the new Hungary became the center of debate in the second half of the 1920s, at least among (mainly) academic experts in jurisprudence and public administration – participants in other spheres of the economy and social management only very rarely expressing an opinion (Hencz 1973). The viewpoint of Kuno Klebelsberg, the then minister of education, on the subject of development of intellectual centers outside Budapest could be considered a rare exception. Indeed his words published in *Pesti Napló* on the 15 September 1927, may be justifiably read as a criticism of state policy during the whole of the twentieth century:

> In Budapest the 'Lágymányos Pool' is the last open area and so either there will be a university-city there or, on the basis of foreign examples, we should consider the possibilities that the hubs of our scientific life should be relocated to Szeged and Debrecen. [...] Is it only Budapest which can take a share of all state institutions and construction free of charge? This system cannot be sustained any longer bearing in mind the principle of equitable distribution.
>
> (Klebelsberg 1928: 75)

Despite the fact that the inter-war period saw the decentralization of economic and cultural development being advocated by several intellectual groups, professional organizations and even elements of government, there were no major changes in the regional structure of the Hungarian economy and society.

In the 1950s signs of regional development were barely detectable at all, apart from the fact that developed industry was not limited exclusively to the capital, and the ratio of industrial workers there had decreased to 44 per cent. New industrial regions emerged, mainly in the Hungarian Uplands area, with Miskolc as its center. Industrial centers were established in the areas of Nógrád, Pécs-Komló, Tatabánya and Várpalota – Hungary's northeast to south-west directional industrial axis was formed.

The extremely centralized state and economic system could not accept that underdeveloped regions or settlements were attempting to go ahead on their own initiative. The council system, introduced in 1950, dismantled the otherwise underdeveloped local government system of the settlements and decreed that the sole task of these councils would be to carry out orders from the center.

The subsequent reform of economic administration in 1968 opened up a new era for regional development. To a certain extent, decentralized economic decisions supported geographically dispersed development, and an increasingly large part of the settlement network became affected by the modern economy. In 1971, a new regional development policy was set by means of two decisions of the Council of Ministers. For the first time in the history of Hungarian spatial development, a socio-political aim was set: the alignment of the living conditions of the population in the different regions of the country. It took some years, however, before administrative reform was followed by spatial and settlement reforms, with considerable differences also in the content of those reforms. In the meantime, opponents of reform were preparing a strong counteroffensive leading to re-centralization. For example, changes to the financial arrangements for local authorities undermined the economic basis of local government (at least as had originally been planned.) By the 1970s, central interference had increased still further – a negative response to increasing economic difficulties.

Economic regulations introduced by the reforms had their effect only rather indirectly – direct impacts were much more limited. Such reforms included the creation of the central spatial development fund, amounting to some 2.5 billion forints during the fourth 5-year plan. Of this sum, 800 million forints were spent for the transfer of the industry from the capital, 400 millions on the industrial re-structuring of the mining areas, while the rest was earmarked to promote the industrialization of underdeveloped regions (Enyedi 1983).

The fact that industrial companies dispersed a significant number of manufacturing units into rural towns and the larger villages had an important impact. Indeed, from the late 1960s to the middle of the 1970s a very strong regional redistribution of industrial production took place (with little changing since, at least as far as the regional spread of industry is concerned.) Yet even then the fundamental dominance of the metropolitan center remained undiminished. Thus, for example, 40 per cent of rural industrial units had their headquarters in Budapest; a figure rising to 70 per cent in the case of the machine industry. Moreover, it was often the case that simpler, less modern, unprofitable and often polluting activities were allocated to undeveloped areas, while R&D, organizational and decision-making functions were concentrated in corporate headquarters. To this extent it may be argued that the overall effect of these changes was to recreate a new form of underdevelopment in which the underdevelopment was indicated, as previously, not by a lack of industry, but rather by its old-fashioned structure and technology.

Table 11.2   Concentration intensity of some indicators in the capital[1]

Category	1938[2]	1985	2004
Industrial employees	3.86	1.18	1.22
Employees in the financial sector	3.14	1.65	1.99
Number of students in higher education	3.00	2.50	2.22
Number of R&D specialists	4.75	3.67	3.14

1) On the basis of the allocation quotient (for example, in 2004 the number of employees in the R&D sector was three times more concentrated in the capital than the population ratio);
2) The ratio of the population was calculated on the basis of 1941 data.
Source: *The Hungarian Statistical Yearbook* and *The Regional Statistical Yearbook*. The author's own calculations fusing different years and pages.

The 40 years of a centrally planned economy produced an ambiguous situation with regards the development of Hungary's regional structure. Delayed industrialization – several elements of which resembled the industrialization of the West European peripheries – contributed to a slowdown in the growth of regional imbalances, but also blocked the spatial dissemination of regional driving forces. The reason for this was unquestionably political in origin. We cannot speak of decentralization in real terms, since the regional establishment of industry was not linked to the devolution of power. The narrow concept of decreasing regional disparities, concentrating on the superficial indicators of underdevelopment attached to infrastructure, favored the survival of the redistribution system.

After the transformation, and in spite of the fact that important changes took place in all areas of activity with a bearing on regional development, the driving forces of real decentralization did not assert themselves. In the 1990s the Spatial Development Act did establish new institutions and provided a number of policy tools, but simultaneously market forces introduced new differentiation processes in the regional structure of the country. This was despite the fact that the concentration level of post-industrial regional driving forces was as high as had been experienced in earlier development periods (Table 11.2).

The increase of regional disparities

Broadly speaking, the regional structure of the Hungarian economy cannot currently satisfy the competition requirements of the post-industrial era and of European integration. During the twentieth century the notions, concepts and political slogans of decentralization proved a failure. The obstacles to progress in almost every attempt at decentralization were increased both by the combined resistance of central government and sectoral leadership, and by the historically shaped provincial form of behavior of the country's regional public administration system. Thus, despite the fact that the key statements since the 1920s have stressed the need for major cities

Table 11.3 The distribution of students in higher education among the regional centers, 1938–2003

H. E. Center	Student numbers			Distribution, %		
	1938	1985	2003	1938	1985	2003
Budapest	7,178	44,900	159,501	54.3	45.2	43.4
Debrecen	1,103	7,291	23,055	8.3	7.3	6.3
Miskolc	312	3,953	13,143	2.4	4.0	3.6
Pécs	1,342	6,480	23,150	10.1	6.5	6.3
Szeged	1,151	8,999	27,000	8.7	9.1	7.4
Others	2,142	27,721	121,095	16.2	27.9	33.0
Total	13,228	99,344	366,944	100.0	100.0	100.0

Source: The author's own calculations on the basis of *The Hungarian Statistical Yearbook* 1938: 296–297; *Regional Statistical Yearbook* 1985: 95, 2003: 137–145.

to create for their own regions, short-term political elites have continually obstructed the possibility of any critical mass being created (apart from their own county seat) which could have become a force for the devolution of power (Konrád and Szelényi 2000). Even today it is possible to cite examples of decisions being generated in county seats motivated solely by short-term expediency. Some three-quarters of a century later, Klebelsberg's dilemma was resolved (not by accident) by university campuses lined up around the Lágymányos 'Muddy Pool', while in the provincial intellectual centers, institutions of higher education are forced to integrate (formally) in order to obtain relatively trivial amounts of funding. Indeed, given the current regional structure of Hungarian higher education and research, it is a misnomer to talk of future knowledge-based regional development, when the size and the weight of the larger university centers is so unsuited to this task (Table 11.3). The four largest university centers after Budapest provide instruction for only one quarter of Hungary's university students: the comparable figure for European countries of approximately the same size ranges between a third and a half of all students (Figure 11.1).

In Hungary, regional economic, social and infrastructural disparities are continuously growing both among counties and regions (Table 11.4). The changes in performance can, first of all, be explained by the relative levels of industrial production. In the period 2001–2003 the value of investment into manufacturing industry in Pest County was €1.3 billion, in Győr-Moson-Sopron County €0.4 billion, in Somogy €0.1 billion, and in Szabolcs €0.2 billion. Similar discrepancies can also be noted in industrial exports. Three-quarters of the industrial production of Győr-Moson-Sopron and two-thirds of that of Fejér County reaches foreign markets, while from the counties of Baranya and Tolna, only one-quarter does so. The exports of the Audi Hungária Company in Győr are 14 times higher than the combined exports

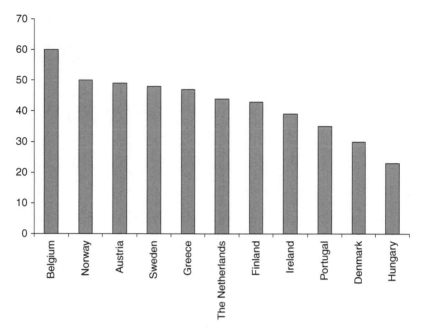

Figure 11.1   The share of the four largest university centers outside the capital of numbers of students in higher education, 2004, %
Source: International Handbook of Universities 2004. The author's design.

of all industry in Baranya County (formerly a highly industrialized county dominated by mining and light industries).

The emigration of young professional intellectuals from the regional centers is a further warning sign. Well-qualified university graduates cannot find jobs requiring high qualifications – an obvious threat to the development of a knowledge-based economy. It is a common complaint that the universities produce too many graduates, but we should also consider whether the economy has been intellectualized to the required level? Developing business services, R&D and international functions – which currently show up weakly in the regions – might result in 1000s of highly qualified jobs, and these could clearly serve the development of the economy.

Modifying these trends is recognized as being the key to the modernization of Hungary, since they are a major reason for the weakening competitiveness of the country. A country characterized by an over-concentration of modern regional development driving forces is not capable of establishing an active and competitive cohesion policy.

The Hungarian regions occupy positions in various groups of the European ranking list. The Central Hungarian region can be found at the end of the

Table 11.4 Changes in the performance capacity of the regions, 1994–2002

Region	GDP per capita, 1994		GDP per capita, 2002			Growth rate, 1995–2001, per cent
	'000 Ft	As percentage of national average	'000 Ft	As percentage of national average	As percentage of EU25 average	
Central Hungary	619	147	2,701	164	96	5.2
Budapest	768	182	3,494	212	118	7.9
Central Transdanubia	365	86	1,462	89	52	4.6
West Transdanubia	424	100	1,703	103	61	4.3
South Transdanubia	353	84	1,204	73	43	2.6
North Hungary	292	69	1,050	64	37	2.3
North Great Plain	311	74	1,062	64	38	3.0
South Great Plain	350	83	1,136	69	40	1.6
Total	422	100	1,648	100	73	4.0

Source: Regional Statistical Yearbook 1994, 2004.

middle third of this ranking list together with Corsica (France), Sardinia (Italy), the Highlands and Islands region of Scotland, Castile and Leon (Spain), and Namur (Belgium). The second most developed Hungarian region, Western Transdanubia, stands at the head of the bottom third of the ranking list. This group of regions is exclusively from the Cohesion countries and includes the North, Central and Alentejo regions of Portugal, and the Peloponnese and Thrace (Greece). The position of the Central Transdanubian region is similar and analogous with some Greek and Portuguese regions and with other, more developed, East European regions. The remaining Hungarian regions, alongside other, exclusively East European, regions are ranked in the middle of the bottom third.

If we regard Budapest as a separate region, then, with its €24,000 per capita GDP – 113 per cent of the EU average – it would feature in the group of the 50 most developed regions in the company of Madrid, Hanover, Liguria, Upper Austria and Bradford.

The formal renewal of Hungarian regional policy

Since 1990 a series of reforms have been introduced decentralizing the state administration, re-establishing the autonomy of local governments and delegating to them broad responsibilities in delivering local public services. The reforms of the early 1990s, and in particular the reform of local government, were characterized by the strengthening of the role of locality (municipalities, local communities) at the expense of the counties. The emphasis of this first wave of reforms was on democracy and autonomy from the central state, while efficiency and rationality, important concerns in Western European states (Stewart and Stoker 1995), were rather neglected. Fragmentation, low level of efficiency and a near doubling of the number of local government units were the main outcomes of this first wave of reforms.

Act XXI on Regional Development and Physical Planning, enacted in 1996 following a long period of preparation, may represent the start of radical changes in Hungary's regional development. That is to say, the laws establishing regime change and the market economy had not so far taken into consideration the fact that transformation has not proceeded in identical fashion among the regions. The forces of the market economy produced favorable changes in the capital and the western border regions; on the other hand, they drove the heavy industry and agricultural areas into crisis. At the beginning of the 1990s it became obvious that those regions unable to modernize themselves on their own needed state subsidies – just as in the West European market economies.

The main policy-making relevant feature of the Act was the creation of a three-tier system of regional development councils at the county, regional and national levels of government, in parallel with the public administrative structures. Additionally, the main territorial and institutional innovation has

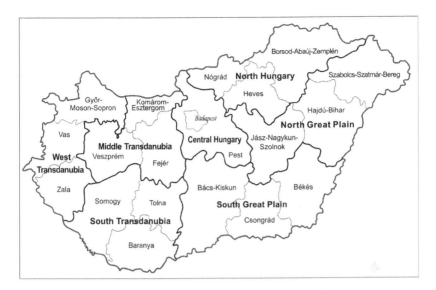

Figure 11.2 NUTS 2 regions in Hungary in 2006

been the establishment, in 1999, of seven planning regions forming the new NUTS 2 units (Figure 11.2).

The establishment of the regions was intended to create a forum for interest intermediation and policy formulation closer to the central state. In practice, however, the limited role of both local public actors and pressure groups (chambers, NGOs etc.) in the regional development councils after the 1999 amendment of the Act, as well as the key role of sectorally minded central state officials in the regional development councils, has substantially decreased their role as an alternative locus of interest articulation at the meso-level of governance. Therefore, the county level remains the pre-eminent locus of interest representation for the main actors in terms of interest representation (Figure 11.3).

Nonetheless, the importance of the first Regional Development Act is illustrated by the fact that it has made possible decentralized development and the incorporation of the concepts of social justice and impartiality into politico-economic decisions. To fulfill these basic constitutional requirements the Act established institutions and made decisions regarding financial tools. Hungarian policy was the first in East Central Europe to elaborate comprehensive regulation for the regional modernization of the country. However, the Regional Development Act and the Parliamentary Decree on the Concept of Regional Development – due to incomplete reforms in other spheres of social administration – could not in themselves bring about the necessary change of direction. Thus, although European Commission reports on Hungary have, since 1998, continuously warned

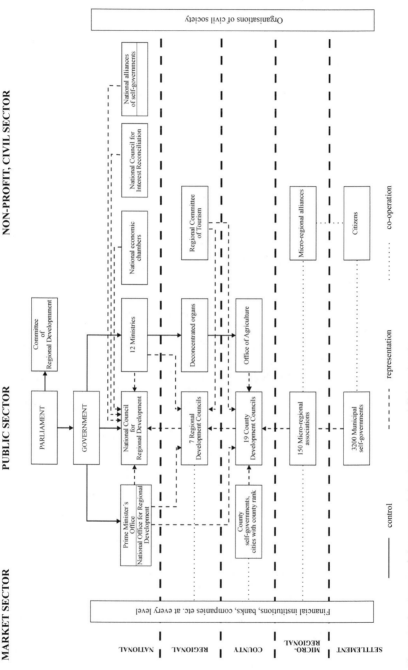

Figure 11.3 Actors of the regional development at different levels
Source: Horváth 2004.

about the gaps in the country's regional policy, these were always subject to the narrow political interests of the Hungarian government of the day. In most accession countries, Regional Development Acts were introduced and both central and local institutions of regional policy were established. In Hungary, however, the Act was amended unfavorably and central government's administration organization for regional development was changed several times (a similar amendment was introduced only in Romania). All of this serves to give the impression that, in Hungary, the concepts of regional development are used only under pressure from the EU and that the sole real aim is to ensure that formal targets are met. However, even if that was the case, by the second half of the 1990s, regional policy had developed a certain momentum as the numerous professional groups active in regional matters had begun to elaborate a large number of regional strategies, concepts and programs. By the early 2000s, however, these efforts had begun to run out of steam, with faith in the viability of decentralization being undermined by the central government's passivity and further attempts to recentralize.

Disappointment peaked with the National Development Plan, which, contrary to original expectations, contained only one regional operative program for the 2004–2006 period. In the Czech Republic and Poland almost 40 per cent of the subsidy available for development was directly at the disposal of the regions, while in Hungary this proportion was 18 per cent. Following the subsequent abandonment of the earlier regional concepts, pro-regionalists, losing hope, became interested in traditional mechanisms, reviving lobbyist bargaining, something which they had previously wished to leave behind. Instead of becoming Europeanized, Hungarian regional policy fell into the trap of provincialism.

Today, resources are fragmented, while the strategies and programs of the regions and counties alike are not considered significant. The relatively small, although continuously expanding, regional development resources are contested by micro-regional stakeholder groups and, as a result of occasional alliances and bargains – effectively based on existentialist motives – resources are spread thinly over different areas of the county. Meanwhile, many continue to gaze piously and hopefully toward the heavens – and so it is perhaps small wonder that they cannot see the neighboring county, town or university, and that there is no ongoing debate about the fulfillment of common aims, since their leaders are each busy lobbying in Budapest, sometimes vying with each other for peanuts.

Cooperation in regional development decisions

The rationale of the Act on Regional Development is based on the concept of partnership. However, it also takes into consideration the basic thesis that regional development is not the result of separate actions or decisions but the product of a large number of market participants playing a common game. The operation of the market economy partly depends upon individual decisions, but collective (governmental or other group) choices also have an important role. The new regional development practice in Western Europe also had difficulties with the organization of partnerships, with almost a decade being required before lessons or models were available for potential transfer.

West European analysis of the general and specific features of successful partnership continues to hold vital lessons for Hungarian regional development (Bennett and Krebs 1994; Leonardi and Nanetti 1990). In particular, the results of the LEDA (Local Employment Development Action) programs of the European Union (EU) between 1986 and 1991 served as a basis for an important analysis by Bennett and Krebs (1994) (based on the analysis of 214 programs in 33 regions.) The key findings may be summarized as follows.

The first characteristic feature is that the type of partnership and the leading actors and the participants in them show noticeable differences in different region types. In less developed regions the local authorities and the mayor are the key figures in development actions, while in the rural areas the number of participating actors is much increased. The most diversified partnerships are to be seen in the industrially deteriorating regions, and here the number of actors is the highest. The leading positions within the programs in most cases are in the hands of regional and local government, but the development agencies and economic chambers also play an important role.

The second characteristic feature, especially important in Hungary, is that universities and research institutions currently participate in development programs as often as the financial and the private enterprise sectors, proving that development is innovative in character. We cannot overlook the fact that in one half of the programs the regional authority plays the leading role, although this potential key player is currently inadequate in Hungary. Consequently, building partnerships in Hungarian circumstances will almost certainly prove challenging.

The third characteristic is the multi-faceted nature of the cooperation activities: partnership is not exclusively financial but rather includes a host of different relationships across a wide range of regional development actors.

The fourth characteristic feature is linked to the cascade connection between the elements of the cooperation network. Although participants are closely linked together in cooperation, depending on the activities and on the type of region, dominant partnerships can be seen. The most frequent forms of cooperation involve groups of local authorities – regional government – and other local actors.

Consequently, the key to success in decentralized regional economic development is control over local development projects, and the new domestic regional development system must also face this problem. The circle of activities which have an influence on regional development is widening, the development factors most appropriate for a given area need to be selected from the wide range of programs available, and partners need to be found to carry out and finance them.

The new regional development system in Hungary also increases the number of the development tasks, widening both the circle of participants and the channels of finance. Consequently, the structure of the institutional system, and the rules of operation and competency need to be examined from the standpoint of whether they represent sufficient organizational power. In our opinion, the internal operational system and powers of most regional development actors means that they are still incapable of organizing efficient partnerships. Local authorities are perhaps best prepared for participation in regional development programs, although the office structure of larger cities and the committee structure of their assemblies still do not fit the differentiated tasks emerging in these settlements. County councils can only be a very modest player, while the chambers – absorbed in building up their own organizations – can in no way be regarded as a dynamizing force. The county development councils, therefore, continue to find themselves in a difficult situation with potential partners more interested in obtaining subsidies rather than in combining their own resources to facilitate genuine cooperative action (Pálné Kovács et al. 2004).

Although the new Act on Regional Development provided a theoretical opportunity for introducing West European-style regional development practice into Hungary, taken together, the fetishism surrounding the autonomy of settlement, infrastructural underdevelopment and – last but not least – the development practice followed in recent years in Eastern Hungary, all suggest that county councils will tend to prioritise infrastructural development. But this approach is insufficient. Traditional infrastructural development is inadequate for the task of creating jobs, bringing about a reasonable increase in export capacity and digging out the roots of underdevelopment. Rather, market institutions, product and technology development, the financial infrastructure of rural enterprises and financial organizations capable of combining scattered resources are needed in each region of Hungary. Suitable responses to these key issues of modernization and competitive readiness can be given only within the framework of a comprehensive decentralization policy.

The new paradigm and the institution of the region

The region is a territorial unit serving the sustainable growth of the economy and the modernization of the spatial structure, having independent financial resources, following an autonomous development policy and equipped with rights of self-government. On the basis of this definition (whose components have naturally changed in different ways in the various periods of European development) regions so far do not exist in Hungary, except as naturally defined by certain geographers (Tóth 2004). Form without content is incapable of influencing the regional structure of the country in a favorable direction, decentralizing the new regional driving forces and establishing the basis for multipolar development. The region defined as the framework of regional research is incapable of organizing the regional driving forces of the twenty-first century without competencies, institutions and tools. Hungary needs regions since European regional development proves unequivocally that the region as the sub-national administration level, based on concepts of self-government, with its economic capacities and structural potential is:

- the optimal spatial framework for the assertion of regional policy, targeting economic development;
- the appropriate area for the operation of post-industrial regional organizational forces and the development of their reciprocal connections;
- the important setting for the enforcement of regional and social interests;
- the most appropriate size of spatial unit to construct modern infrastructure and the professional, organizational, planning and executive institutions of regional policy; and,
- the defining element of the decision-making process of the EU's Regional and Cohesion Policy.

Such a decentralized state structure system can be established organically as a result of complex, legal regulation. The concepts providing its pre-requisites should be fixed in the constitution (or, lacking consensus, in a decentralization law), laying down the reciprocal share of competencies between state and region, contributing to the mitigation of spatial differences and creating equal opportunities for accessing public services, fostering economic decentralization, and delegating rights and resources to local authorities and the regions.

The need for regionalization in contemporary Hungary is not simply a by-product of developments in public administration or EU membership. At stake, rather, is the growth of the Hungarian economy, the modernization of the country, a decrease in regional differences and the future positions to be occupied in the European division of labor. Regionalism might be the new power for initiating modernization in Hungary at the beginning of the twenty-first century. Yet the current regional institutional system of spatial development is unable to fulfill even its original aims. The regional agencies basically have the task of collecting projects, and so they serve to execute the central will and not to realize regional ideas. In the performance of the regional agencies considerable differences can be seen between innovative and traditional execution-oriented agencies. Research suggests that the strongest opposition to true decentralization comes from government ministries. Research also indicates that while most of those involved in the creation of regions support reform in theory, they are not convinced that the current regional borders have been well defined. That said, it is clear that it would be difficult if not impossible to create more acceptable regional borders than the current ones. Dispute over delineation should certainly not be allowed to distract attention from the basic issues – that is, the functions and rights that should be delegated to the regions by the central state administration delegate. The difficulties faced here are formidable with central ministries proving resistant to change. But why should central state administration assess applications for a couple of million forints? Why is working out the vital sectoral operative programs not the most important task for central state administration? Why are there no well-elaborated, long-term development concepts?

Not only operative, but also important strategic planning tasks, could and should be delegated to the regions. In particular because, in the new programming period, the 'traditional' methods being suggested by the center – the still centralist logic of testing methods in one corner of the country before 'rolling them out' to others – cannot be used. Rather, each region should work in its own way. The successful EU member states are those where the country is developing along various regional trajectories.

Throughout the development of Hungarian regionalism, the interests of economic and societal actors are apparent in addition to political reasoning. In the period of the planned economy, establishing an optimal market size played a role, albeit to a limited extent. Large corporations weighed regional factors while organizing their subsidiaries. However, the spatial proximity of such units didn't result in their efficient cooperation, and the interior economic cohesion of various regions did not strengthen or develop. Elements of vertical control remained dominant in economic administration.

By the mid-1980s, developments outside the state borders – in particular the organizing of cross-border cooperation agreements by EEC member states – had raised the possibility of greater weight being given in Hungary to spatial considerations. The Alps-Adriatic Working Community, spurred on by Italian initiatives, became a notable Central European venue of institutionalized inter-regional cooperation. The founding Italian, German and Austrian regions wished to involve Eastern European economies in their cooperative activities, and administrative units of Hungary became the first in Eastern Europe to become members of the Working Community. Participation in its working groups widened the international experiences of Hungarian county officials. At the beginning of transformation, these representatives hoped that democratic governance would also result in the decentralization of exterior political and economic competencies. This was also the hope of various economic actors operating in the western territories of the country. Unfortunately, changes in the Hungarian political system weren't supportive of the aims of institutionalized paradiplomacy. While Hungary currently plays an active role in organizing cross-border cooperations (18 have been registered as of 2006), their effects on economic development have been negligible.

There has been no meaningful progress in regionalizing public administration either. Although parties have made declarations about regionalism and the decentralization of state organization in election programs, their promises were quickly forgotten once they found themselves in government. One exception occurred in 2006, when the Socialist-Liberal government brought a law on creating administrative regions before parliament. The opposition, however, was not supportive, and since the law required a two-thirds majority, it could not be enacted.

Political arguments against regional public administration focus on unfavorable changes in the accessibility of services, with opponents of regionalism stressing that the new administrative level would be more distant from citizens, and that access to quality services would become more difficult. Fears about the weakening of local democracy are also prominent, with opponents predicting constraints on local autonomy and a reduction of financial support for municipalities. Occasionally, arguments against regions also demonstrate a degree of Euro-skepticism, with populist groups viewing the establishment of regions as merely as an obligatory formal requirement set by the European Commission. Naturally, these simplistic, politically motivated views are erroneous. Transforming the by now obsolete unitary state into a decentralized one involves transferring competences down from the central governments to the regions, rather than up from the municipalities: indeed, establishing regional public administration would also require the strengthening of local services.

Possible future images

One of the most frequent elements in professional and political argument supporting comprehensive reform of Hungarian public administration is the need to match the structural framework of regional development functions with EU requirements. The view that the region is the optimal measure for regional development is widely held – not only because of the involvement of NUTS 2 regions in relation to Structural Funds, but also because in Hungary counties are quite incapable of achieving success in the economic competition of the European regions. Consequently, the strengthening of the regions in relation to spatial development is regarded as necessary even where there might be doubts regarding the viability of total regional reform in the near future.

Undoubtedly, the most successful organizational model for managing economic and spatial development would be a directly elected, self-governing authority where the region is a complex unit with multi-layered functions and institutions. However, regardless of the organizational model adopted, we may state in general terms that the following elements stand out in laying the foundations of regional competitiveness:

- strategic alliances;
- public and private partnerships;
- inter-sectoral coordination;
- entrepreneurial activity by the public sector;
- inclusion of local actors in solving actual economic and social problems;
- support and strengthening of synergies and system integration; and,
- capacity to renew the organization.

To catalyze these functions, to integrate the various resources and actors, and to foster and build up networks are the tasks of regional government. This involves a more active assumption of responsibility than would be necessary with a liberal-market model, but one which is significantly less centrally directed and less hierarchical than the welfare model. In the current economic development period, regional authorities need to say not what must be done, but rather, how and with whom.

By way of summary, we can state that decentralization, the spread of non-governmental inter-sectoral forms, networking and complexity are the key terms which characterize the management of regional policy in general. The main objective is not the creation of a new layer of local government, but the realization of these requirements. In those cases where regional-local authorities are operating, it would be appropriate that they have planning rights delegated to them. At the same time it is questionable whether such a body, no matter how democratically accountable, would satisfy partnership requirements. It should, therefore, be guaranteed that the concept of partnership be asserted in the planning process, at the very least in a consultative capacity. The planning arrangement mechanism can even be regulated by regional authorities, although it would be safer to introduce some form of compulsory regulation for this purpose, for example through the establishment of parallel evaluatory bodies. There is, in actual fact, a solution available based on the practices of other EU member states in which the central law details those bodies that must be included in the planning process, although the decision as to the forms and details of the process remain within the competency of the planning bodies themselves. Consequently, the current regional development councils, with only minor changes to their composition and spheres of authority, could remain central – and worthwhile – institutions of the Hungarian regional institutional system.

Regional authorities could take over the resource distribution role currently played by development councils at regional and county level. Regarding resources, regional authorities would decide in terms of size and targets, depending on whether there will be county-level distribution and whether county regional development councils will survive. In addition to size, further highly important issues are the responsibility for resource allocation and the operation of the different subsidizing systems – and in which procedural order and by the use of which mechanisms local authorities carry these things out. Presumably, even in respect of the distribution of national resources, it is not practical to carry out direct institutional management of project systems. Should the body be given a role in operating normative, state-subsiding systems, the rules and aims of distribution and application should appear in institutional decisions, and then the body should also be endowed with controlling rights.

Obviously, this body could make decisions regarding project applications that it had initiated itself, including the self-financing part. In consequence, authority over domestic resources means not only the power to distribute those resources, but also to finance self-initiated projects. From this point of view, it would be highly important that the regional authority itself become the initiating partner for the economic and private sectors, as well as the local authorities of the settlements.

Issues relating to planning and finance include the mechanism to be used for the harmonization of central, regional and private resources to be collected for the projects aiming for EU support. The introduction of planning contracts on the basis of the French example – already applied by Poland in its regional development policy – would also be expedient. Regions might have a role of key importance in the signing of the planning contracts, since only directly elected regional authorities can be considered to be a legitimate partner and to carry sufficient weight to set against that of central government. The main question is the mechanism for the harmonization of regional and central priorities, the linking of resources and the assertion of common priorities. In planning contracts it is possible to agree on common development priorities, including the level and form of state intervention (by subsidy, loan or loan guarantee etc). This pattern is convenient, even in the respect that the subsidy from the state can be also planned alongside the region's own resources.

The planning contracts would be a part of the state budget and would have the result that, unlike the operational budgets, they would cover periods longer than a year and could be modified with much greater difficulty. Details of the planning contracts could even be defined as a part of a separate law on planning. The establishing of regional authorities would have the obvious advantage that the acceptance of both physical plans and development plans would fall within the sphere of authority of the same body. The body itself could decide what sort of agreement and procedural order should be followed in carrying out the dual planning exercise.

It is important to emphasize that there is a need to establish regional authorities, irrespective of whether they may be required by the EU. Independent of the EU's Structural Funds, the organization of regional authorities can – above all – create regional actors equipped with the necessary rights and responsibilities in order to develop and manage the economy of the region, and create an environment favorable to regional marketing, international networking, human resource development, education and training.

12
The Regions of Poland

Grzegorz Gorzelak with Anna Tucholska

Poland is a unitary, decentralized state, in which the decentralization process is still under way. The territorial administrative system has varied over time; however, traditions of 'self-government' have deep historical roots. Poland is a territorially differentiated state, although this differentiation (in terms of GDP per inhabitant) is not greater than that in other European countries of a similar size. Regional differentiation, however, been growing more rapidly during the last 15 years than in West European countries; a process also witnessed in other post-socialist countries. Polish society displays a low level of regional identification, although the regional differences in values and attitudes are clearly visible. Historical factors are of the greatest importance in explaining these differences. Poland's accession to the European Union (EU) opened up new possibilities for the development of the entire country as well as its regions. Following decentralization, Polish territorial units will enjoy a relatively high degree of autonomy in taking advantage of the funds channeled to Poland by the EU and in building upon international economic cooperation.

The elaboration of these points will provide the structural underpinning of this chapter. It will begin with some reflection on the evolution of the administrative system in Poland and the traditions of self-government. An overview of the regional structure of contemporary Polish economy and society will follow. The discussion will conclude with a survey of the outlook for regional development in Poland following the country's membership of the EU.

Territorial structures

Any discussion of Poland's internal territorial divisions must bear in mind that, historically speaking, the country's external boundaries have been in an almost constant state of flux. Poland borders have shifted eastwards and westwards, gaining or losing direct access to the Baltic Sea. After the third partition in 1795, Poland ceased to exist as an independent state, with the tripartite division between Russia, Prussia and Austria established during the Vienna Congress in 1815 lasting until 1918, when Poland regained its full independence. During most of the subsequent period – with the exception of the years between 1975 and 1999 – Poland has been divided into between 10 and 20 regional units (see Table 12.1 for an overview). The current system was established as a second stage in the reintroduction of territorial self-government that had been abandoned during the period of the real socialism in Poland (from 1948 to 1989).

The change of the political system in 1989 and the reintroduction of full local government on the local level brought the issue of regional government once again to the fore, this time in incomparably more favorable conditions. Demands for new regions were already extant as early as 1990: local government, it was argued, should be supplemented by democratic regional government, as part of an entirely new territorial structure. These arguments stressed the need for new regional boundaries and a reduced number of regional units. Because of this, they generated considerable opposition from powerful local elites whose objections served to paralyze political elites at the national level. As result, the reformist government of T. Mazowiecki simply abandoned the issue of new regions, concentrating instead on the reform of local government. Neither did subsequent governments wish to risk a potentially divisive and destabilizing debate about the reform of the territorial organization of the state.

Table 12.1   Territorial administrative structures in Poland after 1918

Period	Number of:			Constitutional system
	Voivodships	powiats	municipalities	
1918–1939	16 (plus 1 city)	279 + 13	3195	self-governmental – state control
1944–1950	14 (plus 2 cities)	299	3005	state
1950–1975	17 plus from 2 to 5 cities)	391	from 8800 in 1954 to some 4500 by 1973 2366 in 1973	full state control
1975	49	powiats abolished	from 2327 to 2121	state control with some elements of self-government
since 1999	16	307 (317) + 65	2489	all 3 tiers: full self-government, state present on the regional level

These were not completely lost years, however, since specialists and experts continued to work on ideas for a new structure. The Institute of Public Affairs was the main think tank concerned: a broad team of experts preparing a draft blueprint of a new system of regional government. This in turn formed the basis for legislation brought forward by the parliament elected in 1997. The center-right government formed after that election promised to introduce 'four great reforms', the reform of the administrative organization of the Polish state among them (the others being reform of the pensions system, the education system and healthcare.) The decision was taken to return to a three-tier pattern, with big regions and an intermediate tier of *powiat*, and their constitutional organization, settled upon.

There were several reasons for the reform. The most important one stemmed from the conviction that strong regions would increase the competitiveness of the Polish economy and at the same time allow the development of more efficient public administration. It was argued that many functions could not be adequately performed by either the central government or by the weak, small administrative regions that were subordinate to it. It was suggested that such functions as institution building, support for academic and scientific research, promotion, direct partner-like relations with investors, infrastructure development etc. could only be performed by genuine, strong and competent regional government. According to this line of reasoning, the *powiat* was an intermediary layer between the big region and the small municipality; an efficient provider of services which could not be efficiently performed at the very local level.

At the end of 1998, after a lengthy legislative process, the three-tier system of territorial organization was established, to be introduced by 1 January 1999. This included 16 regional units (*voivodships*), although a more rational system would have been composed of 12–13 units. The boundaries of the new regions were drawn in a way that showed great resemblance to the old system of 17 *voivodships* that had been abandoned in 1975. The number of the districts (*powiats*) – 308 (later increased to 315) so-called 'country' *powiats* and 65 so-called 'town' *powiats*[1] – established also mirrored closely the pattern that had prevailed until 1973 – and was again was too many. In both cases the decision to establish too many units was a response to bottom-up pressure by regional and local elites defending their administrative status: pressure to which the national legislative and executive bodies succumbed in most cases. The current *powiat* resembles the traditional territorial units that have a long (some 400 years') history in Poland: units that were designed according to the principle that all its localities should be accessible from the respective administrative center during a day's roundtrip on a horseback or in a horse cart. Though it is obvious that this principle is hopelessly outdated, political arguments, supported by the power of tradition, nevertheless led to the overproliferation of *powiats* (Gorzelak 2001).

There has been a dispute in Poland as to whether the boundaries of the new territorial units (*voivodships* and *powiats*) should be drawn in a way that accommodates and respects patterns of social identification with particular territorial units. As research demonstrates, however, such identification is rather weak and is limited to only a few regional and local cases. The main exception at the regional level is in Upper Silesia, where an ethnic group of Silesians – with a local dialect – still form a substantial part of the regional population. Estimates indicate that several hundred thousand people identify themselves as 'Silesian', while over 170,000 ascribed Silesian nationality to themselves in the 2002 census (although, according a verdict of the Supreme Court, there is no justification for acknowledging the existence of such a nationality). Weaker regional identification can be found in 'Greater Poland' (Poznań region). There are some local ethnic groups scattered around Poland, as well, some of which use local dialects (the Highlanders in the south and the Casubians in the north being the most prominent among them).

The weakness of regional/local identification in Poland may be attributed to the historic instability of Polish boundaries and the mass migrations caused by the resulting shifts in the country's territory, as well as the accelerated urbanization and industrialization of the socialist period. This was the main reason for the general acceptance of the unitary territorial and constitutional structure of Poland: a federal system would not have a sound social and historic basis.

The constitutional order and the regions

According to the legislation in force, the region in Poland is:

- a unit of the country's territorial organization;
- a component of the decentralized system of public authority; and,
- a regional self-governing community.

The provisions of the Constitution do not refer directly to the country's territorial organization, understood as an administrative delimitation of the boundaries of territorial units. However, the fundamental law gives the territorial units the status of self-governing communities (municipality – *gmina*, district – *poviat* and region – *voivodship*). This is implied by Article 15 of the Polish Constitution, which provides that 'the territorial system of the Republic of Poland shall ensure the decentralisation of public power'. This provision is elaborated further in Article 164, stipulating that:

1. The municipality (*gmina*) shall be the basic unit of local government; and,
2. Other units of regional and/or local government shall be determined by a parliamentary act.

The unitary nature of the state determines the scope of the region's autonomy as a self-governing public authority (Article 3 of the Constitution stipulates that 'the Republic of Poland shall be a unitary state'). However, the Constitution does not therefore directly regulate the principles on which regional governments operate; it only provides general statements which are applicable to all units of local government (see Table 12.2).

Table 12.2 The main constitutional premises regulating the operation of local and regional governments in Poland

Article	Regulation
Art. 16 (2)	Local government shall participate in the exercise of public power. The substantial part of public duties which local government is empowered to discharge by statute shall be done in its own name and under its own responsibility.
Art. 163	Local government shall perform public tasks not reserved by the Constitution or statutes to the organs of other public authorities.
Art. 165 (1) and (2)	1. Units of local government shall possess legal personality. They shall have rights of ownership and other property rights. 2. The self-governing nature of units of local government shall be protected by the courts.
Art. 166 (1) and (2)	1. Public duties aimed at satisfying the needs of a self-governing community shall be performed by units of local government as their designated duties. 2. If the fundamental needs of the state shall so require, a statute may instruct units of local government to perform other public duties. The mode of transfer and manner of performance of the duties so allocated shall be specified by statute.
Art. 167 (1–4)	1. Units of local government shall be assured public funds adequate for the performance of the duties assigned to them. 2. The revenues of units of local government shall consist of their own revenues as well as general subsidies and specific grants from the state budget. 3. The sources of revenues for units of local government shall be determined by statute. 4. Alterations as to the scope of duties and competences of units of local government shall be made in conjunction with appropriate alterations as to their share of public revenues. The statute referred to in (3) above is the Revenues of Units of Local Government Act of 13 November 2003 (Dz.U.03.203.1966).

Table 12.2   (Continued)

Article	Regulation
Art. 169 (1–4)	1. Units of local government shall perform their duties through constitutive and executive organs. 2. Elections to constitutive organs shall be universal, direct, equal and shall be conducted by secret ballot. The principles and procedures for submitting candidates and for the conduct of elections, as well as the requirements for the validity of elections, shall be determined by statute. 3. The principles and procedures for the election and dismissal of executive organs of units of local government shall be specified by statute. 4. The internal organizational structure of units of local government shall be determined, within statutory limits, by their constitutive organs. The statute referred to in (2) above is the Elections Statute to the Gmina Councils, Poviat Councils and Voivodship Parliaments (Sejmiks) Act of 16 July 1998 (Dz.U.03.159.1547 as amended).

Source: Prepared by Anna Tucholska.

The administrative structure of Poland is regulated by the Act on the Introduction of the Basic Three-Tier Territorial Organisation of the Country of 24 July 1998 (Dz.U.98.96.603),[2] which established, as of 1 January 1999, 16 regional entities and delimited their boundaries by specifying the units of the basic territorial organization (*gminas*) which made up individual regions. The precise territorial organization defining the boundaries of all the territorial units (*gminas, powiats* and *voivodships*) was introduced by the prime minister's announcement of 22 June 2001 *establishing the list of gminas and powiats incorporated by individual voivodships* (M.P.01.20.325).[3]

One of the crucial competencies vested in *voivodship* governments (and similarly to *powiats* and *gminas*) is the right to enact local laws, that is regulations which are binding in the territory of a given *voivodship*. Such regulations can be made on the basis of relevant legal norms, including the act on *voivodship* self-government, and acts of substantive law. The responsibility for making these regulations lies with the Sejmik (i.e. *voivodship* parliament), the constitutive organ of the *voivodship*, and is subject to the *voivod's* (i.e. regional governor's) supervision. On the strength of the *voivodship* self-government act, and by virtue of competencies vested by other statutes and within their statutory limits, the Sejmik can adopt acts of local law that shall be binding in all or part of the *voivodship's* territory.

The competencies and responsibilities of the Polish regions

The basic piece of legislation regulating the scope of activities of the regional government is the aforementioned Voivodship Self-Government Act, which provides that the economy, and economic and civilizational development are the main fields of regional activity: provision of public services remains the reponsibility of local governments (*gminas* and *powiat*). Article 14 of the Voivodship Act lists 15 areas for which responsibility has been delegated to the *voivodship* authorities (see Table 12.3).[4] Above all else, the region is the basic unit responsible for programming economic development; its role is to create conducive conditions for regional development though the formulatation of regional policies. In this regard, the main tasks of the *voivodship* include:

- Formulating the *voivodship*'s development strategy which is then implemented via *voivodship* programs;
- Implementing the *voivodship*'s development policy, which includes the maintenance and development of social and technical infrastructure having regional (*voivodship*) significance;
- Supporting and carrying out activities aimed at improving the level of education among the public, fostering the development of science, and encouraging cooperation between the scientific and economic sectors;
- Fostering technological development and innovation;
- Supporting the development of culture; and,
- The protection and rational use of the national heritage and its assets.

According to the subsidiarity principle, the *voivodship* performs an ancillary role in the execution of public duties exceeding the capacity (financial or organizational) of local governments. It is responsible for duties that are not entirely local in nature, such as the maintenance of *voivodship* roads or the running of academic and research establishments of regional significance.

Given this key role in programming development, international cooperation and participation in international organizations, as well as the implementation of the community law, also fall under the purview of regional authorities.

Polish regions have become increasingly active in international associations and organizations, as well as regional institutions (e.g. the Chamber of Regions of the Congress of Local and Regional Authorities of Europe, Committee of the Regions). The Polish legal system has rather strict provisions as regards initiating regional cooperation, and makes such cooperation conditional on regional compliance with the national laws, the state's foreign policy, as well as the statutory competencies of the regions. It also requires that proposed cooperation and its forms should be approved by the minister for foreign affairs. At the same time, international cooperation between

Table 12.3 Legal basis for the activities of regional governments related to development programming and international cooperation

Area of activity		Competencies and activities	Legal basis
Programming development	Adopting regional development strategies	The *voivodship* government formulates the *voivodship* development strategy, which in particular includes the following objectives: 1) to cultivate the sense of Polish identity, develop the national, civic and cultural awareness of citizens, cultivate and foster the sense of local identity 2) to stimulate economic activity 3) to improve the level of competitiveness and innovation of the region's economy 4) to protect the assets of the cultural and natural environment while taking into account the needs of future generations 5) to develop and maintain spatial order. The *voivodship* development strategy, formulated by the *voivodship* government, upon its adoption (in the form of a resolution) by the *voivodship* parliament (Sejmik), is then notified to the minister for regional development.	Voivodship Self-Government Act of 5 June 1998 (Dz.U.01.142.1590 as amended)
	Cooperation with government administration bodies in programming development	The Joint Committee deals with issues related to the operations of the local government bodies and the state's policies vis à vis such bodies, as well as local government matters which remain within the scope of activity of the European Union and other international organizations of which Poland is a member. This includes such issues as: – working out a common stance of the government and the local government on the identification of economic and social priorities related to regional development and the operation of the *voivodship* government; – carrying out reviews and evaluations of the legal and financial conditions of the operation of local and regional governments; – evaluating the performance of local and regional governments in terms of EU integration processes, including the absorption of EU funds by units of local government;	Joint Committee of the Government and Local Government and Representatives of the Republic of Poland in the Committee of the Regions of the European Union Act of 6 May 2005 (Dz.U. of 23 May 2005 No. 90, item 759). This Act repealed and replaced the Ordinance of the Council of Ministers on establishing the Joint Committee of the Government and Local Government of 5 February 2002 (Dz.U.02.13.124. of 18 February 2002)

		– analyzing information about proposed drafts of legislation, programs and other government documents relating to local government;	
		– giving opinion on the drafts of primary legislation, programs and other government documents relating to local government.	
		The Joint Committee's members from the regional governments ensure that all the *voivodships* are represented in the Committee of the Regions.	
International cooperation	Participation in international local and regional associations cross-border cooperation	The Constitution provides that the units of local government have the right to associate.	The Constitution of the Republic of Poland of 2 April 1997 (Dz.U.97.78.483)
		Units of local government have the right to join international associations of local and regional communities, and to cooperate with local and regional communities of other states.	Act on the Principles of Joining International Associations of Local and Regional Communities by Units of Local Government of 15 September 2000 (Dz.U.00.91.1009 of 28 October 2000). It came into force on 29 January 2001. On its basis, four announcements of the minister for interior and administration were issued – annual lists of units of local governments who joined international associations of local and regional communities, and lists of units of local governments who withdrew from international associations of local and regional communities
		Units of local government can join associations and participate in them within the scope of their competencies, while complying with Polish national law, the state foreign policy and its international obligations.	
		Formulating strategies, principles and forms of cooperation in the document entitled Priorities of Voivodship's International Cooperation.	
		Voivodships can cooperate with the regional communities of other countries while complying with Polish national law, the state foreign policy and its international obligations within the scope of their competencies.	Voivodship Self-Government Act
		Voivodships can participate in the operations of international regional institutions and are represented in such institutions on the terms and conditions stipulated in the agreements concluded by the national organizations bringing together units of local government.	European Framework Convention on Cross-border Cooperation between Communities and Local Authorities (so-called Madrid Convention) (Dz.U.93.61.287).
		The document Priorities of Voivodship's International Cooperation can be passed, and the *voivodship's* international initiatives, such as draft agreements on regional cooperation, can be launched with the consent of the minister for foreign affairs.	European Charter of Border and Cross-Border Regions
			European Charter of Local Self-Government (Dz.U.94.124.607).
			European Charter of Regional Self-Government

Source: Prepared by Anna Tucholska.

regions is becoming both a more important and more visible component of the developmental policies of the Polish *voivodships*.

The legislation pertaining to Structural Funds is regulated both by EU laws and Polish regulations. Community law must be applied, and in case of any discrepancies or doubts (i.e. when a given situation is regulated differently by the national and EU law), it prevails over the national law. *Voivodship* governments have the task of ensuring that the regions themselves, as well as business entities and community organizations, are all well prepared for the absorption of EU Structural Funding, on the same principles which apply to all beneficiaries of this form of assistance. In this context, the key task of the regional authorities is to inspire and prepare adequate operational programs.

Most Polish regions have established their representations in Brussels.[5] The role of these offices – usually staffed by one or two persons – is to follow the changes in the EU laws and regulations and to promote the regions within the international environment. The latter involving attempting to attract FDI, increase the number of tourists and establish cooperation with other regions of the EU. In short, and in the words of one of their number (that of Lódzkie Voivodship), the offices aim at 'creating a positive image of the region in Europe and acquisition of information, often available only in Brussels' (http://www.lodzkie.pl/bruksela/en/tasks/index.html).

Regional development of Poland after 1989

Poland is a country with wide regional disparities. The ratio of disparities in the GDP per capita, which is a summary measure for assessing the level of economic development, is higher than 1 to 4 between the country's 44 NUTS 3 regions – in the case of the relation between Warsaw and the Chełm and Zamość subregion. After inclusion of six cities which represent the NTS 3 level into the subregions which surround them, the scale of these disparities falls to approximately 3.6 to 1 – the relation between Warsaw and the Warsaw subregion to the Chełm and Zamość subregion. Considerable disparities can also be observed within individual regions, especially those with large cities. For instance, in 2001, the span between Warsaw and the Radom region, all part of the Mazowieckie *voivodship*, was 3.9 to 1, while in the Małopolskie *voivodship* the ratio of GDP values per capita was 2.5 to 1, and in Wielkopolskie, 2.6 to 1 (Gorzelak 2005).[6]

Inter-regional disparities in Poland are not, however, greater than in other European countries.[7] Moreover, viewed from this broader perspective, it is important to point out that despite the considerable expenditures incurred by the EU in trying to narrow regional differences across member-states, it is difficult to state beyond doubt whether regions are converging or diverging (EC 2004; also Rodriguez-Pose and Fratesi 2004). In the Polish case, these differences in GDP per capita can be explained by a by-product of two factors – gross value added per person employed in individual sectors and the share of these sectors in the total employment structure. Since the share of agriculture in eastern regions is much higher than in the western regions, the former have lower GDP values than the latter. In addition, non-metropolitan areas display much less effective socioeconomic structures than those in large cities,[8] which have the highest levels of GDP per inhabitant.

Poland's post-socialist transformation has proceeded according to a clear regional pattern. It was the deepest and fastest in metropolitan regions, which were able to replace their former industrial potential with the growth of specialized services. In contrast, former industrial regions declined, while rural areas have not changed their relative situation.

Differentiated social and occupational structures, as well as dissimilarities in migration history, produce regional differences in social attitudes and behaviors, which are notably manifested in electoral behaviors. This was clearly observed in the political preferences toward the EU, as expressed in the accession referendum in 2003. In this case, the boundary of the regained territories represents a strikingly distinct line, dividing the *powiats* whose inhabitants expressed a particularly strong support for Poland's EU membership from those *powiats* that formed part of the Polish state in the inter-war period, where pro-EU sentiment was weaker. In many eastern *powiats*, more votes were cast against accession than in favor.

Generally speaking, when the progress of individual regions since transformation is measured against their level of development at the start of that process, regional development processes appear to be differentiated along two different spatial dimensions (Gorzelak 2005):

1. **Large cities – the rest of the country.** This is a new manifestation of the traditional division between rural and urban areas. By now, however, urban status and the dominance of the non-agricultural sectors of the economy alone are no longer indicators of the development potential. Rather, it is only the very large cities (mainly Warsaw, as well as Poznań, Kraków, Wroclaw and Tricity) who have diverse economy structures, are connected with Europe via relatively well-developed transport and telecommunication infrastructure, are furnished with various institutions, including research and development centers, and have a relatively well-educated population, that are able to establish contacts with the competitive global economy. The diffusion of development from a large city around its vicinity does not exceed a 30km radius (in the case of Warsaw, and probably even less in the case of other large cities), whereas the area in a 50–100km radius is characterized by the 'draining' of resources from the metropolitan region to its metropolitan center (cf. e.g. Gorzelak and Smętkowski 2005).
2. **East-west.** This a *longue durée* dimension; one strongly determined by historical factors. Since the Middle Ages, the western part of what is now

Poland has demonstrated a higher level of development than the eastern part (for instance the Romanesque style did not reach beyond the Vistula River). This division was further reinforced by the partitions, the boundaries of which are even today visible in the country's social and economic space. Since the transformation, eastern Poland has been much less able to adapt to the challenges of an open, competitive, knowledge-based economy. The current regression of some of Poland's eastern regions is largely due to this structural backwardness and the inability of these regions and non-metropolitan central regions to satisfy the requirements of contemporary, open economy.

Trends across both these dimensions are creating ever wider inter-regional disparities; reacting to the challenges created by this situation may be regarded as the main task facing the regional policy in Poland.

Regional policy

As was the case in other post-socialist countries (see Bachtler et al. 2000), during the entire decade of the 1990s regional polices in Poland were extremely weak and subordinated to the sectoral policies of the national governments. In fact, there were only a few measures and instruments applied that could have been labeled as 'regional policy', such as the establishment of 16 special economic zones and the introduction of special measures in those areas threatened by structural unemployment.

The creation of (relatively) strong regional government with some autonomous powers introduced a previously non-existing partner for the central government. Since then, the state's regional policy – as weak as it was – has been supplemented by the development policies of the 16 *voivodships*. The principles of these policies were formulated in the 16 regional strategies prepared by the respective *voivodship* authorities in 1999 and 2000. Very recently these strategies have been updated and supplemented by 15 Regional Innovation Strategies (the Mazowieckie *voivodship* being the only exception).

In the period 2001–2004, Polish regional policies were based on the principle of 'regional contracts' (Gorzela, 2001). The contract was a product of two fundamental documents: the national strategy for regional development, prepared by the government (for the period 2001–2006) and the various regional strategies prepared by the regional governments. On the basis of the national regional development strategy, the government elaborated its 'support program', specifying the goals of the state regional policy, the amounts of money to be spent on it, and the distribution of these funds among the priorities and the regions. Table 12.4 outlines the priorities adopted in the first support program 2001–2002 (later extended to 2003):

Table 12.4 The priorities of the Support Programme, 2001–2002

Priority	Per cent of funds appropriated
Development and improvement of infrastructure supporting the competitiveness of regions	50
Restructuring of the economic base of regions and creating conditions for its diversification	15
Development of human capital	12
Support for regions that need stimulus and are endangered by marginalization	18
Development of inter-regional cooperation	5

Source: The National Strategy for Regional Development 2001–2006.

The total sum assigned to the state's regional policy is distributed according to these priorities. It is divided among the regions according to the following principles:

- 80 per cent according to population size;
- 10 per cent to those regions comprising territories (composed of *powiats*) with GDP per head smaller than 80 per cent of the national average; and,
- 10 per cent to those regions comprising territories (composed of *powiats*) with unemployment higher than 150 per cent of the national average.

The regions thus knew how much money they were going to receive from the state and were able to put forward proposals (compatible with the state's stated priorities) on the basis of the goals and tasks outlined in their own regional strategies. The 16 regional contracts were subsequently replaced by the Integrated Regional Operational Programme, which has been in force for the first period of Polish membership in the EU – from May 2004 until the end of 2006.

Polish regions within the EU

The pre-accession funds

Poland was one of the first countries to benefit from pre-accession EU funds, with the PHARE program, in particular, not only an important source of funds, but also of experience and knowledge about the EU procedures. Several pre-accession projects were directly connected to regional and local development. One of the first such programs – Municipal Development and Training in Poland – helped in the development of training facilities for the newly elected local officials. The STRUDER program, launched in 1993, channeled support into five Polish regions that demonstrated particular serious development problems and handicaps. Germany also directed some €50 million annually into regions in western Poland through the PHARE CBC Poland program.

The integrated operational programme for regional development 2004–2006

After Poland's accession to the EU the country was able to benefit from Structural Funds and the Cohesion Fund. The Integrated Regional Operational Programme of 2004–2006 was among the few programs to implemented in the first membership period. Directly implemented by the regions themselves, the program's priorities were:

1. Development and modernization of infrastructure in order to enhance the competitiveness of the regions. Within this priority, the following were considered to be the most important priorities:

   - modernization and development of the regional transport system;
   - environmental protection infrastructure;
   - the facilities of tertiary education institutions;
   - public infrastructure supporting tourism and culture development;
   - information society infrastructure; and,
   - the development of urban public transport in the main agglomerations of Poland.

2. Strengthening Human Resource Development in the regions, concentrating on:

   - the development of competencies linked to the requirements of the regional labor market and lifelong learning opportunities;
   - equalizing opportunities through scholarships;
   - vocational re-orientation for people leaving agriculture;
   - vocational re-orientation of the workforce affected by the restructuring process;
   - entrepreneurship; and,
   - Regional Innovation Strategies and knowledge transfer.

3. Local Development with assistance was focused on the following:

   - development and restructuring of rural areas;
   - areas of industrial decline and restructuring; and,
   - urban areas threatened by marginalization, including former industrial and military sites.

In addition to the forms of targeted investment noted above, there was also to be investment in micro enterprise start-ups and local educational and social infrastructure.

4. Technical Assistance was directed to the institutions involved in IOPRD implementation (IOPRD – Managing Authority at the Ministry of the Economy, Labour, and Social Policy, Marshal Offices, Voivodship Offices, Voivodship Labour Offices, Regional Financial Institutions).

The total costs of the IOPRD are some €4.08 million (including almost 3 billion from the EU), which will amount to some one third of the total transfers to Poland from the Structural Funds and the Cohesion Fund in the period 2007–2013.

Given that the regional programs are being implemented by the regions themselves and are rooted in their regional development strategies, and given also the decentralized management structure of the IOPRD, it is clear that we are witnessing an important step on the decentralization path.

Regional operational programs 2007–2013

The programming effort is still underway. The change of the government in fall 2005 meant not only the political change, but also brought about some discontinuity in structuring the means and ways of using the Structural Funds and the Cohesion Fund in the new programming period 2007–2013. However, due to the fact that the priorities for Poland's development are – in many cases – relatively obvious, there were continuities between the strategies of the incoming and outgoing governments.

From the point of view of the role of regions one important decision had been maintained. Instead of one regional operational program, in the period 2007–2013 there will be 16 such programs, one for each of the Polish regions. Additionally, a special program for the five eastern regions – the least developed ones – will be launched. It will be managed by the government and financed from the sectoral programs, rather than depleting the funding available for other regional programs.

The National Strategic Reference Framework for 2007–2013 specifies the following goals for the regional development of Poland:

a) *More effective use of the endogenous potential of the largest metropolitan centers.* The policy directions which can promote the achievement of this goal include continued support for the development of the metropolitan functions (including research, educational and cultural functions) of the country's major urban centers, the development of their technical infrastructure to enhance their attractiveness for investment, and the connection of all the urban centers via a network of motorways and dual carriageways. On the one hand, this will foster the competitiveness of the regions where such centers are located, and on the other hand it will accelerate the diffusion of developmental processes.

b) *Accelerated development of Poland's eastern regions (voivodships).* To ensure the success of the cohesion policy in Poland and, in the wider European context, to include these areas in the processes aimed at generating growth and employment, the poorest of the country's regions (Lubelskie, Podlaskie, Podkarpackie, Świętokrzyskie, Warmińsko-Mazurskie) will be given special attention. In addition to those activities expected to improve the competitive advantage of every regions, these regions will be subject to an integrated program of spatial, regional and sectoral policies, focusing on encouraging the kind of accelerated structural changes that is of cardinal importance given their low levels of economic activity and low attractiveness (for external investment).

In particular, the development of these areas will depend on the success of efforts to:

- improve the quality of human capital and enhance spatial and geographical mobility;
- improve the performance of institutions responsible for the programming, direction and implementation of developmental activities;
- expand the metropolitan functions of the main centers of socioeconomic growth and connect these centers with the similar main centers in the country, as well as with European networks;
- promote selected regional products; and,
- upgrade the transport infrastructure as regards the connections between the main urban centers and the town–country connections, and as regards improving accessibility to mass transport systems.

c) Problem areas – counteracting their marginalization and peripheralization. The overriding goal of activities in the problem areas is to support changes that can ensure sustainable development by counteracting the marginalization processes of selected groups of regions. Such problem areas include border areas and areas threatened with natural disasters, as well as post-industrial and post-military zones.

The National Strategic Reference Framework adopted by the government in February 2006 assigns 26.8 per cent of funding (some €16 billion) to the programs that are to be administered by the 16 regional authorities, plus a further 7 per cent of total public funding to a horizontal program for the development of the five least developed regions to be administered by the central state. Additionally, €5.46 billion of the social funds will be managed regionally.[9] Taking these three items together, and estimating the GDP of particular regions within the period 2007–2013, we can (roughly) estimate the share of funds assigned to regions within their prospective GDP. This is shown in Table 12.5.

As can be seen, the least developed regions will receive much greater shares of their GDP in support than those with a higher GDP. This clearly indicates an equity-driven regional policy for the coming period for Poland,

Table 12.5 Regionally addressed EU funds as per cent of prospected regional GDP, 2007–2013

Voivodships (capital city)	EU funds as per cent of regional GDP	Voivodships (capital city)	EU funds as per cent of regional GDP
Dolnośląskie (Wrocław)	1.0	Podkarpackie (Rzeszów)	2.1
Kujawsko-pomorskie (Bydgoszcz)	1.2	Podlaskie (Białystok)	2.0
Lubelskie (Lublin)	2.2	Pomorskie Gdańsk)	1.0
Lubuskie (Zielona Góra)	1.3	Śląskie (Katowice)	0.8
Łódzkie (Łódź)	1.0	Świętokrzyskie (Kielce)	2.1
Małopolskie (Kraków)	1.0	Warmińsko-Mazurskie (Olsztyn)	2.4
Mazowieckie (Warszawa)	0.6	Wielkopolskie (Poznań)	0.8
Opolskie (Opole)	1.2	Zachodniopomorskie (Szczecin)	1.2
Poland			1.1

Source: Own estimates based on data from the Ministry for Regional Development.

which does not necessarily follow the most recent development within the European Commission. The regional distribution of the sectoral operational programs, which will consume another one-third of all funds coming to Poland in the period 2007–2013 is not yet known.

Conclusion

Polish regions have acquired serious competencies in programming regional development. They have become partners for both the national government and international institutions such as the European Commission, European organizations and collective bodies. With competencies come responsibilities. Until Poland's membership in the EU, Polish regions have not had sufficient funds to implement the policies that were to put into effect their development strategies. The greater availability of EU funds – in the form of one integrated program for regional development in the period 2004–2006 and 16 regional operational programs in the subsequent programming period – enabled the regions not only to prepare strategies, but also to put them into practise.

The final outcomes remain to be seen, and are likely to vary, not least because absorption capacity varies considerably across the regions. Generally speaking, however, the regions have a great deal of autonomy in directing funds to particular priorities and projects. It is therefore likely that it is they, rather than the central government or the European Commission, who will be held to account for both successes and failures. The Polish regions are gradually coming of age.

Notes

1. These are relatively large cites (over 100,000 population) and cities that had been the capitals of the former *voivodships*, which assume the responsibilities of a *powiat* (so the city council is at the same time the *powiat* council, and the city mayor is also the chief executive of the *powiat* administration). In most cases such cities are surrounded by 'country' *powiats*.

2. *Dziennik Ustaw* (Journal of Laws).

3. *Monitor Polski* (Official Gazette).

4. These are the following: 1. public education, including tertiary education; 2. promotion and protection of health; 3. culture and protection of historic monuments; 4. social welfare; 5. family policy; 6. modernization of rural areas; 7. spatial planning; 8. environmental protection; 9. water economy, including flood control, and in particular provision of equipment and maintenance of *voivodship* flood-control depots; 10. mass transport and public roads; 11. physical culture and tourism; 12. protection of consumers' rights; 13. defence; 14. public security; 15. counteracting unemployment and activation of the local labor market.

5. Only five Polish regions are the members of the Assembly of European Regions: Kujawsko-Pomorskie, Małopolskie, Mazowieckie, Śląskie, Wielkopolskie.

6. It should be borne in mind that real disparities in the GDP values between a large city and the surrounding area are smaller due to the fact that many people commute to work and that, in many cases, business activity is only formally registered in the city.

7. It should be pointed out that, naturally, the scale of differences depends on the number of units included in the comparison: the more the units, the smaller their size, and the greater the disparities.

8. The shares of persons employed in agriculture are overstated because many of them do not work on a full time basis. This, however, does not disprove the thesis on the fundamental significance of structural differences for regional disparities in the GDP level, but rather sustains it.

9. The total inflow of EU funds to Poland in the period 2007–2013 will reach some €90 billion. This can be roughly divided into three almost equal parts: funds allocated regionally and mostly managed by the regions themselves (displayed in Table 12.5); sectoral operational programs, managed by state agencies; and funds transferred within the framework of Common Agricultural Policy, distributed according to the area of agricultural land.

13
Accommodating European Union Membership: The Regional Level in Bulgaria

Martin Brusis[*]

Bulgaria has been a highly centralized unitary state since its creation in 1878. Its unitary structure has contributed to the survival of Bulgaria as a state in a region where national borders cut across ethnic boundaries and statehood conflicts still pose risks to peace and stability. This state tradition constitutes the broader legitimatory framework for a model of government and society that does not know a regional level in the sense of sub-national territorial-administrative units endowed with a constitutional status, political weight and social basis. Key areas of statehood, such as finance, domestic security, defense or education have been firmly controlled by national ministries that have been reluctant to transfer powers to the more localized layers of government established after the transition to democracy in 1990/1991.

Bulgaria's accession to the European Union (EU) has provided strong incentives for changes to this model. One of the most important change processes concerns the regional level that is exposed to the opportunities and challenges of a multi-level system of governance as the country accommodates to membership in the Union. A growing body of research has shown that European integration induces an emergence of regions as political actors in member states; however this tendency is moderated by domestic institutional arrangements and actor constellations.

The present chapter explores the status and situation of the regional level in Bulgaria in view of Bulgaria's EU membership. It begins by analyzing the constitutional position of local and regional units of government and administration. To what extent have these units – municipalities, district administrations and planning regions – become actors or channels representing local and regional interests and providing input into national European policies and at the EU level?

The main finding is that regional and local interests have so far been only weakly institutionalized in Bulgaria's constitutional order, public administration and political process. The weakness of regional and local structures constrain the role these structures play in the European constitutional debate and in the domestic implementation of EU policies. Moreover, this weakness corresponds to the apparent absence of 'region' as a differentiating feature of Bulgarian society. Finally, the chapter seeks to explain why the incentives of EU membership have not caused a fundamental change of governance in Bulgaria, thereby identifying fiscal restrictions, domestic party politics and the ambivalent role of the EU as factors complementing the impact of state traditions.

Sub-state governmental structures

The Republic of Bulgaria is, according to its 1991 Constitution, a unitary state with local self-government. The Constitution does not specifically envisage regional self-government and underscores the unitary nature of the state by explicitly prohibiting the existence of autonomous territorial formations (Art. 2). Two administrative-territorial units are distinguished in the Constitution. The municipality (*obshtina*) represents the basic territorial unit of local self-government (Art. 136). In addition, the Constitution defines the district (*oblast*) as an administrative-territorial unit entrusted with the conduct of regional policy, the implementation of state government on a local level, and the ensuring of harmony of national and local interests (Art. 142). That said, the Constitution does not specifically preclude the creation of elected self-government at the regional level. Rather, it leaves this decision to the legislature by stating that the territorial division, other administrative territorial units and bodies of self-government shall be establishable by law (Art. 135) (Ivanov et al. 2002: 207). This provision may be read as a constitutional permission to create regions and regional self-government.

There are, however, doubts as to whether this permission includes the district level since the Constitution explicitly assigns the administration of the district to a district governor (*oblasten upravitel*) (Art. 143). The Constitution also constrains the creation of a regional level by prescribing that changes in the form of state structure or form of government require the approval of a grand national assembly, i.e. an enlarged parliamentary assembly specifically elected to amend the Constitution (Art. 158). The Constitution's openness and ambiguity with respect to regional (self-) government indicates that its drafters in 1991 did not agree on a definite model of administrative-territorial organization (Ivanov et al. 2002: 207). Regarding the organization of district government, the Constitution stipulates a prefectoral model. A district governor, who is appointed by the Council of Ministers, shall ensure the implementation of the state's policy, the safeguarding of national interests, law and public order, and shall exercise administrative control (Art. 143).

To prepare for the accession to the EU, Bulgaria in 2000 created planning regions (*rayonite za planirane*) corresponding to the NUTS 2 level of the classification of territorial statistics applied in the EU. These regions constitute territorial units for regional development planning in the framework of the Structural Funds, the EU's most important financial program, which supports the economic convergence of its less developed member states.

Planning regions, administrative districts and municipal self-governments can be seen as institutionalized units on which a representation of regional interests may be built. Given the lack of a constitutionally enshrined regional level, the following sections study the extent to which a representation of regional interests has evolved alongside these units.

Municipalities

Local self-government was re-established in 1991 when the Grand National Assembly adopted a new Constitution and the Law on Local Self-Government and Local Administration (ZMSMA). The first democratic local elections were held in October 1991. In contrast to other Central and East European countries, Bulgaria has not experienced a fragmentation of municipalities since the political transition. The number of municipalities has been relatively stable, some 265 in 2005. High legal obstacles and financial disincentives have discouraged local communities from further proliferation.

With an average size of 30,000 residents and 420 km², Bulgarian municipalities are larger than most municipalities in other European countries. They are composed of numerous individual settlements (*naseleni mesta*), on average 20 per municipality. Due to their composite nature and size, Bulgarian municipalities have 'to a large extent the character of regional self-government' (Boev 2002: 113). The relatively large size of the municipalities and the principle of the direct election of mayors have ensured that mayors are influential political figures, enjoying substantial organizational capacity and strong political legitimacy. Many mayors have taken a national political role in parliament or government (Djildjov 2002: 84).

A second channel of local interest representation consists in the national and regional associations of municipalities. All 265 Bulgarian municipalities are organized in the National Association of Municipalities of the Republic of Bulgaria (NSORB), established in 1996. The NSORB is an entity of private law with voluntary membership, but it is assigned public functions by various laws. The governments of Prime Ministers Simeon Sakskoburggotski and Sergei Stanishev acknowledged the NSORB as a partner by concluding formal policy agreements at the beginning of their terms of office, in December 2001 and October 2005 respectively.

By 2005, ten regional associations of municipalities were also in existence. They are also entities of private law and date back to 1992 (Djildjov 2002: 78). In recent years, development agencies such as USAID and the

UNDP have fostered their creation. While regional associations have been organized on a geographical basis, their membership cuts across district boundaries.

Despite these organizational and political power resources, municipalities have not been particularly successful in representing local interests on the national level. The initial decentralization introduced by the Law on Local Self-Government and Local Administration was not backed up by a concomitant decentralization of financial resources. Local government expenditures declined from 11 to 5 per cent of GDP and from 21 to 14 per cent of the consolidated state budget in the period between 1991 and 2004 (Ivanov et al. 2002: 173; LGI 2004). In 2007, local government expenditure amounted to 19.2 per cent of total public expenditure (MS 2008: 21). Until 2007, municipalities had not been granted the right to determine the rates of local taxes and the types and rates of local fees. In February 2007, the parliament amended the Constitution to entitle municipal councils to set the rates of local taxes and fees in accordance with rules defined in a law (Art. 141(3–4)).

This broader trajectory of reluctant decentralization provides the background against which one can observe and assess the role of municipalities with respect to inputs in EU-policy-making on the national and EU level.

Individual municipalities have not taken a role in EU policy-making, except for the capital Sofia, which established representation in Brussels in October 2004. The NSORB also established representation in Brussels in the same year and participates as an observer in the Committee of Regions as well as being a member of the Congress of Local and Regional Authorities attached to the Council of Europe (CLRAE). While these structures facilitate paradiplomatic activities, the NSORB did not make a publicly visible contribution to the debate on the Constitutional Treaty. Rather, the Association has hitherto focused its paradiplomacy on engaging EU bodies for its domestic objectives.

For example, the Committee of Regions and the NSORB agreed to establish a Joint Consultative Committee (JCC) in December 2001. This body was endorsed by the Bulgarian government and the EU in 2002 and functioned in the framework of the Europe Agreement between Bulgaria, the EU and its member states. The JCC comprised representatives of the Committee of Regions and the municipalities of Bulgaria and met twice a year between December 2003 and December 2006. The JCC has urged the Bulgarian government to strengthen the role and powers of local and regional authorities by implementing meaningful fiscal decentralization, including the right to determine local tax rates, involving municipalities in the management of the Structural Funds and enabling them to co-finance development projects.

The NSORB and the government seem to agree that the main role of municipalities and their national association is in implementing EU policies rather than in shaping them. While local government representatives were excluded from the accession negotiations or the domestic preparation of negotiation positions, the NSORB has participated in the government's domestic communication strategy.[1] In July 2004, the NSORB adopted a municipal action plan for the accession of Bulgaria to the EU. The plan was intended to harmonize municipal legislation with EU requirements, to deliver municipal services meeting EU standards, to improve the administrative and programming capacity of municipalities, and to ensure transparency and control of municipal activities (NAMRB 2004).

In October 2005, the Stanishev government concluded a new agreement with the NSORB, agreeing to prepare the municipalities for Bulgaria's EU membership.[2] The agreement envisaged increasing the administrative and financial absorption capacity of the local level with regard to EU funds, 'to concretise the commitments made by the national level and their impact on the practice of Bulgarian municipalitites', to support municipal projects for transferring good European practice for the delivery of local services, and to limit the negative effects of Bulgaria's EU membership for municipalities. In particular, the government agreed to include representatives of local government in the planning, programming, management, monitoring and evaluation of programs and projects financed from the EU's pre-accession Cohesion and Structural Funds.[3]

By participating in the monitoring, evaluation and review of Bulgaria's regional development policy, the NSORB is involved in an important area of EU-related policy-making. In June 2006, the government committed itself to co-opting the NSORB in the committees charged with monitoring the implementation of the Structural Funds (MS 2006).

Regional associations of municipalities were formed to represent their common interests in relation with the national government, promote regional development, train municipal employees and representatives, and facilitate a knowledge transfer among municipalities. However, while regional associations may be interpreted as examples of bottom-up regionalization, their impact has so far been rather limited. In general, cooperation between municipalities has, according to Bulgarian observers, been uncoordinated and, in many cases, of a merely formal nature (Mollov et al. 2004: 40). Municipalities mostly cooperate in common infrastructural projects, especially in waste management (FRMS 2006: 8).

Most municipalities and the NSORB neither promote the strengthening of a regional level or the introduction of regional self-government, nor do they explicitly oppose such a reform. The NSORB's strategic priority is to enhance the financial resource base and legal powers of municipalities.[4] NSORB representatives have viewed a regional level of government as associated with a recentralization. Central government initiatives have hitherto, according to the NSORB, aimed at transferring powers from the municipalities to the regional level rather than from ministries to the regional level. Both district governors and planning regions are seen as units of the state administration that do not represent municipal interests.

Notwithstanding NSORB initiatives, the representation of Bulgarian local and regional interests in the emerging multi-layer system of EU governance still depends heavily on central government advocacy. A study prepared by government officials and independent advisors accordingly suggests that 'If local government institutions want to successfully represent their interests on the EU level, they need to cooperate and act in a consensus with national government' (Mollov et al. 2004: 27).

Districts

Districts are, on average, 4000 km² large and comprise 280,000 residents. The 28 districts existing today were established in 1999, replacing the nine districts that had existed since 1987. The average number of municipalities per district is 9.4. Districts have been classified as NUTS 3 units while their boundaries reflect the physical geography of the territory, traditional cultural and economic ties, as well as the social, technical and transport infrastructures (ZATURB Art. 5). The boundaries of districts (and municipalities) are determined by the president, on a motion from the Council of Ministers (Art. 98 Constitution, ZATURB Art. 26). A change of the boundaries of districts must be in accordance with the boundaries of the existing municipalities (ZATURB Art. 26).

The Law on Administration and the Statute on District Administrations stipulates that district governors may suspend the execution of unlawful acts of municipal councils and refer them to the courts. District governors may repeal the unlawful acts of mayors of municipalities, for the repeal of which no special procedures are provided. Their decisions may be appealed against in the courts. In practice, district governors have frequently intervened in the functioning of municipalities (Ananieva 2002: 100). Their legal role is, however, not confined to supervising municipalities, but also involves coordination between the deconcentrated bodies of central government and local government.

Moreover, district governors are also envisaged as advocates of regional interests in the framework of regional development. This function is, however, somewhat problematic, as admitted in a strategy paper produced by the Ministry of Regional Development and Public Works:

> Some of the problems of the existing system of district governors and the uncertainties related to decisions to be taken are probably linked to the dual function of the district governor – the fusion of the role of a 'representative of the state' on the regional level, exercising control functions characterizing certain state organs, with the roles of an advocate and guarantor of interests linked to regional development, functions assigned by the Regional Development Law. These latter roles are specifically political, concern the territories of the district and the municipalities located there, and are typical for elected organs.

(MRRB 2005: 17)

District governors and their deputies are political appointees who are accountable to the Council of Ministers. Incoming governments used to fill these positions with their loyal supporters. Contrary to previous practice, the Stanishev government has appointed former mayors and councilors to two thirds of the posts. Since 2005 district governors have met every 2 months with the NSORB to exchange information and address conflicts in the relations between district administrations and municipalities.[5]

District administrations manage, *inter alia*, state-owned property, coordinate between the municipalities and the deconcentrated units of line ministries, support the local mayors and police authorities in sustaining public order and combating crime, assist municipalities in implementing delegated tasks of the central government, oversee the legality of administrative acts issued by municipalities, establish organizations to implement Bulgaria's EU integration policy in the district and prepare regional development plans. District administrations are legal persons and their budgets are part of the budget of the Ministry of State Administration and Administrative Reform. In 2004, the size of their staff was approximately 1 per cent of total government employment, whereas the total staff of municipalities amounted to 26 per cent of government employment (MSA 2005: 46).

The deconcentrated units of line ministries have continued to be institutionally separated from the district administrations, even though integration would facilitate a broader integration of regional and sectoral policies (Djildjov 2001: 93–94). A structural obstacle to such an integration has been the incongruence between the districts and the jurisdictions of deconcentrated units. The territorial organization of these deconcentrated services is based on various laws and decrees, and does not follow clear and consistent criteria (MRRB 2005: 11).

The introduction of directly elected district or regional levels has been discussed among experts and politicians (Djildjov 2002). Three institutional options may be tentatively distinguished in this debate, although none of these options has hitherto been fully elaborated, at least according to available information. One option would be the direct popular election of district governors.[6] This would require amending Article 143 of the Constitution that stipulates the appointment of district governors by the Council of Ministers.

A second option would be the creation of directly elected district assemblies or councils in addition to, and as partners of, the existing district-level state administration.[7] District governors would become responsible for managing the state administration and implementing the decisions of elected assemblies/councils.[8] Most district governors tend to favor the establishment of directly elected councils as partnership institutions for participation in the Structural Funds.[9] A third option appears to be the establishment of directly elected bodies at the level of planning regions rather than districts (Marinov 2001: 32). This option is promoted as being less costly than establishing 28 self-governing bodies.[10] However, as of March 2009, no directly elected bodies had been established at the regional or district level. The Sakskoburggotski government (2001–2005) declared its resolve to establish 'a second level of self-government in accordance with the requirements of European integration' in its program declaration.[11] While the public administration reform strategy of 2003 and the decentralization strategy of 2005 renewed this commitment, no draft legislation was prepared to amend the Constitution or define the role of directly elected regions. The Stanishev government (2005–2009) did not mention the creation of regional self-government in its manifesto. Its decentralization strategy from June 2006 was confined to analyzing the feasibility of establishing regional self-government, but does not suggest any further steps (MS 2006). Rather, the strategy sought to strengthen the capacity and coordinating role of district governors and administrations. However, as integral parts of the state's administration, district governors and their offices at best function as proxy representatives for local and regional interests in respect of EU policy-making. The general organizational capacity of district administrations certainly appears to be too limited to enable any interest representation beyond the national level.

Planning regions

Bulgaria has established six planning regions as NUTS 2 level territorial units for the planning, programming and implementation of the Structural Funds of the EU (see Table 13.1). These regions each comprise three to six districts and respect the boundaries of these districts (2004 Law on Regional Development, Art. 6). The planning regions were initially set up in 2000 by a decree of the Council of Ministers in order to complement Bulgaria's first Law on Regional Development from 1999. A second Law on Regional Development adopted in 2004 (ZRR) included a list of planning regions. As the north-western and south-eastern planning region had fewer than 800,000 inhabitants, they did not comply with the minimum population size required for a NUTS 2 region, necessitating a revision of the ZRR.[12] The modified law was adopted on 15 May 2008 and complemented the division into six planning regions by a division into two large planning regions corresponding to the NUTS 1 level.

The 2004 Regional Development Law has established regional councils for development (*regionalni saveti za razvitie*) attached to the NUTS 2 planning regions. These councils prepare draft regional development plans and preliminary evaluations of projects included in Bulgaria's National Operational Programme for Regional Development. While the plans specify regional policy objectives, the Operational Programme sets out the measures to be co-financed from the Structural Funds.

Regional development councils consist of representatives from central state ministries and agencies, all the governors of those districts that form part of the planning region, one representative of the municipalities of each

Table 13.1 Geographic, social and economic parameters of planning regions (2003)

Planning regions	Area (km²)	% of the total area of the country	Population (persons)	% of the national total	Population density (persons/ km²)	Number of districts	Number of municipalities	GDP p.c. (USD, current prices)	Registered unemployment rate
Bulgaria	**111001.9**	**100.0**	**7801273**	**100.0**	**70.3**	**28**	**264**	**2546**	**14.25**
North-western	10288.2	9.3	512593	6.6	49.8	3	32	2242	23.38
North Central	18320.0	16.5	1165806	14.9	63.6	5	41	2172	16.07
North-eastern	19923.4	17.9	1285803	16.5	64.5	6	49	2171	18.61
South-eastern	14647.6	13.2	782653	10.0	53.4	3	22	2308	14.64
South Central	27516.2	24.8	1944382	24.9	70.7	6	68	2071	14.91
South-western	20306.5	18.3	2110036	27.0	103.9	5	52	3582	7.56

Source: Cadastre Agency; National Statistical Institute, current demographic statistics.

district within the planning region, and representatives of employers and trade unions. The discretion and influence of regional development councils is rather limited since the regional development plans approved by them are only drafts for the Finance Ministry and the Ministry of Regional Development and Public Works. The two ministries are free to adapt these proposals before they jointly submit them to the Council of Ministers for approval. Regional and local representatives are not directly involved in the preparation of the National Operational Programme for Regional Development and the National Development Plan. Moreover, the composition of regional development councils ensures that central government representatives and district governors constitute a majority in all regions.

The current planning regions may be characterized as artificially created institutions that do not reflect a regionally differentiated domestic economic, social or political infrastructure, and that have been specifically designed to comply with EU requirements and ensure the absorption of EU funds (cf. also Barna et al. 2005).

Interacting with European programs

The weakness of regional and local structures in Bulgaria and the lack of familiarity with EU membership explain why Bulgarian regional and local government bodies have little experience in implementing EU regulations and directives. Municipalities and district administrations were entitled to participate in all three EU programs assisting the EU accession preparations: the PHARE program (administrative capacity-building, regulatory convergence with the EU's legislation and socio-economic cohesion), SAPARD (rural and agricultural development) and ISPA (infrastructural projects in the environmental and transport sectors).[13] A survey conducted by UNDP in all Bulgarian municipalities and district administrations in April 2006 showed that 38 per cent of the municipalities had established organizational units dealing with EU-related projects (Marinov and Garnizov 2006: 204). Most district administrations lacked the capacity to deal with EU projects and 72 per cent of all municipalities did not have any approved projects under the three pre-accession funds (UNDP 2004: 181). The large, developed and urban municipalities had the greatest amount of experience with the pre-accession funds.

The limits of local discretion in implementation may be illustrated with the example of regional development policy, the policy area where the EU exerts the most substantial financial influence through its Structural Funds. A comparison between the 1999 and 2004 Laws on Regional Development shows how the discretion of municipalities and district administrations has been reduced. The 1999 Law on Regional Development established district councils for regional development that consisted of local mayors and councilors and assisted the district governor in preparing district development plans. These plans formed the basis of a National Plan for Regional Development that was prepared by the Ministry of Regional Development and Public Works (MRRB) and adopted by the Council of Ministers.

In contrast, the 2004 Law on Regional Development confined the district development councils to elaborating district development *strategies* that had to be approved by the regional development councils and had to take into account the objectives set in advance by the National Strategy for Regional Development. Whereas the previously existing Regional Development Council was a cabinet-level advisory committee involving the NSORB, the newly established 'Partnership Board' was attached only to the MRRB. The planning and programming tasks were fully assigned to the MRRB and the Ministry of Finance, corresponding to the more centralized management approach of the EU Commission.

The May 2008 amendment to the Regional Development Law charged the MRRB with implementing regional development policy – a provision that can be seen as contradicting the constitutional provision that entrusts the district with the conduct of regional policy (Art. 142 of the Constitution).[14] Moreover, the MRRB units for technical coordination and management of regional programs and plans that had been integrated into the district administrations were dissolved and replaced by NUTS 2 level units subordinated to the minister. The 2004 Law, and the 2008 amendment, document a recentralization process in the course of which the central government has withdrawn participation opportunities from the municipalities. This recentralization does, however, also reflect the deficient absorption capacity of the local level outlined above.

Public attitudes

Local or regional attitudes toward European integration and the role of regions within that process do not appear to have been the subject of specific research in Bulgaria. This is not only due to the lack of a broader infrastructure of social science research. It also indicates the fact that Bulgarian scholars did not attach much importance to the regional dimension of society, politics or social structure, which in turn reflects the lack of discernible distinctive regional identities and regionally differentiated communities in Bulgaria (cf. e.g. Genov and Krasteva 1999). Two exceptions to this general situation are the Eurobarometer surveys and the national Human Development reports published by the UNDP office in Bulgaria.

The national Eurobarometer surveys for Bulgaria have repeatedly reported a comparatively high rate of support for the country's EU membership, amounting, for example, to 84 per cent of the population in October 2005.[15] As in other EU accession countries, support for EU membership has been consistently higher among the urban population than in rural areas, which can be explained by the greater number of highly educated persons in cities.

The national Human Development report of 1999 contains more detailed data from an opinion survey that was conducted in November 1998 and March 1999 in order to map the aspirations of citizens with respect to local government (UNDP 1999). This survey concluded that decentralization and local self-government mattered little for most people. 'On the whole, over one-third of respondents felt that life was the same everywhere in Bulgaria. More regionally-minded respondents were found in larger communities (42%), business respondents (37%) and those with a higher education (46%). But the overall perception that life is the same everywhere confirms a lack of local vision for regional peculiarities' (UNDP 1999: 39).

The accession negotiations and the diffusion of EU-related activities to the local level since the beginning of the decade seem to have caused people to pay more attention to the role of municipalities in European integration. According to a Eurobarometer survey carried out in fall 2005, 62 per cent of the Bulgarian citizens believed that local governments should make more effort to involve citizens in EU affairs.[16] While this expectation was less frequently articulated than in the average of the new EU member states, it indicated a growing awareness of the role municipalities could or should play in European integration.

Explaining the weakness of regional structures

Bulgaria's municipalities possess only limited capacity – mainly through their national association – to provide inputs into the debate and preparation of EU policies both on the national level and European level. Districts and planning regions lack even this capacity and have always been integral parts of the state administration and traditional bureaucratic hierarchy. Municipalities and districts have gathered some experience in managing EU projects, but their financial resource base continues to be modest and their discretion in regional development has become even more limited. Neither have the various decentralization or regionalization initiatives discussed in this chapter fundamentally changed this model of governance. Five main reasons may be identified to explain the persistent weakness of decentralized or regional structures in Bulgaria.

1. Bulgaria's economic collapse in the mid-1990s was overcome by establishing a currency board that imposed fiscal discipline as a constraint to all reforms of public policy. The introduction of the currency board in 1997 empowered advocates of centralized government and in particular the Ministry of Finance. Finance ministry officials argued that decentralization would jeopardize fiscal and monetary stability as municipalities would likely overspend and incur debt (Marinov 2001: 35; Minkova 2004). Decentralization would be less efficient and would provide more opportunities for corruption (Djildjov 2002). The priority attached to fiscal discipline and the

perceived lack of financial management skills in municipalities have also weakened public finance arguments in favor of decentralization, such as arguments highlighting the benefits of tax and services competition between municipalities.

2. Local and regional interest representation has been constrained by the divisions of central-local party politics. Risking a bold simplification, one may characterize Bulgaria's party system as shaped by five main forces: the Bulgarian Socialist Party (BSP), the successor of the state socialist regime party; its main adversary, the liberal-conservative Union of Democratic Forces (SDS); the center-right law-and-order party, Citizens for European Development (GERB), established in 2006; the Movement of Rights and Freedoms (DPS), advocating the interests of Bulgaria's ethnic Turkish and Muslim minorities (approximately 10 per cent of the population); and the National Movement of Simeon II. (NDSV), a party established in 2001 to promote the leadership of Simeon Sakskoburggotski, the son of Bulgaria's last tsar (Karasimeonov 2002). The first democratically elected governments were dominated by the BSP and DPS, except for a 1-year period of an SDS-led government in 1991–1992. Following the economic crisis of 1996/1997, the SDS (and its electoral coalition) won the 1997 parliamentary elections and governed the country for a full legislative period. The NDSV emerged as the leading political party in the 2001 elections, forming a coalition government with the DPS and co-opting two BSP-affiliated politicians as ministers. This coalition and cooperation evolved into a formal three-party coalition led by the BSP when the latter became the strongest party in the June 2005 elections.

The political constellation at the local level has been somewhat more stable over successive local elections, with the BSP dominating mainly the rural municipalities, the SDS and recently GERB being most successful in Sofia and other big cities, and the DPS controlling settlements with ethnic Turkish or Muslim majorities. The rural-urban cleavage on the local level reinforced the initial bipolarity between post-communists and anti-communists on the national level, thereby limiting the scope for 'non-partisan' local interest articulation.

While none of the major parties principally opposed decentralization, 'the left party [BSP] is to a greater extent supporting decentralization, insists on conducting decentralization at the lowest possible level, they spend the budget by re-allocating it to the less developed and distant regions; the right party [SDS] is much more interested in the problems at the level of the region, the regional development issues and it strives to concentrate the resources and to fund the bigger projects in the already developed regions which have a greater development potential' (Djildjov 2002: 83).

When NDSV took over government in 2001, it lacked any basis in local government institutions. Facing an erosion of parliamentary and public support in the run-up to the 2003 local elections, NDSV politicians hesitated to embark upon an ambitious fiscal decentralization project they increasingly perceived as serving the political interests of BSP- and SDS-controlled municipalities.[17]

3. Regionalization has been perceived as jeopardizing Bulgaria's cohesion as a state. The collapse of neighboring Yugoslavia and the conflictual history of Bulgarian-Turkish relations in connection with the ethnic Turkish minority in Bulgaria have nurtured fears about a disintegration of the state (Vassilev 2001). These concerns induced the Grand National Assembly to insert two articles in the Constitution that prohibit the existence of autonomous territorial formations and the creation of parties on an ethnic basis. Political representatives of the ethnic Turkish minority have respected these provisions and focused their political strategy on participating in government, rather than calling for regional autonomy.

The DPS does not consider itself an ethnic party and has sought to promote minority interests by strengthening individual rights and freedoms and non-discrimination on the one hand, and supporting the decentralization of government and rural economic development on the other. An autonomous region for ethnic Turks would not only violate the Constitution and be disapproved of by the Bulgarian public, but would also be incompatible with the dispersed settlement structure of Bulgaria's ethnic Turkish and Muslim communities. Most of the ethnic Turkish and Muslim Bulgarians live in two geographically separate rural areas in south-eastern and north-eastern Bulgaria. While there are sizeable communities in the Kurdzhali, Razgrad, Targovishte and Silistra districts, a local majority exists only in Kurdzhali.

Nevertheless, the perceived threat of disintegration has accompanied the debate on a second level of self-government and is likely to restrict the powers of possible self-governing bodies (Djildjov 2002: 87). The ethnopolitical dimension of territorial-administrative issues became visible in the public protests that occurred in August 2005 against the appointment of DPS-affiliated district governors in predominantly ethnic Bulgarian districts such as Varna. Responding to the conflict, two liberal opposition parties proposed the introduction of direct elections for district governors. A politician argued that 'there is no danger from minority groups if a territorial division into six regions is adopted. In such a constellation the results would replicate those of the parliamentary elections and this risk would cease to exist.'[18]

4. Administrative traditions of centralized government and patronage politics can be seen as background variables contributing to the reluctance of incumbent governments to decentralize (Brusis 2004). Since local civil society has developed weakly in Bulgaria as well as in other south-east European countries, public accountability mechanisms have been insufficient particularly on the local level. This has led incumbent politicians and leading administrative officials to trust more in formal-legal hierarchies or in

informal, personalized patron-client relations as methods of ensuring compliance (Verheijen 1999). If a party controls the financial, organizational and staff resources of a central ministry, it faces incentives to retain these resources rather than to transfer powers to the local level. Bribing constitutes a currency for managing these relations and for ensuring upper-level support, but corruption is also a risk associated with decentralization under conditions of weak local accountability.

Patronage and centralism are embedded in a political culture and in collective identities that lack an awareness of regional diversity and regional distinctiveness. There do not seem to be distinctive, articulated regional identities that would contrast with Bulgarian national identity on the one hand, or local identity on the other. The above-mentioned UNDP opinion survey from November 1998 found that 39.5 per cent of Bulgaria's citizens thought that life was the same everywhere in Bulgaria (UNDP 1999: 61).

5. Decentralization initiatives have stalled because the EU has not included decentralization as a part of its accession conditionality (Hughes et al. 2004). EU cohesion policy is based on a notion of partnership between national governments on the one hand, and regional and local governments as well as economic and social actors, on the other. The cohesion policy and the 'partnership paradigm' imply a mandatory adaptation insofar as EU accession countries have to set up structures to manage the Structural Funds, including bodies that may act as 'partners' of central government and regional units of planning and territorial statistics that correspond to NUTS 2. However, there are no formal rules for the constitutional status of the regional level, which is ultimately due to the fact that the regional levels of government in EU member states vary greatly in terms of their legal status, administrative functions and political weight. Lacking harmonized, formal rules, the EU Commission has confined itself to expressing non-mandatory expectations with regard to the creation of regions and regional self-government.

After 2001 the EU Commission advocated a more centralized approach for the management of the Structural Funds, realizing the lack of administrative capacity at the local and regional levels of accession countries (Keating 2003). The scenario of ten states acceding in 2004 implied that the new members would have only 2 years to absorb grants from the Structural Funds, posing additional strains on their administrations. In view of these difficulties, the Commission asked the accession countries to develop only one countrywide Operational Programme for Regional Development instead of several regional operational programs on the level of NUTS 2 regions.

The Commission planned to review the management of the Structural Funds in 2009 and consider an eventual decentralization for the period from 2010–2013. In its annual monitoring reports, the Commission has repeatedly criticized the weakness of regional and local partnership structures in

Bulgaria and the lack of a decentralization strategy. Given the threat of a postponement of the accession, this critique contributed to the government's decision to adopt a decentralization strategy in June 2006. However, the Commission did not oppose (and might indeed have encouraged) the more centralized planning and programming arrangements of the 2004 and 2008 amendments to the Law on Regional Development.

Statements by representatives of the Sakskoburggotski and Stanishev governments indicate that they deliberately abstained from including municipal taxation powers in their constitutional amendments prior to accession because the EU did not identify decentralization as a requirement for membership. The amendment packages of 2003, 2005 and 2006 were designed to meet EU requirements and to comply with EU legislation. Municipal taxation powers were constitutionally enshrined only after accession.

Conclusion

This chapter has explored the status and situation of Bulgaria's regional level against the background of a centralized unitary state tradition on the one hand, and the regionalization incentives of European integration on the other. It has found that existing regional structures are only weakly institutionalized, decentralization initiatives have had limited impact, and that EU-driven regional units are still artificial and imposed institutions. These capacity constraints have largely prevented Bulgarian regional structures from an active participation in the European constitutional debate, for example. The future of the regional level in Bulgaria depends on how the five factors accounting for the weakness of the current regional structures will develop.

The constraints necessitated by the currency board regime are likely to become less rigid since the more substantial EU funds available after accession will require the provision of national funds to co-finance investments. Access to these funds does not necessarily imply a relaxation of overall fiscal discipline, but it is likely to gradually loosen the linkage between fiscal discipline and centralized expenditure management as the programming and partnership principles imply the involvement of numerous stakeholders, cooperation and the development of project management capacity outside the Ministry of Finance. One indication of such a development is the constitutional amendment of February 2007 that removed the constitutional barriers to municipal taxation rights.

The success of decentralization initiatives presupposes a broad consensus among Bulgaria's political forces as constitutional amendments require a qualified majority in the National Assembly. While the major parties generally support further decentralization, a consensus remains susceptible to partisan divisions between central and local government or to parties with special concerns such as support for smaller municipalities.

The ethnopolitical cleavage has become more polarized with a right-wing extremist party (Ataka) entering parliament in 2005 and is thus more likely to affect debates about regionalization, reducing the politically 'admissible' scope of decentralization.

There have been enormous efforts to improve the professional qualification and ethics of Bulgaria's civil service, but overcoming an inherited administrative culture obviously takes time as well as requiring measures to stop the brain-drain of qualified civil servants. Moreover, it also requires efforts to train the political leadership of ministries, seeking to replace patronage habits with an appreciation of merit and performance. Although the EU has opted for centralized management of the Structural Funds, elements of the partnership model are now in place and will contribute to its diffusion (Marinov and Malhasian 2006: 48). Thus, some of these causal factors are likely to facilitate stronger regional and decentralized structures in Bulgaria, but the persistence of several impeding factors suggests that any future regionalization will continue to be an incremental process.

Notes

* This paper has benefited from the generous hospitality and support provided by the 'Wales in a Regional Europe' research center at the University of Wales and the Bertelsmann Foundation's readiness to provide the author with the necessary time to carry out the research. The Economic Policy Institute in Sofia assisted in organizing interviews with Bulgarian experts and in providing access to the data base of 'Capital'. Marina Dimova, Aleko Djildjov, Ginka Kapitanova, Mina Shoylekova, Emil Savov, Ginka Tchavdarova and other Bulgarian experts and officials have devoted their time for interviews and provided valuable comments and materials without which this paper would not have been possible. The author wishes to thank all these colleagues and institutions.

1. Interview with Ginka Kapitanova, Foundation for Local Government Reform, 7 September 2005. Accession negotiations began on 15 February 2000 and took until 15 June 2004.
2. http://www.namrb.org/doc/sporazumenieMS.pdf (accessed 14 March 2006).
3. Mediapool (Bulgarian internet news service), 13 October 2005.
4. Interview with Ginka Tchavdarova, executive director of the NSORB, 1 June 2006; 'Strategicheski plan na Nacionalnoto sdruzhenie na obshtinite na Republika Bulgaria 2006–2013'. www.namrb.org/?act=cms&id=26 (accessed 11 March 2006).
5. Interview with Ginka Tchavdarova, executive director of the NSORB, Sofia, 1 June 2006.
6. Capital 3/2005; Mediapool, 30 August 2005.
7. Mediapool, 8 September 2005; 20 November 2006.
8. Interview with Aleko Djildjov, 1 June 2006.
9. Capital 45/2002.
10. Interview with an official in the Ministry of Regional Development and Public Works, 7 September 2005.

11. Upravlenska programa na pravitelstvoto na Republika Bulgaria'. http://www.government.bg/ (accessed 1 November 2003), 117.
12. The NUTS classification system did not exist as part of the formal EU legislation when Bulgaria established its NUTS 2 regions in 2000. It was first codified in Regulation No. 1059/2003 of 26 May 2003 (*Official Journal of the European Communities L154/1*).
13. http://europa.eu.int/comm/enlargement/financial_assistance/index_en.htm (accessed 11 March 2006).
14. Interview with Aleko Djildjov, 1 June 2006.
15. Standard Eurobarometer Bulgaria. http://europa.eu.int/comm/public_opinion/standard_en.htm (accessed 11 March 2006).
16. Eurobarometer 64. http://europa.eu.int/comm/public_opinion/archives/eb/eb64/eb64_anx.pdf (accessed 11 March 2006).
17. Capital 44/2002.
18. Interview with Veselin Metodiev, deputy president of a liberal-conservative opposition party, Mediapool, 30 August 2005.

14
Conclusion: Europe's Persisting Regions

Roger Scully and Richard Wyn Jones

After the detailed analysis presented in the 12 individual country chapters, the purpose of this concluding chapter will be to assess what we have learned already, and to draw out any further lessons that can be gleaned. Thus, this chapter will first summarize the contributions of the previous chapters. We will then discuss the broader, more general lessons to be learned from the material presented. Finally, we will present some concluding thoughts on the future of Europe's regions.

The individual chapters

As indicated in the introduction, our 12 country chapters sought to examine cases that varied widely among the EU's 27 member-states. Of these, we began with perhaps the most regionalized of all of them, Belgium. Wilfried Swenden's analysis emphasizes the inter-relationship between Europeanization and regionalization: how, in Belgium's case, the process of European integration has both facilitated but also limited the role of the regions. While the former dimension is to some extent common to all the other chapters in this book, Belgium provides perhaps the most striking evidence of the way in which European structures and procedures can limit the more expansive and ambitious regionalizing agendas. The structural imperative to arrive at a single Belgian position in European negotiations – or otherwise risk complete irrelevance – forces regional actors that are otherwise largely (and increasingly) autonomous to seek consensus. Moreover, it is only European imperatives that maintain a role for the Belgian state in many policy areas that have, otherwise, been wholly devolved to the regions. Resentment in Flanders, in particular, at this state of affairs, thus led Swenden to question whether or not the ultimate effect of the interaction between the dynamics of regionalization and Europeanization might be the complete unravelling of the Belgian state.

Romain Pasquier's chapter tells a distinctly different story. It is the story of a continuing search for an appropriate and lasting structure and role for the regions in France. This is rendered difficult not only because of that state's Jacobin, centralist traditions but also because of continued competition between the regional and more local levels. The chapter's discussion of this latter theme was but the first of a number during the course of this book. As the other side of the Jacobin coin, so to speak, the power and status of the local levels in France is so deeply entrenched that, as Pasquier has shown, attempts to regionalize the French state have (thus far, at least) tended to have the paradoxical effect of strengthening local government rather more than empowering the regional level itself.

The constitutional entrenchment of Germany's well established and powerful Länder is in considerable contrast to the position in France. However, as Carolyn Moore has shown, and echoing the experience of Belgium, European integration creates very significant limits on the more powerful regions in particular. German attempts to provide mechanisms at the federal level to compensate for this have proved a poor substitute for competences lost to the EU. It is not surprising, therefore, that the German Länder, previously among the most active proponents of the regional 'third' layer, have rowed back from their previous vanguard role. However, as Moore demonstrates, it is not only the Länder that are frustrated: the federal level also finds itself frustrated by the ways in which Germany's federal structure complicates and weakens the state's position in European-level debates and negotiations.

Italy is another one of the original 'six' EU member-states. However, as shown by Giandomenico Falcon and Daria de Pretis, despite this long membership the constitutional position of Italian regions has in recent times been changing substantially, most notably with the constitutional reforms of 2001 which modified that section of the Italian Constitution (Title V) that underpins the role of the country's autonomous, regional and local authorities. Falcon and de Pretis provide an overview of these developments, paying especially close attention to the role of the Italian regions in the implementation of European rules and regulations, as well as the regions' role in attempting to influence the content of European decisions. With Italy, we see a system very much still in flux and this chapter represents not only a helpful summary of developments to date, but will also act as an important baseline against which future developments may be measured.

In analyzing the situation in Ireland, Katy Hayward not only looks at a state that was part of the first wave of European enlargement, she also enables us to consider a country which has very little modern tradition of regionalism. As the title of the chapter suggests, Hayward views Irish regionalism as very much a pragmatic and instrumentalist development almost wholly designed to lever in European structural funding: the divide into regions serving to multiply the amount of financial support received. Finance aside, given its technocratic, highly bureaucratic and top-down nature, it is perhaps little wonder that Hayward talks of the 'largely inauspicious beginnings of Irish regionalism'.

In light of its highly asymmetrical structures of devolution, analysis of the UK focused specifically on the most powerful of its regions, Scotland. Noreen Burrows' contribution, and in particular her discussion of the meanings of 'region' in the context of Scotland, nicely illustrated the difficulties, complications and contradictions associated with its use. Rhetorically at least, Europe was an important element in pro-devolution arguments and the development of a Scottish European strategy was an important priority for the Labour-led administrations formed in the first two terms of the Scottish parliament. This was not least, of course, because the (then) opposition Scottish National Party has long-advocated 'Independence in Europe', and Labour was thus keen to prove that Scotland's voice could be heard at the European level without it having to resume its status as an independent state. Scotland is perhaps an exemplary instance of how the European dimension can itself contribute to debates amongst regional regionalizers about the form and extent that regional empowerment should take.

Spain was part of the third wave of enlargement. Here, Europeanization, democratization and regionalization have proceeded very much together. However, the Spanish state has nonetheless been challenged by powerful regional regionalist movements. Francesc Morata's chapter examines the relationship between European integration and the Spanish 'State of the Autonomies'. Particularly fascinating is the way in which regional access to European institutions has proven to be a crucial bargaining chip in negotiations between regionalist parties and state-wide parties when the former have held the balance of power in the Spanish parliament. Morata concludes with an examination of the European implications of the recently (2006) redrafted Catalan Statute of Autonomy: this takes on particular significance because, if past practice as described in Morata's chapter is any guide, where Catalonia (and the Basque Country) lead, the other Spanish autonomous regions will eventually follow.

In Sweden, which was part of the fourth enlargement in 1995, the development of a regional layer has gone hand in hand with Europeanization and with the related transformation of a distinctly centralist welfare state. Anders Lidström's chapter pointed to the particular challenges of finding a structure and role for regions in an already populated and settled governmental landscape, especially so when regional identities are largely absent (even if there are clear regional differences in attitudes toward European integration, for example).

The four final chapters all examined states that joined the EU from Central or Eastern Europe in 2004 and 2007. All had formerly been part of the Soviet bloc. Tarvo Kungla's chapter considered one of the smallest of all the enlarged EU's member-states, Estonia. Estonia's small size, and its apparent lack of suitability for a regional level of government, makes it a particularly interesting case to examine: not least because it is one of many small states in the EU of 27. However, as Kungla pointed out, it is not simply questions of scale that limit the role of the regional layer in such contexts. In Estonia, as in other member-states, concerns about the ways in which an empowered regional layer may provide a forum for the demands of minority national groups – in this case, those of the Russian minority – also act as a significant constraint.

Gyula Horváth's analysis explored the peculiar challenges facing regionalism in Hungary. This was a country which, even prior to being submerged into the Soviet bloc, was a particularly centralized country. Horvath has provided a telling critique of the impact of this unipolarity on the country's socio-economic development, and made an impassioned plea for taking regionalism seriously. Along with Anna Tucholska, Grzegorz Gorzelak has given a detailed picture of regional structure in post-transformation Poland. However, while there can be no doubt that substantial progress has been made, from a regionalist perspective, in terms of the gradual empowerment of that country's regions, Gorzelak's discussion of the processes of spatial differentiation present in contemporary Poland – and the resultant inequalities and disparities in rates of socio-economic development – leaves the reader under no illusions about the magnitude of the challenges with which Poland and its regions are faced.

It is, perhaps, entirely fitting that Martin Brusis' analysis of the regional layer in Bulgaria is our final country chapter. Bulgaria is one of the Union's most recent members; it is also another Eastern European country whose very centralist state-tradition actually predates the Soviet era. The difficulties of establishing an effective layer in a shifting and unpredictable national political context, and in the face of rival pressures from above (in particular the Ministry of Finance) and below (a local government layer intent on maintaining its own powers and prerogatives) are made very apparent. It is little wonder that Brusis concludes that Bulgaria's regional structures 'are only weakly institutionalized, decentralization initiatives have had limited impact and EU-driven regional units are still artificial and imposed institutions'.

The contrast between the first and the concluding case-study chapters could hardly be more marked and graphically underlines the huge gulf separating the strongest and weakest European regions. A final, perhaps provocative, thought is that while neither Belgium nor Bulgaria are typical, is it not the case, in the Europe of 27, that it is Bulgaria rather than Belgium that is in fact closer to the norm?

The broad lessons

It should be abundantly clear by now that we cannot point to any single, or simple, model of 'regional Europe'. The picture is far more variegated, and neither the influence of Euro-regionalism nor any other forces have been able to push Europe's polities toward a homogenous set of sub-state regional structures across all 27 EU member-states. The structures of regional government across Europe clearly differ along several dimensions, among the most salient of which are:

- the *constitutional status* of regions: to what degree is their existence embedded within the fundamental governing principles of the state itself?
- The *powers, autonomy* and *governing/administrative capability* of regional structures: are they genuine centers of power in their own right?
- The extent to which regional structures attract the *diffuse institutional support* of the public in those regions: are regions essentially viewed as (at best) just another layer of government machinery, or do they in some way constitute the institutional embodiment of widespread public attachment to the region as a distinct entity?

As we have seen, regions within contemporary Europe differ along all these dimensions. Many of these differences run *between* different countries. However, some of them, as we have seen perhaps most clearly in the cases of Spain and the UK, run *within* EU member-states. These within-state differences appear to reflect substantial asymmetries in levels of regional attachment inside states; that is, they follow primarily from differences in the degree of 'regional regionalism', rather than coming from influences at the European or state levels.

The forces of Euro-regionalism have appeared in this study to be somewhat weaker than might have been expected. They are by no means irrelevant: the many references to them attest to this. But they have not been sufficient, in themselves, to establish more than some rather anaemic regional structures in the absence of any determined state- or regional-level regionalizing impetus. In general, the EU appears to have had much less of a regionalizing impact than was suggested by the Europe of the Regions agenda of the 1980s and 1990s. Furthermore, evidence from some of the chapters in this volume has identified clearly a gradual change of attitudes among some prominent regional actors toward what might be termed the European regional project. In the case of both the Länder and various other regionalist movements, this has taken the form of a distinct cooling toward any notion of the Europe of the regions and a maximalist vision of the integration process. These developments become easier to understand and explain when reframed in terms of the different regionalizing dynamics. So, for example, the regional-regionalists of the Länder seem to have concluded that the constitutionally entrenched state-regionalism of the Bundesrepublik offers stronger guarantees for their position than does the weaker, more amorphous force of Euro-regionalism. Moreover, in some respects the EU actively works against the interests of regions, the more powerful of them in particular. European-level recognition and empowerment of regions pales beside the fundamental assumption of the most powerful centers of EU decision-making that they be based upon the representation of a united state interest.

The impact of state-regionalizing forces has varied very substantially, depending on a number of factors. One is very simply the size of the state. Small countries like Ireland and Estonia have significantly less 'space' for a regional level of government between the local and state levels than a country like Germany. However, other considerations, often quite idiosyncratic in nature, are also in play. The UK's lack of a formal constitutional text makes it essentially impossible to give an embedded status to the regional level in Scotland, Wales and Northern Ireland – even if politically they are nigh-on unassailable. And even a factor like size is far from wholly uniform in its impact. Witness the case of France: a large state by European standards, but one where a combination of Jacobin centralism and a strong attachment to specific localities has left little space into which a strong regional level could be inserted.

Even the forces of regional-regionalism are far from uniform in their shape and direction. Distinct senses of regional attachment do not spring from the same type of source, or manifest themselves in the same way. Often – as in the much-celebrated examples of Catalonia, Scotland and Flanders – regional autonomy can be seen to be a manifestation, or indeed an absolute minimum fulfillment, of a sub-state nationalism. But not all sub-state nationalisms wish for regional autonomy – witness the overwhelming rejection of it by the Welsh in 1979, and their only marginal endorsement of it 18 years later. Nor are regional pressures necessarily a reflection of some form of 'primordial' identity. A regional level bearing little relationship to any 'national' identity and perhaps having little historical grounding can still become one which attracts considerable public support, as the example of post-war German federalism strongly indicates. Regional regionalism varies considerably, therefore, not only in strength but also in character. It can thus hardly be surprising that Europe's regions look so unalike.

The future for Europe's regions?

Much of the stress in the preceding pages thus far has been on the puncturing of some of the more extravagant expectations surrounding the role of regions within the European Union (EU) of the future. However, as the chapters collected in this book vividly underline, this is very far from the whole story. Quite the opposite, in fact: even if maximalist hopes of a 'Europe of the regions' have been disappointed for the foreseeable future, the regional level still plays a vitally important role in European governance.

Indeed, we would argue that dissipating some of the hype that has previously surrounded the future of European regionalism allows us to bring into clearer focus the *actual* contribution made by the regional level. This contribution is likely to continue. In the Union's larger states, regions will continue to play significant (although variable) roles in terms of domestic governance, as well as often having a vital role in the delivery of European policies. This is ensured, in the case of the former, by the nature of various state governmental traditions, and in the latter by the huge size of the contemporary Union of 27. Given the relatively small size of the Union's bureaucracy, the Commission relies on the resources and local knowledge of 'lower' level bureaucracies. In fact, it could hardly operate effectively without them. Thus, even if the hopes of the regional-regionalists of REGLEG and various political parties and movements for a much more significant role for regions in the European policy-making process seem destined to be disappointed, regions will almost certainly continue to play an indispensable, if more modest, role. In that sense, what has been referred to here as Euro-regionalism is alive and well.

So is state-regionalism, at least among the larger states of the 27. One important factor has already been alluded to, and is taken up again in several of the chapters that follow, namely the continuing belief among policy-makers and academics alike that the regional level offers particular advantages in terms of the organization and promotion of economic development. Given that uneven economic development across the territory of the state is an issue for all but the smallest and most prosperous EU members, the continuing belief in the importance of the regional level as a driver of economic development is significant.

With an expanded Union also a Union in which the gap between richer and poorer regions is greater and more obvious than ever, and the need for effective measures to bring about 'convergence' even more apparent, this is precisely an issue in which regionalist dynamics at all three levels may well overlap and reinforce each other. At any rate, regional-regionalism remains in rude health in many parts of the Union. There seems little reason to believe that this will change, especially if one accepts arguments to the effect that globalizing trends actually have the seemingly paradoxical effect of heightening more localized consciousness. Certainly, contemporary developments in Scotland and Belgium suggest that, in these cases at least, regional-regionalism has developed a powerful internal momentum.

Except, perhaps, in a few instances like that of Belgium, Europe's regions have not generally come to play the sort of role that some envisaged for them in the 1980s and early 1990s. Indeed, across Europe regions often do not play very similar roles. Nor do they always play a role as prominent as that which many regions might wish for. However, to conclude from this that regions are unimportant or marginal to the politics and life of Europe would be to miss out on much of what is most important about the political dynamics of today's evolving and ever complex Europe.

Bibliography

Acha, B. (2006), 'Eusko Alkartasuna: A Party in Search of a Third Space' in L. De Winder, M. Gómez-Reino and P. Lynch (eds), *Autonomist Parties in Europe: Identity Politics and the Revival of the Territorial Cleavage.* vol. 1. Barcelona: Institute de Ciènces Polítiques i Socials, 65–100.

Adinolfi, A. (2004), 'Nuove scadenze delle direttive comunitarie nelle materie di competenza regionale: verso le "leggi comunitarie regionali"?' *Rivista di diritto internationale* 3, 759–765.

Adshead, M. (2003), 'Policy Networks and Sub-national Government in Ireland' in M. Adshead and M. Millar (eds), *Public Administration and Public Policy in Ireland: Theory and Methods.* London: Routledge, 108–128.

Alberti, E. (2005), 'Las Comunidades Autónomas en la Unión Europea: las nuevas perspectivas del Tratado Constitucional y la participación interna' in E. Alberti, L. Ortega and J. A. Montilla, *Las Comunidades Autónomas en la Unión Europea.* Madrid: Centro de Estudos Políticos y Constitucionales, 11–42.

Aldeoca, F. and Keating, M. (eds) (1999), *Paradiplomacy in Action: The Foreign Relations of Subnational Governments.* London: Frank Cass.

Alen, A. and Muylle, K. (2003), *Compendium van het Belgisch Staatsrecht, Deel 1B.* Mechelen: Kluwer.

Allik, J. (2003), 'Kas nüüd tuleb toeline haldusreform?' *Postimees,* 4/06/2003.

Amin, A. (1994), 'Post-Fordism: Models, Fantasies and Phantoms of Transition' in A. Amin (ed.), *Post-Fordism: A Reader.* Oxford: Blackwell, 1–39.

Ananieva, N. (2002), 'Political Decentralization and Local Self-Government in the Republic of Bulgaria: Constitutional Principles, Practice and Problems' in *Decentralizing Government.* Zagreb: Friedrich-Ebert-Foundation, 96–103, http://library.fes.de/pdf-files/bueros/kroatien/50255.pdf (accessed 21/06/10).

Anderson, J. et al. (2003), 'Why Study New Borders?' in J. Anderson et al. (eds), *New Borders for a Changing Europe.* London: Frank Cass.

Ansvarskommittén (2003), *Ang. EU:s Påverkan på Svensk Statsförvaltning.* Underlags-PM 11/06/2003.

Arnswald, S. (2000), *EU Enlargement and the Baltic States: The Incremental Making of New Members.* Helsinki: Ulkopoliittinen Instituutti & Institut für Europäische Politik.

Asquith, A. and O'Halpin, E. (1998), 'The Changing Roles of Irish Local Authority Managers' *Administration* 45(4), 76–92.

Astone, F. (2004), *Le amministrazioni nazionali nel processo di formazione e di attuazione del diritto comunitario.* Torino: Giappichelli.

Bachtler, J., Brown, R. and Raines, P. (1999), 'Evaluation of Nordic-Scottish Cooperation' Regional and Industrial Policy Research Paper, No. 35. European Policies Research Centre, University of Strathclyde.

Bachtler, J., Downes, R. and Gorzelak, G. (eds) (2000), *Transition, Cohesion and Regional Policy in Central and Eastern Europe.* Aldershot: Ashgate.

Badiello, L. (2004), 'La representación funcional en Bruselas: evolución, funciones y perspectives' in F. Morata (ed.), *Gobernanza Multinivel en la Unión Europea.* Valencia: Tirant lo Blanch, 125–143.

Baldersheim, H., Sanberg, S., Ståhlberg, K. and Øgård, M. (2001), 'Norden in Europe of the Regions: A Summary of Perspectives and Results' in K. Ståhlberg (ed.),

The Nordic Countries and Europe II: Social Sciences. Copenhagen: Nordic Council of Ministers.

Balme, R. and Bonnet, L. (1994), 'From Regional to Sectoral Policies: The Contractual Relations between the State and the Regions in France' *Regional Politics and Policy* 4(3), 51–91.

Balme, R. and Le Galès, P. (1995), 'Stars and Black Holes: French Regions and Cities in the European Galaxy' in M. Goldsmith and K. Klausen (eds), *European Integration and Local Government.* Chelteham: Edward Elgar, 146–171.

Barna, C., Panchugov, C., Tatar, M. and Todorakov, V. (2005), 'Europeanization of Regions and the Partnership Principle: The Bulgarian Case' *Südosteuropa* 53(4), 557–572.

Barrington, T. J. (1976), 'Can there be regional development in Ireland?' *Administration* (special issue on 'Administrative Structures for Regional Development') 24(3), 350–365.

Bartole, S., Bin, R., Falcon, G. and Tosi, R. (2005), *Diritto regionale.* 2nd edn. Bologna: Il Mulino.

Beluszky, P. (1999), *Magyarország településföldrajza.* Budapest: Dialóg Campus Kiadó.

Bennett, J. (2008), 'EU Funding – What is Available and How it Can be Accessed', presentation by director of NASC Brussels office to Galway City Council workshop on EU Funding, 17 April 2008.

Bennett, R. J. and Krebs, G. (1991), *Local Economic Development: Public–Private Partnership Initiatives in Britain and Germany.* London: Belhaven Press.

Bennett, R. J. and Krebs, G. (1994), 'Local Economic Development Partnerships: An Analysis of Policy Networks in EC-LEDA Local Employment Development Strategies' *Regional Studies* 28(2), 119–140.

Benz, A. and Eberlein, B. (1999), 'The Europeanization of Regional Policies: Patterns of Multilevel Governance' *Journal of European Public Policy* 6(2), 329–348.

Berg, Linda and Lindahl, Rutger (2007), *Svenska kommuners och regioners kanaler till Bryssel.* Stockholm: Svenska institutet för europapolitiska studier.

Bertelsmann Stiftung (2004), *Die Europafähigkeit des deutschen Bundesstaates. Diskussionspapier zum Föderalismus-Reformdialog.* Berlin: Bertelsmann Stiftung http://www.bertelsmannstiftung.de/bst/de/media/xcms_bst_dms_14822__2.pdf. (accessed 21/06/10).

Berti, G. and De Martin, G. C. (2001), *Le autonomie territoriali: dalla riforma amministrativa alla riforma costituzionale.* Milano: Giuffrè.

Beyers, J. and Bursens, P. (2006), 'The European Rescue of the Federal State: How Europeanization Shapes the Belgian State' *West European Politics* 29(5), 1057–1078.

Bienintesi, F. (2004), 'L'evoluzione della legge comunitaria nella prassi applicativa e nelle riforme istituzionali' *Rassegna parlamentare* 4, 849–911.

Billiet, J and Maddens, B. (2007), 'Belgische Gesellschaft und die "Gemeinschaften"' in J. Koll (ed.), *Belgien: Geschichte-Politik-Kultur-Wirtschaft.* Münster: Aschendorff Verlag.

Blair, Stephen (2004), 'Mid-term Evaluation of the Southern and Eastern Regional Operational Programme', presentation by the director of the S&E Regional Assembly to Institute of Public Administration Conference, Dublin, January 2004.

BMW (2006), 'Border, Midland and Western Regional OP Progress Report to December 2005' http://www.bmwassembly.ie/news/reports.asp?doc=reports (accessed 21/06/10).

BMW and SERA (2008), 'Submission on the Future of EU Cohesion Policy'. Border Midland and Western and Southern and Eastern Regional Assemblies http://www.

bmwassembly.ie/news/publications/Future%20of%20EU%20Cohesion%20Policy.
pdf. (accessed 21/06/10).

Boev, J. (2002), 'Bulgaria: Decentralization and Modernization of the Public Administration' in G. Péteri (ed.), *Mastering Decentralization and Public Administration Reforms
in Central and Eastern Europe*. Budapest: Local Government and Public Service
Reform Initiative, 95–119.

Bogetic, Z. (1997), 'Bulgaria' in T. Ter-Minassian (ed.), *Fiscal Federalism in Theory and
Practice*. Washington: International Monetary Fund, 615–633.

Bona Galvagno, F. (2005), *Commento alla legge 4 febbraio 2005, n. 11*. Roma: Presidenza
del Consiglio dei Ministri.

Borras-Alomar, S., Christiansen, T. and Rodriguez-Pose, A. (1994), 'Towards a "Europe
of the Regions"? Visions and Reality from a Critical Perspective' *Regional Politics and
Policy* 4(2), 1–27.

Börzel, T. A. (2001), 'Europeanization and Territorial Institutional Change: Toward
Cooperative Regionalism' in M. G. Cowles, J. Caporaso and T. Risse (eds), *Trans-
forming Europe: Europeanization and Domestic Change*. Ithaca, NY: Cornell University
Press.

Börzel, T. A. (2002), *States and Regions in the European Union: Institutional Adaptation in
Germany and Spain*. Cambridge: Cambridge University Press.

Börzel T. A. (2003), *Environmental Leaders and Laggards in the European Union: Why There
is (not) a Southern Problem*. Ashgate: London.

Börzel, T. A. (2005a), 'Europeanization: How the European Union Interacts with its
Member States' in S. Bulmer and C. Lequesne (eds), *The Member States of the European
Union*. Oxford: Oxford University Press, 45–69.

Börzel, T. A. (2005b), 'What can Federalism Teach Us About the European Union? The
German Experience' *Regional and Federal Studies* 15 (2), 245–257.

Börzel, T. A. and Risse, T. (2003), 'Conceptualizing the Domestic Impact of Europe' in
K. Featherstone and C. Radaelli (eds), *The Politics of Europeanization*. Oxford: Oxford
University Press, 55–78.

Börzel, T. A. and Risse, T. (2007) 'Europeanization: The Domestic Impact of EU Politics'
in K. E. Joergensen, M. Pollack and B. Rosamond (eds), *Handbook of European Union
Politics*. London: Sage, 483–504.

Bourne, A. K. (2003a), 'The Impact of European Integration on Regional Power' *Journal
of Common Market Studies* 41(4), 597–620.

Bourne, A. K. (2003b), 'Regional Europe' in M. Cini (ed.), *European Union Politics*.
Oxford: Oxford University Press, 278–293.

Boyle, M. (2000), 'Euro-regionalism and Struggles over Scales of Governance: The Politics of Ireland's Regionalisation Approach to Structural Fund Allocations 2000–2006'
Political Geography 19, 737–769.

Brunazzo, M. (2005), *Le Regioni italiane e l'Unione europea: accessi istituzionali e di politica
pubblica*. Roma: Carocci.

Brusis, M. (2002), 'Between EU Requirements, Competitive Politics, and National
Traditions: Re-creating Regions in the Accession Countries of Central and Eastern
Europe' *Governance: An International Journal of Policy, Administration, and Institutions*
15(4), 531–559.

Brusis, M. (2003), 'Regionalisation in the Czech and Slovak Republics: Comparing
the Influence of the European Union' in M. Keating and J. Hughes (eds), *The
Regional Challenge in Central and Eastern Europe: Territorial Restructuring and European
Integration*. Bruxelles: P.I.E.-Peter Lang, 89–105.

Brusis, M. (2004), 'Europeanization, Party Government or Legacies? Explaining Executive Governance in Bulgaria, the Czech Republic and Hungary' *Comparative European Politics* 2(2), 163–184.

Bukowski, J., Piattoni, S. and Smyrl, M. (eds) (2003), *Between Global Economy and Local Society: Political Actors and Territorial Governance*. Lanham, MD: Rowman and Littlefield.

Bulmer, S. (2007), 'Theorizing Europeanization' in P. Graziano and M. P. Vinck (eds), *Europeanization New Research Agendas*. Houndmills: Palgrave Macmillan.

Bulmer, S. and Lequesne, C. (eds) (2005), *The Member States of the European Union*. Oxford: Oxford University Press.

Bulmer, S., Jeffery, C. and Paterson, W. E. (2000), *Germany's European Diplomacy: Shaping the Regional Milieu*. Manchester: Manchester University Press.

Bulmer, S., Burch, M., Hogwood, P. and Scott, A. (2006), 'UK Devolution and the European Union: A Tale of Cooperative Asymmetry?' *Publius: The Journal of Federalism* 36(1), 75–93.

Bungs, D. (1998), *The Baltic States: Problems and Prospects of Membership in the European Union*. Baden-Baden: Nomos.

Burche, M., Gomez, R., Hogwood, P. and Scott, A. (2005), 'Devolution, Change and European Union Policy-making in the UK' *Regional Studies* 39(4), 465–475.

Burrows, N. (2000), *Devolution*. London: Sweet and Maxwell.

Burrows, N. (2002), 'Nemo me impune lacessit: The Scottish Right of Access to the European Courts' *European Public Law* 6, 45–68.

Burrows, N. (2006), 'Scotland in Europe: Empowerment or Disempowerment?' in A. McHarg and T. Mullen (eds), *Public Law in Scotland*. Edinburgh: Avizandum, 45–66.

Bursens, P. (2002), 'Why Denmark and Belgium Have Different Implementation Records' *Scandinavian Political Studies* 25(2), 173–195.

Bursens, P. (2004), 'Enduring Federal Consensus: An Institutionalist Account of Belgian Preferences Regarding the Future of Europe' *Comparative European Politics* 2(3), 339–357.

Bursens, P. (2007), 'State Structures' in P. Graziano and M. P. Vinck (eds), *Europeanization New Research Agendas*. Houndmills: Palgrave Macmillan.

Bursens, P. and Helsen, S. (2003), 'Multi-Level Governance in de Praktijk: naar een efficiënte aanpak van het Belgische Europa-Beleid' *PSW Working Paper, 2003/1*. Department of Political Science, University of Antwerp.

Caciagli, M. (2003), *Regioni d'Europa: Devoluzioni, regionalismi e integrazione europea*. Roma: Laterza.

Caliandro, F. (2004), 'Poteri sostitutivi, obblighi comunitari ed assetto delle fonti normative dopo la riforma del Titolo V della Costituzione' *Rivista italiana di diritto pubblico comunitario* 2, 435–456.

Califano, L. (2005), 'Stato, regioni e diritto comunitario nella legge n. 11/2005' *Quaderni costituzionali* 4, 860–863.

Callanan, M. (2002), 'The White Paper on Governance: The Challenge for Central and Local Government' *Administration* 50(1), 66–85.

Callanan, M. (2003a), 'Local Government and the European Union' in M. Callanan and J. F. Keogan (eds), *Local Government in Ireland: Inside out*. Dublin: Institute of Public Administration, 404–428.

Callanan, M. (2003b), 'Regional Authorities and Regional Assemblies' in M. Callanan and J. F. Keogan (eds), *Local Government in Ireland: Inside out*. Dublin: Institute of Public Administration, 429–446.

Cammelli, M. (2001), 'Amministrazione (e interpreti) davanti al nuovo titolo V della Costituzione' *Le Regioni* 6, 1273–1304.

Cannizzaro, E. (2005), 'La riforma della "legge La Pergola" e le competenze di Stato e Regioni nei processi di formazione e di attuazione delle norme dell'Unione europea' *Rivista di diritto internazionale* 1, 153–156.

Caporaso, J., Cowles, M. G. and Risse, T. (2001), *Transforming Europe: Europeanisation and Domestic Change.* Ithaca: Cornell University Press.

Caravita, B. (2002), *La Costituzione dopo la riforma del Titolo V: Stato, Regioni e autonomie fra Repubblica e Unione Europea.* Torino: Giappichelli.

Caretti, P. (1997), 'Sviluppo regionale' in M. P. Chiti and G. Greco (eds), *Trattato di diritto amministrativo europeo.* Milano: Giuffre.

Caretti, P. (2003), 'Potere estero e ruolo "comunitario" delle Regioni nel nuovo titolo V della Costituzione' *Le Regioni* 4, 555–574.

Carroll, W. and Byrne, T. (1999), 'Regional Policy and Ireland' in J. Dooge and R. Barrington (eds), *A Vital National Interest: Ireland in Europe, 1973–1998.* Dublin: Institute of Public Administration, 172–185.

Cartabia, M. and Violini, L. (2005), 'Le norme generali sulla partecipazione dell'Italia al processo normativo dell'Unione Europea e sulle procedure di esecuzione agli obblighi comunitari. Commento alla legge 4 febbraio 2005, n. 11' *Le Regioni* 4, 475–512.

Carter, C. and McLeod, A. (2005), 'The Scottish Parliament and the European Union: Analysing Regional Parliamentary Engagement' in S. Weatherhill and U. Bernitz (eds), *The Role of Regions and Sub-national Actors in Europe.* Oxford: Hart Publishing, 67–89.

Carter Caitriona and Pasquier Romain (2006) 'European Integration and the Transformation of Regional Governance: Testing the Analytical Purchase of "Europeanisation"', *Queen's Paper on Europeanization,* n. 1.

Cassetti, L. (2004), 'Il regionalismo italiano e la multilevel governance dopo le recenti riforme costituzionali' *Le Istituzioni del federalismo* 1, 111–122.

Cavalieri, P. (2006), *Diritto regionale.* 3rd edn. Padova: Cedam.

Cavalieri, P. and Lamarque, E. (2004), *L'attuazione del nuovo titolo V, parte seconda, della costituzione: Commento alla legge 'La Loggia' (Legge 5/6/2003, n. 131).* Torino: Giappichelli.

CEC (1997), *Agenda 2000 Volume 2: Reinforcing the Pre-accession Strategy.* Brussels: Commission of the European Communities.

CEC (2004), 'A New Partnership for Cohesion: Convergence, Competitiveness, Cooperation. Third Report on Economic and Social Cohesion'. Brussels: Commission of the European Communities.

CEMR (1999), 'White Paper on Consultation Procedures of Local and Regional Authorities in Europe'. Brussels: Council of European Municipalities and Regions.

Chardon, M. (2005), 'Art. 23 als "institutionalisiertes Misstrauen": Zur Reform der europapolitischen Beteiligung der Länder in den Beratungen der Bundesstaatskommission' in *Jahrbuch des Föderalismus 2005.* Tübingen: Europäisches Zentrum für Föderalismus-Forschung.

Chieffi, L. (2003), *Regioni e dinamiche di integrazione europea.* Torino: Giappichelli.

Chieffi, L. (2004), 'La nuova dimensione costituzionale del rapporto tra Regioni e Unione europea' *Democrazia e Diritto* 2, 87–114.

Christiansen, T. (2005), 'Towards Statehood? The EU's Move Towards Constitutionalisation and Territorialisation' ARENA Working Paper, 21. Oslo: ARENA.

Christiansen, T. and Jorgensen, K. E. (2004), 'La gobernanza transregional en la nueva Europa' in F. Morata (ed.), *Gobenanza Multinivel en la Unión Europea*. Valencia: Tirant lo Blanch, 369–393.

Chubb, B. (1992), *The Government and Politics of Ireland*. 3rd edn. London: Longman.

Cole, A. (2006), *Beyond Devolution and Decentralisation: Building Regional Capacity in Wales and Brittany*. Manchester: Manchester University Press.

Collins, N. (1987), *Local Government Managers at Work*. Dublin: Institute of Public Administration.

Collins, Neil and Quinlivan, Aodh (2005), 'Multi-level Governance' in John Coakley and Michael Gallagher (eds), *Politics in the Republic of Ireland*. London: Routledge (in association with PSAI Press, 4th edn), 384–404.

Committee of the Regions (2000), *Preparing for the Enlargement: Devolution in the First Wave Candidate Countries, COR Studies E-4/99*. Luxembourg: Office for Official Publications of the European Communities.

Committee of the Regions (2003), *Devolution in the European Union and the Candidate Countries*. Brussels: European Union Committee of the Regions.

Constitution Unit (2005), *Monitor*. London: University College of London.

Costa, O. (2002), 'Les représentants des entités infra-étatiques auprès de l'Union: Processus de professionnalisation diversifiés et intérêts communs' in D. Georgakakis (ed.), *Les métiers de l'Europe politique: Acteurs et professionnalisations de l'Union européenne*. Strasbourg: PUS, 147–168.

Cowles, M. G., Caporaso, J. and Risse, T. (eds) (2001), *Transforming Europe: Europeanization and Domestic Change*. Ithaca, NY: Cornell University Press.

Coyle, C. (1997), 'European Integration: A Lifeline for Irish Local Authorities?' in M. J. F. Goldsmith and K. Klausen (eds), *European Integration and Local Government*. Cheltenham: Edward Elgar, 75–94.

Coyle, C. and Sinnott, R. (1993), 'Regional Elites, Regional "Powerlessness" and European Regional Policy in Ireland' in R. Leonardi (ed.), *The Regions and the European Community: The Regional Response to the Single Market in the Underdeveloped Areas*. London: Frank Cass, 71–105.

D'Atena, A. (2003a), *L'Europa Delle Autonomie: Le Regioni e l'Unione Europea*. Milan: Giuffrè.

D'Atena, A. (2003b), 'Materie legislative e tipologia delle competenze' *Quaderni costituzionali* 1, 15–24.

D'Atena, A. (2005a), 'Modelli federali e sussidiarietà nel riparto delle competenze normative tra l'Unione europea e gli Stati membri' *Il diritto dell'Unione Europea* 1, 59–74.

D'Atena, A. (2005b), *Le Regioni Dopo il Big Bang: il Viaggio Continua*. Milan: Giuffrè.

Deeg, R. (1995), 'Germany's *Länder* and the Federalization of the European Union' in C. Rhodes and S. Mazey (eds), *The State of the European Union, Volume 3: Building a European Polity*. Harlow: Longman, 197–216.

Degen, Manfred (2005), 'Wir haben hier keine offizielle Rolle, aber wir machen was draus' FinanzReport Online, März 2005.

Department of the Environment and Local Government (DELG) (2003), 'Implementing the National Spatial Strategy: Preparing Regional Planning Guidelines. Guidance notes'. Dublin: Department of the Environment and Local Government.

Department of Foreign Affairs (DFA) (2005), 'The European Constitution, White Paper'. Dublin: Stationery Office.

Der Spiegel (Online) (2006), 'EU will deutschen Lotto-Staatsvertrag kippen', 21 October 2006. http://www.123recht.net/article.asp?a=18585&ccheck=1 (accessed 21/06/10).

De Rynck, S. (1996), 'Europe and Cohesion Policy Making in the Flemish Region' in L. Hooghe (ed.), *Cohesion Policy and European Integration: Building Multi-Level Governance*. Oxford: Oxford University Press, 129–162.

Deschouwer, K. (1999), 'From Consociation to Federation: How the Belgian Parties Won' in R. K. Luther and K. Deschouwer (eds), *Party Elites in Divided Societies: Political Parties in Consociational Democracy*. London: Routledge, 74–107.

Deschouwer, K. (2006), 'And the Peace Goes On? Consociationalism and Belgian Federalism in the Twenty-first Century' *West European Politics* 5(29), 815–911.

Detlef, J. and Storsved, A.-S. (1995), 'Legitimacy Through Referendum? The Nearly Successful Domino-strategy of the EU-referendums in Austria, Finland, Sweden and Norway' *West European Politics* 18(4), 18–37.

Deutscher Bundestag, Rechtsausschuss, Stenografischer Bericht. 2nd Meeting, Berlin, 15 and 16 May 2006.

Deutsches Institut für Wirtschaftsforschung (DIW) (2006), *Stellungnahme zum Entwurf eines Gesetzes zur Änderung des Grundgesetzes (BT-Drucksache 16/813) und zum Entwurf eines Föderalismusreform-Begleitgesetzes (BT-Drucksache 16/814)* http://www.diw.de/deutsch/dasinstitut/info/2006/20060531_stellungnahme_foerderalismusre form.pdf.

De Winter, L., Gómez-Reino, M. and Lynch, P. (eds) (2006), *Autonomist Parties in Europe: Identity Politics and the Revival of the Territorial Cleavage*. In 2 vols. Barcelona: Institut de Ciències Polítiques i Socials.

Die Tageszeitung (2006), 'Die Kleinen haben Angst vor Konkurrenz', 8 May.

Die Zeit (2004), 'Interview mit Bundeskanzler Gerhard Schröder', 18 November.

Djildjov, A. (2001), 'Preporaki, vazmozhnosti i perspektivi' in A. Djildjov, F. Hauser and V. Marinov (eds), *Pregled na regionalnata politika v Balgariya: Sastoyanie, ocenka i perspektivi*. Sofia: Fondaciya za reforma v mestnoto samoupravlenie, 81–114.

Djildjov, A. (2002), 'Methods and Techniques of Managing Decentralization Reforms in Bulgaria' in G. Péteri (ed.), *Mastering Decentralization and Public Administration Reforms in Central and Eastern Europe*. Budapest: Local Government and Public Service Reform Initiative, 75–92.

Duran, P. (1998), 'Le partenariat dans la gestion des fonds structurels: la situation française' *Pôle Sud* 8, 114–139.

Edvi Illés, A. and Halász, A. (1921), *Magyarország gazdasági térképekben*. Budapest: Pallas Nyomda.

Elazar, Daniel (1987), *Exploring Federalism*. Tuscaloosa: University of Alabama Press.

Elias, A. (2006), 'From "full national status" to "independence" in Europe: The Case of *Plaid Cymru – The Party of Wales*' in M. Keating and J. McGarry (eds), *European Integration and the Nationalities Question*. London: Routledge, 193–215.

Elias, Anwen (2008), 'Whatever Happened to the Europe of the Regions? Revisiting the Regional Dimension of European Politics' *Regional and Federal Studies* 18(5), 483–492.

Enyedi, Gy. (1983), *Földrajz és társadalom [Geography and society]*. Budapest: Magvető Könyvkiadó.

Eppler, Annegret (2006a), 'Die Europafähigkeit Deutschlands in der Diskussion: Bundesstaatskommission und Ratifizierung des Vertrags über eine Verfassung für Europa' in Michael Borchard and Udo Margedant (eds), *Der deutsche Föderalismus im Reformprozess*. Sankt Augustin: Konrad-Adenauer-Stiftung, 73–100.

Eppler, Annegret (2006b), 'Föderalismusreform und Europapolitik' *Aus Politik und Zeitgeschichte* 50, 18–23.

Estonian Ministry of Interior (2003), 'Regionaalhalduse reformi kontseptsioon: Projekt' Available at http://www.siseministeerium.ee/failid/haldusreformi_projekt. rtf (accessed 21/06/10).

Eurobarometer (1991), 'Eurobarometer Survey 36: Regional Identities and Perceptions of the Third World'. Brussels: Commission of the European Communities.

Eurobarometer (2004a), 'Eurobarometer Survey 62.0: Standard Survey'. Brussels: European Commission.

Eurobarometer (2004b), 'Eurobarometer Survey 62: The Constitutional Treaty, October–December 2004'. Brussels: European Commission.

Eurobarometer (2006), 'Eurobarometer Survey 65: Standard Survey'. Brussels: European Commission.

European Commission (2001), 'Regular Report on Estonia's Progress toward Accession'. Brussels: Office for Official Publications of the European Communities.

European Commission (2004), '21st Annual Report on National Implementation on EU law COM (2004) 839'. Brussels: Commission of the European Communities.

European Commission (2005), 'Plan-D for Democracy, Dialogue and Debate COM (2005) 494'. Brussels: Commission of the European Communities.

European Commission (2006a), 'Progress in Notification of National Measures Implementing Directives' http://ec.europa.eu/community_law/eulaw/pdf/mne_country_ 20061107_en.pdf (accessed 21/06/10).

European Commission (2006b), 'White paper on a European Communication Policy COM (2006) 35'. Brussels: Commission of the European Communities.

Fabbrini, S. (2003), *L'europeizzazione dell'Italia: L'impatto dell'Unione Europea sulle istituzioni e sulle politiche italiane*. Roma-Bari: Laterza.

Falcon, G. (2001a), 'La "cittadinanza europea" delle Regioni' *Le Regioni* 2, 327–342.

Falcon, G. (2001b), 'Modello e "transizione" nel nuovo titolo V della parte seconda della Costituzione' *Le Regioni* 6, 1247–1272.

Falcon, G. (2002), 'Funzioni amministrative ed enti locali nei nuovi artt. 118 e 117 Costituzione' *Le Regioni* 2/3, 383–398.

Falcon, G. (2004), *Stato, regioni ed enti locali nella legge 5 giugno 2003, n. 131*. Bologna: Il Mulino.

Falcon, G. (2005), 'La sentenza n. 303 del 2003 e il problema della leale collaborazione' in L. Violini (ed.), *Itinerari di sviluppo del regionalismo italiano: primo incontro di studio Gianfranco Mor sul diritto regionale*. Milan: Giuffrè, 157–162.

Farrell, Grant Sparks (2003), 'Southern and Eastern Operational Programme – Mid Term Evaluation Report'. Dublin: Department of the Environment and Local Government.

FDI/CIR (2002), *Fiskalna Decentralizacia v Bulgaria: Fokusirane na debata*. Sofia: Fiscal Decentralization Initiative Central and Eastern Europe/Centar za ikonomichesko razvitie.

Featherstone K. (2003), 'Introduction: In the Name of Europe' in K. Featherstone and C. Radaelli (eds), *The Politics of Europeanisation*. Oxford: Oxford University Press.

Featherstone, K. and Radaelli, C. (eds) (2003), *The Politics of Europeanisation*. Oxford: Oxford University Press, 57–82.

Ferrari, G. F. and Parodi, G. (2003), *La revisione costituzionale del Titolo V tra nuovo regionalismo e federalismo*. Padova: Cedam.

Finn, G. (2004), 'An Overview of the Mid-term Evaluation of the BMW Regional Operational Programme,' presentation by the director of the Border, Midlands and Western (BMW) Regional Assembly to the Institute of Public Administration Conference, Dublin, January 2004.

Florenzano, D. (2004), *L'autonomia regionale nella dimensione internazionale: Dalle attività promozionali agli accordi ed alle intese*. Padova: Cedam.

Fouéré, Y. (1980), *Towards a Federal Europe: Nations or States?* Swansea: Christopher Davies.

Fournis, Y. (2005), *Les Régionalismes en Bretagne: La Région et l'Etat (1950–2004)*. Bruxelles: Peter Lang.

Frankfurter Allgemeine Zeitung (*FAZ*) Online (2006), 'EU-Streit über ARD und ZDF eskaliert', 13 December. http://www.faz.net/s/RubE2C6E0BCC2F04DD787CDC 274993E94C1/Doc~EE3C510EE8FF144999C29A917D0B56DB1~ATpl~Ecommon~ Scontent.html (accessed 21/06/10).

FRMS (2006), *Mezhduobshinskoto kooperirane, naglasi, problemi i vuzmozhnnosti za razvitie (Sociologichesko prouchvane)*. Sofia: Fondacia za reforma v mestnoto samoupravlenie.

Gambino, S. (2003a), *Diritto regionale e degli enti locali*. Milan: Giuffrè.

Gambino, S. (2003b), *Il 'nuovo' ordinamento regionale: competenze e diritti*. Milan: Giuffrè.

Gemeinsame öffentliche Anhörung des Rechtsausschusses des Deutschen Bundestages und des Ausschusses für Innere Angelegenheiten des Bundesrates zur Föderalismusreform, Stenografischer Bericht. 18th meeting, Berlin, 31 May 2006.

Genov, N. and Krasteva, A. (1999), *Bulgaria 1960–1995: Trends of Social Development*. Sofia: National and Global Development.

Gilowska, Z., Wysocka, E., Ploskonka, J., Prutis, S. and Stec, M. (1997), *Model ustrojowy województwa (regionu) w unitarnym panstwie demokratycznym*. Warsaw: ISP.

Gomez-Reino, M. and Pasquier, R. (2004), 'Les partis régionalistes et nationalistes en Europe du Sud' *Pôle Sud*, special issue, 20.

Gorzelak, G. (2001), 'Decentralisation of the Territorial Organisation the Polish State'. Paper to Regional Studies Association Conference, Gdansk.

Gorzelak, G. (2005), 'Poland's Regional Policy and Disparities in the Polish Space' *Regional and Local Studies*, special issue, 39–74.

Gorzelak, G. and Smetkowski, M. (2005), 'Metropolis and Its Region – New Relation in the Information Economy'. Paper presented to Regional Studies Association Conference in Aalborg http://www.regional-studies-assoc.ac.uk/events/280505papers.asp (accessed 21/06/10).

Graziano, P. (2003), 'La nuova politica regionale italiana: il ruolo dell'europeizzazione' in S. Fabbrini (ed.), *L'europeizzazione dell'Italia: L'impatto dell'Unione europea sulle istituzioni e le politiche italiane*. Roma-Bari: Laterza, 80–107.

Graziano, P. and Vinck, P. (eds) (2007), *Europeanization: New Research Agendas*. Basingstoke: Palgrave Macmillan.

Grémion, P. (1976), *Le Pouvoir Périphérique*. Paris: Seuil.

Gren, J. (2002), 'New Regionalism and West Sweden: Change in the Regionalism Paradigm' *Regional and Federal Studies* 12(3), 79–101.

Groppi, T. and Olivetti, M. (2003), *La Repubblica delle autonomie: Regioni ed enti locali nel nuovo titolo V*. Torino: Giappichelli.

Grosse Hüttmann, M. (2005), 'Wie europafähig ist er deutsche Föderalismus?' *Aus Politik und Zeitgeschichte* 13/14, 27–32.

Grosse Hüttmann, Martin (2006), 'Föderalismus jenseits des Staates? Entwicklung und Modellcharakter des EU-Mehrebenensystems' in Michael Borchard and Udo Margedant (eds), *Der deutsche Föderalismus im Reformprozess*. Sankt Augustin: Konrad-Adenauer-Stiftung, 137–162.

Gustafsson, B. (1995), 'Foundations of the Swedish Model' *Nordic Journal of Political Economy* 22, 5–26.

Haesly, R. (2001), 'Euroskeptics, Europhiles and Instrumental Europeans European Attachment in Scotland and Wales' *European Union Politics* 2(1), 81–102.

Häggroth, S. (2000), *Local Governance: The Case of Sweden.* Stockholm: Hjalmarson and Högberg.

Hajdú, Z. (2004), 'Carpathian Basin and the Development of the Hungarian Landscape Theory Until 1948'. Centre for Regional Studies (HAS), Discussion Papers, 44.

Harvie, C. (1993), *The Rise of Regional Europe.* London: Routledge.

Haughey, C. (1989), Speech by an Taoiseach (prime minister) to the Irish Council for the European Movement. UCD, Dublin, 2 October 1989.

Herce, J. and Sosvilla-Rivero, S. (2004), 'European Cohesion Policy and the Spanish Economy', Working Paper. Madrid: Fedea.

Hencz, A. (1973), *Területrendezési törekvések Magyarországon.* Budapest: Közgazdasági és Jogi Könyvkiadó.

Himsworth, C. (2007), 'Devolution and Its Jurisdictional Asymmetries' *Modern Law Review* 70(1), 31–58.

Hofmann, H. (2006), 'Die Vorschläge der Bundesstaatskommission im Spiegel notwendiger Reformen der Finanzverfassung' in M. Borchard and U. Margedant (eds), *Der deutsche Föderalismus im Reformprozess.* Sankt Augustin: Konrad-Adenauer-Stiftung, 37–72.

Holmes, M. and Rees, N. (1995), 'Regions within a Region: The Paradox of the Republic of Ireland' in J. B. Jones and M. Keating (eds), *The European Union and the Regions.* Oxford: Clarendon Press, 231–246.

Hooghe, L. (ed.) (1996), *Cohesion Policy and European Integration: Building Multi-level Governance.* Oxford: Oxford University Press.

Hooghe, L. (2004), 'Belgium: Hollowing the Center' in U. M. Amoretti and N. Bermeo (eds), *Federalism and Territorial Cleavages.* Baltimore: Johns Hopkins University Press, 55–92.

Hooghe, L. and Marks, G. (2001), *Multi-Level Governance and European Integration.* Lanham, MB: Rowman & Littlefield.

Hooghe, L. and Marks, G. (2004), 'Gobernanza estatocéntrica y gobernanza multinivel' in F. Morata (ed.), *Gobernanza Multinivel en la Unión Europea.* Valencia: Tirant lo Blanch, 51–85.

Horváth, G. (1998), *Európai Regionális Politika.* Budapest–Pécs: Dialóg Campus Kiadó.

Horváth, G. (2004), 'Regional Challenges and Policy Responses in Central and Eastern Europe' in G. Enyedi and I. Tózsa (eds), *The Region: Regional Development Policy, Administration and E-government.* Budapest: Akadémai Kiadó, 149–191.

Huang, M. (2001), 'Carving Out a New Estonia' *Central Europe Review* 3(2), 15 January http://www.pecina.cz/files/www.ce-review.org/01/2/amber2_2.html (accessed 21/06/10).

Hudson, C. (2005), 'Regional Development Partnerships in Sweden: Putting the Government Back in Governance?' *Regional and Federal Studies* 15(3), 311–327.

Hudson, C. (2006), 'Regional Development Partnerships in Sweden: A Way for Higher Education Institutions to Develop Their Role in the Process of Regional Governance?' *Higher Education* 51, 387–410.

Hughes Hallett, A. and Scott, A. (2003), 'Scotland and EMU: Constraints on Policy Discretion in a Globalised Economy' *Scottish Affairs* 45, 44–59.

Hughes, J., Sasse, G. and Gordon, C. (2001), 'The Regional Deficit in Eastward Enlargement of the European Union: Top Down Policies and Bottom Up Reactions', ESRC

Working Paper 29/01 http://www.one-europe.ac.uk/pdf/w29gordon.pdf (accessed 21/06/10).

Hughes, J., Sasse, G. and Gordon, C. (2004), *Europeanization and Regionalization in the EU's Enlargement to Central and Eastern Europe: The Myth of Conditionality*. Basingstoke: Palgrave Macmillan.

Huyse, Luc (1971), *Passiviteit, Pacificatie en Verzuildheid in de Belgische Politiek*. Antwerpen: Standaard Wetenschappelijke Uitgeverij.

Illner, M. (2002), 'Multilevel Government in Three East Central European Candidate Countries and Its Reforms after 1989', EUI Working Paper, 2002/7.

International Association of Universities (2004), *International Handbook of Universities, 17th edition*. London: Palgrave Macmillan.

Ireland (1999), 'National Development Plan 2000–2006', Dublin: Stationary Office, http://www.ndp.ie/documents/publications/ndp_csf_docs/NDP_complete_text.pdf (accessed 21/06/10).

Ireland (2007), 'National Development Plan 2007–2013: Transforming Ireland – A better Quality of Life for All'. Dublin: Stationery Office http://www.ndp.ie/documents/ndp2007-2013/NDP-2007-2013-English.pdf (accessed 21/06/10).

Ivanov, S., Tchavdarova, G., Savov, E. and Stanev, H. (2002), 'Does Larger Mean More Effective? Size and the Function of Local Governments in Bulgaria' in P. Swianiewicz (ed.), *Consolidation or Fragmentation? The Size of Local Governments in Central and Eastern Europe*. Budapest: Local Government and Public Service Initiative, 167–218.

Izquierdo, J.-M. and Pasquier, R. (2004), 'Les formations ethno-régionalistes en France: une exception européenne' *Pouvoirs locaux* 63, 15–17.

Janikson, K. and Kliimask, J. (1999), 'Regional Policy in Estonia' in M. Brusis (ed.), *Central and Eastern Europe on the Way to the European Union: Regional Policy-Making in Bulgaria, the Czech Republic, Estonia, Hungary, Poland and Slovakia*. Munich: CAP Working Paper, 65–89.

Jans, M. T. and Tombeur, H. (2000), 'Living Apart Together: The Belgian Intergovernmental Co-operation in the Domains of Environment and Economy' in D. Braun (ed.), *Public Policy and Federalism*. Aldershot: Ashgate, 142–176.

Jáuregi, G. (2005), 'La paticipación de las comunidades autónomas en la Unión Europea' *Revista Catalana de Dret Públic* 31, 137–172.

Jeffery, C. (1997a), 'Farewell the Third Level? The German Länder and the European Policy Process' in C. Jeffery (ed.), *The Regional Dimension of the European Union*. London: Frank Cass, 55–75.

Jeffery, C. (ed.) (1997b), *The Regional Dimension of the European Union: Towards a Third Level in Europe*. London: Frank Cass.

Jeffery, C. (2003), 'The German Länder and Europe: From Milieu-Shaping to Territorial Politics' in K. Dyson and K. H. Goetz (eds), *Germany and Europe: A Europeanised Germany?* Oxford: Oxford University Press, 97–108.

Jeffery, C. (2004a), 'Regions in the EU: Letting Them In and Leaving Them Alone', Online Paper XX-04. The Federal Trust http://www.fedtrust.co.uk/uploads/constitution/jeffery.pdf (accessed 21/06/10).

Jeffery, C. (2004b), 'Regions and the Constitution for Europe: German and British Impacts' *German Politics* 13(4), 605–624.

Jeffery C. (2005), 'Regions and the European Union: Letting Them In and Leaving Them Alone' in S. Weatherhill and U. Bernitz (eds), *The Role of Regions and Sub-National Actors in Europe*. Oxford: Hart.

Jeffery, C. (2006), 'The Regional Rescue of the Nation-State', Inaugural Lecture, Chair of Politics, University of Edinburgh.

Jeffery, Charlie (2008), 'Groundhog Day: The Non-Reform of German Federalism, Again' *German Politics* 17(4), 587–592.

Jerneck, M. and Gidlund, J. (2001), *Komplex flernivådemokrati: Regional lobbying i Bryssel*. Malmö: Liber.

Jouve, B. and Warin, P. (2000), *La Région, Laboratoire Politique*. Paris: La Découverte.

Kaldmäe, M., Poom, A., Alamets, U., Kampus, K., Ristkok, P., Roots, K. and Tärnov, J. (2003), *Local Government in Estonia*. Draft document prepared for Estonian Ministry of Internal Affairs (available from www.juhan.ell.ee/english/materials/ELLkogumik_ MK.doc (accessed 21/06/10).

Karasimeonov, G. (2002), *Novata partijna sistemat v Bulgaria*. Sofia: GoreksPres.

Kassim, H. (2005), 'The Europeanization of Member State Institutions' in S. Bulmer and C. Lequesne (eds), *The Member States of the European Union*. Oxford: Oxford University Press.

Keating, M. (1998), *The New Regionalism in Western Europe: Territorial Restructuring and Political Change*. Cheltenham: Edward Elgar.

Keating, M. (1999), 'Asymmetrical Government: Multinational States in an Integrating Europe' *Publius: The Journal of Federalism* 29(1), 71–86.

Keating, M. (2001), *Plurinational Democracy: Stateless Nations in a Post-Sovereignty Era*. Oxford: Oxford University Press.

Keating, M. (2003), 'Regionalization in Central and Eastern Europe: The Diffusion of a Western Model' in M. Keating and J. Hughes (ed.), *The Regional Challenge in Central and Eastern Europe: Territorial Restructuring and European Integration*. Brussels, Peter Lang, 51–68.

Keating, M. (2004a), 'Introduction' in M. Keating (ed.), *Regions and Regionalism in Europe*. Cheltenham: Edward Elgar, xi–xv.

Keating, M. (2004b), 'Regions and the Convention on the Future of Europe' *South European Politics and Society* 9(1), 192–207.

Keating, M. and Hughes, J. (eds) (2003), *The Regional Challenge in Central and Eastern Europe: Territorial Restructuring and European Integration*. Bruxelles: P.I.E.-Peter Lang.

Keating, M. and Jones, B. (eds) (1985), *Regions in the European Community*. Oxford: Oxford University Press.

Keating M. and Loughlin, J. (eds) (1997), *The Political Economy of Regionalism*. London: Routledge.

Keating, M., Loughlin, J. and Deschouwer, K. (2003), *Culture, Institutions and Economic Development: A Study of Eight European Regions*. Cheltenham: Edward Elgar.

Kerremans, B. (2000a), 'Regieren im Mehrebenensystem und Bundesstaatlichkeit: Zur Mitwirkung der subnationalen Ebene Belgiens im Rat der EU und an der Regierungskonferenz 1996/1997' in Europäisches Zentrum für Föderalismus-Forschung Tübingen, *Jahrbuch des Föderalismus 2000*. Baden-Baden: Nomos, 479–509.

Kerremans, B. (2000b), 'Determining a European Policy in a Multi-level Setting: The Case of Specialized Co-ordination in Belgium' *Regional & Federal Studies* 10(1), 36–61.

Kerremans, B. and Beyers, J. (1998), 'Belgium: The dilemma between Cohesion and Autonomy' in K. Hanf and B. Soetendorp (eds), *Adapting to European Integration: Small States and the European Union*. Harlow: Longmann, 14–35.

Kettunen, P. and Kungla, T. (2005), 'Europeanization of Sub-national Governance in Unitary States: Estonia and Finland' *Regional and Federal Studies* 15(3), 353–378.

Kivimägi, T. (2003), 'Kommentaar: Maavolikogu on surnud, elagu maavolikogu!' *Postimees*, 30 June.

Klebelsberg, K. (1928), 'Budapest, Szeged és Debrecen, mint tudományos székvárosok' in K. Klebelsberg (ed.), *Neonacionalizmus*. Budapest: Atheneum Irodalmi és Nyomdaipari, 71–76.

Koenig, T., Daimer, S. and Finke, D. (2008), 'The Treaty Reform of the EU: Constitutional Agenda-Setting, Intergovernmental Bargains and the Presidency's Crisis Management of Ratification Failure' *Journal of Common Market Studies* 46(2), 337–363.

Kohler-Koch, B. (2002), 'European Networks and Ideas: Changing National Policies', European Integration Online Papers (EIoP), 6 http://eiop.or.at/eiop/texte/2002-006a.htm (accessed 21/06/10).

Kommission von Bundestag und Bundesrat zur Modernisierung der bundesstaatlichen Ordnung (2003), *Einsetzungsbeschlüsse von Bundestag und Bundesrat*, Bundestag Drucksache 15/1685, Berlin: Deutscher Bundestag.

Kommission von Bundestag und Bundesrat zur Modernisierung der bundesstaatlichen Ordnung (2003), *Stenografischer Bericht 3: Sitzung*. Berlin, 12 December 2003.

Kommission von Bundestag und Bundesrat zur Modernisierung der bundesstaatlichen Ordnung (2004), Kommissionsdrucksache 0034 'Der Ministerpräsident des Landes Rheinland-Pfalz Kurt Beck: Hintergrundinformationen der rheinland-pfälzischen Landesregierung zur Ländermitwirkung in EU-Anglegenheiten im Zusammenhang mit dem Reformüberlegungen zu Art. 23 GG', 24/03/2004.

Kommission von Bundestag und Bundesrat zur Modernisierung der bundesstaatlichen Ordnung (2004), Kommissionsdrucksache 0041 'Bundesregierung: Position zu Art. 23 GG', 29 April 2004.

Kommission von Bundestag und Bundesrat zur Modernisierung der bundesstaatlichen Ordnung (2004), Kommissionsdrucksache 0045. 'Föderalismusreform: Positionspapier der Ministerpräsidenten', 6 May 2004.

Kommission von Bundestag und Bundesrat zur Modernisierung der bundesstaatlichen Ordnung (2004), Projektgruppenarbeitsunterlage 1/16, 27 September 2004, 'Auswärtiges Amt, Bundesministerium der Finanzen: Stellungnahme zur "Europatauglichkeit", Article 23 GG und Umsetzung von EU-Recht'.

Kommission von Bundestag und Bundesrat zur Modernisierung der bundesstaatlichen Ordnung (2004), *Stenografischer Bericht 3: Sitzung*, Berlin, Freitag, 14 Mai 2004.

Konrád, G. and Szelényi, I. (2000), *Urbanizáció és területi gazdálkodás*. Szeged: JGYF Kiadó.

Kottmann, J. (2001), 'Europe and the regions: sub-national entity representation at Community level' *European Law Review* 26(2), 159–176.

Kumar, K (2003), 'Britain, England and Europe: Cultures in Contra-flow' *European Journal of Social Theory* 6(1), 5–23.

Kungla, T. (2002), 'Europeanization of Territorial Structures in Central and Eastern European Countries' Tartu University EuroCollege Discussion Papers, 3.

Laffan, B. (2000), 'Rapid adaptation and light coordination' in R. O'Donnell (ed.), *Europe: The Irish Experience*. Dublin: Institute of European Affairs, 125–147.

Laffan, B. (2001), 'Organising for a Changing Europe: Irish Central Government and the European Union' *Blue Paper* 7. Dublin: Policy Institute, Trinity College Dublin.

Laffan, B. and Payne, D. (2001), *Creating Living Institutions: EU Cross-Border Co-operation after the Good Friday Agreement*. Armagh: Centre for Cross-Border Studies.

Lafont, R. (1967), *La Révolution Régionaliste*. Paris: Gallimard.

Landtag von Baden Württemberg (2006), 'Mitteilung der Landesregierung: Bericht über die Europapolitik der Landesregierung im Jahre 2005/6'. Drucksache 14/315, 19 September.

Le Galès, P. and Lequesne, C. (eds) (1997), *Les Paradoxes des Régions en Europe*. Paris: La Découverte.

Lein-Mathiesen, J. (2004), 'Nordic Regional Lobbying in Brussels' in S. Dosenrode and H. Halkier (eds), *The Nordic Regions and the European Union*. Aldershot: Ashgate.

Leonardi, R. and Nanetti, R. Y. (eds) (1990), *The Regions and European Integration: The Case of Emilia-Romagna*. London: Pinter.

Letamendia, F. (ed.) (1999), *Nacionalidades y Regiones en la Unión Europea*. Madrid: Fundamentos.

LGI (2004), 'Assessment of the Draft 2005 State Budget in Light of the Fiscal Decentralization Reform Program'. Sofia: Local Government Initiative.

Lidström, A. (1999), 'Sweden: The End of the "Swedish model"?' in J. Loughlin (ed.), *Subnational Democracy in the European Union: Challenges and Opportunities*. Oxford: Oxford University Press, 319–342.

Lidström, A. (2005), 'Urban-regional Cooperation: The Case of Umeå in Sweden' in F. Hendriks, V. van Stipdonk and P. Tops (eds), *Urban-regional Governance in the European Union*. The Hague: Elsevier, 45–63.

Lieven, A. (1993), *The Baltic Revolution: Estonia, Latvia, Lithuania and the Path to Independence*. New Haven: Yale University Press.

Lindahl, R. (2005), 'Svensk opinion om EU-medlemskapet' in S. Holmberg and L. Weibull (eds), *Lyckan kommer, lyckan går: SOM-rapport, 36*. Göteborg: SOM-institutet, Göteborgs universitet.

Local Government Denmark (LGDK) (2002), 'Eesti: Riiklik järelevalve ja omavalitsuste audit'. Kopenhaagen: Local Government Denmark http://www.siseministeerium. ee/public/Eesti_riiklik_j_relevalve_ja_omavalitsuste_audit_20070223110204.doc. (accessed 21/06/10).

Loughlin, J. (1996), ' "Europe of the Regions" and Federalization of Europe' *Publius: The Journal of Federalism* 26(4), 141–162.

Loughlin, J. (1997), 'Representing Regions in Europe: The Committee of the Regions' in C. Jeffery (ed.), *The Regional Dimension of Europe: Towards a 'Third Level' in Europe?* London: Frank Cass.

Loughlin, J., Lidström, A. and Hudson, C. (2005), 'The Politics of Local Income Tax in Sweden: Reform and Continuity' *Local Government Studies* 31(3), 351–366.

Lynch, P. (2004), 'Regions and the European Convention on the Future of Europe: Dialogue with the Deaf?' *European Urban and Regional Studies* 11(2), 199–207.

Mabellini, S. (2004), *La Legislazione Regionale: tra obblighi esterni e vincoli nazionali*. Milan, Giuffrè.

MacCarthaigh, M. (2007), *The Corporate Governance of Regional and Local Public Service Bodies in Ireland*. Dublin: Institute of Public Administration.

MacCarthaigh, M. (2008), *Government in Modern Ireland*. Dublin: Institute of Public Administration.

MacDonald, R. and Hallwood, P. (2004), *The Economic Case for Fiscal Federalism in Scotland*. Glasgow: Fraser of Allander Series.

MacDonald, R. and Hallwood, P. (2006), 'The Economic Case for Fiscal Autonomy: with or without Independence'. The Policy Institute.

Mäeltsemees, S. (2000), 'Local Government in Estonia' in T. M. Horváth (ed.), *Decentralization: Experiments and Reforms*. Budapest: Open Society Institute & Local Government and Public Service Initiative, 64–113.

Maesschalk, J. and Van Der Walle, S. (2006), 'Policy Failure and Corruption in Belgium: is Federalism to Blame?', *West European Politics* 29 (5), 999–1017.

Magone, J. M. (2003), 'The Third Level of European Integration: New and Old Insights' in J. M. Magone (ed.), *Regional Institutions and Governance in the European Union*. Westport CT: Praeger, 1–28.

Magyar Statisztikai Évkönyv (1938), Budapest: Központi Statisztikai Hivatal.

Manganaro, F. (2006), *I Rapporti Giuridici Internazionali degli enti Locali*. Torino: Giappichelli.

Mangiameli, S. (2001), *La Riforma del Regionalismo Italiano*. Torino: Giappichelli.

Mangiameli, S. (2003), 'Sull'arte di definire le materie dopo la riforma del Titolo V della Costituzione' *Le Regioni* 1, 337–344.

MAP-Ministerio para las Administraciones Públicas (1995), *La Participación de las Comunidades Autónomas en los Asuntos Comunitarios Europeos*. Madrid: MAP.

Marin, B. (1990), *Governance and Generalized Exchange: Self-Organizing Policy Networks in Action*. Frankfurt: Campus/Westview Press.

Marinov, V. (2001), 'Savremenno sastoyanie na politikata na regionalno razvitie v Bulgaria' in A. Djildjov (ed.), *Pregled na Regionalnata Politika v Bulgaria: Sastoyanie, ocenka i Perspektivi*. Sofia: Fondaciya za reforma v mestnoto samoupravlenie, 7–63.

Marinov, V. and V. Garnizov (2006), 'Ocenka na kapaciteta na obshtinite i oblastnite administracii za uchastie v usvoavaneto na sredstva ot Strukturnite fondove i Kohezionnia fond na ES'. Sofia UNDP. www.undp.bg (accessed 15 March 2009).

Marinov, V. and Malhasian, D. (2006), *Partnership in Structural and Cohesion Funds Absorption: A Comparative Review of the Practices of Selected EU Member States and Lessons Learned for Bulgaria*. Sofia: UNDP.

Marks, G. (1996), 'Politikmuster und Einflusslogik in der Strukturpolitik' in M. Jachtenfuchs and B. Kohler-Koch (eds), *Europäische Integration*. Opladen: Leske and Budrich.

Marks, G., Haesly, R. and Mbiaye, H. A. D. (2002), 'What Do Subnational Offices Think They are Doing in Brussels?' *Regional and Federal Studies* 12(3), 1–23.

Marshall, A. J. (2002), 'European Regional Policy and Urban Governance: Assessing Dublin's Experience'. ECPR Joint Sessions, workshop 12. Turin, March 2002.

Martines, T., Ruggeri, A. and Salazar, C. (2005), *Lineamenti di Diritto Regionale*. 7th edn. Milan: Giuffrè.

Maurer, A. and Becker, P. (2004), *Die Europafähigkeit der Nationalen Parlamente*. Berlin: Stiftung Wissenschaft und Politik.

McGauran, Anne-Marie, Verhoest, Koen and Humphreys, Peter (2005), 'The Corporate Governance of Agencies in Ireland: Non-Commercial National Agencies'. Dublin, Institute of Public Administration, Committee for Public Management Research Report No. 6.

McGowan, L. and Murphy, M. (2003), 'Europeanisation and the Irish Experience' in M. Adshead and M. Millar (eds), *Public Administration and Public Policy in Ireland*. London: Routledge, 182–200.

Millan, B. (1997), 'The Committee of the Regions: In at the Birth' *Regional and Federal Studies* 7(1), 5–10.

Ministry of Finance of the Republic of Estonia (2003), 'Eesti Riiklik Arenukava Euroopa Liidu Struktuurifondide Kasutuselevõtuks – ühtne programmdokument 2003–2006' http://www.fin.ee/doc.php?6129 (accessed 21/06/10).

Ministry of Finance [Sweden] (2004), 'Supplementary terms of reference for the Committee on Public Sector Responsibilities'.

Minkova, M. (2004), *Defining the New Role of the Regions in Overseeing and Coordinating Regional Development in Bulgaria*. Budapest: CEU Center for Policy Studies.

Mitchell, J. and Leicester, G. (1999), 'Scotland, Britain and Europe: Diplomacy and Devolution' *The Scottish Council Foundation Occasional Paper* 12.

Mollov, B., Shikova, I. and Dimova, M. (2004), *Podgotovkata na mestno i regionalno nivo za chlenstvoto na Bulgaria v Evropeyskia Sayuz: Predprisaedinitelni programi i Strukturni Fondove*. Sofia: Ministerstvo na vanshnite raboti.

Moore, C. (2006a), '"Schloss Neuwahnstein"? Why the Länder Continue to Strengthen their Representations in Brussels' *German Politics* 15(2), 192–205.

Moore, C. (2006b), 'Conflicts in Representing the Regions in Brussels: The Case of Wales' *Regional Studies* 40(7), 793–799.

Morata, F. (2001), 'El Estado de las Autonomías' in M. Alcantara and M. A. Martinez (eds), *Política y Gobierno en España*. Valencia: Tirant lo Blanch, 121–150.

Morata, F. (2003), 'La Gouvernance à Niveaux Multiples et la Coopération Subnationale en Euope' in A. Sedjari (ed.), *Gouvernance et Conduite de l'Action Publique au XXI siècle*. Paris: L'Harmattan.

Morata F. (2004), 'Gobernanza Multinivel y Regiones' in F. Morata (ed.), *Gobernanza Multinivel en la Unión Europea*. Valencia: Tirant lo Blanch.

Morata, F. and Muñoz, X. (1996), 'Vying for European Funds: Territorial Restructuring in Spain' in L. Hooghe (ed.), *Cohesion Policy and European Integration*. Oxford: Clarendon Press.

Morata, F. and Ramon, R. (2005), 'Regiones y Constitución Europea' *Quaderns de Treball* 44/05. Barcelona: IUEE/UAB.

Morata, F. and Rodríguez, P. (2008), 'Els actors de l'Euroregió Pirineus-Mediterrània: Xarxes, Percepcions i Expectatives'. Working paper online, 19. Bellaterra: IUEE http://www.iuee.eu/pdf-publicacio/144/pWMGTqlfsYyIVt3WqGxf. PDF (accessed 21/06/10).

Morgenroth, E. (2008), 'Economic Integration and Structural Change: The Case of Irish Regions' in Christiane Krieger-Boden, Edgar Morgenroth and George Petrakos (eds), *The Impact of European Integration on Regional Structural Change and Cohesion*. London: Routledge, 49–71.

MRRB (2005), 'Strategia za decentralizacia v Bulgaria, obedinyavascha decentralizacia na pravomoschia i finansovata decentralizacia'. Sofia: Ministerstvo za regionalnoto razvitie i blagoustrojstvoto.

MS (2006), 'Strategija za decentralizacia'. Sofia: Ministerski savet. Reshenie 424/2006, 5 June 2006 http://www.government.bg. (accessed 21/06/10).

MS (2008), 'Godishen doklad za ispalnenieto na Strategiata za decentralizacia i na Programata za izpalnenie na Strategiata za decentralizacia prez 2007 g., Ministerski Savet – Savet po decentralizacia na darzavnoto upravlenie'. Sofia, June 2008 http://www.decentralization.government.bg/?id=14 (accessed 15/03/2009).

MSA (2005), 'Annual Report for the Public Administration 2004'. Sofia: Minister of State Administration.

Munro, K. (2006), 'Among friends' in *Holyrood: 150th Issue Commemorative Volume*. Edinburgh.

Nagel, K. J. (2004), 'La actuación de las regiones en la política europea: un análisis comparado' in F. Morata (ed.), *Gobernanza Multinivel en la Unión Europea*. Valencia: Tirant lo Blanch, 245–284.

NAMRB (2004), 'Municipal Action Plan for the Accession of Bulgaria to the EU'. Sofia: National Association of Municipalities of the Republic of Bulgaria.

Naß, K.-O. (1989), 'The Foreign and European Policy of the German Länder' *Publius: The Journal of Federalism* 19(4), 165–184.

National Forum on Europe (2005), 'Fifth Report: A model of democratic engagement'. Dublin: National Forum on Europe secretariat.

National Treasury Management Agency (2002), 'Ireland: Information Memorandum', March 2002 http://www.ntma.ie/Publications/Ireland_Information_Memorandum_2002.pdf (accessed 21/06/10).

Négrier, E. (1998), 'Une action publique sans coopération politique: Le style languedocien de la politique régionale' *Pôle Sud* 8, 41–53.

Négrier, E. and Jouve, B. (eds) (1998), *Que Gouvernent les Régions d'Europe?* Paris: L'Harmattan.

Nemes Nagy, J. (1987), *A Regionális Gazdasági Fejlődés Összehasonlító Vizsgálata.* Budapest: Akadémiai Kiadó.

Norgaard, O. and Johannsen, L. (1999), *The Baltic States After Independence.* Cheltenham: Edward Elgar.

O'Hara, P. and Commins, P. (2003), 'Ireland and the Future of Europe: A Regional Perspective' in B. Reynolds and S. Healy (eds), *Ireland and the Future of Europe: Leading the Way towards Inclusion.* Dublin: CORI Justice Commission, 29–64.

Olle, V. (2001), *Kohalikust omvalitsusest Eesti Vabariigis 1918–1940.* Tartu: a. Tartu Ülikool.

Olsen, J. P. (2002), 'The Many Faces of Europeanization' *Journal of Common Market Studies* 5, 921–952.

Olsson, J. and Åström, J. (2004), 'Sweden' in S. Dosenrode and H. Halkiev (eds), *The Nordic Regions and the European Union.* Aldershot: Ashgate, 77–92.

Onida, V. and Cartabia, M. (1997), 'Le Regioni e la Comunità europea' in M. P. Chiti and G. Greco (eds), *Trattato di Diritto Amministrativo Europeo.* Milan: Giuffré.

Oscarsson, H. (2004), 'Det delade landet' in H. Oscarsson and S. Holmberg (eds), *Kampen om Euron.* Göteborg: Statsvetenskapliga institutionen, Göteborgs universitet.

O'Sullivan, T. (2003), 'Local Areas and Structures' in M. Callanan and J. F. Keogan (eds), *Local Government in Ireland: Inside Out.* Dublin: Institute of Public Administration, 41–81.

Õunapuu, J. (2003a), 'Haldusreform teeb Eesti tugevamaks' *Postimees*, 4 August.

Õunapuu, J. (2003b), 'Reform saab üha selgemaks' *Postimees*, 10 September.

Pajno, A. (2003), 'Il rispetto dei vincoli derivanti dall'ordinamento comunitario come limite alla potestà legislativa nel nuovo Titolo V' *Le Istituzioni del federalismo: regione e governo locale* 5, 813–842.

Palermo, F. (1999), *Il Potere Estero delle Regioni.* Padova: Cedam.

Palermo, F. (2002), 'Titolo V e potere estero delle Regioni: i vestiti nuovi dell'imperatore' *Le Istituzioni del federalismo: regione e governo locale* 5, 709–732.

Palermo, F. (2006), 'Se lo stato non si fida delle regioni' http://www.affarinternazionali.it/articolo.asp?ID=150 (accessed 21/06/10).

Pálné Kovács, Ilona, P., Paraskevopoulos, C. J. and Horváth, G. (2004), 'Institutional "legacies" and the Shaping of Regional Governance in Hungary' *Regional and Federal Studies* 14(3), 430–460.

Parry, R. and MacDougall, A. (2005), 'Civil Service Reform Post Devolution: The Scottish and Welsh Experience' *ESRC Devolution Briefing* 17.

Pasquier, R. (2002), 'Quand l'Europe frappe à la porte des régions: Européanisation et mobilisations régionales en France et en Espagne' *Politique Européenne* 7, 159–177.

Pasquier, R. (2003a), 'La régionalisation française revisitée: Fédéralistes, mouvement régional et élites modernisatrices (1950–1964)' *Revue française de science politique* 53(1), 101–125.

Pasquier, R. (2003b), 'From Patterns of Collective Action to the Capacity for Governance in French Regions' in J. Bukowski, S. Piattoni and M. Smyrl (eds), *Between Global Economy and Local Society: Political Actors and Territorial Governance*. Lanham, MD: Rowman and Littlefield, 67–90.

Pasquier, R. (2004a), *La Capacité Politique des Region:*. *Une Comparaison France/Espagne*, preface by Yves Mény. Rennes: Presses Universitaires de Rennes.

Pasquier, R. (2004b), '1986–2004: dix-huit ans de démocratie régionale: Vers une maturité politique des régions française ?', *Les Cahiers de l'Institut de la Décentralisation 7*.

Pasquier, R. (2005), 'Cognitive Europeanization and the Territorial Effects of Multilevel Policy Transfer: Local Development in French and Spanish Regions' *Regional and Federal Studies* 15(3), 295–310.

Pasquier, R. (2006), 'The Union Démocratique Bretonne: The Limits of Autonomist Expression in Brittany' in L. de Winter, M. Gomez-Reino and P. Lynch (eds), *Autonomist Parties in Europe: Identity Politics and the Revival of the Territorial Cleavage, Volume 2*. Barcelona: Institut de Ciències Politiques i Socials, 79–100.

Pérez-Nievas, S. (2006), 'The Partido Nacionalista Vasco: Redefinining Political Goals at the Turn of the Century' in L. De Winder, M. Gómez-Reino and P. Lynch (eds), *Autonomist Parties in Europe: Identity Politics and the Revival of the Territorial Cleavage, Volume 1*. Barcelona: Institute de Ciènces Polítiques i Socials, 31–63.

Per-Jakez, H. (1975), *Le Cheval d'Orgueil*. Paris: Seuil.

Perkmann, M. (2005), 'The Emergence and Governance of Euroregions: The Case of the EUREGIO on the Dutch-German Border'. Paper presented at a workshop on 'Euroregions, experiences and lessons' at the Institut Universitari d'Estudis Europeus, Barcelona.

Peters, G. B. and Pierre, J. (2001), 'Development in Intergovernmental Relations: towards Multi-Level Governance' *Policy and Politics* 29(2), 131–135.

Petersson, O., Hermansson, J., Micheletti, M. and Westholm, A. (1997), *Demokrati över gränser: Demokratirådets rapport 1997*. Stockholm: SNS Förlag.

Pettersen, P. A. (1996), 'The 1994 EU Referendum in Norway: Continuity and Change' *Scandinavian Political Studies* 19(3), 257–281.

Pitino, A. (2005), *Verso una Nuova Legge Comunitaria*. Torino: Giappichelli.

Pizzetti, F. (2002), *Il Nuovo Ordinamento Italiano fra Riforme Amministrative e Riforme Costituzionali*. Torino: Giappichelli.

Pizzetti, F. (2003), 'La ricerca del giusto equilibrio tra uniformità e differenza: il problematico rapporto tra il progetto originario della Costituzione del 1948 e il progetto ispiratore della riforma costituzionale del 2001' *Le Regioni* 4, 599–628.

Plaid Cymru (1999), 'Cyrchu at y Gymru newydd: maniffesto Plaid Cymru 1999/Working for the new Wales: the manifesto of Plaid Cymru, The Party of Wales 1999. Caerdydd: Plaid Cymru' <http://news.bbc.co.uk/hi/english/static/events/wales_99/manifestos/plaidcymru.html (accessed 21/06/10).

Poirier, J. (2002), 'Formal Mechanisms of Intergovernmental Relations in Belgium' *Regional and Federal Studies* 12(3), 24–54.

Pouvoirs Locaux (2003), *Décentralisation: 'Acte deux', scène un…* Special issue of *Pouvoirs Locaux* 59.

Pozun, B. (2001), 'Little Country, Big Problem: Slovenia's Regions' *Central and Eastern Review* 3(3), 22 January http://www.ce-review.org/01/3/pozun3.html (accessed 21/06/10).

Profeti, S. (2006), 'La sfida europea delle regioni italiane: quattro strategie a confronto' *Rivista italiana di politiche pubbliche* 1, 39–69.

Putnam, R. (1988), 'Diplomacy and Domestic Politics: The Logic of Two Level Games' *International Organization* 42(3), 427–460.

Radaelli, C. M. (2000), 'Whither Europeanization? Concept Stretching and Substantive Change' European Integration online Papers (EIoP), 8 http://www.eiop.or.at/eiop/texte/2000-008a.htm (accessed 21/06/10).

Radaelli, C. M. (2003), 'The Europeanization of Public Policy' in K. Featherstone and C. M. Radaelli (eds), *The Politics of Europeanization*. Oxford: Oxford University Press, 27–56.

Ramon, R. (2006), 'Multi-level Governance in Spain: Building New Patterns of Subnational Participation in the Council of Ministers of the EU'. Working paper presented at the Research Seminar of the Institut Universitari d'Estudis Europeus, Barcelona.

Ramon, R. (2007), 'España y la Política Agrícola Común' in F. Morata and G. Mateo (eds), *España en Europa, Europa en España (1986–2006)*. Barcelona: CIDOB.

Redwood, J. (1999), *The Death of Britain?* Basingstoke: Palgrave Macmillan.

Rees, Nicholas, Quinn, Bríd and Connaughton, Bernadette (2004), 'Ireland's Pragmatic Adaptation to Regionalization: The Mid-West Region' *Regional and Federal Studies* 14(3), 379–404.

Rodriguez-Pose, A. and Fratesi, U. (2004), 'Between Development and Social Policies: The Impact of European Structural Funds in Objective 1 Regions' *Regional Studies* 8(1), 97–113.

Roig, E. (2004), 'Continuidad y Refundación; Deliberación y Decisión: el proceso de la Convención y la reforma de los Tratados' in E. Alberti and E. Roig (eds), *El Proyecto de Nueva Constitución Europea*. Valencia: Tirant Lo Blanch, 17–131.

Rokkan, S. and Urwin, D. (eds) (1982), *The Politics of Territorial Identity: Studies in European Regionalism*. London: Sage.

Ronchetti, L. (2005), 'Sweden' in Procedures for Local and Regional Authority Participation in European Policy Making in the Member States. Brussels: Committee of the Regions, 260–268.

Rose, L. E. and Ståhlberg, K. (2005), 'The Nordic Countries: Still the "Promised land"?' in B. Denters and L. E. Rose (eds), *Comparing Local Governance: Trends and Developments*. Basingstoke: Palgrave Macmillan, 83–99.

Ruggiu, I (2004), 'Le politiche della devolution scozzese: unus rex unus grex una lex?' *Le Regioni* 6, 1267–1306.

Ruubel, N. (2002), 'The Capacity of Estonia to Administer EU Structural Funds'. Department of Public Administration, University of Tartu (unpublished).

Sandberg, S. (2005), 'Den folkvalda regionala nivån ställning i Norden' in P. Tallberg (ed.), *Självstyre på Lokal och Regional Nivå. Skåne och Västra Götalandsregionen*, 103–128.

Sandberg, S. and Ståhlberg, K. (2000), *Nordisk Regionalförvaltning i Förändring*. Åbo: Åbo Akademi.

Scharpf, F. (2005), 'No Exit from the Joint Decision Trap? Can German Federalism Reform Itself?' MPIfG Working Paper 05/8 http://www.mpi-fg-koeln.mpg.de/pu/workpap/wp05-8/wp05-8.html (accessed 21/06/10).

Scharpf, Fritz (2008), 'Community, Diversity and Autonomy: The Challenges of Reforming German Federalism' *German Politics* 18(4), 509–521.

Schmidt, V. (2003), 'The European Union: Democratic Legitimacy in a Regional State?' *Journal of Common Market Studies* 42(5), 975–997.

Schmidt, V. (2006), *Democracy in Europe: The EU and National Polities*. Oxford: Oxford University Press.

Schrijver, F. (2006), *Regionalism after Regionalisation: Spain, France and the United Kingdom*. Amsterdam: Amsterdam University Press.

Scott, A. (2005), 'The (missing) Regional Dimension to the Lisbon Process'. Scotland Europa Discussion Paper, 27. Brussels: Scotland Europa.

Scottish Executive (2004), 'The Scottish Executive's European Strategy: Framework for the Executive's Work on EU Issues over the Next Four Years' http://www.scotland. gov.uk/Publications/2004/01/18759/31717 (accessed 21/06/10).

Scottish Executive (2007a), 'Participation and Engagement in Politics and Policy Making: Building a Bridge between Europe and its Citizens' http://www.scotland.gov.uk/ Publications/2007/01/23145406/0 (accessed 21/06/10).

Scottish Executive (2007b), 'Attitudes towards the European Union and the challenges in communicating "Europe": Building a Bridge between Europe and its Citizens' http://www.scotland.gov.uk/Publications/2007/01/23145439/0.

Scottish Executive (2007c), 'Young People's Views on Participation and Their Attitudes towards the European Union: Building a Bridge between Europe and its Citizens' http://openscotland.gov.uk/Publications/2007/01/23145514/0 (accessed 21/06/10).

Scottish Executive (2007d), 'Building a Bridge: Scottish Executive Report on Communicating Europe to Its Citizens' http://www.scotland.gov.uk/Publications/2007/03/ 19134334/0 (accessed 21/06/10).

Scottish Executive EU Office (SEEUO) (2007), 'Forward Look 2007' http://www. scotland.gov.uk/Topics/Government/International-Relations/Europe/15181/ fwdlook2007 (accessed 21/06/10).

SERA (2006), 'Annual Report and Accounts 2005'. Waterford: Southern and Eastern Regional Assembly http://www.seregassembly.ie/publications/pub_docs/ annual_report_2005(en).pdf.

SERA (2008), 'Southern and Eastern Regional Assembly Annual Report and Accounts 2007'. Waterford http://www.seregassembly.ie/publications/pub_docs/ annual_report_07_(en).pdf (accessed 21/06/10).

Smith, A. (2006), 'The Europeanization of the French State' in A. Cole, P. Le Galès and J. Levy (eds), *Developments in French Politics*. Basingstoke: Palgrave Macmillan, 105–121.

Smyrl, M. (1997), 'Does European Community Regional Policy Empower the Regions?' *Governance: An International Journal of Policy and Administration* 10(3), 287–309.

Sollander, S. and Öhrvall, R. (2004), *Ja och Nej till Euron: Folkomröstningen om Euron 2003*. Stockholm: Statistiska Centralbyrån.

State Chancellery of Estonia, Office of European Integration (2000), 'National Programme for the Adoption of the Acquis 2000' http://www.riigikantselei.ee/failid/ NPAA2000_Estonia.pdf (accessed 21/06/10).

Statskontoret (2005), *EU:s Påverkan på Kommuner och Landsting*. Stockholm: Statskontoret.

Stellungnahme des Bundesrates 18.02.05. ,Entwurf eines Gesetzes zu dem Vertrag vom 29: Oktober 2004 über eine Verfassung für Europa'. Drucksache 983/04 (Beschluss). Berlin: Deutscher Bundesrat.

Stewart, J. and Stoker, G. (eds) (1995), *Local Government in the 1990s*. London: Macmillan.

Stoiber, Edmund (2004), 'Grußwort des Bayerischen Ministerpräsidenten Dr. Edmund Stoiber anlässlich der Eröffnung der Bayerischen Vertretung in Brüssel am 29', September http://www.bayern.de/Presse-Info/Reden/2004/rede_040929 (accessed 21/06/10).

Svenning, O. (2005), *Göran Persson och hans Värld*. Stockholm: Norstedts förlag.

Svenska Kommunförbundet/Landstingsförbundet (2001), *Six Years in the EU – The Consequences for Sweden's Municipalities, County Councils and Regions 1995–2000*. Stockholm: Svenska Kommunförbundet och Landstingsförbundet.

Svensson, B. and Östhol, A. (2001), 'From Government to Governance: Regional Partnerships in Sweden' *Regional and Federal Studies* 11(2), 25–42.

Sveriges Kommuner och Landsting (2008), 'Medlemmarnas internationella engagemang'. Stockholm: SKL.

Swenden, W. (2002), 'Asymmetric Federalism and Coalition-Making in Belgium' *Publius: The Journal of Federalism* 32(3), 67–88.

Swenden, W. (2006), *Federalism and Regionalism in Western Europe: A Comparative and Thematic Analysis*. Basingstoke: Palgrave Macmillan.

Swenden, W. and Jans, M. T. (2006), 'Will it Stay or Will it Go? Federalism and the Sustainability of Belgium' *West European Politics* 29(5), 888–894.

Taagepera, R. and Misiunas, R. J. (1983), *The Baltic States: Years of Dependence 1940–1980*. London: Hurst.

Területi Statisztikai Évkönyv (1985), Budapest: Központi Statisztikai Hivatal.

Területi Statisztikai Évkönyv (1994), Budapest: Központi Statisztikai Hivatal.

Területi Statisztikai Évkönyv (2003), Budapest: Központi Statisztikai Hivatal.

Területi Statisztikai Évkönyv (2004), Budapest: Központi Statisztikai Hivatal.

Thiesse A.-M. (1997), *Ils Apprenaient la France: L'exaltation des Régions dans le Discours Patriotique*. Paris: Maison des sciences de l'homme.

Tiberi, G. (2005), 'La riforma della legge "La Pergola"' *Quaderni costituzionali* 3, 671–674.

Tierney, S. (2006), 'Scotland and the Union State' in A. McHarg and T. Mullen (eds), *Public Law in Scotland*. Edinburgh: Avizandum, 25–45.

Töller, A. (2006), 'How European Integration Impacts on National Legislatures: The Europeanisation of the German Bundestag'. Harvard University, Center for European Studies Working Paper Series 06.2, Cambridge: MA.

Toniatti, R., Palermo, F. and Dani, M. (2004), *An Ever More Complex Union: The Regional Variable as a Missing Link in The EU Constitution?* Baden-Baden: Nomos.

Tóth, J. (2004), 'Kell-e nekünk régió?' *Mindentudás Egyeteme* 3, 193–212.

Trench, A. (2004), 'Devolution: the Withering Away of the Joint Ministerial Committee' *Public Law*, 513–517.

Trench, A. (2005), 'Central Government's Responses to Devolution'. ESRC Devolution Briefing, 15 http://www.devolution.ac.uk/pdfdata/Briefing%2015%20-%20Trench.pdf (accessed 21/06/10).

Uibopuu, H.-J. (1991), 'Estland unter der Sowjetherrschaft und auf dem Wege zur Unabhängigkeit' in B. Meissner (ed.), *Die Baltischen Nationen: Estland, Lettland, Litauen*. Köln: Markus, 119–138.

UNDP (1999), *National Human Development Report Bulgaria: Volume 2*. Sofia: United Nations Development Program.

UNDP (2004), *Assessment of Municipal and District Capacities for the Absorption of the EU Structural and Cohesion Funds*. Sofia: United Nations Development Program.

Vassilev, R. V. (2001), 'Post-communist Bulgaria's ethnopolitics' *The Global Review of Ethnopolitics* 1(2), 37–53.

Verheijen, T. (1999), 'The Civil Service of Bulgaria: Hope on the Horizon' in T. Verheijen (ed.), *Civil Service Systems in Central and Eastern Europe*. Cheltenham: Edward Elgar, 92–130.

Verhofstadt, G. (2006), Speech by Prime Minister Verhofstadt at the Center for Strategic and International Studies in Washington http://www.diplomatie.be/en/press/speechdetails.asp?TEXTID=47831 (accessed 21/06/10).

Viks, K. (2002), 'Europeanisation and Transformation of Public Administration: The Case of Estonia'. Institut für Europäische Politik working paper http://www.iep-berlin.de/fileadmin/website/03_Forschung/Eurpaeisierung/viks-europeanisation-estonia.pdf (accessed 21/06/10).

Vink, M. P. and Graziano, P. (2007), 'Challenges of a New Research Agenda' in P. Graziano and M. T. Vinck (eds), *Europeanization: New Research Agendas*. Basingstoke: Palgrave Macmillan.

Violini, L. (2005), 'Legge "La Loggia" e partecipazione delle Regioni ai processi decisionali comunitari: la Corte (a buon diritto) assolve le scelte legislative, benché incompiute' *Le Regioni* 1/2, 226–235.

Vlaamse Standpunten (2003), 'Voorbereiding van de Vlaamse Standpunten voor de Intergouvernementele Conferentie 2004'. Research report commissioned by the Flemish government; general co-ordinator K. Lenaerts.

Wakefield, J. (2005), 'The Plight of the Regions in a Multi-layered Europe' *European Law Review* 30(3), 406–419.

Wallace, H. (1977), 'Institutions in a Decentralised Community' in B. Burrows, G. Denton and E. Edwards (eds), *Federal Solutions to European Issues*. London: Macmillan.

Wallace, W. (2005), 'Post-sovereign governance' in H. Wallace, W. Wallace and M. A. Pollack (eds), *Policy-Making in the European Union*. Oxford: Oxford University Press.

Watts, R. L. (1989), 'Executive Federalism: The Comparative Perspective' in D. P. Shugerman and R. Whitaker (eds), *Federalism and Political Community: Essays in Honour of Donald Smiley*. Peterborough, Ontario: Broadview Press, 439–459.

Weatherhill, S. (2005), 'The Challenge of the Regional Dimension in the European Union' in S. Weatherhill and U. Bernitz (eds), *The Role of Regions and Sub-national Actors in Europe*. Oxford: Hart, 1–33.

Weatherill, S. (2005), 'Finding a Role for the Regions in Checking the EU's Competence' in S. Weatherill and U. Bernitz (eds), *The Role of Regions and Sub-national Actors in Europe*. Oxford: Hart, 131–156.

Weatherill, S. and Bernitz, U. (eds) (2005), *The Role of Regions and Sub-national Actors in Europe*. Oxford: Hart.

Weber, E. (1977), *Peasants into Frenchmen: The Modernization of Rural France 1870–1914*. London: Chatto and Windus.

Whelan, N. (1976), 'Considerations Relevant to Central Government' *Administration* (special issue on 'Administrative Structures for Regional Development') 2(3), 283–301.

Woelk, J. (2003), 'La partecipazione diretta degli enti substatali al processo decisionale comunitario: Considerazioni comparative' *Le Regioni* 4, 575–598.

Wright, J. (2006), *The Regionalist Movement in France, 1890–1914: Jean-Charles Brun and French Political Thought*. Oxford: Clarendon Press.

Wyn Jones, R. (2007), *Rhoi Cymru'n Gyntaf: Syniadaeth Plaid Cymru. Cyfrol 1*. Caerdydd: Gwasg Prifysgol Cymru.

Yuill, D., Mendez, C. and Wishlade, F. (2006), *Cohesion Policy Reform: The Implications for Spain*. Glasgow: European Policies Research Centre, University of Strathclyde.

Index

Please note: locators in **bold** type indicate figures or illustrations, those in *italics* indicate tables and those with 'n' refer to notes.